CONSTITUENT IMAGINATION

Constituent Imagination

Militant Investigations // Collective Theorization

Edited by Stevphen Shukaitis + David Graeber

with Erika Biddle

AK Press

Oakland // Edinburgh // West Virginia

Constituent Imagination: Militant Investigations // Collective Theorization
Edited by Stevphen Shukaitis + David Graeber

ISBN 978-1-904859-35-2
Library of Congress Number: 2006924199

For more information and ongoing projects:
http://www.constituentimagination.net
info@constituentimagination.net

Cover Design: Haduhi Szukis
Layout: C. Weigl

AK Press
674-A 23rd Street
Oakland, CA 94612
www.akpress.org
akpress@akpress.org
510.208.1700

AK Press U.K.
PO Box 12766
Edinburgh EH8 9YE
www.akuk.com
ak@akedin.demon.co.uk
0131.555.5165

Printed in Canada on 100% recycled, acid-free paper by union labor.

Contents

:: Communities of/in Resistance ::

:: Education & Ethics ::

Acknowledgements

Writing acknowledgements for a volume like this is an absurd but necessary task. Absurd because, if one were to properly thank everyone who has provided inspiration and ideas, the result would be a volume composed mainly of extended thank yous; necessary because without vibrant communities of resistance there would be no point is assembling a book like this. Militant investigation is an inherently collective and social process and, for this reason, trying to credit individuals for ideas is difficult in the same way that attempting to claim ownership over them is. It is for our *companer@s* around the world, from the recuperated factories of Argentina to the Italian social centers, from joyful festivals in the streets to building new communities in and beyond the classroom, that we research, write, and teach.

Having said that we would still like to acknowledge the efforts of people without whom this project never would have seen the light of day. Special thanks to Yvonne Liu, Nate Holdren, Jim Fleming, Ben Meyers, and Jack Z. Bratich for on-going conversations and friendship. Thanks to Stefano Harney, Campbell Jones, and everyone else from the University of Leicester Centre for Philosophy and Political Economy. Much respect to Stephen Dunne and Eleni Karamali who helped co-edit the "Inscribing Organized Resistance" issue of ephemera (www.ephemeraweb.org) that grew out of this project. An extra special thanks to Sophea Lerner for being such a caring and wonderful person during the process of putting this book together. Thanks to Andréa Schmidt, the Institute for Anarchist Studies and the wonderful folks at AK Press for their support of the project. And thanks to the Snydersville Diner for a seemingly endless supply of coffee and tasty slices of pie that provided excellent encouragement during the process of editing and revising.

The front cover image is from the Faculty of Social Sciences at the University of Buenos Aires in Argentina. Fittingly enough, someone has spray painted both "*Manicomo*" (madhouse) and "*4 Imagacion al Poder*" (All power to the imagination), which succinctly summarizes the ambivalent nature of forms of radicalism embedded in the university. The image facing the Introduction is one of Dave Eden's tattoos, taken during a particularly joyous weekend of reveling in Canberra, Australia (of all places).

Ambrose Bierce once described the imagination as "a warehouse of facts, with poet and liar in joint ownership." With that in mind, we dedicate this book to all those who steal moments from the weight of the present to dream and dance towards a better tomorrow. All the poets, liars, dreamers, heretics, and brethren of the new free spirit, cheers to you.

Gracious thanks for permission to reprint articles that have appeared elsewhere in English: "Continental Drift: Activist Research, From Geopolitics to Geopoetics" (*Framework* Issue 4 December 2005); "Do It Yourself...and the Movement Beyond Capitalism" (*Radical Society* Volume 31, Number 1 2004); "Something More on Research Militancy: Footnotes on Procedures and (In)Decisions" (*ephemera* Volume 5, Number 4 November 2005); and "Autonomy, Recognition, Movement" (*the commoner* Number 11 Spring / Summer 2006).

We would also like to thank the following people for the images (listed by page number) that hopefully make this volume more interesting to look at than it would be otherwise: Haduhi Szukis (10, 250), RadicalGraphics.org (36), the Dissent Network! (110), and Gaye Chan (178).

How to Use This Book

Method is nothing else than reflective knowledge, or the idea of an idea...the foundation which must direct our thoughts can be nothing other than the knowledge of that which constitutes the reality of truth, and the knowledge of the understanding, its properties and power. —Baruch Spinoza

This is not a book that has been designed to sit on a shelf; its primary purpose is not to be used as a citation or reference in important sounding journals that no one reads. It is a text intended for use as a tool to gather experiences, examples, and materials that can further the development of the constituent power of lived imagination that will transform the world around us.

Militant research is not a specialized task, a process that only involves those who are traditionally thought of as researchers. It is an intensification and deepening of the political. Militant research starts from the understandings, experiences, and relations generated through organizing, as both a method of political action and as a form of knowledge. With this in mind, individuals and groups are encouraged to send their stories and experiences of conducting militant research to info@constituentimagination.net.

New materials and information will be added to the website for this project regularly: http://www.constituentimagination.net. Suggestions of materials, resources, and links are always welcome and encouraged.

Introduction

Stevphen Shukaitis + David Graeber

Thoughts. Provocations. Explorations. Forms of investigation and social research that expand possibilities for political action, proliferating tactics of resistance through the constituent power of the imagination. Walking, we ask questions, not from the perspective of the theorist removed and separate from organizing, but rather from within and as part of the multiple and overlapping cycles and circuits of struggle. For the removed theorist, movements themselves are mere abstractions, pieces of data to be categorized, analyzed, and fixed. The work of militant investigation is multiple, collectively extending forms of antagonism to new levels of understanding, composing flesh-made words from immanent processes of resistance. Far from vanguardist notions of intellectual practice that translate organizing strategies and concepts for populations who are believed to be too stupid or unable to move beyond trade union consciousness, it is a process of collective wondering and wandering that is not afraid to admit that the question of how to move forward is always uncertain, difficult, and never resolved in easy answers that are eternally correct. As an open process, militant investigation discovers new possibilities within the present, turning bottlenecks and seeming dead ends into new opportunities for joyful insurgency.

A beautiful example of this is John Holloway's book, *Change the World Without Taking Power*. Holloway, a soft-spoken Scottish political philosopher, was associated with the "Open Marxism" school developed at the University of Edinburgh where he taught in the 1970s and '80s. In 1991, he moved to Mexico where he took a position with the Instituto de Humanidades y Ciencias Sociales in the Universidad Autónoma de Puebla. After the Zapatista rebellion broke out in 1994, he quickly became one of its chief intellectual supporters. In 1998, he helped compile a book of essays on the Zapatistas called *Zapatista! Reinventing Revolution in Mexico*; this was his attempt to think through the implications of this new revolutionary paradigm, one which rejected classic Marxist ideas of vanguardism and the very project of trying to seize state power for one of building autonomous communities rooted in new forms of direct democracy, using the categories of Marxist theory. The result was an extremely dense book. At certain points, it reads like a mixture of Marxist jargon and lyric poetry:

> In the beginning is the scream. We scream.
>
> When we write or when we read, it is easy to forget that the beginning is not the word, but the scream. Faced with the mutilation of human lives by capitalism, a scream of sadness, a scream of horror, a scream of anger, a scream of refusal: NO.
>
> The starting point of theoretical reflection is opposition, negativity, struggle. It is from rage that thought is born, not from the pose of reason, not from the reasoned-sitting-back-and-reflecting-on-the-mysteries-of-existence that is the conventional image of the thinker.
>
> We start from negation, from dissonance. The dissonance can take many shapes. An inarticulate mumble of discontent, tears of frustration, a scream of rage, a confident roar. An unease, a confusion, a longing, a critical vibration.[1]

More than anything else, it's a book about knowledge. Holloway argues that reality is a matter of humans doing and making things together: what we perceive as fixed self-identical objects are really processes. The only reason we insist on treating objects as anything else is because, if we saw them as they really are, as mutual projects, it would be impossible for anyone to claim ownership of them. All liberatory struggle therefore is ultimately the struggle against identity. Forms of knowledge that simply arrange and classify reality from a distance—what Holloway refers to as "knowledge-about"—may be appropriate for a vanguard party that wants to claim the right to seize power and impose itself on the basis of some privileged "scientific" understanding, but ultimately it can only work to reinforce structures of domination. True revolutionary knowledge would have to be different. It would have to be a pragmatic form of knowledge that lays bare all such pretensions; a form of knowledge deeply embedded in the logic of transformational practice.

Furious debates ensued. Leninists and Trotskyites lambasted the book as utopian for adopting what they considered a naïve anarchist position—one that was completely ignorant of political realities. Anarchists were alternately inspired and annoyed, often noting that Holloway seemed to echo anarchist ideas without ever mentioning them, instead writing as if his positions emerged naturally from a correct reading of classic Marxist texts. Others objected to the way he read the texts. Supporters of Toni Negri's Spinozist version of Marxism denounced the book as so much Hegelian claptrap; others suggested that Holloway's argument that any belief in self-identical objects was a reflection of capitalist logic seemed to imply that capitalism had been around since the invention of language, which ultimately made it very difficult to imagine an alternative.

In Latin America, where the battle was particularly intense, a lot of the arguments turned around very particular questions of revolutionary strategy. Who has the better model: the Zapatistas of Chiapas or Chavez's Bolivarian Revolution in Venezuela? Were the Argentine radicals who overthrew four successive regimes in December of 2001 right to refuse seizing power, to reject the entire domain of formal politics and try to create their own autonomous institutions? Or had they allowed an opportunity for genuine revolutionary change to slip through their grasp? For many in the global justice movement in Europe and North America, the book provided the perfect counterpoint to Michael Hardt and Negri's *Empire*, then being hailed in the media as the bible of the movement. Where Hardt and Negri were drawing on an Italian autonomist tradition that saw capital not as imposing itself on labor but as constantly having to adjust itself to the power of workers' struggle, Holloway was arguing that this approach did not go nearly far enough. In fact, capital was labor and capitalism the system that makes it impossible for us to see this. Capitalism is something we make every day and the moment we stop making it, it will cease to exist. There were endless Internet debates. Seminars and reading groups were held comparing the two arguments in probably a dozen different languages.

What we want to draw attention to is that this debate was carried out almost completely amongst activists. Holloway himself was a bit surprised on discovering teenage anarchists were taking his book with them while hopping trains or attending mass mobilizations. "It's a very difficult book," he admitted to a journalist who interviewed him in 2002, adding he was "surprised and gratified" that so many young people had taken an interest in it.[2] Meanwhile, in the academy, it was as if all this had never happened. Holloway's book was not widely assigned in courses or read in graduate seminars. In fact, most Marxist scholars seemed unaware that John Holloway even existed. Mention his name and one would almost invariably be greeted by blank stares. It was as if the debate was happening in another universe. In some ways, perhaps it was.

It's important to note this was not because this book is mainly concerned with practical advice to activists. Actually, it contains almost none. It's a work of philosophy; a theory of knowledge that concedes the author has no idea how one would actually go about putting its theories into practice. On the other hand, as a theory of knowledge it is daring, sophisticated, and quite brilliant. So why was it ignored in the academy? The obvious response is slightly scandalous. What makes Holloway unusual is not that he is writing theory but that he is writing theory that explicitly argues that writing theory is not enough. In the academy, theories of action are acceptable. Theories that argue that writing itself is a form of political action are acceptable (in fact they are greatly appreciated). Theories that are in effect calls to political action beyond the academy pass by as if they never were.

The Peculiar Drama of the Imperial Academy

Granted what we are saying is particularly true of the American academy, one increasingly cut off from the rest of the world. For that reason it is perhaps fitting that a great many of the materials in this volume come from the US (as well as Canada and the UK). Hopefully, they will start conversations and motions in new directions in engaged research, which in general have been occurring elsewhere (particularly in Italy, Spain, and South America) for much longer. Empire always produces a certain blindness. In the case of the United States, one form this takes is a strange obliviousness to the fact that our university system, though the largest in the world, is not only no longer producing social theory the rest of the world is particularly interested in, it's hardly even importing any. Ask a social scientist in France to name an American social theorist, the only ones likely to come readily to mind are turn of the century Pragmatists and '50s sociologists like Erving Goffman and Harold Garfinkel, and possibly Judith Butler.

True, during the Cold War, there was a determined effort, led by sociologists like Talcott Parsons, to create some kind of hegemonic US-centered social science largely based on developing Max Weber as a theoretical alternative to Marx. That dissolved after the worldwide student rebellions of the late '60s. In the US, this was followed by a huge inrush of French theory, a kind of French invasion. For over a decade there was a flood of new theoretical heroes one after the other: Lacan, Levi-Strauss, Deleuze, Foucault, Lyotard, Kristeva, Derrida, Cixous, De Certeau, and so on. Then somehow the spigot dried up. It's not that France was no longer producing theorists, it was just that (with few exceptions) American scholars were not interested in them. Instead, for the last fifteen or twenty years, the American academy—or the part that fancies itself to be the radical, critical, subversive branch of it—have for some reason preferred to endlessly recycle the same body of French theory: roughly, reading and rereading a set of texts written between 1968 and 1983. There are all sorts of ironies here. Aside from the obvious one, that a group of people so obsessed with intellectual fashion do not seem to notice they are recycling ideas from thirty years ago—rather like music fans who feel they are the quintessence of cool even though they listen exclusively to classic rock—there's the very fact that those American academics who see themselves as the most subversive of all structures of received authority have been spending most of their time establishing and preserving an authoritative canon.[3] Meanwhile, any number of major intellectual trends in Europe (for instance Critical Realism in the UK, the MAUSS group in France, Luhman's Systems Theory in Germany) that are widely discussed in Brazil, for instance, in America seem to pass by almost completely unnoticed. True, this is only a part of the picture. The American academy, as Jack Bratich points out later in this volume, has always been divided between the administrative and critical functions.

The former has been running great guns (sometimes all too literally) and has generated a great deal of theory—various strains of economics, rational choice theories and the like—that are directly involved in maintaining neoliberal institutions, justifying and providing technologies for various administrative bureaucracies, staffing everything from NGOs to advertising agencies. Here ideas really are flowing out of America again and have had an enormous influence over the rest of the world—even if for the most part they have been rammed down the throats of administrative bureaucracies by the threat of coups, bribery, intimidation, the manipulation of international debt (and, recently, outright military conquest).[4] The scions of the critical left meanwhile often seem uninterested in the phenomenon, engaging in heated debates about epistemic violence without having very much to say about the more literal violence often being planned and justified on the other side of the quad.

Perhaps this is exactly what one should expect from a dying empire. Or perhaps from any empire, dying or not. Great empires are not known for promoting intellectual creativity. They tend to be more interested in questions of law and administration. American universities are at this point primarily concerned with training the staff for various global bureaucracies (government, NGOs, corporations) and, secondarily, providing for the reproduction of what right-wing populists like to call the "liberal elite," an increasingly endogamous and inward-looking caste who dominate what passes for American culture. If they have found an intellectual formula that successfully justifies and facilitates that, why would there be need to change it?

Or is there something wrong with universities in general?

On the other hand one could just as well ask: why is it we assume that creative and relevant ideas should be coming out of universities in the first place? The modern university system has existed only a few hundred years and during most of that time, universities were not places that much fostered innovation or the questioning of received knowledge. They were largely places for compiling and redacting received knowledge and teaching students to respect authority. The old-fashioned stereotype of the professor as a greybeard pedant fussing over some obscure interpretation of a Latin epode, unaware of or disdainful of the world around him, was not really that far from the truth. For the most part, universities were dominated by figures who were scholars but in no sense intellectuals.

This has not changed as much as we'd like to think. Graduate school is not on the whole meant to foster creativity or encourage students to produce new ideas. For the most part, it's designed to break students down, to foster insecurity and fear as a way of life, and ultimately to crush that sense of joy in learning and playing with ideas that moved most students to dedicate their lives to the academy to begin with. For this it substitutes an imperative for obsequiousness, competitiveness, and slick self-presentation that is referred to as "professionalization."[5] Graduate school is designed to produce academic functionaries who when they finally do have tenure, and can say whatever they want, are almost certain not to have anything too dramatic or relevant to say. Of course there are always those who refuse to be crushed. The majority are kicked out or marginalized; a select minority promoted to superstar status and treated as charismatic heroes so obviously exceptional that their very existence serves to remind mere mortals of their limitations. And the casualization of academic labor, of course, has made all this even worse.

From this perspective, what we saw in the '60s was something rather unusual: a brief moment when the model changed. Universities were supposed to encompass intellectual life, intellectual life was to be creative and politically radical. By now the pretense is wearing thin. In US universities, the only folks coming up with really innovative ideas in the social or cultural field are involved with postcolonial studies—expats and intellectuals with roots in the global south, a group that will most likely increasingly abandon imperial universities as American power itself begins to fade. The realignment is already starting to happen. The largest departments for American studies, for example, are currently in universities in India and China. For present purposes, this matter is something of an aside. The critical thing is that universities were never meant to be places for intellectual creativity. If it happens, it's not because it is especially conducive to them, but only because if you pay enough people to sit around thinking, some new ideas are bound to get through. This raises an interesting question: Where do new ideas actually come from? In particular, where do new ideas about the nature of social life originate?

We're anarchists, so of course our immediate impulse is to say: "But of course, they emerge from social movements, or from the unleashing of popular creativity that follows moments of revolutionary upheaval." Or as Robin D.G. Kelley puts it, "Revolutionary dreams erupt out of political engagement: collective social movements are incubators of new knowledge."[6] Clearly there is some truth in this. Consider the outpouring of creativity that followed the Russian revolution—not only in the arts, but especially in social theory: whether the psychological theories of Lev Vygotsky and Alexander Luria, the dialogism of the Bakhtin circle, or even the folklorism of Vladimir Propp or structural linguistics of the Prague School.[7] It's all the more impressive when one considers how brief was the window for creativity, before the innovators began to be murdered, sent to camps, starved or killed in world wars, or simply shut down by Stalinist orthodoxy. Still it seems that things are a bit more complicated. Especially if one is speaking of social theory, new ideas are even more likely to emerge from the frustration of revolutionary hopes than from their fulfillment.[8]

As Robert Nisbet pointed out half a century ago, sociology rose from the wreckage of the French revolution. Almost all of its early themes—community, authority, status, the sacred—were first singled out by reactionary critics of the revolution like Louis-Gabriel Bonald, Edmund Burke, or Joseph de Maistre, who argued these were precisely the social realities that Enlightenment thinkers had treated as so many bad ideas that could simply be brushed away. As a result, they argued, when revolutionaries inspired by Enlightenment teachings tried to put their ideas into practice, the result was inevitably catastrophic. These themes were then picked up by authors like St. Simon and Comte and eventually fashioned into a discipline. Similarly, Marx wrote *Capital* in the wake of the failure of the revolutions of 1848 largely in order to understand what it was about capitalism that made it so resilient. The entire history of Western Marxism, from Lukács through Gramsci and the Frankfurt School, has been a series of attempts to explain why the proletariat in the most advanced industrial nations did not rise up in arms. Whatever you might think of this tradition, none but the most hardened Stalinist would deny that it was extraordinarily creative.

There's a peculiar pattern of inversions here. Universities were founded as places for the celebration of art and culture; they still like to represent themselves that way in brochures and promotional literature. Over the last two hundred years, however, they have become ever more focused on economics and administration. In the case of revolutionary movements, things have developed very much the other way around. What began as workers' organizations grappling with immediate economic issues have, as workers consistently appeared willing to act against their own economic interests, been forced to grapple more explicitly with the nature of symbols and meanings—even as their theorists continue to insist they are ultimately materialists. One can already see this in Marx's *Capital*, a book that begins not with an analysis of material infrastructure but with a long and utterly brilliant symbolic analysis of monetary value. Western Marxism quickly became a tradition of cultural analysis. State socialist regimes were obsessed with cultural issues as well but they exhibited remarkably bad faith in this regard. In their ideological statements, they invariably proclaimed themselves ardent economic determinists and insisted that the domain of ideas is just a reflection of material forces. Then they proceeded to lock up anyone who disagreed with them on this point, or for that matter anyone who composed art or poetry that didn't meet their approval. As many have pointed out, there's a bit of a contradiction here. If they really believed art and ideas were epiphenomena, this sort of behavior would be completely pointless. By mobilizing such enormous material resources to suppress even the whisper of dissent, they acted as if they attributed an enormous power to ideas. So one could say that by the mid-twentieth century most branches of Marxism, for better or worse, not only believed that there was a domain of ideas separate from practice (already a pretty dubious proposition in our opinion), but that ideas had extraordinary political power. Capitalists, even while they espoused some variety of philosophical idealism, acted as one would if they really believed in material determinism. They didn't lose a lot of sleep worrying about art and philosophy but saved their energies for maintaining control over the means of production, on the assumption that if they did so, the rest would more or less take care of itself.

All this helps explain why so much of the radical theory of today—including the vast majority of concepts drawn on in this book—trace back to France and Italy. These countries were, especially in mid-century, trapped inside an extraordinary situation of suspense, where a permanently stalled revolution produced an apparently endless outpouring of theoretical innovation.

Demanding the Impossible (Why France?)

It's commonplace nowadays to say that at the Yalta conference on the division of Europe after World War II, Churchill and Roosevelt "sold out" Eastern Europe by allowing Stalin to keep everything occupied by the Red Army within the Communist orbit. This happened of course, but what's usually left out is that in exchange, the Soviets told Communist resistance forces poised to seize power in Italy and France to hold off and refused to give meaningful support to Communist partisans who did try to seize power in Greece, even after the Western powers rushed in aid to the fascist colonels who eventually crushed them. Had the fate of Europe been left to purely internal forces the postwar division might have looked completely different. It presumably would have been not an East-West split but a North-South split. Those countries bordering on the Mediterranean (with the exception of Spain and Portugal already lost to fascist regimes) would be socialist, and those of the north from England and Germany to Poland and Lithuania would be allied with the capitalist powers (with the probable exception of Scandinavia). What those southern European regimes would have ended up looking like—something along the lines of Yugoslavia or some kind of parliamentary socialism, for example?—we will never know. The important thing here is the fact that it *didn't* happen.

In France, the moment of opportunity quickly faded. The United States government rushed in money and support for a right-wing nationalist regime that quickly began implementing most of the major planks of the left-wing program, nationalizing banks and instituting universal health care. There followed two decades of great prosperity. The university system expanded rapidly. The Communist Party (PCF) soon found itself with a lock on the votes of the industrial workers and control over the union bureaucracy, but no broader electoral support. Over time, Communist functionaries came to a de facto acceptance of their status within the overall structure of power. At the same time, their official ideology was straight Soviet-line. Intellectuals who supported the party were obliged to at least pay lip service to an extremely orthodox, hidebound version of Marxism. The only alternatives were to join the world of squabbling Trotskyite sects, detach oneself from any meaningful tie to mass-based social movements, or give up on politics entirely. Even Foucault joined the PCF. Most remained on the Left and tried to reach some sort of compromise. The temptation to remain politically engaged was strong since this was an environment where (much as in Eastern Europe) ideas actually were taken seriously but where (unlike in Eastern Europe) the state provided intellectuals with generous grants and never shot them. Intellectuals were left with a situation where they were free to say whatever they liked, where broad sections of the public were actually interested in their opinions, but where the main thing they had to talk about was the lack of revolutionary transformation.

What followed is a story that's been told many times before and there's no reason to rehearse it in any detail. We don't really need to map out the succession of intellectual trends (Existentialism, Structuralism, Poststructuralism...), intellectual heroes (Sartre, Levi-Strauss, Foucault...) or even to go into a detailed account of the events of May '68, when a campus insurrection led to a series of wildcat sympathy strikes in factories around France that paralyzed the country and briefly seemed to herald a genuine social revolution. That promise was, as we all know, not to be. It was betrayed most dramatically by the PCF itself whose unions joined with the government to do everything in their power to bring employees back to work and the population back under the control of the administrative apparatus. In doing so, they managed to destroy any remaining illusion that the party might ever be a revolutionary force and therefore any legitimacy it might still have had among the intellectual classes. In the wake of the failed revolt there followed an even greater surge of innovative theoretical writings, one that lasted for more than a decade. This is the body of texts that has now become the canon of American social and cultural theory.

Here we can add something to the conventional account. What is referred to in France as *"la pensée soixante-huit"* or "68 thought," and in America as "French theory," consists—as authors like Peter Starr have pointed out—largely of attempts to explain why the insurrectionaries failed and why revolution in the traditional sense of the term was no longer possible. Or, alternately, why it never was possible. Or, why the insurrectionaries had not failed, because really they were avatars not of communism but of consumerism, or individualism, or the sexual revolution, or maybe something else. There was a dazzling array of arguments. Again, there would be no point in trying to rehearse them all. What many fail to notice is that few of these arguments were entirely new. For the most part they drew on the same themes and theoretical concepts that had been put forward in the streets during the insurrection: the rejection of bureaucratic organization, the liberation of desire and the imagination, and the imperative to unveil the hidden structures of domination that lay beneath every aspect of everyday life. Even though the insurrectionaries took them in much less pessimistic or individualistic directions. In this sense, calling it "68 thought" is not entirely deceptive. Daniel Cohn-Bendit later claimed that he and the other rebel spokesmen hadn't really invented anything: they were just repeating slogans and arguments they'd read in the works of the Situationist International, *Socialisme ou Barbarie*, and the anarchist journal *Rouge et Noir*. However, this is precisely where '68 marks a great intellectual rupture. If one goes to an anarchist bookstore or infoshop in almost any part of the world, this is what one is still likely to find: There will be works by and about the Situationists (particularly Guy Debord and Raoul Vaneigem), and the *Socialisme ou Barbarie* authors (certainly Cornelius Castoriadis, occasionally even Claude Lefort), alongside others continuing in the same tradition, and anarchist journals of every sort. Usually equally striking in their absence will be the work of the most famous poststructuralist authors like Michel Foucault, or Deleuze and Guattari.

The absence of the latter can be partly attributed to the fact that they are so easily available elsewhere. University bookstores are crammed full of the stuff and rarely carry anything by the authors likely to be found in infoshops. It is very hard to avoid the conclusion that the readership for French theory has effectively split in two. Activists continue to read the works immediately preceding May '68: works that anticipated revolution. They also continue to develop them. Academics continue to read and develop the works from immediately afterwards. The result is two different streams of literature. Activists do draw from the academic stream to a certain degree, but the academics almost never read the other one.

Let us provide a small illustration. One of the first French Marxist scholars to concern himself with the liberation of ordinary life from structures of alienation (commuting, consumerism, dead time) was Henri Lefebvre, a sociologist whose book, *Critique of Everyday Life*, came out as early as 1947. He was eventually expelled from the Communist Party. In 1957, his teaching assistant Jean Baudrillard convinced Guy Debord and Raoul Vaneigem (known at the time as sometime-artists, sometime-essayists and political agitators) to attend a course of lectures Lefebvre was offering on the subject of daily life at Nanterre. The ideas set out in those lectures had an enormous influence on the manifestos of the Situationist International that began to appear in the early '60s, during which time all four men became great friends. There were eventually falling outs (there always were with the Situationists), but one can observe the same themes in Baudrillard's dissertation work *The System of Objects* (1968), as in Debord's *Society of the Spectacle* (1967) and Vaneigem's *Revolution of Everyday Life* (1967)—the latter two were also considered the two most important texts for the rebellion. Debord and Vaneigem focused on what they called "the spectacle," seeing the passivity of consumer audiences before the TV screen as the most concrete and explicit form of the relation created by the entire commodity system that renders us all obliging audiences to our own lives. The spectacle breaks down and destroys any sense of life as art, adventure, or community (all living "totalities" in their language), and then hooks us into the system by selling us dead spectral images of everything we have lost. Where Baudrillard used semiotic theory to describe how the consumer system operated by a total, all-embracing logic, Debord tried to map out the mechanics of "spectacular capitalism" and the ways to strike back against it through artistic subversion and creation of systems of insurrectionary self-management. Vaneigem wrote books directly addressed to young people, describing the immediate textures of daily life under capitalism in a style that mixed high theory, catchy slogans, and bitter satire as well as imagining insurrectionary alternatives.

After '68, Baudrillard abandoned Marxism, having decided that its logic was merely a mirror of capitalism. He's now considered one of the first great avatars of postmodernism—though a rather unusual one, since he never abandoned the idea that capitalism was a giant totalizing system that renders consumers passive and helpless before it, only the idea that there was any meaningful way to strike back. Resistance, he argued, is impossible. The best we can hope for is a certain "ironic detachment." Debord allowed the SI to collapse and tried to drink himself to death, eventually committing suicide. Vaneigem never stopped writing (he spent a good deal of his later life researching Medieval heresies) and continues to put out radical tracts to this day.

The striking thing here is the reception these three theorists had in the academy. What follows is a little experiment using the online academic search engine Jstor (jstor.org), which compiles major academic journals in the English language. We took the simple expedient of searching by discipline for the number of academic articles that mentioned each of the three authors by name. The results were striking:

	Baudrillard	Debord	Vaneigem
Language & Literature	348	80	3
Art & Art History	75	34	7
Sociology	51	5	0
History	45	10	1
Anthropology	22	3	0
Philosophy	21	3	0
Political Science	20	1	0
Economics/Business	11	0	0

The figures more or less speak for themselves.[9] Baudrillard is considered canonical and is regularly cited in all disciplines, even if many authors often only cite him in order to disagree with him. Debord is seen as a minor figure in art or literary studies, and is almost unknown outside them. Raoul Vaneigem might as well never have been born.

This is interesting for any number of reasons. If you ask a scholar in, say, a cultural studies department what they think of the Situationists, you are likely to witness some kind of intellectual brush of the hand. The usual response is a dismissal of them as silly '50s or '60s Marxists, along the lines of the Frankfurt School who believed that capitalism was an all-powerful system of production and consumers were hapless dupes being fed manufactured fantasies. Eventually, you will then be told, students of popular culture came to realize this position was elitist and puritanical. After all, if one examines how real working people actually live, one will discover that they construct the meaning of their lives largely out of consumer goods but that they do it in their own creative, subversive fashion and not as passive dupes of marketing executives. In other words, real proletarians don't need some French bohemian pamphleteer to call on them to subvert the system, they're already doing it on their own. Hence, this sort of literature is an insult to those in whose name it claims to speak. It doesn't deserve to be taken seriously.

This is one reason we think the case of Baudrillard is so telling. After all, if Debord and Vaneigem are being elitist, Baudrillard is obviously a thousand times more so. Debord and Vaneigem at least thought it was possible to strike back against the spectacle. Baudrillard no longer does. For him, we are nothing but helpless dupes and there's nothing we can do about it; except, perhaps, to step back and admire our own cleverness for at least (unlike the pathetic fools still insisting they can change things) having figured that out. Yet Baudrillard remains an academic superstar. One has to ask: if the cultural studies folks are right to dismiss the Situationists as elitists with contempt for the real lives of non-academics, why is it that non-academics continue to buy their books? Why is it that non-academics are pretty much the *only* people who continue to buy their books? Because it's not just info-shops. Since the late '70s, Situationist ideas, slogans and forms of analysis have become so thoroughly inscribed in the sensibilities of punk rock that it's almost impossible to listen for very long to certain strains of counter-cultural music without hearing some catchy phrase taken directly from the works of Raoul Vaneigem. The Situationists have managed to become *part* of popular culture while cultural studies has remained completely trapped in the academy. It is these practices of do-it-yourself cultural production that Ben Holtzman, Craig Hughes, and Kevin Van Meter describe in this volume as forms for developing post-capitalist social relations in the present.

The obvious conclusion is that it's precisely Baudrillard's elitism that makes him palatable for academics, because it's the kind of elitism that tells its readers not to do anything. It's okay to argue that it's not necessary to change the world through political action. It's okay to argue it's not possible. What's not okay—or anyway, what's considered tiresome and uninterest-ing—is to write works that cannot be read as anything but a call to action. Debord *can* be read simply as a theorist, though it requires a good deal of willful blindness. In the case of Vaneigem it's nearly impossible. Hence, in the eyes of the academy: Debord is a minor figure and Vaneigem does not exist.

We are not writing to say either of these two traditions is superior, let alone that one should efface the other. Just about every contributor to this volume draws on both. We do want to insist on two things. The first is that both traditions are equally intellectually legitimate. The university does not have any kind of monopoly over insight or theoretical sophistication. The second is that these ideas can only be understood within their social context. The Situationists developed perhaps the single most unsparing critique of the alienation of capitalist life. As members of an artistic collective that turned increasingly toward political action, they became prophetic voices for that intuition that has always existed in the revolutionary Left—that the experience of unalienated production in art can somehow be fused to the tradition of direct action to point to a way out. It is this tradition that Gavin Grindon traces through from the Surrealists and the College of Sociology to the actions against the G8 that occurred in 2005 in the fields of Scotland. Castoriadis, in turn, is the great philosopher of the revolutionary imagina-tion; from him we get the power to create something out of nothing that seems to crop up at moments of crisis and upheaval, which developed into a theory of revolutionary "autonomy"—in the literal sense, the power of com-munities to make their own rules.

The post-'68 reaction challenged a series of the key terms—the subject, totalities, dialectics, alienation, even (in its traditional sense) power—and effectively removed them from the mix. This was part of a general purging of Marxist categories. The disillusionment with Marx is not in itself entirely surprising considering the previous dominance of the French Communist Party and the almost universal revulsion against its role in the events of May '68. But here too, this can be seen as radicalizing certain trends that had already existed within Marxist thought well before '68. It was primarily a rejection of Hegel and the Hegelian notion of the subject. If the emphasis on structures of domination within everyday life traced back to activist circles, the desire to scrub away everything that smacked of dialectics traced to Louis Althusser, the philosopher who in the '50s became the chief academic stalwart of the PCF. Althusser is famous for arguing that there was an epistemic break in *Capital* where one could detect the exact moment where Marx abandoned his early dialectical concerns with alienation and developed instead a scientific understanding of society. He often argued for a Marxism that would be founded not on Hegel but Spinoza and was also the first to insist that the very notion that we think of ourselves as subjects, as beings with free choice and free will, is an illusion created by larger structures of domination. Incidentally, he was also the mentor of a certain Michel Foucault. One might say that poststructuralism is largely Althusser without the Marx.

True, in their first book, *Anti-Oedipus* (1968), Gilles Deleuze and Felix Guattari were still writing in the classic mode of trying to save Marx from his latter-day interpreters. Before long though, Marx apparently vanished. Similarly Michel Foucault, who used to boast he had been out of the country during the events of May '68, quickly abandoned claims of affinity with Maoism to build a career around a series of strategic rejections of traditional Marxist interests and assumptions. All sorts of previously orthodox figures tried to outdo one another in their rejection of some aspect of their previous orthodoxy. The most dramatic case, perhaps, was Françoise Lyotard, who was previously best known for leading the breakaway faction that had split from the *Socialisme ou Barbarie* group in protest when they abandoned the principle that only the industrial proletariat could lead the revolution. (His new group was called *Communisme ou Barbarie*.) By 1979, Lyotard announced that we had begun the transition to a new age, which he dubbed "postmodernism," marked by an attitude of suspicion towards all metanarratives (aside from, presumably, the one he was now proposing). Marxism, and also nationalism, for example, were increasingly becoming relics of an antiquated age—a claim that one would think would be considered more of an historical irony considering it was announced in a "report on knowledge" offered up to the government of Québec.

What one sees here is how the emphasis shifted from the factory and capital to the questions about how subjects are created through an endless variety of discourses on forms of power or production outside those domains we normally think of as the economy: in the family, clinics, asylums, bodies, prisons, literary texts. These domains were not seen as refractions of, or subordinate to, the logic of capital, but rather as part of the shifting ground made up of fractured fields of power, without a center or coordinative bond. Sometimes this was seen as the simple truth of power, other times it was seen as marking the truth of a new stage of history that itself emerged in the wake of '68. Either way, this eliminated any space for a politics of alienation because there never was a natural state from which to feel estranged, or anyway, there isn't any more. Either way, we are merely the product of an endless series of discourses.

Poststructuralism has added an enormously rich vocabulary to the human sciences: disciplinary systems, discourses and truth-effects, subject formation, rhizomatic structures, war machines, desiring machines, panopticism, territorializations and deterritorializations, flows, biopolitics, nomadology, simulacra, governmentality, etc. While all this has come to dominate critical theory in the American academy and to various degrees elsewhere as well, and in many cases there used to justify political withdrawal, it's not as if activists have found it entirely useless. As we've said, activists seem much more likely to draw from the academic stream than the other way around.

We Want Everything, or the Italian Laboratory

While French theory from the '60s and '70s has been the staple of the global academy for years, interest in Italian radical theory from this period is more recent. Historically, the situation in Italy was in many ways similar to France. Here too the Communist Party played a principal role in the resistance during World War II, and was poised to seize power afterwards, when it seemed the only major political force untainted by association with fascism. The Italian Communist Party was also ordered to stand down by Stalin, and ended up playing the loyal opposition within a social democratic regime dominated by parties of the Right. Italy was unique in at least two crucial ways. First, the Italian party was that of Antonio Gramsci. After the war it threw itself into a classic Gramscian war of position, building strategic alliances and cultural hegemony based upon the idea of the autonomy of the political. Perhaps as a result, the Italian Communist Party remained far larger than the French Communist Party even in its heyday. It was often very close to the majority party, even if the US-supported Christian democrats always managed to control the government. As in France, the result was that the party dominated the labor bureaucracy, but it also increasingly drifted away from the immediate bread-and-butter concerns of factory workers, continually sacrificing them for broader political imperatives. This leads to the second key difference: the structure of the Italian academy meant that

'68 had a very different impact. Rather than creating a moment of exaltation followed by collapse, the alliance between students and workers was in a sense institutionalized. At the very least, activists, researchers, and factory workers continued to talk to one another. The result was a series of intense overlapping cycles of struggles lasting over ten years. Some of the organizational structures that emerged during this period—most famously, the squats and occupied social centers—endure to this day.

It's often said that in Italy, 1968 happened twice: first in '68 and then in '77. It would probably be more accurate to say it never completely ended: even if the fierce government repression after the occupations and uprisings of '77 had the effect of destroying much of the organizational infrastructure and landed thousands of activists and hundreds of intellectuals in jail, or sent them fleeing to foreign exile.[10] Here it might be helpful to recall an argument of Immanuel Wallerstein that genuine revolutionary moments, even if they seem to take place in one country, are always worldwide in scope. The French revolution in 1789 or Russian revolution in 1917 might well have had just as powerful long-term effects on Denmark or Mexico. The revolutions of 1848 and 1968 did not succeed in taking over the state apparatus anywhere but they caused convulsions across the world that marked genuine breaks in history. Afterwards things were not the same. In the case of the revolutions of '68, this was, according to Wallerstein, a rejection of states and state bureaucracies as instruments of the public will. So it's appropriate, perhaps, that in Italy, where '68 took such institutional legs, what started as "workerism" ultimately came to be known as "autonomism."

The body of theory generated by this particular frustrated—but not completely frustrated—transformation was also different from France. Where one saw a gradual movement away from Marxism in France, in Italy it was marked by a "return to Marx," a rejection of Gramscian theories of cultural hegemony[11] and an attempt to reexamine Marx's original texts—*Capital* and the *Grundrisse*—in the light of contemporary conditions. The range of concepts that emerged from all this—class composition, the social factory, revolutionary exodus, immaterial labor, the general intellect, constituent power, the state form, real subsumption, the circulation of struggles, and so on—have permanently enriched the revolutionary tradition. It is a language and a conceptual apparatus that is just as complex and challenging as poststructuralism. It would be vain to try and summarize it, but we thought it important to stress two areas where, in our opinion, the autonomist tradition has made extraordinarily important contributions.

One of the greatest achievements of autonomist theory has been to remove class struggle from the back burner of social theory. Generations of political Marxists have tended to give lip service to the notion that it should be important, and then go on to write history as if the real driving force in almost anything—imperialism, the factory system, the rise of feminism—was the working out of contradictions within capital itself. Capital was always the prime actor in the historical drama; workers' organizations were left to scramble to adjust to its latest depredations. Against this, Mario Tronti, one of the first theorists of Italian workerism, proposed what he termed a "Copernican shift." Let us, he said, re-imagine history from the assumption that resistance is primary and it's capital that must always readjust. The results were surprisingly compelling. Rather than seeing the neoliberal offensive that began in the late '70s and peaked in the early '90s as an unstoppable capitalist offensive against the social gains embodied in the welfare state, and then imagining working class organizations as its defenders, it became possible to see welfare state capitalism had itself been destroyed and delegitimized by popular revolts in the '60s. What was '68, after all, if not a rebellion against the stifling conformity and engines of bureaucratic control, against the factory system and work in general, in the name of individual freedoms and the liberation of desire? Capital first stumbled and then was forced to turn the rebels' weapons against them saying, in effect, "You want freedom? We'll show you freedom! You want flexibility? We'll show you flexibility!" Class struggle consists of dynamic moments of composition—in which the working class creates new structures, alliances, forms of communication, cooperation—and decomposition, through which capital is forced to turn some of these tools back on it, so as to introduce hierarchies and divisions that destroy working class solidarity. In Italy, this made it much easier to understand the paradoxical role of the Italian Communist Party that ultimately became an agent of capitalism, and the main force in imposing the Italian version of neoliberalism.

Another major contribution was the argument that the growth of what came to be referred to as "new social movements" and "identity politics" starting in the late '60s—whether the women's movement, ethnic or racially based movements, gay rights, or lifestyle-based groups like punks and hippies, movements no longer centered on the factory or capitalist workplace— did not mean that the logic of capitalism was no longer important. Rather, the logic of the factory (exploitation, discipline, the extraction of surplus value) had come to subsume everything. But so did labor power: the extension of capitalist controls into every aspect of human life paradoxically meant that capital no longer had any space in which it was completely dominant. This line of argument culminated in Toni Negri's famous claim that in effect we are already living under communism because capitalism has been increasingly forced to make its profits parasitically, leeching off of forms of cooperation (like language or the Internet) that were developed almost entirely outside of it. Whatever one may think of the particulars, this sort of argument is once again groundbreaking in its insistence on putting capitalism in its place.

It is not that '68 was a failure. Capitalism is a global system; it would never have been possible to liberate a bounded territory like France or Italy anyway. Rather, capitalism has been forced to claim credit for our victories, and even sell them back to us. The fact that feminism, to take an obvious example, has been co-opted and corporatized does not mean that the Women's Movement was a failure or a capitalist plot. Under the current domain of real subsumption, everything is co-opted. This in turn means that capitalism is increasingly administering social forms that are not in their essence capitalist at all.

One need hardly remark how different all this is from the reaction to '68 in France, with its retreat from Marx—although the social transformations being considered were quite similar: the introduction of post-Fordist industrial systems, emphasis on individualistic consumerism, and so on. In the academy—as in the corporate media (which interestingly tends to let the academy be the judge of what counts as a radical idea)—none of this left a trace. Or: not until very recently. During the '70s, '80s and '90s, in the English-speaking world "Italian theory" still referred almost exclusively to Gramsci. As others have noted, Gramsci was a critical figure for cultural studies at the time, as his work provided the bridge for a discipline founded by Marxists (it originally emerged from worker's education programs) to move away from its Marxist legacy and towards a kind of broad "postmodern" populism and institutionalization in the university.[12] Meanwhile in Italy, things were moving in almost exactly the opposite direction. There are other reasons the academy found it hard to deal with all this. The academy tends to seek out heroic individuals. French theory is always presented to us, much like classic Marxism, as the invention of specific heroic thinkers. It's not very difficult to do. One of the remarkable things about autonomist theory is that it is extremely difficult to represent it that way. It's so obviously a collective creation, taking shape through endless formal and informal conversations between activists, researchers, and working people.

When a new wave of Italian theory finally did start to appear on the radar, it always took the form of ideas attributed to heroic individuals. First Giorgio Agamben (one of the few radical Italian philosophers who was not involved in social movements and did not base himself in Marx). After Seattle, it was the turn of Toni Negri—admittedly the single most prolific and influential theorist to emerge from Autonomia—whose book *Empire*, co-written with Michael Hardt, came out in English in 2000 (and in Italian, curiously, somewhat later). Negri was the perfect bridge, since he was as much an avatar of French '68 thought as of Italian workerism. While his ideas had originally taken shape within autonomous circles in Italy in the '50s and '60s, he spent years in Paris in the '70s as a disciple of Althusser, and made something of a life's work of giving theoretical flesh to Althusser's project of removing the Hegelian element from Marx and reinventing Marx as a follower of Spinoza. During the years of repression in Italy immediately following '77, Negri was arrested and eventually convicted, quite ridiculously, with the full support of the PCI, of being the intellectual force behind the Red Brigades. He fled to Paris in 1983 and did not return to Italy until 1997—just as the alterglobalization movement was coming into gear. There he quickly established himself as the rather controversial intellectual voice for direct action groups like Ya Basta! and the Disobedienti. In the course of all this, Negri had adopted a great deal of the poststructural conceptual apparatus: postmodernity, biopower, deterritorialization, and so on. Hence, *Empire* was the perfect book to make autonomist ideas palatable in a university setting. In accord with the logic of the academy, all of these ideas were attributed personally to Negri.

At the same time, a few other Italian autonomist thinkers (Paolo Virno, Franco "Bifo" Berardi, Maurizio Lazzarato) have at least appeared dimly on the academic horizon, though their work is more likely to be known from webpages created by aficionados than in seminars and official reviews. Nevertheless it is critical that these webpages exist. While the standard line that the organization of the globalization movement is modeled on the Internet has always been wildly overstated (and in many ways the opposite is the case), the Internet certainly has provided unparalleled opportunities for the circulation of ideas. As intellectual labor increasingly moves away from the academy, new forms of circulation can only become increasingly important.

Global Circuits, Local Struggles

Since the 1970s it has become increasingly difficult to treat these different ideas as national traditions, precisely because their development has occurred through increasingly large networks and patterns of circulation. Perhaps this is related to the emergence of what Tiziana Terranova, drawing from the traditions of autonomist thought, calls a "network culture," or a global culture that is characterized by an abundance of informational output that "unfolds across a multiplicity of communication channels but within a single informational milieu."[13] Fittingly enough, during this period the emerging electronic architecture of what would become the Internet switched from a method of packet switching and data transmission based on closed circuits to forms of protocol based on a model of an open network. During the early '70s, the gains of social struggles from the '60s were met with capitalist counteroffensives by all means possible—from the tactical usage of inflation, to food shortages, to rapid increases in currency speculation (especially after the decoupling of the dollar from the gold standard). While radical social movements have always exhibited a strong degree of internationalism, during this period it became more possible than ever before for practical ongoing collaboration, mutual campaigns, and the development of new ideas to emerge collectively in widely dispersed geographic areas.

One striking example of this can be seen with the Wages for Housework campaigns that began in the early '70s. In 1972, Mariarosa Dalla Costa (who was involved in Potere Operaio and help to found Lotta Continua) and Selma James (who was involved with the struggles for independence in the West Indies and feminist organizing in the UK) published a book called *The Power of Women and the Subversion of Community*. Their arguments, drawing from their experiences of struggles and debates emerging within the feminist movement, provided a crucial turning point for reorienting organizing strategies. Through its understanding of the work of housewives as a key component of class struggle, it developed a method for understanding the organizing of a whole host of struggles not usually considered within the confined notion of the industrial proletariat (housewives, the unemployed, students, agrarian workers), as interconnected and important. By focusing on a demand for recognition of housework as work, this opened the door for a renewed consideration of forms of social protagonism, and the autonomy of forms of struggle, to develop what Dalla Costa and James described as "not a higher productivity of domestic labor but a higher subversiveness in the struggle."[14]

These arguments led to the founding of Wages for Housework campaigns across the world. Their writings were translated into multiple languages. This focus on the importance of considering unwaged labor in the discourse on capitalism filtered through various networks and connections. For instance, these arguments proved extremely significant for a number of individuals in New York City in this period, who would go on to form a collective (with a corresponding publication) called Zerowork. These currents mutated and crossbred with similar currents developing at the time, from the collaboration between the IWW and Surrealism emerging in Chicago in the late '60s to debates around the nature of class struggle that occurred in the UK in the '80s. Zerowork, which would over time morph into the Midnight Notes collective, came to draw from the experiences of its members in Nigeria to describe the creation of new enclosures founded upon an ongoing process of primitive accumulation that was backed by the IMF and other state agencies. These arguments, in turn, would come to be used by many in the revived global justice movement that has become more familiar through the media in recent years.

What we want to emphasize are the ways that the constant circulation of ideas, strategies, and experiences occurring across ever-increasing geographic areas have produced new connections and collaborations that are often ignored and under-appreciated by the allegedly critical and subversive academics one might logically think would take the greatest interest in their development. It might be of historical interest to map out the many connections and routes these genealogies of resistance contain, but that is not the task at hand right now. What is most striking to us are the ways this living history and the memories of struggles have been taken up, reused, reinterpreted, and redeployed in new and creative directions. The contents of this book draw together many strands and lineages, and tease them out in different directions to create new possibilities. Colectivo Situaciones, for instance, draws inspiration from Italian currents of radicalism and the writing of Baruch Spinoza, not to mention the rich tradition of struggles in Argentina and Latin America. In their piece for this book, they engage in dialogue with Precarias a la Deriva, a Madrid-based feminist collective. Maribel Casas-Cortés and Sebastián Cobarrubias draw from the experiences and ideas of Precarias a la Deriva and Bureau d'études to map strategies of resistance as teaching assistants in North Carolina; Angela Mitropoulos uses Mario Tronti's ideas to consider the nature of autonomy and refusal in organizing around migration and border issues in Australia; Harry Halpin sits in a tree somewhere outside of Edinburgh contemplating the ambivalent nature of technological development and forms of organizing; Gaye Chan and Nandita Sharma are in Hawai'i, drawing inspiration from another set of radicals, the Diggers, to use the planting of papayas to create new forms of the commons. They are all reclaiming existing traditions through new practices.

Again, what is important to us is not necessarily to draw out all the different and multiple connections that exist, as interesting as that might be. What we want to do here is draw from these histories, experiences, and moments to ask questions about methods through which social research creates new possibilities for political action. That also means we wish to explore the ways in which militant praxis and organizing are themselves modes of understanding, of interpreting the world, and expressing modes of social being.

Research draws upon the multivector motion of the social worlds we inhabit and develops methods for further movement within that space, whether it's using militant ethnography within the globalization movement in Barcelona or applying autoethnographic methods as a homeless organizer in Toronto. As Graeme Chesters and Michal Osterweil describe, it's a question of forging a space, ethic, and practice appropriate to where we find ourselves, whether in a classroom or university space, a social center, a factory, or knitting at a summit protest. There is no pure social space in which new practices and ideas will emerge from an ideal revolutionary subject that we only need to listen to. Our lives are constantly distributed across a variety of compromises with institutions and arrangements of power that are far from ideal. The question is not to bemoan that fate but rather to find methods and strategies of how to most effectively use the space we find ourselves in to find higher positions of subversiveness in struggle.

This is a process of finding methods for liberating life as lived imagination from the multiple forms of alienation that are reproduced through daily life and throughout society. Alienation in this sense is not just something that exists from a lack of control in one's workplace, or a process that divorces one from being able to control one's labor. Rather, as all of society and our social relations are creatively and mutually co-produced processes, alienation is lacking the ability to affect change within the social forms we live under and through. It is the subjective experience of living within structures of the imagination warped and fractured by structural violence. This violence occurs not only in striking forms (prisons, wars, and so forth), but also through the work of bureaucratic institutions that organize people as "publics," "workforces," populations, etc.; in other words, as aggregated segments of data whose form is imposed rather than mutually constituted and created. From census surveys and marketing research to even sometimes the most well-intended social movement research, research finds itself used as a tool to categorize and classify; it becomes part of the process of organizing forms of knowledge that are necessary to the maintenance of alienating structures, from the most horrific to the most mundane.

Constituent power is what emerges most fully and readily when these institutional structures are shattered, peeling back bursts of time for collective reshaping of social life. It is from these moments that archipelagoes of rupture are connected through subterranean tunnels and hidden histories, from which one can draw materials, concepts, and tools that can help guide us today, wherever we might find ourselves. Trying to put a name on the directions of tomorrow's revolutionary fervor is for that reason perhaps a bit suspicious, even if well-intended, because the process of tacking a name on something is often the first step in institutionalizing it, in fixing it—it is the process that transforms the creativity of the constituent moment back upon itself into another constituted form and alienating structure.

But if we are not trying to come up with definitive versions of reality (naming the world in order to control it), what are we doing? This question of rethinking the role of thought and knowledge production as a part of organizing, of appreciating multiple perspectives rather than universal truths and plans, is exactly what the contributors for this volume are doing. It would be silly to think that in this volume such a question could be definitively answered, or that it would be possible to capture and represent the vast experiences, accumulated practices, and knowledges that have been developed by organizers and militant researchers. Just the sheer amount of excellent proposals and submissions received for this project indicated to us how much interest in the pursuit of new forms of engaged research practice has grown. They simply all couldn't fit in one book (although perhaps in an encyclopedia devoted to the subject).

The point is to use these developments to construct new possibilities, to follow the paths of our collective wanderings in ways that we could not have even dreamed of before starting this project. These hastily sketched maps and guides will orient our directions. We are stashing reserves of affective mental nourishment and conceptual weapons under our belts as we find new paths and passages. Eduardo Galeano once observed that "Utopia is on the horizon: I walk two steps, it takes two steps back. I walk ten steps and it is ten steps further away. What is utopia for? It is for this, for walking."[15] What then is theory for? It is a question that is best answered through walking, through a constant process of circulation and movement that we begin here, following in the footsteps of many who have come before us.

Notes

1. John Holloway, *Change the World Without Taking Power: The Meaning of Revolution Today* (London: Pluto Press, 2002).

2. John Ross and John Holloway, "A Visit with John Holloway: Change the World Without Taking Power," *Counterpunch*, April 2nd, 2005. Available at http://www.counterpunch.org/ross04022005.html

3. Granted, in recent years there have been a few new names. At times it seems as if there's a continual debate over who will be the newest hip French theorist: Alain Badiou, Jacques Rancière, etc. Not surprisingly, in these conversations a prolific and brilliant author and activist like Michael Onfray, who set up a free university in northern France, is not even mentioned (nor for that matter have *any* of his many books been translated into English).

4. One cannot attribute the prestige of neoliberal theory exclusively to force. It has been adopted quite enthusiastically along with American business models in some circles in Europe. But to some degree we would argue that this is the reflected prestige of empire. If the U.S. did not have the institutional dominance that it does, it's hard to imagine this would still be happening.

5. See in particular *Social Text* 79, Vol 22, no. 2, *Turning Pro: Professional Qualifications and the Global University*, eds. Stefano Harney and Randy Martin (Summer 2004).

6. Robin D.G. Kelley, *Freedom Dreams: The Black Radical Imagination* (Boston: Beacon Press, 2002).

7. And this in a country that before the revolution had produced no social theory at all, though it did produce a number of great novels.

8. They also seem to emerge especially from the margins of the academy, or moments when professional thinkers were in dialogue with someone else: artists, workers, militants, etc.

9. In each discipline, the pattern is remarkably consistent: Baudrillard is always the most frequently cited, Debord is cited far less, and Vaneigem is not cited at all. True, Vaneigem gets a bit of a bump in Art and Art History, for example, but it turns out all seven articles were published in a single special issue of the journal *October* dedicated to Situationism. Similarly, Debord

gets a small bump in History—but this is because it's hard to talk about the events of May '68 in France without mentioning the Situationist influence on the student insurrectionaries, not because historians are using his ideas. Even here, Baudrillard, who played no significant role in such events, is cited three times more than both of them put together, and Vaneigem, whose book was if anything more important, is still effectively ignored. Aside from the historical references, the Situationists are viewed as artistic and literary figures, not social thinkers. Outside art and literature, Debord is cited only a very small number of times and Vaneigem is never cited once.

10. This history of struggles and ideas is well-documented and described by Steve Wright in *Storming Heaven: Class Composition and Struggle in Italian Autonomist Marxism* (London: Pluto Books, 2002).

11. Richard Day, *Gramsci is Dead: Anarchist Currents in the Newest Social Movements* (London: Pluto Press, 2005).

12. Nick Thoburn, *Deleuze, Marx, Politics* (London: Routledge, 2003).

13. Tiziana Terranova, *Network Culture: Politics for the Information Age* (London: Pluto Press, 2004), 1.

14. Mariarosa Dalla Costa and Selma James, *The Power of Women and the Subversion of Community* (Brighton: Falling Wall Press, 1972), 36.

15. Quoted in: Notes From Nowhere, *We Are Everywhere: The Irresistable Rise of Global Anticapitalism* (London: Verso, 2003), 499.

:: MOMENTS OF POSSIBILITY //
GENEALOGIES OF RESISTANCE ::

:: MOMENTS OF POSSIBILITY //
GENEALOGIES OF RESISTANCE::

Action is a struggle to constitute the world, to invent it.... To act is
at once a form of knowledge and a revolt...[it] is precisely the search
for and the construction of the common, which is to say the affirmation of absolute immanence. —Antonio Negri

Moments of possibility, of rupture—Yves Fremion calls them the "orgasms
of history." From Greek slave revolts to the San Francisco Diggers, from
the Brethren of the Free Spirit to the Dutch Provos, these social explosions
unleashed the power of collective imagination in ways that are almost never
appreciated by conventional histories. Emerging without leaders or guidance from institutional structures, they open windows to the possibility that
everything could change at once and the world be made anew. In these moments, borders that separate people burst open into renewed periods of social
creativity and insurgencies. Workers talk to and organize with students, artists collaborate with housing organizers, the very boundaries between these
categories blur as singular antagonisms combine and recombine. Where
before there were multiple but separate struggles, these same struggles are
multiplied, transformed, fused, and increased exponentially in their presence and potentialities. That is not to say that they are homogenized or combined into one thing, but rather complementarities and affinities are weaved,
dancing new strategies through the social fabric.

These new forms reveal glimpses of a future world, of the possibilities for liberation existing in the present. We can trace the connections between them, a genealogy of resistance that draws together hidden histories
and points towards the future. Each contains difficulties and complications,
places where it was necessary to take a leap of faith and risk the impossible.
It is from these moments, these spaces of creation, that we can learn the
most. From the College of Sociology turning festivals and the sacred into
resistance to punk DIY culture creating new social relations and forms of
production, these moments embody not just practices to adapt and creatively
redeploy, but are in themselves ways of understanding the world and forms
of research in action.

To treat practices as forms of knowing, and knowledges as forms of
doing, means rejecting the idea that theory and practice can ever truly be
separated: they are always interconnected and woven through each other.

All too often and easily, the understanding embodied in organizing is not appreciated for the forms of knowledge it contains; likewise theorization often becomes detached from the location of its production and circulation. In these moments of possibility, these openings in the flow of history, boundaries and distinctions break down, forming an archipelago of possibility and the understanding that it is our task to extend today into tomorrow.

Continental Drift: Activist Research, From Geopolitics to Geopoetics

Brian Holmes

How does a world come together? How does a world fall apart? Neoliberal globalization made those opposite questions into one—and September 11 showed that the answer will never be a perfect synthesis. Locating yourself against the horizons of disaster, then finding the modes and scales of intervention and turning them into lived experience, are the pathways for intellectual activism in the contemporary world-system.

Neolib Goes Neocon

A double dynamic is at work in geopolitics today, one that destroys what it constructs and dissolves what it unifies. And that's exactly what we all have to deal with. One prime example is the enlargement of the European Union (EU), right up to the fiasco of the ultraliberal constitution. The end of the historic split with the East now appears as the beginning of the Core Europe/New Europe divide, with the social-democratic bastions of the West seeking shelter from the global market, while post-Communist states refuse any speed checks on the road to riches. But the absence of a democratic constitution only favors corporate lobbies and big power deals, leaving national parliaments as a smokescreen over the real decisions.

An even more striking case is the self-eclipsing rise of the WTO, which just yesterday seemed fated for the role of world government. No sooner was the international trading regime consolidated than tariff wars sprang up between the US and the EU, protests flared around the globe, and the process of bloc formation gathered steam, with negotiations for both the

FTAA and a renewed Mercosur in Latin America, moves toward an expanded ASEAN system (joined by China, Japan, and South Korea) and finally
the Venezuelan proposal of ALBA, calling for a leftist "dawn" after the sun-
down of free trade. But as any historian remembers, trading bloc formation
was the prelude to the global conflicts of the 1940s.

For the strangest embrace of contradictory forces in the world today,
consider the symbiotic tie between industrialized China and the financialized
United States. China constantly struggles to produce what the US constantly
struggles to consume—at an ecological risk that no one can even measure.
To make the wheel of fortune go on spinning, the Chinese loan their manufacturing profits back to the US, so as to prop up speculation on the almighty
dollar and keep the world's largest market soluble. What will happen if the
Chinese pipeline to the US Treasury stops flowing is anybody's guess; but
as New Orleans floodwaters recede into a domestic quagmire that can only
recall the international disaster in Iraq, America's attempts to save its fading
hegemony look increasingly desperate and uncertain. Levels of conflict are
rising all across the globe, and the problem of how to intervene as a world
citizen is more complex and daunting than ever. The counter-globalization
movements marked the first attempt at a widespread, meshworked response
to the chaos of the post-'89 world system. These movements were an uneasy
mix between democratic sovereigntists, no-border libertarians (the "new
anarchists"), and traditional, union-oriented Keynesians. They could all critique the failures of neoliberal governance, but they all diverged and faltered
before its cultural consequences. And the latter wasted no time coming.

By undercutting social solidarities and destroying ecological equilibri-
ums, the neoliberal program of accelerated capital expansion immediately
spawned its neoconservative shadow, in the form of a military, moral, and
religious return to order. Nothing could have made better cover for the de-
nial of democratic critique, the clampdown on civil liberties, and the continuing budgetary shift from social welfare to corporate security. The backlash against globalization became a powerful new tool of manipulation for
the elites who launched the whole process in the first place. The current
scramble to consolidate regional blocs reflects the search for a compromise
between global reach and territorial stability. Beyond or before the "clash
of civilizations," a feasible scale of contemporary social relations is the
leading question. From this perspective, the free-market policy of the Bush
administration in Latin America is comparable to Al Qaeda's dreams of
an Islamic caliphate in the Middle East. Both seek to consolidate a region.
The networked production system forming around Japan and China, or the
EU's continuous diplomatic courtship of Russia despite flagrant atrocities in
Chechnya, give similar insights into this quest for a workable scale, which is
essentially that of a "continent," however elastic or imprecise the term may
be. Paradoxically, continentalization is not countered but is driven ahead by

global unification. Behind the tectonic shifts at the turn of the millennium lies the accumulated violence of a thirty-year neoliberal push toward a borderless world, wide open for the biggest and most predatory corporations.

Disorienting Compass

The extraordinary breadth and speed of the current metamorphosis—a veritable phase change in the world system—leaves activist-researchers facing a double challenge, or a double opportunity. On the one hand, they must remap the cultural and political parameters that have been transformed by the neoconservative overlay, while remaining keenly aware of the neoliberal principles that remain active beneath the surface. In this effort, the social sciences are the key. Economic geography is crucial for tracing the global division of labor, and grasping the wider frameworks of what European activists now call "precarity." The sociology of organizations reveals who is in control, how power is distributed and maintained in a chaotic world. The study of technics charts out the future in advance, and shows how it operates. And the toolkits of social psychology offer insights into the structures of willful blindness and confused consent that uphold the reigning hegemonies. This kind of analysis is critically important for activist initiatives, which can stumble all too easily into the programmed dead-ends of manipulated ideologies.

Yet the disciplines also have to be overcome, dissolved into experimentation. Autonomous inquiry demands a rupture from the dominant cartographies. Both compass and coordinates must be reinvented if you really want to transform the dynamics of a changing world-system. Only by disorienting the self and uprooting epistemic certainties can anyone hope to inject a positive difference into the unconscious dynamics of the geopolitical order. How then can activist-researchers move to disorient the reigning maps, to transform the dominant cartographies, without falling into the never-never lands of aesthetic extrapolation? The problem of activist research is inseparable from its embodiment, from its social elaboration.

Just try this experiment in public presence: literally trace out the flows of capital, the currents of warfare and the rise and fall of transnational organizations since 1945, using hand-drawn dates and arrows on a conventional Mercator projection. The effect is to build a cartographic frame narrative of the emergence, complexification and crisis of US hegemony since 1945; but at the same time, through gesture and movement, to act out the ways that geopolitical flows traverse living bodies and become part of tactile consciousness, entering what might be termed "felt public space." Intellectual work becomes intensive when it is unmoored from normalizing frameworks, acted out as a social experiment in a self-organized seminar, in a squat or an occupied building, at a counter-summit, on a train hurtling through Siberia.

As supranational regions engulf ever-larger populations and the movement across shifting borders becomes an ever-more common activity, geopolitics is increasingly experienced in the flesh and in the imaginary, it is traced out on the collective skin. This is when geopoetics becomes a vital activity, a promise of liberation.

How to interpret artworks and artistic-activist interventions so as to highlight the forms taken by the geopoetic imaginary? Through analytical work on the dynamics of form and the efficacy of symbolic ruptures, one can try to approach the diagrammatic level where the cartography of sensation is reconfigured through experimentation. This level comes constantly into play whenever it is a matter of translating analysis back into intervention. Because of the transverse nature of global flows, it is possible to draw on the experiences of far away acts of resistance in the midst of one's own confrontations with power, both in its brute objective forms, and in its subtle interiorizations. The relation between the Argentine pot-banging *cacerolazos* and the almost continuous urban mobilizations in Spain, from February 15, 2003, all the way up to the ouster of the mendacious and power-hungry Aznar government in March of 2004, is a large-scale example of this process of transfiguration. And this is the generative side of the contemporary continental drift. To sense the dynamics of resistance and creation across the interlinked world space is to start taking part in the solidarities and modes of cooperation that have been emerging across the planet since the late 1990s.

Just Doing It

If you want to accomplish anything like this kind of research, don't expect much help from the existing institutions. Most are still busy adapting to the dictates of neoliberal management; and the best we could do for the first big round of meshworked critique was to hijack a few of their people and divert a few of their resources. What's more, the open windows that do exist are likely to close down with the neoconservative turn. Self-organized groups will have to generate a collective learning process about the effects of social atomization and economic subjugation—essentially, a new understanding of the forms of contemporary alienation—and they will have to explore the reactions to these trends, whether intensely negative (the fascist and racist closure of formerly democratic societies) or positive and forward-looking (activist interventions, the invention of new modes of social self-management, cultural reorientations, ecologically viable forms of development). Another goal of the critique is to raise the level of debate and engagement in the cultural and artistic sectors—the vital media of social expression—where a narcissistic blindness to the violence of current conditions is still the norm. But the most important aim is to help relaunch the activist mobilizations that became so promising around the turn of the millennium. "Help" is the right word here, because there is no intellectual privilege in the activist domain. Activist-researchers can contribute to a short, middle, and long-term analysis of the crisis, by examining and inventing new modes of intervention at the micro-political scales where even the largest social movements begin.

Who can play this great game? Whoever is able to join or form a mesh-work of independent researchers. What are the pieces, the terrains, the wagers and rules? Whichever ones your group finds most productive and contagious. How does the game continue, when the ball goes out of your field? Through shared meetings in a meshwork of meshworks, through collective actions, images, projects, and publications. And most importantly, who wins? Whoever can provoke some effective resistance to the downward spiral of human coexistence at the outset of the 21st century.

Do It Yourself...
and the Movement Beyond
Capitalism

Ben Holtzman // Craig Hughes // Kevin Van Meter

"The powers that be," Stephen Duncombe wrote, "do not sustain their legitimacy by convincing people that the current system is The Answer. That fiction would be too difficult to sustain in the face of so much evidence to the contrary. What they must do, and what they have done very effectively, is convince the mass of people that *there is no alternative*."[1] Indeed, this outlook of hopelessness was common even among activists of the 1960s era. As one former 1960s activist explained, the idea of "we can change the world" became "what good did it all do anyway."[2] However, even as the political climate during the 1970s worsened, a means of circumventing the powers-that-be emerged through the Do It Yourself (DIY) ethic. DIY is the idea that you can do for yourself the activities normally reserved for the realm of capitalist production (wherein products are created for consumption in a system that encourages alienation and nonparticipation). Thus, anything from music and magazines to education and protest can be created in a nonalienating, self-organized, and purposely anticapitalist manner. While production mostly takes place through small and localized means, extensive and oftentimes global social networks are utilized for distribution.[3] Though DIY is most prominent in the realm of cultural production, it is continually being expanded to reclaim more complex forms of labor, production, and resistance.

DIY has been effective in empowering marginalized sectors of society, while simultaneously providing a means to subvert and transcend capitalism. As a means of re-approaching power, DIY became a way of withdrawing support from capitalism and the state while constructing and experimenting with other forms of social organizing. Through involvement in and expansion of DIY culture, participants have constructed alternatives that are more than symbolic—they have created space for empowerment, non-alienating production, mutual aid, and struggle. DIY is not simply a means of spreading alternative forms of social organizing or a symbolic example of a better society; it is the active construction of counter-relationships and the organization against and beyond capitalism. And as we will demonstrate, the accomplishments of DIY have contributed to its sustained importance to anticapitalist struggle in the United States over the past twenty-five years, particularly in the movement against neoliberalism.

The concept of DIY has been and continues to be debated among its participants.[4] It is fluid and fragmentary, constantly being modified and expanded by its actors.[5] DIY can, however, be understood as a two-step process, first addressing value and then social relationships. It undermines exchange-value while simultaneously creating use-value outside of capitalism. DIY thus becomes synonymous with bringing life to "self-determining labor which capitalism seeks to reinternalize for its own development, but which repeatedly breaks free to craft new kinds of human activity constitutive of new social relations transcending capitalism."[6] When a DIY commodity is produced, it is created for its use-value, rather than for its exchange-value. This is part of the process of undermining capitalism by forming relationships not intended by capitalism—inverting value and undermining the imposition of work that is embodied in capitalist commodities.[7]

While DIY still takes place in a monetary economy, and all the vestigial elements of capital have not left its processes, commodities produced in DIY fashion have expanded their use-values in relation to their exchange-value. Exchange-value is no longer the predominant attribute of the commodity, and use-value—"worth," to its participants—is primary. DIY as a form of activity creates value outside of capitalism. While this is not noncapitalist activity, since a commodity still does exist, it is a first step in the process of going beyond capital.[8]

DIY reconstructs power relationships differently than those found under capital, by abandoning the institutions of capital and the state, and constructing counter-institutions based upon fundamentally different principles and structures.[9] DIY social relationships, especially in regards to production, largely escape all four aspects of alienation that Marx described.[10] "Capital," as Marx notes, is "a social relation," which can thus only be overcome by creating other social relationships.[11] In DIY, we find the process of creating these relationships.

We can see DIY's emergence in the late 1970s as a continuation of struggle against the social factory. "From the plant to the university," as Guido Baldi described, "society becomes an immense assembly line, where the seeming variety of jobs disguises the actual generalization of the same abstract labor."[12] DIY is the struggle of the collective individual against the production of its subjectivity,[13] against its reproduction as a commodity of capitalism.

The Economic Crisis of the 1970s and the Emergence of DIY

By the early 1970s, much of the world was facing economic crisis. The crisis was characterized by the abandonment of fixed exchange rates, a temporary wage/price freeze, and a period of stagflation. As the crisis deepened overt social rebellion waned, though new sites and forms of resistance erupted.[14]

In Britain during the late 1970s, youth, particularly young artists and those from the lower classes, were growing increasingly disenchanted with a state that was unable to respond effectively to the economic crisis—as inflation and unemployment continued to rise.[15] The British public was consumed with "periodic outbursts of 'crisis' or 'doom' rhetoric," as questions about the future, particularly for youth, remained unanswered.[16] Additionally, in response to the economic crisis and declining sales, leisure industries such as music, were "increasingly trying to minimize risk by utilizing established performers at the expense of new performers," limiting innovation and music's ability to reflect the discontent of much of the nation's youth.[17]

These factors contributed to the emergence of a new youth movement: punk. Punk's public emergence, generally marked with the release of the Sex Pistols' "Anarchy in the U.K." in December 1976, sent shock waves throughout Britain, both for its apparently unexplainable, nihilistic character as well as the threat it posed. As one observer noted in 1978, punk as "a social phenomenon...provoked the greatest fears."[18] Punk was almost unanimously denounced by clergymen, politicians, parents, and pundits for its "degeneration of the youth" and its potential to cause an upheaval of British culture and politics. The media both created and reinforced fears, reporting that this new cult must be "expelled—or better still—destroyed at all costs."[19]

Punk, however, did not need to be destroyed—it self-destructed. Indeed, by decade's end, "the Sex Pistols had fragmented...the Damned, the Jam, and the Clash were trying, with varying degrees of success, to bridge the gap between punk antagonism and pop sensibility—it looked like things were being made safe again, opposition was being channeled and recuperated, rebellion commodified."[20]

Punk was apparently dead. However, punk's "death" brought new life to the counterculture. Particularly in the United States, where punk had always been far more apolitical than in Britain, local punk scenes developed in rural communities, suburbs, and cities.[21] These scenes were often linked by one common feature: "the spirit of Do-It-Yourself."[22] Indeed, many of these fledgling scenes placed as their central focus the oft-repeated but rarely followed commitment of earlier punk bands: capitalist influence was not only unnecessary but unwelcome. With this view, punks began to create their own networks of musical and cultural production. These networks hinged on developing substantive ways of abandoning capitalist institutions and building alternative networks and communities.[23]

The Development of DIY Culture and Protest in the 1980s

"Making Punk a Threat Again"—DIY Punk in the USA

In the United States in the early 1980s, the Reagan administration implemented socially and economically destructive policies that seemed targeted at undermining the gains achieved in the preceding cycle of struggle.[24] As Christian Parenti has observed, "Reagan's plan was to cut taxes on the rich, gut welfare, and attack labor."[25] Deindustrialization continued as insecure and low-paying service jobs became more prevalent.[26]

Punks responded to the ill effects of what they were witnessing and often feeling themselves. One form resistance took was song lyrics. These ranged from sophisticated songs of satire, such as Reagan Youth singing: "We are the sons of Reagan (Heil!) / We are the godforsaken (Heil!) / Right is our religion / We watch television / Tons of fun and brainwashed slime / We are Reagan Youth (Seig Heil!)" to more the more simplistic songs, such as Dirty Rotten Imbeciles' "Reaganomics": "Reaganomics killing me / Reaganomics killing you."[27]

Punks also developed more explicit forms of resistance, such as cultural networks organized on principles antithetical to the conservative, individualistic, and pro-corporate environment Reagan was encouraging.[28] The speed with which punks developed these networks was significant. This was eloquently and accurately described by one young punk writing to the journal *Radical America* in 1982:

> Large punk "scenes" as they are called have appeared in the last few years in Brazil, Lebanon, Israel, South Africa, and in almost every city in the US. The scenes are managed by punks, meaning the kids put on shows (all ages, no corporate slugs) in old warehouses, club houses, or anywhere else. Bands make no money, promoters make no money, shows are inexpensive.... Politically, it seems most bands are left wing or anarchistic.... There are literally hundreds of fanzines that people put out expressing their own views and telling the world what's going on.[29]

Punks had developed an international network in which they could start bands, play shows, tour, and release music with little or no corporate influence. Though these activities involved aspects of capitalism such as the use of money, the processes and the relationships that served as their base were distinct from capitalist practices. Indeed, as Robert Ovetz has noted, "the capitalist aspects [were] subordinated to the desires and intentions of those involved in the process." "Another way to look at it," he continued, "would be to see something entirely new growing from within the old, destroying it in the process. Rather than making music to make money, or create work to control people, many…are trying to create a way of living where the making of music and its sharing with others is the predominant characteristic of the way [they] choose to live."[30]

These practices were significant for their ability to foster alternatives to capitalism in Reagan's America. Punk also helped to forge "a new counter-cultural space…a place for a new generation to form critical insights based on its own experience."[31] Further, the DIY ethos informing these actions extended into a variety of areas. As one punk noted, punks "organize gigs, organize and attend demos, put out records, publish books and fanzines, set up mail order distributions for our products, run record stores, distribute literature, encourage boycotts, and participate in political activities."[32] DIY reoriented power often fosters a newly found awareness of individual and collective ability to produce and further social change. The emphasis DIY placed on direct participation advanced the practices and ideals of the movement. One punk described his early involvement as the "realization that people like us all over the world were creating their own culture. A democratic culture was ours for the taking, but as a true democracy implies, we had to participate."[33]

Zines, Empowerment, and Independent Media

One principal means for spreading DIY ideas throughout the punk movement was the production of zines: noncommercial, small-circulation magazines created without desire for profit. Punk zines first emerged as a means to communicate both within and between different scenes and expanded into a forum in which people could discuss issues rarely addressed by the mainstream media. Indeed, in the punk scene in the 1980s, many zines discussed nuclear power/weaponry and US involvement in Central America. Zines also encouraged active participation in these struggles, sometimes by publishing lists of corporations with ties to global atrocities and encouraging boycotts of them (or, often, advocating the boycott of corporations altogether and discussing noncorporate alternatives).[34] Zines were key sources of information about protests, and often encouraged direct engagement as a form of political expression. Indeed, as one San Francisco newspaper reported in 1984, "the punkers, in torn t-shirts and polychromatic hair styles…prefer street theater and spontaneous action to marching with placards."[35]

The significance of zines lies not only in their ability to spread information about political events and actions, but also to encourage both inspiration and empowerment of producers as well as readers. The production of zines is relatively simple—all that is needed by an individual with a desire to express her/himself is access to a photocopier. This, however, is not the only explanation for the contagiousness of their production by punks. Indeed, zine production also offered the opportunity, often for the first time, to significantly develop, express, and share passions, knowledge, and frustrations in an unrestricted forum.

This emancipatory power of zines is evident in the role they played in Riot Grrrl, a radical, feminist, punk movement of young women frustrated with the sexism of punk and greater society, which emerged in the early 1990s. Zines provided an opportunity for women to voice their experiences, opinions, stories, and criticisms of culture in a photocopied "safe space." They could be produced by oneself, allowing grrrls an ability to express what they could not in any other forum or area of their lives. This ability helped to disassemble the feelings of relative powerlessness that had been inflicted upon grrrls (by teachers, parents, boys, the media, and patriarchal institutions of society). As one grrrl expressed it, "Just by going out and doing a zine says something—it means that this thing called 'empowerment' is in effect. Time to make a statement. And it ain't no feeble attempt. These zines scream 'I AM MAKING A DIFFERENCE.'"[36] Indeed, grrrls often cite zines as having empowered them to become involved with clinic defense, Food Not Bombs, gay and women's rights groups, and to attend and organize public demonstrations and direct actions.[37]

Food Not Bombs

Another example of DIY ethics informing resistance is Food Not Bombs (FNB). The central focus of FNB is to reclaim ("recover") food that has or will be discarded by businesses and distribute it publicly in order to help those in need and draw attention to the realities of poverty and military spending. The group formed out of the Clamshell Alliance, a major component of the anti-nuclear struggles during the late 1970s and early 1980s.[38] The originators of FNB were highly influenced by the punk scene, as it "spoke out on issues of war, the ugly corporate culture and the repression of the state," as one founder recalled.[39] The founders were also attracted to and influenced by the DIY ethic of punk, encouraged by the example of other projects that resisted "government or corporate control."[40]

As the cuts in social welfare programs and attacks on labor continued throughout the 1980s and into and through the 1990s, FNB's mission of providing food with a revolutionary intent became increasingly important, and chapters were organized across the United States.[41] Not only was food being served to those hardest hit by the rollback, but it was also being done publicly. As an article by two FNB organizers explained, "Unable to address the real causes of social and economic inequality, business leaders and politicians increasingly feel that if the homeless can be permanently contained within the homeless shelters and rehabilitation programs, then the economic problems of retail businesses and the tourist industry will be miraculously solved."[42]

The act of serving food publicly was itself part of a struggle against the strategy of the ruling classes. Food Not Bombs is informed by the understanding that "giving away free food [is] a strong and direct threat to capitalism."[43] By "recovering" food, FNB groups redefine its use as a weapon against capital.[44] Food is brought back to its original use-value, while its exchange-value is undermined.[45] By organizing food recovery and production as a democratically structured community project, FNB helps to create an alternative model and social space for those involved with and affected by its actions.

The decentralized nature of FNB has also been fundamental to its continued importance. Each chapter (of which there are currently over two hundred internationally) is guided by the basic ideas of the group—non-violence, vegetarianism, direct action, and direct democracy—but functions autonomously. In the place of a centralized organization is an international network of local chapters practicing mutual aid. This non-hierarchical organization prevents too much control from developing in one place, and it also encourages the empowerment of participants by offering them a means to be directly involved in challenging capitalism and furthering social justice.[46]

The intentional dual nature of FNB also reflects the group's DIY spirit.[47] Many see themselves as having a responsibility to resist capitalism through active struggle against capital and the state. This is a prefigurative struggle, working to create a bottom-up, community-controlled, democratic society. As one organizer explained: "The solution to today's problems is the creation of the world we want and the disruption and destruction of the system that exists."[48] Accordingly, activists are putting into practice an alternative way of organizing outside of capitalism. Indeed, the DIY nature of FNB contributes to it being as much an "empowering and such a strong challenge to mainstream culture," as it is a successful and accessible example of anti-capitalism in action.[49]

Reclaim the Streets/Critical Mass

Reclaim the Streets (RTS) and Critical Mass (CM) are also examples of political activities that have grown out of DIY culture. RTS has its roots in the British anti-road struggles that took place in the early- and mid-1990s as well as in London's rave culture.[50] An RTS action appears as if it is a spontaneous party erupting in the middle of a city street, with the number of participants varying from hundreds to thousands. Critical Mass's origins are within the larger radical and bike cultures in San Francisco in the early 1990s.[51] A Critical Mass ride involves any number of bikes riding through the streets, forming a block among a sea of cars. Riders attempt to reclaim public space as a statement against consumption and pollution. Both of these are celebrations in which public space is used "for public ritual, performance, and transformation."[52]

As Duncombe has observed, "both RTS and punk arise out of the same place: DIY culture."[53] The same could be said of Critical Mass. Neither is a spectator sport; they work only if everyone participates.[54] Naomi Klein explains that RTS's "spontaneous street parties are an extension of the DIY lifestyle, asserting as they do that people can make their own fun without asking any state's permission or relying on any corporation's largesse."[55]

RTS and CM have also created activities that do "not encourage the endless deferral of the revolutionary moment."[56] Indeed, both enact the desires and dreams of participants in reality, "creating a space in which it seem[s] that anything [can] happen."[57] Benjamin Shepard and Kelly Moore are correct in understanding RTS and Critical Mass as temporary autonomous zones.[58] However, they must also be seen as experiences that go beyond symbolic action. More than just providing a brief autonomous zone, they also "harness a...direct social power to invent [activists'] own reality."[59] Indeed, as one participant notes, "we demand collaboratively produced public space by going out and actually creating a collaboratively produced public space."[60] With these actions, RTS and CM do not ask power to address their needs nor do they ask permission for their actions (indeed, they are always nonpermitted), they reclaim power from the state in taking action, thus helping to create new avenues for participation in politics and everyday life.

DIY Culture and Movement Against Neoliberalism

All of the examples discussed above have been, both directly and indirectly, at the forefront of the struggle against capitalism in the United States.[61] Indeed, DIY, in the age of neoliberalism, has continued to be an instrumental form of resistance for the current political and economic situation.

Punk has introduced thousands of young people each year to DIY. Song lyrics give voice to anticapitalist critique. Indeed, as the punk band Brother Inferior sang, "Building their empire.... Expanding their hatred, expanding their crimes, expanding their slavery, leading the third world to its demise under salvation's guise."[62] The cultural network of punk—producing zines, records, literature, documentaries, art, social spaces, etc.—has continued to serve as a working example of a noncapitalist social and economic system. DIY punk has also encouraged involvement in explicit political action against capitalism, with thousands of punks participating in the recent protests against neoliberalism.[63]

Zines have played an important role in continuing to educate, empower, and mobilize people in the movement against neoliberalism. They contributed greatly to the organizing efforts of the protests held during the meetings of the World Trade Organization (WTO) in Seattle in 1999. Numerous zines, including those whose focus was primarily outside of politics, "devoted pages to sharing information about globalization of the economy, specifically the role that the [WTO] plays in international trade and labor issues."[64] Though the Internet and face-to-face organizing were also significant, zines served as a principal means by which information and dialogue about the actions spread in the year before the protests took place.

Food Not Bombs and the groups inspired by them have served food at all of the major demonstrations against neoliberalism. In addition, FNB was one of the few movements in the United States that emphasized non-hierarchical, bottom-up organizing throughout the 1980s and into the 1990s. Many of the principal organizers in the movement against neoliberalism "had their start as Food Not Bombs volunteers."[65] As one organizer explains, "Our model of organizing by affinity groups, our history of organizing blockades and other acts of non-violent direct action is now the basis of protests against corporate control."[66] While FNB was not the only group that utilized this form of directly democratic organizing, it is among the most prominent and most credited with sustaining this method "through the dark ages of the US left in the early 80s."[67]

Critical Mass and RTS have also played crucial roles in the large and diverse movement against neoliberalism. Indeed, the celebratory and party-like atmospheres evident in the streets of Seattle to Genoa can be traced, at least partially, to the influence of these groups.[68] Furthermore, both have been a constant presence at these protests. RTS also had direct roles in several of the major international demonstrations against neoliberalism in the years before Seattle.[69] In addition, these groups have proved important for helping to expand and maintain the movement by encouraging continual local action and organizing outside of the large-scale protests. This has contributed to building local communities of resistance and providing outlets for expression and experimentation on a smaller and consistent basis.[70]

The emphasis within DIY cultural production on removing hierarchies between producer and consumer as well as on empowering, informing, and challenging the power held by mainstream media can also be seen in the development of Independent Media Centers (IMCs), which have been the principal means by which the movement against neoliberalism has represented itself. Indeed, every facet of "reporting" is done by movement participants themselves. IMCs have been able to circumvent the relative stranglehold corporate media has held over popular representations of protesters and struggles. IMCs have utilized advancements in technology to overcome the limitations that have plagued previous attempts of movements to produce media.[71] While presentations by the mainstream media remain important, IMCs have provided a means for those engaged in the struggle against neo-liberalism to produce widely disseminable counter-narratives to the discourses of the mainstream media.

IMCs have also made production of media widely accessible to movement participants. Indeed, IMCs' software allows for "anyone with access to the Internet to instantaneously publish their texts, audio, and video files onto the cyber-network's newswires."[72] Thus, IMCs have emerged not only as a source of information and analysis, but also as a forum in which participants can voice their own experiences, opinions, stories, and criticisms. IMCs allow for participants to literally "become the media." Participants are provided with the means to "easily get involved in commenting, editing, highlighting stories, and even managing/facilitating the media production through Indymedia's open, (relatively) transparent grassroots media processes."[73] The result of this has been an international network of over one hundred IMCs, which has developed "not only a diverse global media network, but also a committed network of journalists seasoned in the challenges of covering protests and activism."[74]

In addition, DIY resistance has encouraged the continuation of direct action as a tactic in the struggle against neoliberalism. Direct action has been a crucial strategy of this movement because many of its participants have viewed the institutions of neoliberalism as undemocratic and inaccessible, wherein "transnational capital is the only real policy-maker."[75] Accordingly, in recent years, DIY and direct action have had an intertwined history. As George McKay points out, "[DIY] and non-violent direct action (NVDA) feed each other: NVDA is the preferred form of politics."[76]

With direct action as with DIY, individuals are not asking power to address their needs and concerns through processes of representation—they are carrying out actions on their own behalf in which the means are also the ends. David McNally addresses this point, observing that "the direct action approach is based upon a politics of self-activity. Steering away from appeals to politicians, bureaucrats or other elites to 'help' the downtrodden by doing something for them, it demands and mobilizes, encouraging [people] to act for themselves."[77] The reclamation of streets, the creation of grass-roots media, the "recovery" of and ability to publicly serve food to the hungry have all required participants to forge their own spaces, while struggling to abolish and transcend capitalism. These directly democratic methods of organizing have been the main inspiration for the form that the large-scale direct actions have taken.[78] Accordingly, through these projects, DIY culture has been at the base of resistance to neoliberalism in the United States.

Moving Beyond Capitalism

By moving within and expanding on DIY culture, participants have been able to escape the idea that there is no alternative. As a distinct form of anticapitalist struggle, DIY culture has provided a means of circumventing the power of capitalist structures, while at the same time creating substantive alternatives. This is evident not only in DIY cultural production but in social relationships and the creation of use-values outside and independent of capitalism. They are an extension of the struggles against the social factory and further the recomposition of the marginalized populations.

In a strategic sense, the DIY elements found in the current movements against capitalism are among the most successful. They are highly participatory, practical, positive, constructive, non-ideologically based, and often go beyond simplistic oppositional politics and critique. These elements are actively creating an alternative in the United States (and across the world)—a bottom-up globalization. It is for this reason that discussion of strategy within the movements against capitalism should address DIY.

This essay's purpose is not to portray DIY as a blueprint for a new society. Rather, among our purposes is to expand the definition of politics and political action and to highlight a largely unrecognized contemporary force of activity outside the realm of traditional political action. We see DIY as a political concept, but one based on composition rather than ideology. This concept is flexible, has the potential of being utilized across a broad area of activities and struggles, and is not simply applicable only to those of a particular counterculture or music-oriented youth culture. Ultimately, however, the direction of DIY is up to the participants themselves.

Certain forms of DIY activity have been privileged in this essay, however others exist and need similar attention.[79] Further, this political project is in need of a proper analysis of the success of these activities—which have worked and been sustainable, which are no longer useful, and hence the strategic expansion of those that are successful—in moving beyond capitalism. The forms of resistance that we have discussed have been some of the crucial components to the recent struggles against capitalism. These and similar activities can serve as positive examples of new forms of social relations, and within them, new worlds.

Notes

As with any collective writing project this essay was born of the interweaving differences, knowledges, and common perspectives of its participants. Working separately the authors would not have been able to produce such an article. However, mutual and collective experiences in various social struggles on Long Island created a common point from which the authors could approach the questions this essay sought to answer. This article was originally written at the suggestion of Silvia Federici and slated for publication in the Italian journal *DeriveApprodi* (where it did not appear). The authors wish to thank George Caffentzis, Kenneth Culton, Silvia Federici, Conrad Herold, and Anita Rapone for their comments on earlier drafts as well as David Graeber and Stevphen Shukaitis for inviting us to be a part of this volume.

1. Stephen Duncombe, *Notes from Underground: Zines and the Politics of Alternative Culture* (London: Verso, 1997), 6. Italics in original.

2. Andrew Boyd, "Irony, Meme Warfare, and the Extreme Costume Ball," in *From ACT UP to the WTO: Urban Protest and Community Building in the Era of Globalization*, eds. Benjamin Shepard and Ronald Hayduk (New York: Verso, 2002), 248.

3. Gustavo Esteva and Madhu Shri Prakash note that the argument between localism and globalism—micro and macro—is an outdated way of approaching social organization. Utilizing the Zapatistas as an example, Esteva and Prakash describe how local political action that is then bolstered through international networks is a more effective, responsive, and positive strategy than emphasis simply placed on unilateral "global thinking." Gustavo Esteva and Madhu Shri Prakash, *Grassroots Post-Modernism* (London and New York: Zed Books, 1998).

4. Gilles Deleuze and Felix Guattari, *What Is Philosophy?* (New York: Verso, 1994 [Originally published as *Qu'est-ce qua la Philosophie?* in 1991]). Deleuze and Guattari's "concept" is also helpful in theoretically constructing DIY. DIY does not hold to a classical philosophical or revolutionary tradition, in which an objective position unfolds an ethics, unfolding a politics. Rather it is a "concept" that describes action; its purpose as a concept is to create further action.

5. DIY as a concept does not stand above or outside the activity that it describes. It is not a blueprint for activity, nor is it a priori—it is immanent to the activity, and is part of the ontological construction of the activity.

6. Harry Cleaver, "Kropotkin, Self-Valorization and the Crisis of Marxism," *Anarchist Studies* 2, no. 2 (Autumn 1994), 125.

7. Harry Cleaver, *Reading Capital Politically* (Oakland: AK Press, 2000 [1979]), 82.

8. Here we offer a particular reading of an underutilized passage in Marx's *Capital*, as a point of theoretical intervention to discussion of this activity. Products of human labor always contain use-values regardless of whether they are produced under capital. If the labor which creates the use-value in a product is fundamentally different than labor (imposed work) under capitalism, and is part of a different set of social relations, in this case DIY, then the product is not a commodity, or is a different form of commodity than is usu-

ally found under capital. Specifically, an album produced (and distributed) by a DIY band is a product of different social relations than those that define capital. The possibility of creating and distributing products of human labor—which are products of a different set of productive and distributive relations and hence have different amounts of and relations between use-value and exchange-value—is one possible strategy for moving beyond capitalism. For this section in its entirety see: Karl Marx, *Capital* (New York: Penguin Books, 1976), 131.

9. This is an example of the political concept of exodus. See Paolo Virno, "Virtuosity and Revolution: The Political Theory of Exodus," in *Radical Thought in Italy: A Potential Politics,*. eds. Paulo Virno and Michael Hardt (Minneapolis: University of Minnesota Press, 1996), 188–208.

10. At every level, a different set of relations is taking the place of relations imposed by capitalism. DIY participants are not alienated from the process, product, each other, or their desires. Rather, they are led by their desires: by the desires to communicate, celebrate with others, and have substantive relationships. Karl Marx, *Economic and Philosophic Manuscripts of 1844* (New York: Prometheus Books, 1988), 69–84.

11. Karl Marx, *Capital*, Vol. 1 (New York: Penguin Books, 1990), 932.

12. Guido Baldi, "Theses on the Mass Worker and Social Capital," *Radical America* 6, no. 3 (May–June 1972), 3.

13. Antonio Negri and Michael Hardt, *Empire* (Cambridge: Harvard University Press, 2000), 195–97.

14. That the crisis was largely a response to social struggles is certainly a controversial thesis, but one we find convincing. See *Zerowork: Political Materials I*, (Brooklyn, NY: Zerowork, 1975); George Caffentzis, "The Work/Energy Crisis and the Apocalypse," in *Midnight Notes: Work, Energy, War, 1973–1992*, ed. Midnight Notes Collective (New York: Autonomedia, 1992), 215–71.

15. Unemployment doubled in Britain from 1975–1977. Paul Cobley, "Leave the Capitol," in *Punk Rock: So What? The Cultural Legacy of Punk*, ed. Roger Sabin (London: Routledge, 1999), 176.

16. Dave Laing, *One Chord Wonders: Power and Meaning of Punk Rock* (London: Open Up, 1985), 30.

17. For more on the state of the music industry and its inability to relate to the discontent of youth, see Peter G. Ross, "An Organizational Analysis of the Emergence, Development and Mainstreaming of British Punk Rock Music," *Popular Music and Society* 20, no. 1 (Spring 1996); Kenneth J. Bindas, "'The Future Is Unwritten': The Clash, Punk, and America, 1977–1982," *American Studies* 34, no. 1 (1993).

18. Bruce Dancis, "Safety Pins and Class Struggle: Punk Rock and the Left," *Socialist Review* 39 (May–June 1978), 64. Part of this threat was punk's role, along with reggae, in helping to bring together black and white youth.

19. Cobley, "Leave the Capitol," 173.

20. George McKay, *Senseless Acts of Beauty: Cultures of Resistance Since the Sixties* (London: Verso, 1996), 73.

21. Jeff Goldthorpe, "Intoxicated Culture: Punk Symbolism and Punk Protest," *Socialist Review* 22, no. 2 (April–June 1992), 43–44. It is important to observe that a DIY, anarchist, punk scene developed in Britain in the early 1980s with bands such as Conflict, Crass, and Discharge. For a substantial discussion of Crass, see McKay, *Senseless Acts*, 73–101.

22. Kevin Mattson, "Did Punk Matter? Analyzing the Practices of a Youth Subculture during the 1980s," *American Studies* 42, no. 1 (2001), 73. The DIY spirit had been a part of punk since its inception. However, it was not until punk's "death" that this aspect developed and became substantive.

23. It is important to note that punk is not the only way to trace the development of DIY. During the late 1970s, a similar movement was developing in black ghettos in the form of hip hop. It is also certainly true that there are many historical examples of groups who had understandings similar to those described in this paper: the Industrial Workers of the World, numerous radical feminist groups of the 1960s and 1970s, the Black Panthers, etc. However, it was not until punk in the late 1970s that DIY explicitly developed as a term and as a practice.

24. Reagan's actions were not limited to policy. For example, recall the firing of the Professional Air Traffic Controllers Organization (PATCO) workers, as well as the encouragement of increases in tuition prices and cuts in welfare payments, which were bases (labor, education, and welfare) from which struggles had previously been launched.

25. Christian Parenti, *Lockdown America: Police and Prisons in the Age of Crisis* (New York: Verso, 1999), 38.

26. Michael B. Katz, *The Undeserving Poor: From the War on Poverty to the War on Welfare* (New York: Pantheon, 1989), 128–133. Recent studies have stressed the importance of understanding deindustrialization in a broad historical context, and as a process that didn't simply begin in the 1970s and 1980s. See for example: Thomas J. Sugrue, *The Origins of the Urban Crisis: Race and Equality in Postwar Detroit* (Princeton, NJ: Princeton University Press, 1996); Jefferson Cowie, *Capital Moves: RCA's Seventy-Year Quest for Cheap Labor* (Ithaca and London: Cornell University Press, 1999).

27. Reagan Youth, "Reagan Youth," *A Collection of Pop Classics* (New Red Archives, 1984 [original release]); Dirty Rotten Imbeciles, "Reaganomics," *Dealing With It* (Rotten Records, 1983 [original release]).

28. We are referring to a prominent—though not fully inclusive—field within punk, one that was influenced by the concept of DIY and political action. To be sure, not all of punk was politically radical or even to the Left or at all influenced by DIY.

29. Carl Haynes III, "Letter to the Editor," (circa 1982), *Radical America* 18, no. 6 (1984), 2.
30. Robert Ovetz, "Noize Music: The Hypostatic Insurgency," *Common Sense: Journal of the Edinburgh Conference of Socialist Economists* (1993), 13.
31. Goldthorpe, "Intoxicated Culture," 35–36.
32. Joel, *Profane Existence*, no. 11/12 (Autumn 1991), 10. Quoted in Craig O'Hara, *The Philosophy of Punk: More Than Noise!* (San Francisco: AK Press, 1999), 132.
33. Jason Kucsma "Resist and Exist: Punk Zines and the Communication of Cultural and Political Resistance in America," (Bowling Green: The People's Papers Project, 2003), 82.
34. Mattson, "Did Punk Matter?" 82–83.
35. Ibid., 83.
36. Quoted in Hillary Carlip, *Girl Power: Young Women Speak Out!* (New York: Warner Books, 1995), 38.
37. For the best examples of how zine production encouraged political action in Riot Grrrl, see Kristen Schilt, "'I'll Resist with Every Inch and Every Breath': Girls and Zine Making as a Form of Resistance," *Youth and Society* 35, no. 1 (September 2003), 71–97; Jessica Rosenberg and Gitana Garofalo, "Riot Grrrl: Revolutions from Within," *Signs* 23, no. 3 (spring 1998), 809–841; Caroline K. Kaltefleiter, *Revolution Girl Style Now: Trebled Reflexivity and the Riot Grrrl Network* (PhD diss., Ohio University, 1995).
38. Keith McHenry, "On Food Not Bombs," in *Passionate and Dangerous: Conversations with Midwestern Anti-Authoritarians and Anarchists* ed. Mark Bohnert (St. Louis: Passionate and Dangerous, 2003), 24–25. For a discussion of the Clamshell Alliance, see Barbara Epstein, *Political Protest and Cultural Revolution: Non-violent Direct Action in the 1970s and 1980s* (Berkeley and Los Angeles: University of California Press, 1991), 58–91.
39. Keith McHenry, interview with authors via email, September 23, 2003.
40. Ibid.
41. For one telling example of the crisis labor faced during the 1980s, see the literature on the 1985–86 Hormel strike. Particularly useful are: Peter Rachleff, *Hard Pressed in the Heartland: The Hormel Strike and the Future of the Labor Movement* (Boston: South End Press, 1992) and Neala Schleuning, *Women, Community, and the Hormel Strike of 1985–1986* (Westport: Greenwood Press, 1994). For a Food Not Bombs organizer's take on this period in a larger discussion of his history and social struggles in the late twentieth-century, see: Shawn Sitaro, "Shawn Sitaro Interviews Eric Weinberger," *Z Net*, http://www.zmag.org/eric_we.htm.
42. Keith McHenry and Alex Vitale, "Food Not Bombs." *Z Magazine*, September 1994.
43. Available online at www.zmag.org/ZMag/articles/sept94vitale.htm.
44. McHenry interview, September 23, 2003.

45. This is one of the many reasons why those involved with Food Not Bombs have been constantly harassed by the police. For example, over one hundred were arrested in a period of repression in San Francisco in 1988 and over seven hundred arrests have been made in San Francisco alone since 1992. For an account of the harassment of Food Not Bombs in San Francisco, see Richard Edmondson, *Rising Up: Class Warfare in America from the Streets to the Airwaves* (San Francisco: Librad, 2000), 45–73, 158–213.

46. By creating new social relations for the production and distribution of products of social labor, be it albums or food, we fundamentally alter the relations between use-value and exchange-value contained in commodities. Here Food Not Bombs is taking the food that they serve outside the "medium of exchange." In this, those commodities are altered in relation to their content of use-value, and in some cases might no longer be commodities at all. See endnote 8 for further elaboration.

47. This sort of organization, among other things, also makes FNB harder to target or dismantle.

48. Food Not Bombs also helps us begin to understand the constructive side of the "anti-war" movement. The name is meant to be taken both literally and metaphorically. "Food" implies both the reclaiming and redistribution of a basic requirement for human survival, but it is also the demand for something much more radical—a society structured around human needs. "Not Bombs" represents the demand for a world without war, and more broadly, a world not structured around exchange-values. FNB thus offers a starting point in understanding DIY's importance to the anti-war movement—a topic we hope is explored in a future essay.

49. McHenry interview, September 23, 2003.

50. Ibid.

51. For an article discussing the origins of RTS, see John Jordan, "The Art of Necessity: The Subversive Imagination of Anti-Road Protest and Reclaim the Streets," in *DiY Culture: Party and Protest in Nineties Britain*, ed. George McKay (London: Verso, 1998), 129–51.

52. Chris Carlsson, *Critical Mass: Bicycling's Defiant Celebration* (San Francisco: AK Press, 2002), 7.

53. Benjamin Shepard and Ronald Hayduk, "Public versus Private Spaces, Battlegrounds, and Movements," in *From ACT UP to the WTO*, 201.

54. Stephen Duncombe, interview with authors via email, October 1, 2003.

55. Ibid.

56. Naomi Klein, *No Logo* (New York: Picador, 2000), 317.

57. This quote is by organizer John Jordan in reference to RTS—it holds true for the general DIY culture we have been discussing. Quoted in Jordan, "The Art of Necessity," 151.

58. Peter Gartside, "Bypassing Politics? A Critical Look at DiY Culture," in *Young Britain: Politics, Pleasures and Predicaments*, ed. Jonathan

Rutherford (London: Lawrence and Wishart, 1998), 69.

59. Benjamin Shepard and Kelly Moore, "Reclaiming the Streets of New York," in Carlsson, *Critical Mass*, 195–203. Chris Carlsson, "Cycling under the Radar—Assertive Desertion," in ibid., 82.

60. Stephen Duncombe, "Stepping off the Sidewalk: Reclaim the Streets/NYC," in Shepard and Hayduk, *From ACT UP to the WTO*, 215–28.

61. Unfortunately, length constraints prevent us from significant discussion of two important points. First, the examples of DIY culture we highlight—punk, zines, Food Not Bombs, Reclaim the Streets, Critical Mass, and IMCs—also exist as elements of the movement against neoliberalism in countries across the globe. Second, the limitations of DIY culture, not the least of which have been issues related to race, gender, sexuality, and class within the highlighted examples. We warmly welcome additional research into non-US/UK examples of DIY culture as well as into the limitations of DIY, particularly with respect to race, gender, sexuality, and class.

62. Brother Inferior, "Expansion," *Anthems 94–97* (Sensual Underground Ministries, 1999).

63. See, for example, *Maximumrocknroll* 201 (February 2000), unpaginated.

64. Kucsma "Resist and Exist," 94.

65. McHenry, interview, September 23, 2003. To cite just one example, Naomi Klein has observed how many members of the Ontario Coalition Against Poverty, an influential group that "exists for the sole purpose of empowering the poor and the homeless...first became involved in anti-poverty work... through Food Not Bombs." Naomi Klein, *Fences and Windows: Dispatches from the Front Lines of the Globalization Debate* (New York: Picador, 2002), 38.

66. McHenry, interview, September 23, 2003.

67. Ibid.

68. Naomi Klein has argued that RTS "may well be the most vibrant and fastest-growing political movement since Paris '68," Klein, *No Logo*, 312.

69. For example, twenty-six countries and thirty cities had RTS parties during the Global Street Party of May 16, 1998, which was timed with the convergence of the G8 leaders in England as well as with the fiftieth anniversary of the World Trade Organization. In another example (of many more), on June 18, 1999, RTS and Peoples' Global Action put out a call for international protests during the G8 meeting in Cologne, Germany. For a collection of documents on these actions see "June 18, 1999: Global Protest Against Capitalism," http://www.infoshop.org/ june18.html.

70. See Carlsson, *Critical Mass*.

71. This includes limited resources, an inability to provide fresh information, and powerlessness to make media widely accessible to and influential among the public. See Dorothy Kidd, "'Which Would You Rather: Seattle or Porto Alegre?" paper presented at the "Our Media, Not Theirs" conference in

Barcelona, July 2002.

72. Ana Nogueira, "The Birth and Promise of the Indymedia Revolution," in Shepard and Hayduk, *From ACT UP to the WTO*, 295.

73. Douglas Morris, "Globalization and Media Democracy: The Case of Indymedia," in *Shaping The Network Society*, eds. Douglas Schuler and Peter Day (Cambridge: MIT Press, 2004).

74. Ibid.

75. Olivier de Marcellus, "PGA: Dreaming Up an Old Ghost," in *Auroras of the Zapatistas: Local and Global Struggles from the Fourth World War*, ed. Midnight Notes Collective (Brooklyn: Autonomedia, 2001), 103–15.

76. George McKay, "DIY Culture: Notes Towards an Intro," in *DiY Culture: Party and Protest in Nineties Britain*, 4.

77. David McNally, *Another World Is Possible: Globalization and Anti-Capitalism* (Winnipeg: Arbeiter Ring, 2002), 243.

78. For a discussion of the way that non-hierarchical forms of organization have been the basis of organization in the movement see David Graeber, "The New Anarchists," *New Left Review* 13, no. 61 (January–February 2002), 63–73.

79. We have predominantly discussed areas of cultural production. Space has prevented inclusion of other forms DIY has taken, such as Community Supported Agriculture projects, community gardens, and the extensive number of radically organized infoshops and social centers that have opened over the past twenty years (In the United States, for example, see Longhaul Infoshop [Berkeley, California], Civic Media Center [Gainesville, Florida], Abc No Rio [New York City]). For linkages between struggle and gardening, see Peter Lamborn Wilson and Bill Weinberg, *Avant Gardening: Ecological Struggle in the City and the World* (Brooklyn: Autonomedia, 1999). In addition, it must be stressed again that our discussion privileges examples of DIY that largely (though by no means completely) involve white participants and that there are various examples of DIY (and other anticapitalist actions) that have proliferated within communities of color in the United States—something future research must also address.

Logic and Theory of Inquiry: Militant Praxis as Subject and as Episteme

Antonio Negri
Translated by Nate Holdren + Arianna Bove

In our discussion on historical causality and the ontological genealogy of the concept of Empire, we tried to "subsume under the concept" (in Hegel and Marx's terms) large social movements and the transformations of techniques of government and of the structural *dispositifs* of sovereignty. Thus, we have practiced political science, but not only that. Through this type of analysis we not only tried to track down some functional transitions, but also to grasp the wrong-footedness and contradictions present in the unfolding of these events. However, it must be noted that the route traced until now leaves a series of methodological questions open to us, which must be closely examined.

The first issue concerns the transition determined by the conjugation of the ontological and the institutional (respectively the movement and politics). The relationship between social movements and institutional change takes shape concurrently with the transformation of the very nature of movements. In this sense, the transition is *fundamentally* from the hegemony of material labour to that of immaterial labour; which is to say, the processes internal to the labour force that have transformed the forms of work, existence, and expression.[1] The explanation for historical evolution is to be found within these ontological dimensions of labour. There would not be effective struggles unless they were locked in, linked to, and produced by this profound transformation of labour. Struggles did not develop just around the problems of wage allocation or the quantification, distribution, and antagonism of the relationship between wages and profits: above all, they always revolved around *the intention to liberate labour*. This liberation of labour runs through the process that leads to the hegemony of immaterial labour. The "refusal of work" in the 1960s and 1970s was a positive sign that dovetailed with a refusal of the Taylorist and Fordist labour paradigm and the will to change it. This will produces the discovery of more advanced forms of the productivity of human labour, while also determining better conditions and real possibilities of liberation from exhaustion, impoverishment, and the destruction of bodies that characterises the labour of the mass worker. Taking this analysis further, we encounter new dimensions of labour that invest the whole of life. From the methodological point of view, this shift provides us with an interpretive framework that is internal to these processes and allows us to understand labour not only from the standpoint of productive activity (as economic activity), but also in a framework that integrates affective, communicative, and vital aspects, which is to say, ontological elements. These elements turn life and productive activity into a single and interwoven whole and a single effective reality. (It must be noted that it is extremely important to take on this interpretive standpoint—*from labour to biopolitics*—because it allows us to face up to a series of central problems, such as social reproduction and questions raised by feminism, and to include and treat them within a common discursive fabric.)

The second issue in need of closer examination, particularly from the methodological point of view, is the definition of *multitude*. We defined the multitude not only as a class concept (linked to the experience and transformations of labour) and a political concept (as a democratic proposal oriented toward the construction of new relationships amongst civic singularities), but also as a *dispositif* of power (*potenza*) that extends to life as a whole and is able to express the common, an increased power and a re-qualification of life, production, and freedom.[2] By saying this, we are reasserting that we are going through a long and complex phase of transition and it is difficult to grasp all of its facets. However, the concept of multitude we've elaborated gives us a clue about where to go, increasingly freeing us from all dialectics of sublimation and synthesis (of the Hegelian method of *Aufhebung*). Instead, our method takes the multitude as the ontological threshold and is thus defined as syncopated, interrupted, open, and untimely. *Like the multitude, the method folds onto the event, it is event.*

Thus, a further essential issue is to follow the production of subjectivity, where the latter assists and develops the possible convergence of labour activity and the *construction of the "common."* Here our method starts from below, but when building from below we are confronted by enormous obstacles. In the fourth lesson, in the discussion of war as the last stage of capitalist control, both author and readers was subjected to the vertigo of the present historical phase.[3] The risk is inevitable: it is a matter of moving forward, and the only way to do so is by doing research according to a logic of immersion, of situating ourselves inside the present, always starting from below, where there is no outside. Now, to consolidate ourselves in this perspective, it is necessary to *define cooperation*. We said that linguistic cooperation is the model of postmodern production, not only because, materially speaking, machines function by means of languages, but also insofar as new forms of cooperation between individuals continue to emerge through language. Rather than individuals, we are dealing with singularities that cooperate. However, if linguistic cooperation is productive cooperation, if everything is inside this cooperation, and if, within it, the multitude is a constituent power, then how are diversity and command in the labour process articulated within these flows? What, for example, is the difference between manager and worker and between their respective activities? In explicit methodological terms, the problem is this: how can we evaluate and, if necessary, cut through this development from within? The form of cooperation is not sufficient in itself to solve this problem. From this perspective, it is probably necessary to follow the (Marxian) thread that defines the common as the only thing that can eliminate certain confusions and equivocal lack of differentiations. *The common distinguishes*: it allows us to separate the manager from the worker. In fact, only the affirmation of the "common" enables us to steer the flows of production from within and to separate the alienating capitalist flows from those that recompose knowledge and freedom. The problem will be solved by a practical rupture capable of reaffirming the centrality of common praxis.

Our research must provide forms of antagonism interpreted through new figures of militancy and the convergence of knowledge and action in the construction of the common. One of the most important elements of the discourse on method is *the practical, material determination; the praxis that breaks through a purely critical framework*. Language and cooperation must be traversed *by a practical rupture* and by the establishment of the centrality of common praxis, which is a concrete union of knowledge and action within these processes.

We can also deal with this issue from another perspective and resume the old tradition of *operaismo's discussion of "joint-research"* as the exemplary form of such method. The practice of joint-research was simply the possibility of knowing, through inquiry, workers' levels of awareness and consciousness as productive subjects. If I go into a factory, get in touch with the workers and carry out with them an investigation into the conditions of their labour, the joint-research is obviously the description of the productive cycle and the identification of the functions of each person within that cycle. But at the same time, it is also a general evaluation of the levels of exploitation that each and every one of them suffers, of the workers' ability to react in relation to their consciousness of exploitation in the system of machines and before the structure of command. This way, as the research advances, the joint-research creates outlooks of struggle in the factory and defines threads or devices of cooperation beyond the factory. *Evidently, this is where the hegemony and centrality of praxis in research reside*: this praxis helps our understanding of the cycle of production and exploitation and is enhanced when it determines resistance and agitation, which is to say, when it develops struggles. Thus, it is practically possible to *constitute an antagonistic subject*, because this is what the argument is about. We can start, then, from this old experience of *operaismo* and ask ourselves: what joint-research can be carried out *today*, in postmodernity, under totally transformed conditions of labour and social organization? This is clearly a difficult question, which I cannot answer here; if anything, it is a case of moving forward and working around it.

In fact, if we think about inquiry today in all its practical significance, the important thing is to enhance its *biopolitical premises and settings*. The central elements of inquiry ought to be *bodies*. There is an array of issues that concern the body and corporeal life that need to be brought into play if we wish to constitute, represent, and begin to define any constellation or composition. I believe this issue is of extraordinary importance and arises from the biopolitical method that we are beginning to practice. This method breaks away from the overly rigid, analytical methodologies experimented with by sociology. I call such methods "salami theories," the analytical slicing up of the social body. Today, by contrast, we are probably beginning to confront first and foremost the issue of corporeality (and we do so with great confidence in the power of the body).

Another issue to be dealt with is the need to constitute the object by positing—negatively to start with, yet always and in each instance—its singularity and its thrust towards the common, rather than simply its identity or difference. This methodological cue is new and original: in the past we used to select, analytically isolate, and then point to the *homo oeconomicus*, the aesthetic one, the psychological one, and so on—now we can bring it all together. While we used to move between the processes of determination and the specificity of phenomena (to always wind up stuck between identity and difference), it is now possible to skip this dichotomous pair and to see *the multitude as the common and difference as singularity*. Today, we have the chance to overcome these old dichotomies not only in words but concretely: the contents of differences are enriched in singularities and play together in the common, as in a new frame of activity. The key element of this perspective is the common, that is: the bodies; the logical categories of singularity and how they refer to the common; and the common as ontological presupposition. I think that from this perspective, sociological research ought to keep clarifying the conditions of "commonality" within which a singularity is established. This is crucial if we want to build something. These constellations somehow correspond to the old idea of class "composition," albeit here newly composed within the wealth of a corporeal common.

Although we adopted the biopolitical as our research framework, we never progressed by way of contact with bodies per se. *Each singularity is defined as corporeality,* but biopolitical corporeality is not merely biological: it is also social. For instance, when we deal with an issue like the *precarisation of labour,* we certainly grasp its exhausting physical effects on the labourer—the mobility and flexibility of labour—but we also see the possibilities inherent in the new labour-power.[4] In other words, on one hand, we have the terrible conditions that constrain precarious labour, and, on the other hand, its new potentials. In this way we can grasp precariousness, by fluctuating between identity and difference, while seeing the common as the basis of exploitation and, at the same time, the activity of resistance.

On this note, we shift to practice and the practical option: the *rediscovery of antagonism.* But where exactly is this transition, and where does the option of antagonism lie? The theoretical proposal, from what has been said so far, would identify exploitation in command in the labour process as the expropriation of cooperation; that is, as the ability to block the activity of the multitude. Exploitation is established precisely on the wealth of the common and the productivity of the multitude. It attempts to impede their expression, to silence them, to disembody them, to eliminate them and take away their properties. Here we should grant alienation a strong materiality that relates to every aspect of the body. It is an expropriation and a disembodiment that clashes against singularities and the common, and clearly collides with a practice that springs from the expression of the common and the processes of its construction. I think that the only way to begin to place a stronger emphasis on our research is by insisting on the singular and common configuration of new subjects of production, and on the exploitation that deepens them, advancing from the things that dance and move before our eyes in postmodernity.

Let us posit one last question very openly: what is it that we want? We obviously want democracy, *democracy at a global scale,* that is, for all. The term "democracy" is not a happy one for sure, but we have no others. Every time we say that we want democracy, we seem to fall into a trap because we are immediately asked: but what exactly do you want? Give us a list of all the democratic demands you claim to bring to this platform! I do not think that it is a case of making a list. If anything, on the basis of what has been said we need to start outlining a scheme of what the *desire for democracy, or better yet, for the "common"* is, as a methodological criterion for evaluating the alternative proposals that continue to arise. At times, I am under the impression that a whole series of proposals that had, until recently, seemed completely utopian, today appear increasingly real—as if our awareness of having entered a new epoch has matured. We should draw up something analogous to the *cahiers de doleances,* which were published before the explosion of the French Revolution. These documents presented the complaints of the Third Estate, but were more than simple protestations: they were denunciations of injustices as well as proposals for their solution. *The method that acts from below moves through critique in order to provide a practical response.*

The issue today is how to conceive of a democracy at the global level. A first critical focus (as expounded in *Empire*) demonstrates the development of imperial mechanisms of control, division, and hierarchy. We have also seen how these mechanisms are deployed in the exercise of permanent war. *The real problem* will be that of *augmenting the subversive desire of the common* that invests the multitude, by opposing it to the war, institutionalising it and transforming it into constituent power.

In the course of the previous lectures, we have noted that there are at least three elements capable of defining the multitude in terms of the common. The *first element* relates to social ontology: the affirmation that immaterial and intellectual labour does not call for command in the labour process and that it can create in excess. This *excess* is developed in a "network." From the point of view of the ontology of labour, this means raising the problem of how to guarantee forms of networks for the future democracy. The network is a system of communication in which values of cooperation in the full sense, both productive and political, are formed.

The *second element* is that of the "common," that is, the material premise of production that no longer requires either capital or exploitation in order to exist. From this perspective, *capitalism becomes increasingly parasitic with respect to the accumulation of the common.* The common permits the constitution of being and cannot be reappropriated or privatised by anyone. So while, on the one hand, labour theories show us the inefficiency of command, on the other hand—and paradoxically—social theories show us the inalienable nature of the common. The common is the inalienable matter on which we can build democracy. *The third main element* that configures the multitude is freedom. Without freedom there is no creative labour, *without freedom there is neither cooperation nor common.*

Once these elements are investigated, critique can move onto juridical and bourgeois conceptions of rights and democracy. On this issue, I think that Marx's writings on rights are still valid, especially his critique of Hegel's *Philosophy of Right.* His critique needs to be extended to current democratic rights, to show how formal equality and substantial inequality still constitute their foundation.

This becomes more relevant when we consider the new grounds for a global constitution and a global system of rights. It is crucial to emphasise how the development of capitalism tends to eliminate the efficacy of any regulatory action of nation-states. In modernity, the development of capitalism occurred via the state; but today, in postmodernity, capitalism has reappropriated the whole of the social fabric at the multinational level, and only resorts to nation-state interventions when necessary. When we speak of common property, of networked labour, and of the guarantees of freedom, we have to deal with the process of globalisation. This is extremely important because it helps us firmly reassert that we have moved beyond any guarantees nation-state's once provided, and beyond any illusion of a return to a nation-state's balance of power. Today, democracy must be extended into the relations between multitudes, and must construct new social relations and a new idea of rights in this way. We are not referring here to the abolition of rights, but rather to new juridical forms capable of establishing norms guided by the three principles described above. There must be sanctions against those who wish to re-establish command and introduce criteria of property over or against the network, blocking its access or controlling its nodes. At the same time, there must also be sanctions against those who create technological and/or juridical tools to obstruct the circulation of knowledge and the great "commonality" that can feed production and life.

—

Up to this point, you must think that we haven't spoken of logic. Or perhaps you will concede that I've alluded to it by referring to inquiry, the theory of joint-research, and through my emphasis on the pragmatic behaviours that can and should be developed in the field of social knowledge. But, in fact, we have really spoken of logic. Because we didn't use academic terms, it might seem like we've avoided the issue—but we haven't. So, in order to explain ourselves also in academic terms, to show that even militants can cross our rhetorical fields without difficulty, here comes a scheme, or a high filter of what we have been logically unraveling. In fact, it is a schematic summary of the lecture, complemented by some bibliographic references.

1. The preamble to the discussion of logic as theory of inquiry is found in Marx's *Einleitung*. We also refer here to John Dewey's *Logic: The Theory of Inquiry* [1938]. In his *John Dewey* (Harvard University Press, Harvard: 2001), Alan Ryan demonstrates how the lines of American empirical logic can intersect the lines of Marxian logic. The works of Rodolfo Mondolfo and Sydney Hook recover their relevance today. Briefly, the centrality of praxis is here treated as an epistemological and a political issue. Moreover, in this introduction we have emphasised the relation between language, rhetoric, dialogue, and invention, as they are intertwined in the two dimensions that we like: the Spinozian logic of the common name and the rediscovery of the common name in postmodern logic (on this question, see Kairos, *Alma Venus*, Multitudo, manifestolibri, Roma: 2002).

2. *Inquiry as a logical dispositif.* What does this mean? It means that, in our attempt to construct a logic of research, we have always developed a

theoretical process that goes from the constitution of the object (inquiry), to the dialogical explanation of the constitution of the object (joint-research), to end with the definition of the constitutive subject. We thus see a sort of return of the object to the subject: this has always been the progression of revolutionary logic, as Ryan explains very well in his *John Dewey*, where he outlines the transition from revolutionary liberalism to the New Deal of the US in the 1920s and 1930s. *Mutatis mutandis*, we could refer this "return of the object to the subject" to every revolutionary experience. In the previous lectures, we demonstrated how the logic of the subject lies between causality and the discontinuity of development. The identification of the logic of the event is the main point in our discussion. We can say that the "common name" (the concept) always oscillates between identity and difference, but is also determined in the interstice between singularity and the common. If that is the case, the subject is situated inside a process of production of subjectivity as production of a given temporality and spatiality. But, while we see the formation of the subject in the production of the common (through cooperation), we have also underlined the field of logic's inability to accomplish inquiry by itself. Cooperation in itself does not explain antagonism; so we must start again from the standpoint of antagonism.

3. *Inquiry as ethico-political dispositif.* In the Fordist society of the mass worker, inquiry as an ethico-political *dispositif* was interpreted by joint-research: in joint-research the epistemological and militant/agitating devices were joined together. In this respect, see G. Borio, F. Pozzi, and G. Roggero, *Futuro Anteriore. Dai "Quaderni Rossi" ai movimenti globali.* DeriveApprodi, Roma: 2002. When we refer to inquiry as an ethico-political *dispositif*, we do not avoid the more distinctly cognitive and general epistemological questions; on the contrary, we include and situate them inside a process of collective learning. Somehow, inquiry as an ethico-political *dispositif* is always a *Bildungsroman*. The issue of the formation of the elite is tied to the question of the centrality of praxis, and to the organization of antagonism. A new series of problems arises here, in particular due to historical changes in class composition. What does inquiry as an ethico-political *dispositif* mean in postmodern society: not the Fordist society of the mass worker but that of precarious, mobile, and flexible labour, the society of immaterial services and the hegemony of cooperation? I do not think the answer would be too different from the one regarding the issue of joint-research, from the perspective of method and the constitutive progression of the subject. Throughout the 1990s these issues were dealt with in the journal *Futur Anterior*, published in Paris by L'Harmattan; those who are interested can consult it. As to the process of joint-research in the postmodern scene and on the cooperation of immaterial labourers, see A. Negri et al., *Des entreprises pa comme les autres*, Publisud, Paris: 1993, and A. Negri et al., *Le basin du travail immaterial*, L'Harmattan, Paris: 1996.

4. *Inquiry and the logic of language.* Having established the relationship between inquiry as logical device and the new situation of postmodern production, where language emerges as the fundamental means of production and productive cooperation, it is necessary to redefine inquiry in terms of the logic of language. Paolo Virno, in *The Grammar of the Multitude* and *Il ricordo del presente. Saggio sul tempo storico* (Bollati Boringhieri, Turin: 1999) provides numerous openings on these issues. For my part, in addition to the arguments proposed by Virno, for a close examination of the problem of productive language (and cooperation and singularity), I refer to the works of Bakhtin, where the linguistic constitution of the real is defined in strong materialist terms.

—

Having developed our method in this way, we are again faced with some of the great themes of communism. This means that our method is adequate to *the epochal alternative* where we place ourselves, when *the crisis of neoliberalism* manifests as its alternative *the aims of communism*: the reappropriation of enterprises, the egalitarian distribution of wealth, the collective management of knowledge, etc. For years and years, since the great post-'68 crisis, nobody dared to speak about these things. Today, we begin to speak about them again and to adopt methods that lead to these possibilities of expression, because we know that we live at the threshold of an extreme crisis: faced with either the restoration of a harsh past or the hope for a new world. It is a matter of decision, and it is precisely *around the issue of the decision that the political is born.* Before approaching the issue of decision, we should stretch the imagination on this point and think that in the terrible and bloody period of transition we find ourselves in, everything is possible after all. Imagination and decision must intertwine in the movement of the multitude and the desire of expression that the multitude produces. Inside this imagination, *democratic representation*—which has always been presented to us as the foundation of the guarantee of liberties—is a monstrous mystification to say the least. The imagination of the multitude currently raises the question of *combining sovereign power* (potenza) *with the productive capacity of subjects.* As we outlined it, our discussion on biopolitics leads to this conclusion. But how can the desire of the multitude be organised? How can another democracy be invented? At the national level, democracy no longer exists, and it is unthinkable at the global level. Nonetheless, these un-thoughts are the actuality of desire.... We ought to use the terms of the Enlightenment and conceive of new electoral constituencies at the global level that would no longer correspond to nations, but cross the face of the earth rebalancing the wealthy and poor areas, blacks and whites, yellow and green, etc., hybridising and subverting political borders and limits, using force at the service of the construction of the common. Constituent imagination is what we want. Enlightenment is necessary. But let us return to decision. What does the problem of the relationship between the common experience of the multitude and the ethico-political and juridical concept of decision entail? I think that this can and should be talked about here and elsewhere, but the answer can only be given at the level of the language of the movement, *inside the movement*. After all, these questions only mature in the movement; parties are dead and buried. The movements raise these problems and suggest solutions. Now, on the issue of the decision of the multitude: what is striking in the movements from Seattle to today is that they no longer speak of taking power, but rather of *making power*, of creating another power, and while everyone knows this is utopian, they also know that it has become necessary and realistic due to the vertigo of the current epochal transition. We cannot wait two or three hundred years for the decision of the multitude to become reality!

But this could happen and defeat may be inevitable... In that case, let's leave! The radical nature of constituent power corresponds to exodus as an alternative, a constructive exodus that expresses positive forms of relations between decision and the multitude and thus between freedom and the production of the common. If we cannot construct an alternative power, the multitude can say: strike, desertion, subtraction from power... And the processes *between constituent power and exodus* will interweave and alternate. They are like waves that follow one another. The terms of the multitude's decisions are tough, produced by a tempestuous sea: there is no dulling of the masses for power. There is an ontological insurrection of the multitude. We live the biopolitical.

Notes

1. *Forza Lavoro*: the term used here denotes both "workforce," meaning a set of workers at a given workplace or labor market, as well as "labor power" in the Marxian sense, meaning the capacity to work which workers sell in exchange for wages. –Tr.

2. Negri uses the term "common" to refer to the social resources of cooperation and knowledge created by the changing nature of work and social interaction today. The term "common" is used to distinguish such common resources from "the commons" understood as pre-capitalist shared land holdings and resources. For more on this concept, see Michael Hardt and Antonio Negri *Multitude: War and Democracy in the Age of Empire* (New York: Penguin, 2004). –Ed.

3. This text is part of a set of talks that Negri gave. Here Negri is referring to the lecture immediately prior to this one, entitled "On the Production

of Subjectivity, Between War and Democracy." This chapter as well as the other lectures were printed in *Cinque Lezioni su Impero e Dintorni* (Milano: Raffaello Cortina, 2003). –Tr

4. See endnote 1. –Tr.

Something More on Research Militancy: Footnotes[1] on Procedures and (In)Decisions

Colectivo Situaciones
Translated by Sebastian Touza + Nate Holdren[2]

Translators' Introduction

The translation of this significant article, a fundamental piece insofar as it lays bare the values and principles Colectivo Situaciones invoke in their definition of themselves as militants, calls for a reflection on our role as translators. It is important to share with the reader our urge to dispel any mythical (mis)understanding of the transparency of language. We share Colectivo Situaciones' conviction that abstraction inevitably impoverishes experience. Translation adds one more layer of abstraction. In this sense, we assume the full significance of the Italian adage *traduttore, traditore.* Not because we intend to betray anybody, but because the acknowledgment that every translation is a betrayal is our attempt to keep faith with the concrete situation in which the experience being communicated unfolds. In this introduction, we would like to go through some of the difficulties we had in doing the translation. We hope that by explaining the decisions we made, we will bring the reader closer to the work of Colectivo Situaciones.

We faced our first difficulty when trying to translate the title. We were unsure how to translate the term *militancia de investigación.* This phrase can be translated into English as either "research militancy" or "militant research." At the risk of taking words too seriously (always a risk in translation), it may be useful to spend some time on these two possible translations. "Militant research" implies a continuity with other examples of militant research, those presented in other parts of this volume and elsewhere.

"Research militancy" may sound strange to the English speaker's ear and it is less immediately clear what the term means.

The grammatical difference between these two phrases is a matter of which word defines the activity and which word qualifies it; which word will be the predicate of the other. The difference seems to be one of emphasis. Does the Spanish phrase refer to knowledge production that happens to be radical in some way (militant research)? Or does it refer to radical activism that happens to take the form of knowledge production (research militancy)?

Our indecision brought us to ask Colectivo Situaciones which one of the two expressions they felt more comfortable with. To our surprise—or perhaps not—the response was "both." "We think of our practice as a double movement: to create ways of being militants that escape the political certainties established a priori and embrace politics as research (in this case, it would be 'research militancy'), and, at the same time, to invent forms of thinking and producing concepts that reject academic procedures, breaking away from the image of an object to be known and putting at the centre subjective experience (in this case, it would be 'militant research')."

Situaciones came together as a collective in the late 1990s. Previously they had been involved in El Mate, a student group notable for creating the Che Guevara Free Lecturership, an experiment oriented toward recuperating the memory of the generation of Argentinean and Latin American revolutionaries of the 1960s and 1970s that began at the faculty of social sciences at the University of Buenos Aires and quickly spread throughout several universities in Argentina and abroad. The Argentinean social landscape in which the men and women of Situaciones forged their ideas was a desert swept by neoliberal winds, in which only a few movements of resistance could stand up by themselves. Those were times in which dilettante postmodern thinkers had come to the conclusion that social change was a relic from the past and in which people involved in politics could only see their activity through rarely questioned models.

Research militancy was the response to the need to rebuild the links between thought and the new forms of political involvement that were rapidly becoming part of the Argentinean reality. In the prologue "On Method" of the book *La Hipótesis 891*, Colectivo Situaciones wrote together with the unemployed workers' movement of Solano, the authors distinguish research militancy from three other relations to knowledge.[3] On the one hand, academic research inevitably reifies those it constructs as objects. Academics cannot help leaving outside the scope of their investigation the function of attributing meaning, values, interests, and rationalities of the subject who does the research. On the other hand, traditional political activists—those involved in parties or party-like organizations—usually hold that their commitment and involvement makes their relation to knowledge more advanced than the work done by academics. But their activity is no less objectifying, in the sense that it always approaches struggles from a previously constituted knowledge framework. Struggles are thus regarded not for their value in themselves, but rather in terms of their contribution to something other than themselves—the coming socialist or communist society. A third figure, the humanitarian activist, also relates to others in an instrumental fashion—in the justification and funding of NGOs (nongovernmental organizations)—and takes the world as static, not subject to being radically changed (thus, the best one can hope for is the alleviation of the worst abuses).

Research militancy does not distinguish between thinking and doing politics. For, insofar as we see thought as the thinking/doing activity that deposes the logic by which existing models acquire meaning, thinking is immediately political. On the other hand, if we see politics as the struggle for freedom and justice, all politics involves thinking, because there are forms of thinking against established models implicit in every radical practice—a thought people carry out with their bodies.

This brings us to a second translation difficulty. Two Spanish words translate as the English word "power": *poder* and *potencia*. Generally speaking, we could say that *poder* expresses power as "power over" (the sense it has, for instance, when it refers to state or sovereign power) and *potencia* is defined as "power to," the type of capacity expressed in the statement "I can."[4] To continue with the generalization, it is possible to say that *poder* refers to static forms of power, while *potencia* refers to its dynamic forms. *Potencia* always exists in the here and now; it coincides with the act in which it is effected. This is because *potencia* is inseparable from our capacity—indeed, our bodies' capacity—to be affected. This capacity cannot be detached from the moment, place, and concrete social relations in which *potencia* manifests itself. This is the reason we are arguing, in this article, that anything said about *potencia* is an abstraction of the results. Whatever is said or communicated about it can never be the *potencia* itself. Research militancy is concerned with the expansion of *potencia*. For this reason, a descriptive presentation of its techniques would necessarily lead to an abstraction. Such a description might produce a "method" in which all the richness of the *potencia* of research militancy in the situation is trimmed off to leave only that part whose utilitarian value makes it transferable to other situations.

The thought of practices is enacted with the body, because bodies encounter each other in acts that immediately define their mutual capacities to be affected. History can only be the history of contingency, a sequence of moments with their own non-detachable intensities. Miguel Benasayag argues that act and state—to which correspond *potencia* and *poder*—are two levels of thought and life.[5] Neither of them can be subsumed by the other. Each takes the side of *potencia* or the side of the *poder* (or of the desire for *poder*, as expressed in militants who want to "take power," build the Party, construct hegemonies, etc.).

Potencias found in different forms of resistance are the foundation of "counterpower," but the terms are not the same. Counterpower indicates a point of irreversibility in the development of resistance, a moment when the principal task becomes to develop and secure what has been achieved by the struggle. Counterpower is diffuse and multiple. It displaces the question of power from the centrality it has historically enjoyed, because its struggle is "against the powers such as they act in our situations" (*La Hipótesis 891*, 104). To be on the side of *potencia* is to recognize that the state and the market originate at the level of the values we embrace and the bonds that connect us to others.

Potencia defines the material dimension of the encounter of bodies, while *poder* is a level characterized by idealization, representation, and normalization. Colectivo Situaciones avoid using a name to define their political identity, which would freeze the fluid material multiplicity of militant research by subordinating it to the one-dimensional nature of idealizations. "We are not autonomists, situationists, or anything ending with -ist," they once told us. Identities have normalizing effects: they establish models, they place multiplicity under control, they reduce the multiple dimensions of life to the single dimension of an idealization. They make an exception with *Guevarism*, because Che Guevara clearly preferred to stay on the side of *potencia* and opposed those who calmed down concrete struggles in the name of ideal recipes on how to achieve a communist society.[6]

An investigation into the forms of *potencia* and the social relations that produce it can only be done from a standpoint that systematically embraces doubt and ignorance. If we recognize that the practical thought of struggles is an activity of bodies, we have to recognize as well—with Spinoza—that nobody knows what a body can do. To do research in the realm of *potencia*—to investigate that which is alive and multiple—militant researchers have to abandon their previous certainties, their desire to encounter pure subjects, and the drive to recuperate those subjects' practice as an ideal of coherence and consistency. In this regard, one might say that Colectivo Situaciones seek to concretely embody two Zapatista slogans: "asking we walk," and "we make the road by walking," such that, the act of questioning and collective reflection is part of the process of constructing power.

Research militancy is a form of intervention, a practice that accompanies other practices, or *experiencias*. This is our third translation difficulty. Colectivo Situaciones, like many other activists belonging to the wave of new protagonism in Argentina, use the word *experiencia* to refer to singular, more or less organized groups, with flexible boundaries, involved in an ongoing emancipatory practice. *Experiencias* with whom Colectivo Situaciones have practiced research militancy include: H.I.J.O.S. (the human rights group formed by children of the disappeared); MoCaSE (a *campesino* group); MTD of Solano (a movement within the larger *piquetero* movement, formed mainly by unemployed workers); Grupo de Arte Callejero (a street art group that works very closely with H.I.J.O.S.); the educational community Creciendo Juntos (a free school run by militant teachers); the political prisoners of Néstor Kirchner's government; and a number of other *experiencias* in Argentina, Bolivia, Uruguay, and Mexico. The word *experiencia* connotes both experience, in the sense of accumulation of knowledges of resistance; and experiment, understood as a practice. In this article, when the word *experiencia* displays this double connotation we translate it as experience/experiment.

We keep these words together because we find it important to keep present the experiential dimension to which the word *experiencia* makes reference. An *experiencia* can have territorial characteristics, such as MTD of Solano, whose roots are in a shanty town located in the south of greater Buenos Aires, or it can be more deterritorialized, like Colectivo Situaciones. But in all cases, *experiencias* are defined by a certain form of the life-world, a particular quest to redefine the bonds that define that group of people as a collective in such ways that they produce, in the situation, social relations that are superior to those of capitalism. The construction of a noncapitalist sociability is a key activity for the *experiencias* Colectivo Situaciones works with. For MTD of Solano, for instance, the production of subjective bonds that are different from those of the state and the market is a defining moment of their concept of autonomy. The material basis of support for both the market and the state are the bonds produced at the local level. Thus, one of their most important activities of self-reflection involves the critique of individualist values, contractual relations, and the instrumentalization of life as they appear at the most basic and concrete level. That is, on the same level, in the same temporal and spatial dimension, that *potencia* exists. There are certain types of social bonds that make *potencia* stronger. Others make it weaker. The research militancy theorized and practiced by Colectivo Situaciones is a committed effort to both producing bonds at that concrete level and weaving them in such way that they allow for maximum *potencia*.

Militant researchers work towards making the elements of a noncapitalist sociability more potent. This requires them to develop a particular type of relation with the groups and movements they work with. Following Spinoza, Colectivo Situaciones calls this relation "composition." Composition defines relations between bodies. It does not refer to agreements established at a discursive level but to the multidimensional flows of affect and desire the relationship puts in motion. Thus, research militancy becomes immanent to the *experiencias* it works with. This concrete relation is not achieved through conscious understanding, but by letting oneself be open to the dynamics of affect that define the possibility of *potencia* in the situation.

Here, Colectivo Situaciones moves away from a certain truism pervasive in much of contemporary activist culture, both in Argentina and in North America: the idea that a certain type of communication (be it the use of the Internet, grassroots filmmaking, or any other medium) has an inherent emancipatory effect on people. Communication produces abstractions of experience. The experience itself can only be lived. Even though there is *potencia*, for instance, in the activism that carries out grassroots communication experiments, the *potencia* in the situation cannot be communicated. In this sense, perhaps Colectivo Situaciones would agree with the thesis put forward by Michael Hardt and Antonio Negri, according to which there is no circulation of struggles.[7] Except that, for Colectivo Situaciones, this is not just the case for this point in history. Struggles do not communicate their *potencia*, they never did and they never will. There is, however, the possibility of resonances between struggles and points of resistance, but that is something entirely different. There are resonances between struggles when there are "shared epochal problems" and they face similar obstacles, making possible the transference of "certain knowledges, feelings, and declarations." Thus, there could be resonances between, for instance, Argentinean *piqueteros* and migrant workers in Western Europe, even if there is no actual exchange of words between them.[8]

Colectivo Situaciones makes a crucial distinction between the abstract perspective of "global thinking," and the thought of the situation, for which the experiential dimension is the concrete form of existence of the world. Here, as the Malgré Tout Collective puts it, the choice is clear: either world or situation.[9] The global standpoint is one in which we look at the world as spectators, the mass-mediated outlook that turns us into concerned individuals, concerned about issues that come to us only as representations. The constricted sphere of the situation, however, is one whose configuration we are responsible for. We produce and are produced by the situations we inhabit. Either our practices are those of the individual-spectator, and thus keep in place certain values, bonds, and affects that reproduce the centrality of state power and the pervasiveness of market relations, or we are the persons in situations who are open to producing and maintaining the bonds that assemble a different, noncapitalist sociability.

Research militancy takes an immanent commitment to the situation. The situation, as Colectivo Situaciones understands it, is a sovereign space and time that defines its own senses and subtracts itself from the senses produced by the state and the market. The working hypotheses of research militants are direct elaborations on the exigencies of the situation. In contrast with the academic researcher, the traditional militant, and the humanitarian activist, who are "extrasituational," the militant researcher thinks and acts in the situation.

How to write about the *potencia* of an experience/experiment knowing that its *potencia* will not be transferred into the writing? What kind of writing can at least look for resonances? Certainly not a writing that presents itself as a blueprint, an outline, or as a forecast. The writing has to be anti-pedagogical. Militant research does not teach, at least not in the sense of an explication which assumes the stupidity and powerlessness of those it explains to.[10] Research militancy is a composition of wills, an attempt to create what Spinoza called joyful passions, which starts from and increases the power (*potencia*) of everyone involved. Such a perspective is only possible by admitting from the beginning that one does not have answers, and, by doing so, abandoning the desire to lead others or to be seen as an expert.

Of course, it should be clear that we as translators believe there is much to be learned from Colectivo Situaciones. But it is not a matter of transmitting their ideas, as if copying recipes from a cookbook. Rather, we believe it is a matter of learning to recognize and amplify the *potencia* in our own situations, and so to act in a way that resonates with the practice of Colectivo Situaciones. We hope that our translation helps people make use of the text for their own purposes and in their own situations.

I

This article tells a real story. This story—like so many stories these days—begins with a message, an email. It is signed by a friend from Madrid, who is a member of the group Precarias a la Deriva.[11] The message is addressed to Colectivo Situaciones. She asks us for an article about the collective's experience in Argentina, and more specifically in Buenos Aires. In particular—she tells us—the idea is that we say "something more" about the figure of the militant researcher. Something "more" not so much about the concept, but about the practice. "About the context, about difficulties, knowledges, procedures, notions," our friend says. "Because," she adds, "the piece *On Method*[12] leaves many doubts about concrete questions regarding the workshops."

Our friend suggests that we further elaborate on four fundamental questions: "Decision," "concepts," "procedures," and "knowledges" (know-hows). To begin the exchange, we were told about how each of these questions can narrate a dimension of an experience/experiment: she referred to that of the Precarias a la Deriva.

We tried to understand. Decision: refers to the decision(s) we made in order to produce and develop *research militancy*. A story not so much of Colectivo Situaciones as one of the ways in which we developed the idea of research militancy. Concepts: to show our relation to the notions we use. Not so much explaining them (which would be very boring), but introducing their operation in concrete situations. Procedures: namely, getting inside the material processes that configure the activity of research militancy as such.

Finally, there are the know-hows, which refer to the infinite local knowledges that make possible the creation and development of the procedures.

To be sure, this task turned out to be—then and now—*titanic*. In fact,
we were capable of confronting it, in a very partial way, only because our
friend was willing to maintain a more or less regular correspondence with
us on these issues.[13] As a result of this conversation, "decisions" and "procedures" related to two of the four proposed items were laid down: aspects of
which we will give here central importance.

What follows, then, is an attempt to develop the context and the char-
acterization of some facets of research militancy: not so much by doing a
historico-political description of our circumstances, nor by providing a narration of the concrete experiences we have carried out (both aspects are
partially registered in our publications);[14] rather, the modes in which such
experiences produced a trajectory.

II

The first problem we ran into when we started the correspondence was
that of communication: what does it mean to *communicate*? On one hand,
there is the fundamental, insurmountable impossibility of the nontransfer-
able character of experience. We can tell this and that. We can even tell everything, but there is always something that slips away. And, moreover, there
are differing points of view. How to bring them all together? And even when
this can be done, there is an intensity of experience that can only be captured
fully by being there, physically present, and subjectively involved.[15]

On the other hand, how to communicate what we do, if not by doing?
That is, how to transmit a reflection (a word committed to an experience/
experiment, to certain practices, to living thought) about reflection without
making a metatheory about ourselves?

Moreover, how to explain each singular operation, in all its precarity,
without turning it, in the same exposition, into a technique (our friend shares
this concern: "Suffice it to think of all the Methods, with a capital "M," and
their disastrous consequences")?

In the end, when we reject the word "communication" we don't do so in
the name of an *incommunicability* that would confirm the financial dispersion of experience, but as an impeachment of the accompanying assumptions of the "society of communication." If the ideology of communication
presupposes that "all that is communicable deserves to exist and all that
deserves to exist is communicable," only because technology provides the
means to do it, what is cut out is precisely the affirmation of the experience (as a weave and experiential constellation) that causes the word to be
spoken. From here onwards, to the word "communication" we will oppose
the word *composition* (or processes of interaction, collective valorization,

system of productive compatibilities), understanding as such the sketching of a plane in whose interior the *word* does say *something.*

Finally, something that might be easy to say, however difficult to accept: how to narrate the fact that research militancy is not the name of the experience of someone who does research but that of the production of (an) encounter(s) without subject(s) or, if you prefer, of (an) encounter(s) that produce(s) subject(s)? How to admit the fact that Colectivo Situaciones is not the subject of its own activities, and that the encounters in which it found itself—fortunately—involved were not foreseen, planned, nor implemented at will by those who write this article? (We will come back to this.)

In an era when communication is the indisputable maxim, in which everything is justifiable by its communicable usefulness, research militancy refers to experimentation: not to thoughts, but to the power to think; not to the circumstances, but to the possibility of experience; not to this or that concept, but to experiences in which such notions acquire power (*potencia*); not to identities but to a different becoming; in one word: intensity does not lie so much in that which is produced (that which is communicable) as in the process of production itself (that which is lost in communication). How to say something, then, about all this and not merely exhibit the results of such a process?

III

Let's turn to what our friend from Madrid calls "decision"—and we call experiment, or rather, "indecision." How does research militancy arise? What is that we call militant research? What is it made of? Answering these questions would be more or less like the *history* of the collective. But that history does not exist. In its place we can at best force things a little and reconstruct briefly a trajectory. But how to do it? How to say something interesting about such homely issues?

Toward the end of the 1990s, we began to look at our shared experiences. We found two issues we needed to come to terms with: on one hand, *militant commitment* as a directly political element and the efficacy of our experience thus far; and on the other, our *relation to the university* and the process of generating knowledge. This contradiction is a good starting point.

The group developed in spite of its two tendencies: one that arose by reflecting on its own militant practice, and the other that asked itself about the modes in which political practice is related "from within" to the production of effective knowledges.

There were two figures to interrogate. The first is the remains of the "sad militant"—as Miguel Benasayag (who was a key figure in this period and in many of our decisions) calls it.[16] This figure is always "setting out the party line," and keeping for himself a knowledge of what ought to happen in the situation, which he always approaches from outside, in an instrumental and transitive way (situations have value as moments of a general strategy that encompasses them), because his fidelity is, above all, ideological and preexists all situations.

The other figure is that of the "university researcher," who links himself to his research as to an object of analysis, whose value is strictly related to his capacity to confirm preexisting theses. Here, once again, fidelity to institutional procedures, academic or para-academic, eludes any commitment to the situation.

The issue was, in any case, to transform the very foundations of our practice, the presuppositions on which research stands. Here we can identify a first decision: to create a practice capable of co-articulating involvement and thought.

In turn, this (in)decision implied a whole series of operational resolutions: we had to reorganize ourselves as a smaller group, an intense affective affinity, and reorganize our way of working entirely. This process, which culminated in the formation of the collective, was frenetic during the years 1999 and 2000.

In practical terms, what has research militancy meant for us since then? That politics abandoned power as an image in which to recognize itself and created in its place a more powerful interlocutor. And that our way of thinking was related precisely to practices, that thought and politics depended on the capacity for experience, involvement, and encounter; and that the subject of knowledge or political action could not be conceived as transcendent with respect to situations, but made itself present for us as a result of those encounters. If there was a hinge decision, in this sense, it was that of thinking from and within the situation; that is, without conceiving practices, theories, or subjects a priori.

The emergence of Colectivo Situaciones was directly linked to other practices that emerged in Argentina in the late 1990s, as both cause and product of the social and political crisis[17] that was brewing at the time.[18] We found ourselves involved in the hyper-accelerated dynamic of the crisis (which peaked with the events of December 19 and 20, 2001), and in the dizzying transformations that occurred in the country. In this context, we developed some working hypotheses, which were, perhaps, precarious but suitable at least in order to participate in this process—still open, under very ambivalent forms—in an active way.

At this point in the story, it might be useful to pose some of the questions that we formulated for ourselves in order to ponder the problems of this trajectory. We also aim to avoid a history of "happy decisions," one that would erase every real mark of concrete labor. With what perceptual and conceptual mechanisms is it possible to capture the emergence of these new elements of sociability if they demand a new precise disposition to feel and think? How to link ourselves to the fragility of this emergence, helping its development rather than contributing to its neutralization? What degree of ignorance do we need to arm ourselves with in order to make research a real organizer of our practices and not merely a tactical façade?

According to our friend in Precarias a la Deriva, "the driving force of our militant research is a desire for common ground when the common ground is shattered. That is why it has, for us, a performative-connective function: something like the activity of a communicative Wobbly, of a weaver of affective-linguistic territorialities."

This force that gives impulse to Precarias a la Deriva, that search for the common ground that has shattered, remains for us a fundamental question: how to produce consistency between experiences/experiments of a counterpower that neither emerges as unified nor does it desire an external, imposed, state-like union? How to articulate the points of power and creation without developing a hierarchizing unity in charge of thinking on behalf of everyone, of leading everyone? How to draw lines of resonance within the existing networks without either subordinating or submitting to them?

Research militancy takes shape as a series of operations that, in the face of concrete problems (or of anguish that stubbornness turns into productive interrogations), establish bonds capable of altering our subjectivities and finding some sort of community in the middle of today's radical dispersion. How to provoke interventions that strengthen horizontality and resonances, avoiding both hierarchical centralism and pure fragmentation? And, to continue in this line: how to co-articulate thinking in common with the experiences/experiments that have been elaborating hyperintelligent practices? How to produce authentic compositions, clues that later circulate through the diffuse network of counterpower, without being perceived as an outsider to the experience of thought, but, at the same time, without merging with experience(s) that is/are not directly our own? How to avoid ideologization, the idealization that everything which generates interest is welcome in our times? What kind of writing does justice to the singular situation? What is to be done with the friendships that arise from these encounters and how do we continue them? And, finally, what to do with ourselves, if with each experience/experiment we get further away from our initial subjectivities, without any mode of return?

The list of these (in)decisions gives an idea of the problems that arise among experiences/experiments in militant research. Our friends from Universidad Trashumante say, when they begin a workshop, they know "how to start, but not how to end."[19] If there is a productive (in)decision, it is precisely that of not knowing in advance how are we going to go through all these issues and be ready to face them time and again, to the point that the absence of this insistence speaks more of the collapse of the ongoing experience than of its maturation—or its being overcome.

Indeed, the consistency of the experience that follows the encounter is based more on these procedures than on the invocation of a common ideal. In our experience, the labor of dissolving ossifying ideological cement (be it autonomist, horizontalist, situationist, or multiple) has turned out to be decisive. We hold that idealization is a destructive force. A real, contradictory, rich, and always conflicted experience is placed on the one-dimensional pedestal of the redeeming ideal. Operations are idealized, permitting the experience/experiment to produce an existence. This is, then, transformed into an example to apply anytime and anywhere, as a new set of a priori principles. It is then asked to be able to confirm this ideal for everyone. The fragility of the experience/experiment creates tensions. How to sustain that burden? Later, of course, deception comes and, with it, destruction continues: "I thought this time it really was it, but it was only a fraud." What to do when we are faced with this mechanism of massive adherences and rejections, which elevate and dethrone radical experiments, repeating the consumerist mechanisms of the society of the spectacle? What resources do we have in hand to look after this unexpected front of exteriority to which the ideal subordinates us? What can effectively place us inside these procedures—in their reality—and no longer in their idealization?

Indeed, in our experience, there is a very strong component of working against ideals in their function as promise. That is to say: how to work from the power (*potencia*) of what is and not of what "ought to be?" Above all, when the ideal is a—more or less arbitrary—personal projection to which nobody is obliged to adapt. Research militancy does not extract its commitment from a model of the future, but from a search for power (*potencia*) in the present. That is why the most serious fight is against the a priori, against predefined schemes. Fighting the a priori, then, does not imply giving up for dead any stretch of reality. Nothing needs to die. It does imply, however, a permanent introspective revision over the type of perceptions that we are bringing into play in each situation.

We believe that the labor of research militancy is linked to the construction of a new *perception*, a new working style towards tuning up and empowering (*potenciar*) the elements of a new sociability. Perhaps clay is the metaphor to describe it: it has the capacity to receive affections without opposing resistances, in order to understand the real play of powers (*potencias*). The question is not, then, to configure a center that thinks radical practices, but to elaborate a style that allows us to become immanent to this multiplicity, without being insiders to each multiple: a multiple among multiples, a métier that, while doing its own thing, is involved with the others.

It will be clear, then, that the main (in)decision of research militancy is shared by the multiplicity in which it operates, and does not belong (except in fantasy) to the group that claims to be doing the research, as if it existed before and outside this multiple.

IV

As we noted at the beginning of this article—there are not any procedures outside the situation. To produce a narrative on the activities that the collective carries out, a formalization of its knowledges, would be as pointless as a manual on research militancy, and that is no one's intention.

When one reflects on the work, things appear invested of a coherence and functionality they by no means had at the very moment of their production. That recollection, that anti-utilitarian insistence, is vital for the development of research militancy, at least in our view.

When we talk about workshops and publications as practices of the collective, we immediately find it necessary to remind ourselves that there are no such workshops: just an heterogeneous conglomerate of meetings without any threads of coherence other than those that suddenly spring up from chaos, and without our knowing exactly how to develop them. Something similar happens to the publications: they emerge as provisional needs to invoke the presence of other experiences by which to extend ourselves, but they do not represent a necessary phase of a larger system.

So, we only know how to start. And that very minimally. In fact, all the procedures (mechanisms) that we prepare prove to be authentically inappropriate when confronted with the texture of a concrete situation. Thus, the very conditions of the encounter are somewhat anticipated by the shared will to co-research, it does not matter much what about (the topic might change), as long as on this "journey" we all experience substantial changes, that is, that we emerge with new capacities to empower (*potenciar*) practices.

Whatever it is that sets the conditions, there is a prior functionality of the workshop: to produce an "uncoupling" (in each meeting, again and again) from everyday spatiality and velocity. The disposition to think emerges from allowing thought itself to spatialize and temporalize according to its own requirements.

According to our friend from Madrid, there is, in their "search in the surroundings of the experiences of self-organization, and in approaching them in order to propose work in common, an immediate problem comes up: that of their exteriority to the reality to which they come close, more so when their condition and their biography is so different from that of the people with whom they come in touch with. In fact, to break with the separation between 'we' and 'they' is one of the fundamental challenges of their workshops." Above all, if those encounters are animated by the "search for a radicality not from on high, that clings to the surface of the real; a practice of self-interrogation, of locating problems and launching hypotheses (always from the practices) that would constitute the 'hardcore' of militant research."

But, is this true? Does *difference* inevitably lead to *distance*? What distances and differences are we talking about? And regarding the image of "approaching," to what *perception* does it refer?

We could call "procedures" precisely those forms of "putting into practice" that arise from the questions of coming to terms with *differences*. How to build an *us* of thought, albeit a transient one? How to lay out a common plane as a condition, however ephemeral, of joint production? These questions are as valid for the "close" social experiences/experiments as they are for the "distant" ones.

The movement of the encounter, then, is not so much about getting closer as it is about *elaborating a common plane*. And this refers to a more complex scenario, in which the mutual measurement of "distances" and "proximities" (the "insides" and "outsides") is not simply a matter of one's initial *positions* (of departure), but also of whether one's own *plane* (which includes steps forward and backward, enthusiasms and distrusts, periods of production and depressive lacunae) is drawn or not.

Without a doubt, a plane may be difficult to draw: counterpower exists only as a fold or knot between heterogeneous experiences/experiments. One dynamic is *territorial*, the other more *deterritorialized*. The territory is *impoverished* and the more deterritorialized experiences/experiments are *virtualized* without this common fabric (without this encounter between both). Deterritorialized spatiality and territorial modes are polarities inside the fold of counterpower and their being knotted together is one of the fundamentals of the new radicality. The experiences/experiments more linked to the territory—more concentrated—and those more diffuse—those more nomadic—can, in their dynamic differences, articulate, combine, or interact as occupations of the public sphere by counterpower.

Difference(s), then, call for a more in-depth interrogation. The postmodern impossibility of experience is nurtured by this "festival of difference" (which, strictly speaking, becomes indifference, or dispersion). But that says nothing about the potential of articulation among these experiences.

Moreover, we could ask whether an experience/experiment has value as such—and, in this sense, a profound political character—precisely when it manages to suspend that indifference of differences. When one manages to produce a conjunction (or plane) capable of subtracting itself from the "logic of pure heterogeneity" (which says "differences separate" and "there is no possible connection in the indifferent difference"). An experience/experiment—or situation—would be, then, that which is founded in the articulation of points (as relative as they might be) of a certain homogeneity. The question is neither to erase nor to disguise differences, but to stop them from setting up certain common problems.

Let's go back to our friend from Precarias a la Deriva: "I wonder whether you interrogate yourselves about your own composition and biography, about the position of your equals, and whether doing militant research with others involves self-analysis, above all in order to avoid the trap of a displacement, of not questioning one's own life and one's own practices (and thus introducing a split between militancy and life). In Precarias a la Deriva we consider a primary problem 'starting from oneself,' as one among many, in order to 'get out of oneself' (out of one's individual ego and the radical group to which one belongs) and to encounter other resisting people (hence, what I said above about being both outside and inside, in a dislocated position ourselves)."

Precarias a la Deriva claim to "politicize life from within." To turn life itself from immediate experience into something political, something committed. We would formulate this another way: in order to revitalize politics, it must be immersed in the most immediate multiple experiences. We use these phrases with a certain uneasiness because they sometimes refer to the idea that there is something missing in life and that life still needs to be well-organized. Perhaps it would be better to talk about a politics that measures up to life itself. Even if we did, it wouldn't be enough, because we prefer, without a doubt, a life that disorganizes politics rather than a good politics that manages to organize life, displacing it, proposing transcendental problems to it, determining its priorities and obligations.

But let's go deeper into our friend's questions: why does Colectivo Situaciones look for sites of intervention outside? What truth do we expect to find in different people? Isn't this an escape from the need to politicize our own lives in their everydayness? Moreover, doesn't this just renew the old militancy (classical exteriority) in new forms—in the sense that, beyond rehashed languages and mechanisms, people keep going (approaching) places from outside, hoping for a more or less magical solution to their own subjective and political constitution?

These questions would be rhetorical if we only formulated them in order to refute them. It turns out, however, that these are not questions that can be eliminated in a single stroke. They live inside us and speak to us of certain tendencies whose control completely escapes our manifest intentions. Again and again we must insist on them, because they have no definitive antidote and, moreover, they are tendencies widely favored by the dominant social dynamics. In fact, the main value of formulating them is to force ourselves to work in-depth on the problem of exteriority.

Nevertheless, another image must be considered. Not only that of finite points escaping their tragic destiny of radical exteriority and producing simulacra of "interiority" (the union of the "separate as separate," as Guy Debord says), but also that of points that need (and work) to find resonances with the resonances of others.[20] The distinction might seem hollow, even though it describes opposite paths: in dispersion (exteriority) the alternatives oscillate between "irremediable fragmentation" or "necessary centralization"; but once we draw a plane (something very different than "inside and outside"), consistency refers to a transversality.[21]

Of course, we would still have to resist the accusation of spontaneism. A curious thing, since it's not composition that is spontaneous, but dispersion. And we ask ourselves what to do with it. Is centralization the only viable alternative? Or is the common experience strong enough to prefigure new constituent modes of doing?

This is a fundamental question for research militancy, because the elaboration of a plane is neither spontaneous nor irreversible. Rather, it requires a sustained practice ("procedures" that we could not define abstractly) of collaboration in order to make commonality emerge in (and from) difference (immanence is a strategy of cutting in exteriority). Our obsession with composition is precisely inscribed in this concern about "ourselves," but under a new set of suppositions: dispersal is not overcome through representation. The question of immanence, then, would be: how to be/with/others?

As in a phenomenology, we could then describe the path of research militancy as the manifestation of this rejection of exteriority and spectacle, along with—and as a procedure for—the production of keys for composition, for the construction of modes of immanence.[22]

If collective experience has any meaning for us, it is, above all, in the way it allows us to actively confront, produce, and inhabit the context in which we live and produce: neither as a "subject who knows and explains," nor as the passive individual of postmodernity. This capacity is a way of recognizing ourselves as multiple within a multiplicity, and of coming to terms with a certain mode of being of that multiplicity in practice.

Hence, the strong existential components of research militancy.[23] And the absurdity of pretending that it becomes a task (or, even worse, the fundamental task) of the movement.[24] Research militancy's questions are the same ones that hundreds of groups[25] ask themselves: What new elements of sociability can emerge? Which ones will persist (do they persist?), and which ones disintegrate? What kind of relations (barriers and bridges) are drawn by the state and the market? How do the new resistances emerge? What problems are posed at the different levels?

Now that we are at this point it is, perhaps, possible to perceive the difference between thinking the situation in its universality or simply assuming it locally. When we talk about a situation we are concerned with the mode in which the universal appears in the local, not the local as "part" of the global. That is why the drift of the situation is much more interesting (sinuous) than the locality itself. While the local is defined by a fixed environment and a limited and predefined set of resources—reducing its alliances to neighboring points—the situational is actively produced, determining its dimensions and multiplying its resources. Unlike the local, the situational expands the capacities for composition-affection.[26]

V

While exteriority denotes the spatial impossibility of connection, dispersion is produced by acceleration in the temporal plane, which prevents us from finding a point to stop, to elaborate. In this context, what does politics (a "nocturnal politics," as Mar Traful says) consist of?[27] Are the elements of our practices powerful (*potentes*) enough to become constituent of experience, of a new politics? How do we measure their efficacy? These questions come up because there are practical elements that justify them. But those elements neither explain nor develop the questions.

What would a new type of politics be like? And, more specifically, what exigencies would a new understanding of politics present to research militancy? What can the experience of research militancy contribute to this understanding?

From our angle, these questions refer to the efficacy of forms of action: what kind of intervention is constructed? What does the power (*potencia*) of the act depend upon? Research militancy experiments, as we have said, concern the development of new modules of space-time. It experiments with the becoming-agent (*agenciamiento*) of heterogeneous elements in points of homogeneity that turn dispersive experience (a desert) into a situation in which it is possible to elaborate and produce notions of composition (beyond the discourse of *communication*).

In a concrete situation, intelligence springs neither from erudition nor from cleverness, but rather from the capacity for involvement. In the same way stultification can be explained by very concrete forms of distraction.[28] Hence the possibility of establishing a concrete link between the affective-fabric that operates in a situation and its operational productivity.[29] Thus, what determines the efficacy of the act is not so much the number, quantity, or massiveness of the situations (aggregation capacity), as it is the aptitude for composition of the relations (consistency capacity).

As is evident, what we are suggesting is linked to a very concrete situation: the current Argentinean crisis. Here, a desert blown by violent neoliberal winds blasted existing bonds and intensified the process of dispersion. In the development of a counterpower, we experiment with the tension between new bonds and the massive demand for containment. This tension, in fact, manifested itself as a contradiction between quantitative presence (of dispersed elements waiting to be reunited) and need of a system of new relations capable of sustaining this process of aggregation, no longer as a mere reunification of the dispersed but as a new type of active configuration.

One feature of Argentina in recent months has been the meteoric growth of numerous social groupings, immediately followed by their rapid decomposition. We are not talking about some kind of absurd invalidation of mass actions or organizations, but rather about an interrogation in order to make experiments affective.[30] There is probably no single valid criterion in for efficacy. Each experience/experiment of struggle and creation necessarily produces its own resources and procedures. We only intend to raise the following question: what does "aggregation" add to composition, given that aggregation organizes people and resources according to certain constituent relations (valid at any numeric or geographic scale)?

Hasta Siempre,
Colectivo Situaciones
February 29th, 2004

Notes

1. "Footnotes" refers, literally, to a second level of writing of this article, in which the notes do not constitute a complementary set of references, but rather a fundamental articulation with the central body of the text.

2. The translators are involved in an informal network dedicated to supporting and encouraging translation of radical social movement and theoretical materials. Interested persons may get in touch by emailing notasrojas@lists.riseup.net. –Tr.

3. MTD of Solano and Colectivo Situaciones, *Hipótesis 891: Más Allá de los Piquetes* [Hypothesis 891: Beyond the Roadblocks] (Buenos Aires: Ediciones de mano en mano, 2002). An updated version of this passage will appear as an article in the book *Utopian Pedagogy*, edited by Richard Day, Mark Coté, and Greig de Peuter (Toronto: University of Toronto Press, forthcoming).

4. For further discussion of this distinction, see John Holloway, *Change the World Without Taking Power* (London and Sterling, VA: Pluto Press, 2002). Translators of works by French and Italian philosophers inspired by Spinoza usually run into similar difficulties. See the translator's introduction written by Michael Hardt in Antonio Negri, *The Savage Anomaly: The Power of Spinoza's Metaphysics and Politics* (Minneapolis: University of Minnesota Press, 1991).

5. Miguel Benasayag, a former member of the Argentinean Guevarist guerrilla army PRT-ERP, is now a philosopher and activist residing in Paris. He participates in the collective Malgré Tout and played an important role in the early life of Colectivo Situaciones.

6. Cf. Miguel Benasayag and Diego Sztulwark. *Política y Situación: De la potencia al contrapoder* (Buenos Aires: Ediciones de mano en mano, 2000), 217–21. Diego Sztulwark is one of the members of Colectivo Situaciones.

7. Michael Hardt and Antonio Negri, *Empire* (Cambridge, MA and London, UK: Harvard University Press, 2000), 52–59.

8. For a discussion of the notion of resonance, see "Dignity's Revolt," in John Holloway and Eloína Peláez, *Zapatista! Reinventing Revolution in Mexico* (London: Pluto Press, 1998).

9. "Manifeste," Collectif Malgré Tout. Available online at http://1libertaire.free. fr/malgretout02.html (English translation forthcoming). In 1999, El Mate (Colectivo Situaciones had not appeared yet), Malgré Tout, Mothers of Plaza de Mayo, along with other collectives from Latin America and Europe, gathered in Buenos Aires to form the Network of Alternative Resistance. Their joint declaration outlines several of the principles of Colectivo Situaciones' philosophy. An English translation can be found at http://www.voiceoftheturtle.org/library/nar_manifesto.php.

10. See Jacques Rancière, *The Ignorant Schoolmaster: Five Lessons In Intellectual Emancipation* (Stanford, CA: Stanford University Press, 1991).

11. Precarias a la Deriva, whose name translates as Precarious Women Adrift, are a collective who undertake militant research on precarious and feminine labor, primarily in Madrid. More information on and by the Precarias can be found at http://www.sindominio.net/karakola/precarias. This article originally appeared in a Spanish language collection dedicated to militant research, entitled *Nociones Comunes,* edited by Marta Malo of Precarias a la Deriva. *Nociones Comunes* is available at http://www.nodo50.org/ts/editorial/librospdf/nociones_comunes.pdf.

12. This text is the prologue of *Hipótesis 891. Más allá de los piquetes.*

13. The exchange took place during the last trimester of 2003 and, as we said, constitutes the basis for this text. In our experience, productive friendship turns out to be the greatest source of inspiration, with the bonus of giving us the greatest satisfactions.

14. Many of which can be found at www.situaciones.org.

15. Faced with these deliberations, our friend asks, "Why don't you believe in communicating and publishing texts?" To separate ourselves from the alienating image of communication, in its ingenuous version as a message from one consciousness to another, we suppose that writing, implicit in a practice, in a living thought, is particularly moving for those who search. We experience publication more as a search for (producing-receiving) *resonances* than a transmission of messages. The final goal of publication is, in our case, to extend experimentation, to establish links with experimenters in other places. This bond is incompatible with the pure "will to communicate."

16. The notion of Militant Researcher itself came up, for us, from the encounter with Miguel. See Miguel Benasayag and Diego Sztulwark, *Política y Situación: De la potencia al contrapoder.* Later published in French and Italian under the titles *Du contre-pouvoir* (Paris: La Découverte, 2002) and *Contropotere* (Milan: Eleuthera, 2002).

17. And, yet, it is not productive to reduce the presentation of these experiences/ experiments to their relation—of cause or of effect—to the subsequent social

and political crisis in Argentina. In fact, all these experiments had been pro-ducing an extended elaboration whose fundamental point of origin was the failure of revolution in the decade of the 1970s. In relation to this balance—in which the issue was to maintain a commitment but rediscussing at length the conditions and procedures—a vast spectrum of comrades recreated ideas and ways of approaching struggle. Our participation, at that moment, in the Che Guevara Free Lectureship was inscribed within this fabric.

18   Our first activities had to do with the articulation of our encounters with the experience/experiment of *escraches* by H.I.J.O.S., with the MLN-Tupamaros, with the Peasants Movement of Santiago del Estero (MOCASE), and with the Movement of Unemployed Workers (MTD) of Solano. [The word "escrache" is Argentinean slang that means "exposing something outrageous." *Escraches* are street demonstrations in front of the houses where people involved in hu-man rights violations during the dictatorship live. H.I.J.O.S. is the acronym for Children for Identity and Justice, against Oblivion and Silence. Also, "hi-jos" is the Spanish word for "children." This organization was formed in 1995 by children of the disappeared during the dictatorship (1976–1983). –Tr.]

19   Universidad Trashumante is an itinerant collective based in San Luis, Argentina, whose activities include popular education, the recuperation of popular memory, and the production of grassroots networks. After publishing this article, Colectivo Situaciones published a book based on dialogues with those involved in this experience/experiment: *Universidad Trashumante: Territorios, Redes, Lenguajes* (Buenos Aires: Tinta Limón, 2004).

20   Of course, *outside* and *inside* do not refer to a predefined spatiality, but to different immanent or transcendent ways of conceiving the bond: when we establish bonds with others seeking to create new worlds, are we looking *outside*? Or, put another way, what to do if those "other worlds" already exist in the process of creation, in acts of resistance? Would we sacrifice our *com-mon* being with others in the name of a purely physical vicinity determined by crudely spatial criteria?

21   Which helps understand the *non-institutional* horizon of research militancy.

22   In this sense, both the knowledges produced and the current questions about the *construction of networks* acquire a very precise value: Isn't it valid to look for transversal forms of composition that articulate the social practices of different groups on the basis of what they can have (and defend) in com-mon? It seems clear that these experiments in networks can be very useful in order to know each other (and ourselves) and to relate to each other (and to ourselves), but, what happens when we reach the limit of the tensions that a network can generate? Isn't it necessary, then, to de-center the networks, to produce new nodes, to conceive heterogeneous planes, and to open oneself towards stretches of the network that have not been *made explicit*?

23   *Falling in love* or *friendship* is how we express the feeling that accompanies and envelops *composition*. And, precisely, we experience research militancy

as the perception that something develops between us and in others, at least for a moment; above all, when, instead of being lost in anonymity, this *moment* sparks off other moments, and the memory that is the result of that sequence becomes a "productive resource" of the situation. This is the most persistent feeling we have about the concrete meaning of becoming "something else."

24 Above all, if what we take into consideration is the extent to which research militancy does not seek to "organize others." Not because it renounces organization—there is no research militancy without high levels of organization—but because its problem is posed in terms of a self-organization that collaborates with the self-organization of networks.

25 Shared problems in the face of which there is no subject-object distinction. The researcher is the person who participates in the problematization. And the research objects are problems, ways of posing them, and self-research about dispositions to be able to pose those problems.

26 The exchange with Precarias a la Deriva has for us a fundamental immediate value. Moreover, the exchanges maintained on the basis of this article have left the trace of a certain style of work that it is necessary to deepen and, in this sense, are not very far from what we call "workshops." "Workshops" are, then, just like that. They do not constitute themselves—nor do they aspire to—into the General Staff of the situation: they constitute themselves as a point of encounter capable of thinking and, in the best of cases, elaborating practical hypotheses with the force of an intervention.

27 *Por una política nocturna*, (Barcelona: Editorial Debate, 2002). [There is an online version available at http://www.sindominio.net/ofic2004/publicaciones/pn/indice.html –Tr.]

28 On this, see the very interesting lessons of Joseph Jacotot, brought to us by Rancière in a book that is fundamental for us: Jacques Rancière, *The Ignorant Schoolmaster: Five Lessons in Intellectual Emancipation* (Stanford: Stanford University Press, 1991).

29 In this sense we can fully rehabilitate—from our most immediate experience—the theories that speak about an "affect-value."

30 There is no doubt that the insurrectional actions of the Argentinean December of 2001 opened a new and fertile field of actions and debates of all kinds and, even closely, the same sequence is empowered (*potenciada*) by the revolts that took place in Bolivia in 2003.

The Breath of the Possible

Gavin Grindon

He was surrounded by angry patriots with pepper spray and batons at the ready. To hop down would be to take a beating and maybe a felony charge, so he did the only thing he could: he breathed deep, lifted his arms, and flung himself straight out over the cops and the crowd, stage-diver style. The crowd let out a collective frightened gasp. It was the shocked response of people watching something so daring it looked, at first glance, suicidal.... My heart stopped too in that moment. It seemed both lightning quick and eternal, that one second when the flying anarchist hovered horizontally in the air. When he fell to earth, landing in the arms of his comrades and escaping the police, everything felt different, like we were living in the pages of history, as though in that moment there was a crystal clear delineation of past and future. Something had just Happened...the problems in the world had looked impossible before.... In that incredibly bold leap over the heads of the riot police, the option of saving the world from the jaws of destructive, violent capitalism seemed possible somehow. One quick, bold move—it made other acts of amazing audacity seem possible...if that flying anarchist taught me nothing else, it was that when shit looks absolutely impossible, don't worry. Don't stop to analyse too much. Be courageous. Do what they don't expect. Take a leap. Anything is possible.—Sophia Delaney, "Anarchists Can Fly," in Notes from Nowhere (Ed.), *We Are Everywhere*, 2003.

In her account of this activist's daring leap of faith to escape from the top of a flagpole after having replaced the American flag with a black and red flag, Delaney focuses on what has been an important element in the global justice movement's understanding of itself and its actions: the importance of joy, desire, and mythic moments of potent affect. The focus on these moments owes much to a particular thread of radical theory, which, orienting itself around the concept of festival, found a potential in these moments, and sought to mine it.

From the Surrealists to the Situationists to Reclaim the Streets, throughout the twentieth century an eclectic set of theorists and artists have picked up the gauntlet of festival and developed a line of theory that connects festival's effervescent moment to revolutionary social change. In picking up this thread, they argued that the festival's participatory aesthetic and religious experience held a catalytic potential untapped by the traditional left. Such experience, they argued, was absent in modern society, and its return held the potential for revolutionary social action.

However, it is crucial that the object of both their activism and theory was an experience that, as affectivity, was to some extent beyond rational analysis. This complicates their role as activists in creating such irrational moments of experience as well as their role as theorists attempting to understand the relation between these moments and social revolution.

Between 1937 and 1939, a group calling itself the College of Sociology met intermittently in the café of the Palais Royal and in a bookstore on the rue Guy Lussac in Paris. It was formed by Georges Bataille and Roger Caillois and was influenced by both the new sociology of Emile Durkheim and Marcel Mauss, as well as the Surrealist movement of the 1920s. Like the Surrealists they championed a euphoric subjective experience that was radically different than the dull, profane experience of modern life, and which, they hoped, would revolutionise it.

Instead of the Surrealist experience of "the marvelous," they termed their experience "the sacred," borrowing from Durkheim's *The Elementary Forms of the Religious Life*. For Durkheim, the bounds of what is "other" are always socially determined, and the sacred is experienced as part of a social ritual of transgression. This logic of otherness (to which Bataille gave the name "the heterogeneous"—"the science of the altogether other") finds social expression in the exuberant abandon of religious festivals.[1] The festival's transgression of taboos through the loss of goods and self was intertwined with the personal transcendence of the sacred. Such festivals were exemplified by the "potlatch," which Bataille's tutor Mauss had identified in numerous cultures, or by the ritual sacrifices of the Aztecs. The sacred was then not only a transcendent subjective experience, but also a social phenomenon.

Like the Surrealists, the College of Sociology saw their project as connected to that of revolution. In his essay "The Notion of Expenditure," Bataille argued that this sacred festival experience would make itself felt in modernity through a violent proletarian revolution, inspired not by economic contradictions but by potent emotional forces and inspiring mythic images. The sacred was both end and means. Aside from their Surrealist dream of a society reshaped by the force of the sacred, the College understood radical activity towards this end as bound up with an emotional, affective experience that could not be rationalised. Bataille's heterology was an attempt to engage with this experience in theoretical terms.

Heterology stressed the *primacy* of the other. The sacred was an experience of the unknowable, of pure, irrational affect. Andre Breton compared the sublime experience to an orgasm and a religious transcendence. For Bataille, a late Freudian and briefly a priest-in-training before he lost his faith, it was also a *petit mort*. Rather than the Surrealists' union of the real and the sur-real, Bataille read such experience as a radical atheistic experience of self-loss, a brush with the void. He saw the drive towards otherness, even towards the other of death, as fundamental to the psychological and social organisation of society. Giving the example of a French village, he argued that it was not by accident that it was organised with the church and its graveyard at its centre, and that this centre was the place of sacred experience and religious festivals.

Despite this fundamental centrality, otherness is always that which is outside and cannot be contained by any totalising theoretical knowledge. Bataille's total experience of loss could not be logically built towards: its orgasmic eruption of desire appears in his writing as both the basis and the end of revolutionary activity. His heterogeneity breaks with the Hegelian theory of the dialectic that had been an influence on early Surrealism. Bataille's system began with a constellation of binary oppositions like self-other, profane-sacred and bourgeoisie-proletariat. However, where the dialectic looks to the resolution and synthesis of these binaries, Bataille maintained his interest in the transgressive moment when the negative value triumphs. It is at this point of the sacred's "impossible" experience of the self experiencing its own loss to the other, that Bataille takes his own leap of faith and asserts the negative moment as self-justifying. It is an impossible third space that attempts to step beyond and outside of the dialectic: an other which refuses recuperation.

Advancing a theory of the undoing of theoretical totality is a rather contradictory move, It presupposes a more totalising theory that can encompass this undoing: what Bataille termed "a system of thought exhausting the totality of the possible."[2] Bataille often acknowledges the contradiction: "should I say that under these conditions I sometimes could only respond to the truth of my book and could not go on writing it?"[3] The primacy of the other can only be grounded in the evidence of the experience of the encounter with the other itself. Kojéve would criticise the circularity of Bataille's argument, saying that he was putting himself "in the position of a conjurer who expected his own tricks to make him believe in magic."[4] In reaching the limit of reason, Bataille was forced to turn to faith in the sacred. Faith is an abandonment of the critical self to an idea, and Bataille had abandoned himself to the idea of abandonment. Having seen Surrealism's "mad love" itself as a matter of self-loss, crisis, and undoing, Bataille allowed himself to fall in love with the falling itself.

This became an even more torturous theoretical knot when the College went on to assert that the return of these experiences to modern life was allied to, or even completed, the revolutionary project of the Communists. The theoretical impossibility of the sacred experience found in festivals, which Bataille had put his faith in, was also to be the basis of revolutionary social change. How could such change be built towards or encouraged? Was it a question of simply waiting for the spontaneous explosion of the sacred, or could it be brought somehow into everyday life in the meantime? How could the eruption of the sacred be made *possible*?

This created a problem for the College: how could they accomplish and articulate this leap of faith? How could such a critical impossibility be discussed without betraying it? The College's answer to this problem came in the form of myth. The revolution, bound up with the vertiginous experience of the festival, would take the form of an orgasmic eruption of joy and desire inspired by a powerful investment of emotion in myth. But, as the College turned to focus on myth as a means to radical social change, this faith in sacred experience translated into a flat opposition between activist engagement and theoretical understanding.

The College, like many sociologists of their time, worked with a model of society indebted to natural science. They understood the sacred as the centrifugal force at the centre of any social group and developed a novel notion of activism that entailed the unleashing of this force. Activism then was not simply a matter of forcing political change by practical means, but of playing agent or catalyst in setting loose an unstoppable infection or chain reaction. The College intended to spread a sacred "virus" through the social body that would bring the full explosion of the sacred ever nearer. The sacred, which they argued was both a profound form of transcendent communion and the heart of community, was also closely tied to primitive methods of communication. Activism meant creating myths; myth would be the inspiring, viral agent through which the sacred was communicated and activated in society. The College credited Georges Sorel as an influence, and they shared his understanding of myth as a means of "acting on the present."[5] Myth tapped into the irrational psychological forces at the heart of the sacred, "the primordial longings and conflicts of the individual condition transposed to the social dimension."[6] Myth's stoking of these desires would move subjects to action, drawing them into eruptions of sacred sociality. It was a psychological activism: where the Surrealists had conceived of their "revolution" as a matter of pure sentiment and subjectivity, the College attempted, through myth, to tie these sentiments to a more material notion of revolution. But, as they did this, Bataille found himself back in the tricky position of having to relinquish theoretical enquiry. For myth's activism to be effective in sweeping one up in the experience of the sacred, one had to first believe in the myth. This meant that before he could take on society, Bataille would first have to put his own faith in the myth he had just created and leap into the impossible.

While this convoluted logic may sound rather esoteric, this turn to myth for the inspiration to action is readily evident today. The global justice movement often engages this territory of myth and powerful experience: consider the movement's self-representations, in its exciting and inspiring accounts of protests and actions, not least when it comes to the "great battles" of Genoa, Seattle, Prague, and London, often given iconic monikers like "J18." There has been a particular focus on collections of powerful, first-hand accounts of the experience of these events. Prevalent among these is, for example, the now familiar photographic image of the lone, heroic masked figure, standing perhaps before the massed police, perhaps by a burning barricade, with a flag held high, or a tear gas canister about to be returned to the police. For a group like CrimethInc, there is even a self-conscious theoretical embrace of myth: "So what can we embrace in place of history? Myth.... When we tell tales around the fire at night of heroes and heroines, of other struggles and adventures...we are offering each other examples of just how much living is possible."[7]

In the College's time, sacred experience and myth were politically tricky theoretical tools. If the College wanted a perfect example of the social expression of the sacred as myth-inspired irrational effervescence in the streets, they had to look no further than the events of *Kristallnacht* in November 1938, only fifteen months after the College's first declarations. Sorel, whose ideas about myth they drew upon, himself swayed politically from far left to far right. Caillois observed, "At present, all the movements that show mythological characteristics display a real hypertrophy of this festival or ritual function." But the examples he gave were "the Hitlerian movement or the Ku Klux Klan."[8] Engaging with myth's political ambiguity, the College argued that these forces had been all too effectively appropriated by the Right while at the same time being completely ignored by the deterministic materialism of the orthodox Left.

Since the global justice movement's inception, and its articulation of the ideas of festival, joy, and myth, our own times, too, have become darker and more pessimistic. Bataille's co-location of sacred experience and sudden social change might describe the agonistic, orgasmic moments of political and religious martyrdom central to fundamentalist terrorism. It might even be used to reflect upon the mythic status of September 11th and its accompanying images, in the discourses of both Islamic and American fundamentalism, which put faith before critical analysis in the service of reaction.

Eagleton does just this in *Holy Terror* when he argues that "Terrorism is…a Dadaist or Surrealist 'happening' pushed to an unthinkable extreme."[9] He claims that the social realisation of sublime experience comes in the form of an unambiguous terror, in the "shock and awe" of the terrorist act, as "the Real stages an impossible appearance in reality itself."[10] Similarly, Retort argue that the terrorists of September 11th embraced and hijacked capitalism's own logic of mythic representation, understanding only too well its cold and cruel logic: "Terror can take over the image-machinery for a moment—and a moment, in the timeless echo chamber of the spectacle, may now eternally be all there is." After September 11th, an influential American conservative think tank asserted that it was now a question of winning "the battle of the story." Some activists, such as those of the *smart meme* project,[11] have responded to these developments by asserting the need to build new counter-myths, to "create effective memes—self-replicating units of information and culture…viral by nature."[12] In light of all this, the College's engagement with the political ambiguity of myth seems uncannily timely. How are we to understand the radical potential of myth and affect in this context, when the potential of festival seems to have been outflanked by contesting social forces?

Eighteen years after the College's last meeting, another small but far more famous group of theorists, the Situationist International, took up many of the College's concerns, and focused particularly on the competing political uses of these irrational forces. The Situationists, reacting against the College's turn from history to myth, tended to see such representations as a form of reification. Looking back on Surrealism's embrace of myth, Raoul Vaneigem wrote:

> The "spectacle" is all that remains of the myth that perished along with unitary society: an ideological organisation whereby the actions of history upon individuals themselves seeking…to act upon history, are reflected, corrupted and transformed into their opposite—into an autonomous life of the non-lived.[13]

The "spectacle" was the term Guy Debord developed to understand capital's ability to recuperate new forms of thought and representation, created by people like the Surrealists, in terms of the totality of alienating capitalist relationships pervading society. Debord attempted to grasp this complex social totality of division and contradiction by employing a powerfully dialectical Marxism, and it is interesting to see the Situationists' attempt to theorise and create autonomous spaces of inspiring, aesthetic experience in light of Bataille's earlier battle against Hegel's logic for an affective, subjective space.

Although myth had become spectacle, the Situationists did not give up on the realm of affect. They described their own project for creating spaces outside of and opposed to the totality of the spectacle as the creation of "situations." Defined as "a moment of life concretely and deliberately constructed by the collective organisation of a unitary ambiance and a game of events,"[14] a situation was an affective experience defined by participation rather than spectatorship. This space was understood in terms different than those of the College of Sociology. Rejecting the College's Freudianism and Nietzscheanism, the Situationists turned away from a sublime experience of crisis and apocalypse and back to the early Surrealists' demand for a unifying and total aesthetic experience. The total, playful re-determination of social organisation; the ultimate situation would be the revolution itself and the new society it embodied.

When it came to describing the possibility for an immediate, total life outside and against the spectacle, Debord's account of reification made things very difficult for the Situationists. Because the spectacle's logic could turn any partial opposition into a passively consumed image, the Situationists decided it was essential to initiate a total refusal of the society of the spectacle. But, having set this scene, it became increasingly difficult for the Situationists to move from instances to a totality of refusal. How could a situation lead to a revolution when, its partial nature allows it to be reified by capitalist social relations and made complicit with the spectacle? Total revolt seemed both necessitated and precluded by the spectacle's power to recuperate anything short of absolute refusal. The Situationists portrayed myth's affectivity as caught in the dead hands of the spectacle and yet also as the potent force at the centre of a new world. The spectacle and the situation were represented within their theory as two competing totalities that could not be reconciled. They went so far as to define radical social change as a competition between artists and authorities over who would develop new technologies of conditioning. Like the College's sacred, the situation had become an impossible space.

A common critique of this emphasis on totality is that it is disabling and that it had an awkward relationship both to the Situationists' focus on aesthetics and to their avowed council communism. Jean Barrot's 1979 *Critique of the Situationist International* argues that "The S.I. explained everything from the spectacle" and, as a result, "one does not know where it comes from, who produces it...by what contradiction it lives and may die."[15] In other words, this focus on the spectacle is at the expense of the real subject who produces capital: the working class. While the Situationists maintained that the spectacle only *appeared* determining and all pervasive, their rigorously totalising theory seemed to presuppose that it was both.

The Situationists' analysis of the power of the spectacle only presents half the picture. There is a discontinuity between this analysis and their insistence on the role of the active subject. Caught in this gulf, the Situationists found themselves in an impossible position. In order to cross this gap, they undertook their own leap of faith. To quote the graffiti on the walls of Paris in 1968, they said it was necessary to "demand the impossible."

This placement of the affective moment alongside the impossibility of the theoretical subject is not so much symptomatic of an impasse as it is a leap of faith beyond the limits of their theory. Putting faith in the unscripted realm of the situation means putting faith in the realm of possibility. It was crucial in this respect that the experience of the situation, like the sacred, was a total experience that coincided with a totality of new social relationships. The transcendent terms of aesthetics and religion provided a language for possibility that theory did not. Vaneigem's most poetic moments often coincide with his most urgent demands for a new life:

> People are crushed under the wardrobe.... "The rationality of the wardrobe is always the best," proclaim the thousands of books published every day to be stacked in the wardrobe. And all the while everyone wants to breathe and no one can breathe, and many say, "We will breathe later," and most do not die, because they are already dead. It is now or never.[16]

As a result of this move, the Situationists notoriously lent themselves to heavy mythologisation—a tendency inherited by the global justice movement. As I write this, in the run up to the protests against the 2005 G8 meeting in Scotland, the literature of the groups involved stays true to this spirit: The Leeds May Day Group assert, "Our experiments in new ways of being are limited only by our imagination."[17] The flyers of the Dissent! Network echo this aesthetic of potential, claiming "Everywhere there are willing accomplices desiring to live our adventures" and they bring a Surrealist slant to *Zapatismo* when they state that "As we walk, we dream."[18] This inheritance is clearest in those groups most openly influenced by Situationist approaches, such as CrimethInc, whose flair for lyrically encapsulating radical ideas rivals Vaneigem's own. What these groups have copied is the Situationists' *style*, which more coherently captured radical possibility than their theoretical analysis.

More orthodox strains of Marxism would no doubt see such approaches as nothing more than bare-faced utopianism. Indeed, mass actions are sometimes described as "orgasms of history" that can seem so spontaneous that it becomes difficult to engage with them theoretically.[19] However, the experience of another collection of radicals, the Italian autonomists of the 1960s and 1970s, can help us see that rather than simply constituting an ahistorical utopianism, the openness of dreaming and asking questions is in fact tied to practical political engagement, to walking.

Rather than a distinct group like the College or the Situationists, *autonomia* was a diffuse and heterogeneous nationwide movement that came into existence in Italy in the early 1970s. One current within it, however, the network of Autonomia Operaia (Workers' Autonomy) explored the contested subjective space of resistance and domination that concerned these other groups, but did so not by referring to aesthetic or religious language, but by remaining thoroughly inside the Marxist lexicon, bending and redefining its terminology to rewrite Marxism from within.

The Situationists understood the subject as realising itself as fundamentally other to and outside of the domination of capital. But Autonomia Operaia, for example in Antonio Negri's theory of the socialised worker, understood the subject as necessarily moving and resisting *within* a system of domination that squeezes the subject just as it depends on it. This difference can be more clearly understood in terms of the theory of alienation which each employs.

The Situationists' approach rested on the Marxist concept of reification drawn from *Capital* and developed by Lukács, whereby "social action takes the form of the action of objects, which rule the producers instead of being ruled by them."[20] Reification was a theory of alienation based on an analysis of the logic of the commodity, and *The Society of the Spectacle* generally understood society as divided between the passive subject who consumes the spectacle and the reified spectacle itself. This entailed the knotty problem, described above, of returning to the "impossible" totality of the subject outside of the spectacle.

Autonomia Operaia was instead informed by the turn, in the earlier Italian Marxist current of *operaismo*, to Marx's *Grundrisse* and the development of the real subsumption of labour in order to grasp capital's ability to enclose the world outside work. Marx argued that capitalism is characterised by the development from formal subsumption, in which production remains structurally unchanged but a capitalist collects the surplus value, and real subsumption, in which the new industrial relations of production subsume labour more thoroughly to the production of surplus value and in which workers become automatons who are only one—albeit conscious—part of a productive machine. The theory of the social factory, or the socialised worker, understood the increased time and space outside the workplace not as a realm outside the productive economy devoted to *consumption* and the reificatory logic of the commodity, but as an expansion of the realm of the *production* of surplus value. The Situationists saw all formerly sovereign areas of life as dominated by the reifying logic of commodity *consumption* in the society of the spectacle. Autonomia Operaia saw these areas instead as an expansion of the factory's alienated relations of *production* in the social factory.

This may seem even more dystopian than the Situationists' vision: it does away with the idea of creative space "outside" the relations of capital, however problematic. The College's theory of myth had grasped how fascism spread first not through the rigid structures of the state and economy, but through affective and informal networks and relations. Similarly, the Situationists' notion of radical subjectivity is often read as anticipating the 1968 rebellion, proliferating in spaces invisible to the objective understanding of the state, unions, and Communist party. The social factory thesis now shows capital itself operating on these networks, relying on the subject's formerly autonomous social spaces for the production of surplus value.

However, there was also a positive side to this vision. From this perspective, the Situationists can be seen as granting the spectacle too much power to autonomously recuperate dissent, because they tend to ignore the working class as the subject that actually produces the spectacle and instead focus exclusively on the commodity relation. The autonomist perspective breaks with the Situationists' obsessive concern for totality. The Situationist subject, acting creatively outside the spectacle, but then recuperated by it, is replaced by the autonomist subject whose creativity is caught within and compromised by the machinic relations of the social factory. So, although the real subsumption thesis left Autonomia Operaia in a similar position to the College and the Situationists—insofar as these groups' total opposition between the subject and the objective world placed them in an impossible situation—Autonomia Operaia's positioning of the subject "within and against" capital, and as productive *of* capital, put them in a position that was no longer impossible but "cramped." Thoburn reads this cramped position in relation to Deleuze and Guattari's notion of a minor literature:

> Deleuze and Guattari argue that cramped, impossible conditions compel politics, for if the most personal individual intrigue is always traversed by a wealth of determining social relations, then these social relations must be engaged with, disrupted, politicised, if anything is to be lived.[21]

This moment of engagement and disruption (which Negri terms "self-valorisation") is a leap where the subject asserts itself against the determining social relations of capital and instead constructs others. Despite Autonomia Operaia's thorough analysis of the real subsumption of labour, Negri, recalling the Situationists' impossible demand, asks us to presuppose a radical separateness of labour from these relations when it comes to moving beyond them, even if this entails oversimplifying matters:

> I see it as a moment of intensive rooting within my own separateness. I am other—as also is the movement of that collective praxis within which I move.... It is only by recognising myself as other, only by insisting on the fact of my differentness as a radical totality that I have the possibility and the hope of a renewal.[22]

But despite this request it is clear that, for Negri, this is not a utopian faith in the sacred or the aesthetic but a positive matter of history and materialism:

> It seems to me fundamental to consider the totality of the process of proletarian self-valorisation as alternative to, and radically different from, the totality of the process of capitalist production and reproduction. I realise that I am exaggerating the position, and oversimplifying its complexity. But I also know that this "intensive road," this radical break...is a fundamental experience of the movement as it stands today.[23]

For Negri, theoretical oversimplification in describing this leap allows a more accurate and complex account of material practice. Especially as, in his engaged writing, the urgency of the move *towards* practice is paramount in validating his theory. For example, in *Marx Beyond Marx*, Negri ascribes a scientific methodology to Marx that might seem a little unconventional:

> It is not simply what permits a passive construction of the categories on the basis of a sum of historical acquisitions; it is above all what permits a reading of the present in the light of the future.... To take risks, to struggle. A science should adhere to that. And if occasionally one is an ape, it is only in order to be more agile.[24]

In this context of an agile theory that leaps in order to accommodate the movement of practice, Negri put his faith in the social phenomena around him that illuminated his writing. "The methodological precondition of an initial radical rupture is empirically corroborated by an extensive documentation."[25] The "leap" of these moments of subjective assertion is not a practice simply opposed to theory. It embodies the intimate material negotiations of an engaged, critical subject. The accompanying theoretical leap in describing them is not a matter of utopianism but of historical engagement.

Communism for Negri does not take the form of a prefigurative or post-revolutionary totality, but is embedded in the open material practice of the movement. It is a cramped, not impossible, practice.[26] Where Bataille and the Situationists resisted the logic of the dialectic by seeking to persist in the moment of the "other," Autonomia Operaia instead navigated in the streams of becoming. In either case, the elusive, radical quality these theorists are trying to describe is creative *potential*. For Negri, the more Marxist sounding "invention power"[27] replaces the Surrealist overtones of "creativity" and "desire" in describing the movement from virtuality to materiality.

In describing practices of self-valorisation, the College of Sociology and the Situationist International had recourse to the language of religion and aesthetics. This was a leap of faith away from the aspects of their Marxist theory that suggested such a venture should not be possible. As we have seen in Negri's engagement with Marx, such leaps can be seen not as a turning away from reality, but as intimately related to the overdetermined social conditions of contemporary capitalism. We can recast the impossible gap, more practically, as a cramped space.

Within the global justice movement, groups like the Clandestine Insurgent Rebel Clown Army (CIRCA) or the Tute Bianche embody minor moments of audacity, exploration, and experiment. We can see the minoritarian "performed" by CIRCA as they embrace the figure of the scapegoat or the fool whose exclusion enables social renewal. For Bataille's scapegoat or Deleuze's minor, this exclusion entails a peculiar joyful affect. In the very moment of making themselves vulnerable and open to failure, appearing as ridiculous "bare" subjects, without guard or pretence, the clowns embrace possibility and creativity. "I may be different—a poor scapegoat...an object of ridicule...BUT—you-are-me.... Activist culture is often paralysed by the desire to get things right. The fear of not creating the perfect action/campaign that will change the world.... Yet many classic clown acts are founded on the idea that from failure comes opportunity."[28]

Indeed, despite the great "stories of the battle" of Prague and Genoa, one might sense a recent minoritarian turn in the Global justice movement. In contrast to the apocalyptic sublime that Bataille theorised between two world wars or the Situationists' epic quest for a "Northwest passage," beyond the twentieth century, the global justice movement is often more in synch with the profoundly quotidian folk-mythology of the single steps of the Zapatistas' "Walking, we ask questions." This minor perspective provides a way to think the movement that gets us from here to there, the movement which is, of course, the material substance of the larger, audacious leaps of history which we see crystallised in the myths of Seattle and J18.

In *Hamlet*, Shakespeare used the metaphor of an old mole to bring the spectre of Hamlet's father back down to earth. Marx borrowed this metaphor to understand the virtuality of the spectre of Communism as grounded in the subterranean tunnels of the working class' cycle of struggles. Perhaps the old mole can also materialise "the breath of the possible" that Breton described in his Surrealist tracts and bring our mythology of sacred and sublime moments down to earth too. We can see the minor as grasping the movement of Marx's old mole, not only as an "other" rupturing the surface of everyday life to emerge in visible, potent experiences of self-valorisation (in 1848, 1968, or 1998), but also as an intimate, burrowing recompositional mechanism, digging away at a series of Northwest passages within and against capital.

Aesthetics can create possibilities for thought. Deleuze argued that the Surrealists' method of montage, developed by the cinema, made possible to think beyond what he saw as the false movement of dialectics. It is not surprising then that some theorists have chosen the Surrealist aesthetic to represent radical possibility against the limits of Marxist theory. The Situationists' and the College's leap of faith used aesthetics, which lends itself to describing the impossible and the virtual, to talk about their "impossible" situation. Employing dialectics made it impossible for these theorists to grasp movement, to move from instances of refusal to total revolution. Autonomia Operaia's move away from totality allows us to see the theoretical leap of asserting subjective experience as an attempt to cross the gap to material practice. Similarly inspiring accounts, such as that of our flying anarchist, delineate the possibility of a (in this case quite literal) line of flight just as they describe the material praxis of the movement of movements.

The open nature of these vital moments of affect allows us to grasp the virtuality and possibility of the space of practical political engagement. Thus, we can see, in the figure of the minor, a way to navigate the space between bare-faced utopianism and blank impossibility. As Delaney's account describes, these vital moments of affect are bound up with the creation of possibilities, with living in the pages of history, and in the cramped space of capitalist social relationships.

Notes

1. Georges Bataille, "The Pineal Eye," in *Visions of Excess: Selected Writings, 1927–39*, ed. Allan Stoekl (Minneapolis: University of Minnesota Press, 1988), 84.
2. Georges Bataille, *The Accursed Share, Vols. 2 and 3: The History of Eroticism* and *Sovereignty*, trans. Robert Hurley (New York: Zone Books, 1991), 14.
3. Georges Bataille, *The Accursed Share, Vol.1: Consumption*, trans. Robert Hurley (New York: Zone, 1988), 11.
4. Roger Caillois, "Interview with Gilles Lapouge, June 1970," in *The Edge of Surrealism: A Roger Caillois Reader*, ed. Claudine Frank (Durham and London: Duke University Press, 2004), 143.
5. Georges Sorel, *Reflections on Violence,* trans. Thomas Ernest Hulme and Jack Roth (Glencoe, Illinois: Free Press, 1950), 144.
6. Roger Caillois, "Introduction," in *The College of Sociology 1937–39*, ed. Denis Hollier (Minneapolis: University of Minnesota Press, 1988), 10.
7. CrimethInc Ex-Workers Collective, *Days of War, Nights of Love: CrimethInc For Beginners* (CrimethInc Free Press, 2001), 113.
8. Roger Caillois, "The Function of Myth," in *The Edge of Surrealism: A Roger Caillois Reader*, 119.
9. Terry Eagleton, *Holy Terror* (Oxford and New York: Oxford University Press, 2005), 91.

10. Ibid., 47.

11. Retort, *Afflicted Powers: Capital and Spectacle in a New Age of War* (London and New York: Verso, 2005), 28.

12. See http://www.smartmeme.com

13. Patrick Reinsborough, "Decolonising the Revolutionary Imagination: Values Crisis, The Politics of Reality, and Why There's Going to Be a Common-Sense Revolution in This Generation," in *Globalize Liberation: How to Uproot the System and Build a Better World*, ed. David Solnit (San Francisco: City Lights, 2004), 180.

14. Raoul Vaneigem, *A Cavalier History of Surrealism*, trans. Donald Nicholson-Smith (San Francisco: AK Press, 1999), 5.

15. Situationist International, "Preliminary Problems in Constructing a Situation," in *Situationist International Anthology*, ed. Ken Knabb (Berkeley: Bureau of Public Secrets, 1995), 45.

16. Jean Barrot, "Critique of the Situationist International," in *What Is Situationism? A Reader*, ed. Stewart Home (Edinburgh and San Francisco: AK Press, 1996), 28.

17. Raoul Vaneigem, *The Revolution of Everyday Life*, trans. Donald Nicholson-Smith (London: Rebel Press / Left Bank Books, 1994), 51.

18. Leeds May Day Group, *Summits and Plateaus* (Self-published, 2005). See www.nadir.org.uk.

19. Dissent! Flyer, 2005. See htp://www.dissent.org.uk.

20. See, for example, Jennifer Whitney, *Shattering the Myth of Seattle*, at www.daysofdissent.org.uk/seattle.htm.

21. Karl Marx, *Capital: A Critical Analysis of Capitalist Production, Vol.1*, trans. Samuel Moore and Edward Aveling (London: Allen and Unwin, 1971), 46.

22. Nicholas Thoburn, "Autonomous Production? On Negri's 'New Synthesis,'" in *Theory, Culture and Society* 18, no. 5 (2001), 7–9

23. Antonio Negri, "Domination and Sabotage," in *Italy: Autonomia: Post-Political Politics*, eds. Sylvere Lotringer and Christian Marazzi (New York: Semiotext(e), 1980), 63.

24. Ibid., 62.

25. Antonio Negri, *Marx Beyond Marx: Lessons on the Grundrisse*, trans. Harry Cleaver, Michael Ryan, and Maurizio Viano (Brooklyn and London: Autonomedia and Pluto Press, 1991), 49.

26. Antonio Negri, "Domination and Sabotage," 63.

27. Antonio Negri, "Crisis of the Planner-State: Communism and Revolutionary Organisation," in *Revolution Retrieved: Selected Writings on Marx, Keynes, Capitalist Crisis and New Social Subjects 1967–83*, ed. Red Notes (London: Red Notes, 1988), 147.

28. Kolonel Klepto, *Making War With Love: The Clandestine Insurgent Rebel Clown Army*, at www.clownarmy.org/about/writings.html.

:: CIRCUITS OF STRUGGLES ::

:: CIRCUITS OF STRUGGLE ::

There is nothing simple or mysterious about a cycle of struggle. The class struggle has many circuits, sectors, internal divisions, and contradictions, but it is neither a mystical unity nor a chaotic mess.
– Zerowork Collective

Understanding the multiple circuits and paths running through and composing a cycle of struggles, the ways in which the possibilities within moments of rupture come to reproduce and proliferate themselves, is an important part of militant investigation. By understanding how these cycles and circuits are formed, how they articulate themselves horizontally (across spatial areas) and vertically (through different parts of society), we further understand the power contained within these movements. How and when are the nodes and connections that compose these cycles formed? How intense are the connections? Cycles of struggles form their own geography, unevenly developed and full of potential. Circuits connect with others and replicate, turning cycles of struggles into spirals and opening up new planes of resistance.

We can map the resonances and connections over physical space and encounters, through mediated machinations and communications, through and around the disparate spaces that compose the university, the hospital, the city square, and through all spaces of life. By looking at the different circuits and channels through which information flows, we can see that cartographies of resistance trace the multiple and overlapping spaces and forms of struggle that exist, extending and expanding them. These connections often occur through unexpected routes, from tree-sits to hacklabs, from the post-Fordist workplace that tries to encompass all of life to the detention camp where life itself seems to be denied.

The processes of composition and decomposition, as described, occur through these circuits. In turn, the analysis of the processes and circulation of the knowledges involved becomes part of this process of recomposition. What are the contents, directions, and natures of the struggles? How are these struggles circulated and developed? This process of "imagineering," of deploying images and stories of struggles in other locations, rarely occurs directly, but usually travels through other tangled routes, through circulating references and chains of translation. These new knowledge-practices and possibilities create a collective form of intellectual practice dispersed over time and space.

Drifting Through the Knowledge Machine

Maribel Casas-Cortés and Sebastián Cobarrubias

1. Introduction

In August 2005, the administration of the University of North Carolina at Chapel Hill declared that Labor Day would be cancelled as a holiday for librarians, professors, teaching assistants (TAs), students, and all those involved in classroom instruction. Only certain workers counted as labor and thus would enjoy the national holiday. Frustrated by the administration's arbitrary decision that knowledge-work wasn't real work, a group of grad students, course instructors, and undergrads decided that it was time to make the conversations about workload, usually whispered in the hallways, public. Though none of us cherished Labor Day over May Day this half-cancellation of a work holiday provided the perfect opportunity to call attention to the economic and social role played by the university in our everyday lives and beyond. It was a great excuse to put our questions about work—immaterial and otherwise—into conversation with many others and begin to discuss ways of intervening. Constituting an improvised research team armed with the material of our labor—notebooks, blackboards, cameras, recorders, and chalk—this group of university employees conducted a "stationary-drift" during Labor Day, occupying a corner of one of the busiest parts of the campus for hours. The group interviewed passersby, distributed questionnaires, recorded video, conducted collective discussions, and generated participatory maps on what work and non-work meant for us versus what it meant to the administration. The invitation was made to map out Labor Day on campus and interview each other, starting with the guiding question: "What's your labor like, today and everyday?" All of this in order to discuss and investigate our own conditions of life and work in our temporary territory: the university.[1]

The ad-hoc intervention group generated four audio-taped interviews, three audio-taped collective conversations, fifty surveys and questionnaires, four color-coded maps, one page of conclusions on butcher paper, thirty digital photos, twenty minutes of videotape, and a three-page research log, as well as signs, flyers, and some graffiti. This initial "drift" on Labor Day 2005 became the first step in a plan to carry out a longer militant research project to challenge our own notions of the university and discover new strategies for struggle. September 6th, 2005 became the first public event of "Mapping the University: Drifting through the Knowledge Machine" by the 3Cups Counter-Cartographies Collective.

So what were the findings of your little "laboratory research" experiment?

While the intervention was short, it did open the door to a lot of questions and generated interest among quite a few people as to continuing with explorations of our own territory: the university. The arbitrary decision of who did or didn't deserve a work holiday provided the fruitful tension that we needed to begin a process of rethinking the university as a site of production and not as an ivory tower for the contemplation of the outside world. A broader public intervention could be made to raise attention to the multiple forms of labor at the university, and more generally to the power and political economy of universities in the post-Fordist economy. Some of the initial conclusions from that day focused on two aspects of *inhabiting* the university:

(a) Our spatial understanding of the university as a discrete and untouched entity was totally inadequate for figuring out what was going on and what to do. This notion obscures the multiple roles of universities in employment and flexible labor markets, the knowledge economy and corporate research, defense contracts and recruiting, finance capitalism through loans, university endowments and investments, and gentrification.

(b) Other experiences of campus activism, while necessary, seem insufficient to respond to issues such as new working conditions of a fragmented/temporary labor force. We wanted to start asking questions about possible ways of organizing and acting beyond student solidarity efforts with often faraway causes, as well as rethinking the reasons for the unsuccessful TAs union organizing (especially in North Carolina).

These two initial and interrelated suspicions were all well and good but moving on them was not easy to figure out. If there are so many things going on in the university, such a fragmented population of professors, ground-skeepers, adjunct instructors, food service workers, grad students, under-grads, clerical workers, and so many transformations happening simultane-ously (privatizations, subcontracting, tuition hikes, neocon policing), how could we figure out how it all related, how to tie existing struggles to others and how to provoke new ones?[2]

In order to move these questions forward, some of us took up the inspi-rations provoked by research projects enacted by social movements them-selves. What follows then is a description of two concrete activist research projects that pushed us to take the step of investigating the university. The research strategies developed by the collectives Precarias a la Deriva (from Madrid, Spain) and Bureau d'études/Université Tangente (from Strasbourg, France) produced strong resonances and provoke a chain reaction to start a research project on campus. These aren't random choices, but ones that gave us the necessary tools to investigate the material conditions of academic knowledge production. After presenting these two inspiring examples, we come right "back to school," mapping out the contexts we are facing of uni-versities in the "knowledge economy," and drawing specific reappropria-tions of Precarias a la Deriva and Bureau d'études on how we might move forward.

2. Research Experiments Initiated by Social Movements

An exciting wave of interest in research is rising among social move-ments as a way to understand and reshape the effects of capitalist globaliza-tion in everyday life. Research becomes a political tool to intervene in the processes that are moving us towards a neoliberal world. Different experi-ments of militant/action/radical research had been provoking our imagina-tions and contaminating our practices for a while. It made sense: a way of producing knowledge specifically for social movements in order to evaluate steps taken, to understand new contexts, or to open up new issues of strug-gle. It seemed particularly pertinent to the post-Genoa, post-September 11th, and post-Iraq moments: how to make sense of it all and move forward; how to explore alternative ways of challenging a complex system of oppressions? At times, we were confronted by the difficulties presented by the appar-ent distance between much "research" and "activism." However, we began to see, through many of our own itineraries in movement collectives that dabbled in research, as well as through inspiring examples such as Colectivo Situaciones, that it was possible to think of a form of in-depth research that came from and responded to social movements, whose methods themselves reflected movement politics, and whose results informed on-the-ground re-sistance.[3]

Precarias a la Deriva: Research methods for everyday interventions in a post-Fordist economy

The impact of neoliberal free-trade policies being promoted in Spain since the late '80s produced a harsh process of deindustrialization, followed by a transition towards a post-Fordist economy based on services and finance. The sharp shift in labor patterns included rising unemployment and proliferation of temporary contracts, affecting in singular ways different sectors of society. The "flexibilization" or "casualization" of labor markets required important cuts in labor protection laws and the loss of the multiple benefits guaranteed by the previous welfare-state economy.[4] Discontent with such an aggressive deregulation of labor markets was made explicit through several anti-European Union campaigns organized not only by official labor unions, but fueled by environmental and peasant sectors, immigrant groups, and especially by a frustrated youth filled with promises of neutral-sounding flexible labor but ending up with what became commonly known as *contractos basura* (garbage contracts). The shift in labor conditions was the target of critiques and mobilizations across Europe. European social movements started to coin these (re)emergent labor conditions as precarity.[5] Thus, what in English would be called flexible, casualized, or contingent labor (without any kind of necessary critical connotation) is being politicized in several European countries as "precarious labor," denouncing its fragile and exploitative character and promoting it as a new identity of struggle. *Precariedad* or precarity refers, then, to the labor conditions that arose after the transition from life-long, stable jobs common in industrial-capitalist and welfare-state economies, to temporary, insecure, low-paying jobs emerging with the globalization of the service and financial economy:

> The precariat is to post-Fordism what proletariat was to Fordism: flexible, temporary, part-time, and self-employed workers are the new social group which is required and reproduced by the neoliberal and post-industrial economic transformation. It is the critical mass that emerges from globalization, while demolished factories and neighborhoods are being substituted by offices and commercial areas. They are service workers in supermarkets and chains, cognitive workers operating in the information industry.[6]

Precarias a la Deriva was born out of this intense political moment at one of the places where issues of *precariedad* were being heatedly discussed: Eskalera Karakola, a women's squatted social center located in the Lavapies neighborhood.[7] After reflecting upon their own conditions and participation in the different mobilizations and current debates around labor issues many of the women organizing out of Karakola found that existing modes of analysis and organizing did not correspond well to their situations.

Why precarias *or feminine precarity?*

The first babbles of this action-research project are traced to the context of the general strike taking place in Spain on June 20, 2002 as part of the anti-European Union campaign during the Spanish presidency of the European Union. In the space of the Eskalera Karakola, several women started to share their unease with the general call by the big labor unions to stop all production chains for twenty-four hours. They wanted to be part of a generalized and explicit discontent against labor conditions, but the traditional tactic of the strike assumed an ideal type of worker that was far from their particular conditions. Striking in the context of a per-hour contract, domestic task, temp work, or self-employed job would not have any of the expected effects. Nobody would even realize it. With this frustration as their point of departure, the women involved with Eskalera Karakola started to brainstorm new ways of political intervention adapted to their circumstances.

The discussion ended up with a proposal: the *piquete-encuesta* or the "picket-survey." During the day of the national strike, several small groups of women armed with cameras, recorders, notebooks, and pens were dispersed throughout the city of Madrid. They aimed to hold conversations in the marginal centers of the economy where the strike made little sense: the invisible, non-regulated, temporary, undocumented, house-based sectors of the market. The main theme of the survey centered around the question: "*Cual es tu huelga?*" (What is your strike?) The survey by and of *precarias* stopped the productive and reproductive chain for some time and more importantly gave a temporary opportunity to talk among, and listen to, an invisible and fragmented population. The exchange resulting from that day was inspiring: they opened a potential space for unmediated encounters between otherwise unconnected women, who while sharing similar precarious conditions, had radically different experiences.[8]

Within this effervescence, the research project called "On the drift through the circuits of the feminine precarity" emerged. The object of study and intervention were the labor conditions created by a post-Fordist economy among women, working at different sites of the casualized job market in an urban setting. Through a close engagement with their own experiences, this project would refine the notion of precarity, to articulate a more situated version of it. Thus their research coalesced around the notion of *precariedad femenina* (feminine precarity) as a particular form of flexible labor: gendered but not sexed.[9] This qualification of precarity challenges overly production-centered analyses and offers an understanding able to capture the effects of changing labor conditions in the continuum of production-reproduction. One of this project's analytical contributions consists in breaking the distinction between "labor" and "life" usually maintained by traditional political economy. They analyze how the post-Fordist changes in labor are producing *post-Fordist* lives, looking at the new subjectivities generated. The condition of *precariedad femenina* cannot be reduced only to negative labor conditions pointed out by the notion of the precariat as a cousin of the *proletariat*. This is how they define themselves, acknowledging the multiple character of living as *"precarias"* (the feminine version of *precario*), pointing out how subjects are produced under both oppression and empowerment:

> We are *precarias*. This means some good things (such as the accumulation of knowledge, expertise and skills through our work and existential experiences, which are under permanent construction), a lot of bad ones (such as vulnerability, insecurity, poverty, social instability), and the majority, ambivalent stuff (mobility, flexibility).[10]

Why "derivas" or "drifting?"

Finding collective ways of struggle was one of the main challenges to be addressed, especially focusing on the possibilities of articulation among women who shared the common experience of *precariedad* yet were employed in extremely different types of work from university professors to sex workers to translators to domestic servants. Based on the excitement of the results of the picket-survey, a plan for reconnecting and exploring the diversity of experiences of *precariedad* in a more systematic way started to take shape. They needed research methodologies that would fit their circumstances and be relevant to provoking conflict. Looking for a procedure that would be able to capture their mobile, open-ended, and contingent everyday lives, they found inspiration in the Situationist technique of "drifting." Situationist researchers wander in the city, allowing for encounters, conversations, interaction, and micro-events to be the guide of their urban itineraries. The result was a psychogeography based on haphazard coincidences. This version though was seen as appropriate for a bourgeois male individual without commitments and not satisfactory for a *precaria*. Instead of an exotic itinerary, the *precarias* version of drifting consisted of a situated and directed trajectory through everyday-life settings.

Situationist methods open up unexpected spatial situations which generate realities worth exploring. The Precarias' methods pursue an intentional model of the drift where spaces normally perceived as unconnected are linked. This allows everyday itineraries to become the leading line to follow, making visible underground realities otherwise off the radar for regular discourse. This version of the drift presented itself as a perfect technique, attentive to the spatial-temporal continuum that they were experiencing as women under the new labor conditions. This project then contributed a methodology that could be understood as a feminist version of drifting, a kind of "*derive a la femme.*"

This innovative research methodology generates a political-economic analysis well-informed by current theoretical trends. Precarias' project reviews, criticizes, rescues, and combines different bodies of work not by revering authority, but affectively.[11] Going back and forth between a variety of sources and their actual lived experience allows them to develop a *situated* investigation of the material conditions held in common and the radical differences being lived through.[12] These *feminist drifts* act as circuits articulating fragmented spaces and experimental tours that re-imagine the political as collective interventions in everyday life. They produce participatory cartographies of their collective itineraries, where field research is the temporary expedition following the space-time continuum of singular experiences.[13] Precarias' project is about searching for commonalities and fostering singularities, while maintaining the tension between them. They look for ways to articulate *lo común singular* (the singular in common), to cross-fertilize collective action among radically different specificities.

Bureau d'études/Université Tangente: Hacking cartographies to map power and imagine insurrections

Based in Strasbourg, France, this activist map-making group began around 1998. Its origins are in the radical art world of France at the time. Bureau d'études/Université Tangente (BE/UT) began to experiment with proto-versions of maps and flowcharts of economic networks as a form of public/political art. After several projects, frustration with the political economy of the art world grew. The organizing of the unemployed and squatters movements at the time took the efforts of the BE/UT into even more politically engaged art and work on issues of the "new economy" such as knowledge-work. Reflections on the changing nature of the economy, as well as the increasing prominence of global resistance movements and the calls to articulate a new sort of international solidarity, finally gave this kind of *artivist* group a venue beyond the gallery/museum circuit and pushed the collective toward a long-term engagement with cartography as a way to work on and communicate issues related to the new movements. Large numbers of antagonistic maps, as well as accompanying texts, have been produced for radical analysis and education. These are distributed at counter-summits, No Border camps, Social Forums, communicated directly to local collectives (we picked our first map up at a squat in Barcelona), as well as on their website.[14] Their maps and writings have inspired groups in many places to look into map-making as a form of intervention and tool for struggle.

So what are their maps about—and why maps anyway?

These cartographic representations are often an incredible and dizzying display of institutions, actors, personalities, organizations, and movements: a sort of network map tracing out the links and articulations of both "power structures" (the European Union [EU], global finance, particular corporations) and counterpower flows. For example, in one map called the "European Norm of World Production" one can see icons representing things like the European Commission, which connect to different banks, political institutions, and personalities. Flows of networked links show the associations among this institution and biotech regulations, defense industries, telecommunications, migration policing, etc.

Rather than a defeatist "power is everywhere, there's nothing left to do" response, these maps evoke something else. In many of them, there is a multitude of targets and places where power is being exerted. In the Bureau's work on "European Norms," for example, instead of a vertical pyramid where real power exists at just one point, the very structuring of the EU's quest for a neoliberal/imperial Europe is configured by a vast number of institutions, corporations, laws, etc. The configuration itself is the structure. Thus, there are dozens of possible fracture points: no one struggle is totally primary here. The map gives the impression of being unfinished, that some links are yet to be traced or understood—just as power is reforming itself and morphing in response to popular struggles. This appropriation of cartography provides new ways of thinking, new forms of antagonism, as well as the understanding that no institutions or "sites" of power are bound and self-contained in any simple way. Every powerful institution is made up of its links and flows with other forms of power.[15] The Bureau d'études explains the importance of this type of movement-based research:

> Autonomous knowledge can be constituted through the analysis of the way that complex *machines* function...The deconstruction of complex machines and their "decolonized" reconstruction can be carried out on all kinds of objects...In the same way as you deconstruct a program, you can also deconstruct the internal functioning of a government or an administration, a firm, or an industrial or financial group. On the basis of such a deconstruction, involving a precise identification of the operating principles of a given administration, or the links or networks between administrations, lobbies, businesses, etc., you can define modes of action or intervention.[16]

At the same time that power is mapped one can also follow the itineraries of movement activity with the goal of strengthening autonomous forms of organizing, understanding distinct activist efforts together, or searching for new sites of resistance.

So tell us some more about maps

These mapping strategies seemed relevant to carrying out militant research practices that were tuned to many activist principles. Based on what we've learned from the experiences of Bureau d'études and other mapping collectives, we've tried to draw out some of the benefits of a social movement-based form of cartographic production in order to strengthen and deepen struggles.

Maps are nontextual and nongrammatical. This means that rather than a text or tract where the reader is forced to follow the author's train in a pretty linear way, maps have no rigid beginning or end. While maps definitely show some things while hiding others, they are not bound by the same rules of grammar and syntax. Different map viewers can see different links and orders of things, and can focus on any point of the map at any time without having to turn pages. This nontextual characteristic can also help bridge some constraints of language and literacy (though its hypervisuality may produce other limitations).

Maps are easier to produce or build on in a participatory and collective manner. While co-authoring a text for a collective of any significant size can be quite difficult—simply because sentences are hard to construct with lots of people—map items and icons can be added to in a much easier way. Different people can suggest different items that might be relevant for a map on, for example, a particular corporation, a set of labor relations, a part of the neighborhood, etc. Even when a map is finished, different users can draw on it, adding new items or connecting previously unconnected ones (just think of what one normally might do on a tourist or street map).

Maps are excellent tools for teach-ins and workshops. They are also practical devices for communication among struggles more generally. Partly this is facilitated by their visual nature, except that unlike a film, for instance, you might be able to view an entire map (or maps), and move your attention anywhere on them. This can change the flow of collective discussion and reflection and makes it easy to refer back to previous points.

Maps never need to be considered finished. As mentioned above, people can draw on them or draw new ones. Text boxes can be added. Different maps can be read in conjunction with one another in order to deepen analyses and look for more tools. For example, the Bureau d'études might have a map of different state institutions of governance which includes certain financial institutions, and another map about those financial institutions that follows their connections to other industries and companies.

Activist maps have already been used in many different ways. Sometimes they look more like cartoons meant to communicate a point, a form of agit-prop or "propaganda map"—for instance, the image of an octopus crawling over the earth.[17] Other activist maps are more like street maps for particular protests that designate things like targets, safe zones, and tactical areas.[18] The maps called for here, and enacted by collectives such as the Bureau d'études, go even a step further. They are explicitly intended to apply movement politics to the map-making process, such that the form they take may be pretty funky and unorthodox. The goals are specifically to understand what forms of power we may be up against, as well as what counterpowers we may be able to create.

The maps become a part of activist "growth," if you will. They can act as a way of linking daily experiences and itineraries to broader-scale configurations of economic and political power. It's at this point where we see the connection between the experiences of Precarias a la Deriva, Bureau d'études, and what we hope to enact through the "Mapping the Universities" project.

3. Back to School: An Emerging Activist Research Project at a US Knowledge Machine

For different economic, political, and personal reasons, some of us ended up studying and working at a university located in the jungles of the US South. What we perceived as the isolation of the ghettoized US academy was a source of frustration during the first years of our program. After conversations with others, though, we realized that the isolation was reinforced by the myth of the university as an ivory tower displaced from the "real world" as well as from "real activism." As inhabitants of the university, it was not difficult to see how higher education institutions were contributing to the process of neoliberalization of the economy we'd been fighting all along.

For example, University of North Carolina-Chapel Hill (UNC-CH) is one of about ten universities within a fifty-mile radius of North Carolina that provides the labor force to nearby Research Triangle Park, one of the main hubs of the worldwide knowledge economy, including many multinational corporations. The concentration of PhDs working in the geographical triangle formed by the three most important universities in the area is one of the highest in the world. This is accompanied by a rise in part-time service work under dubious conditions. Duke University is the third-largest private employer in North Carolina, just a bit behind Wal-Mart, and is referred to by local citizens of Durham as the "plantation." This pole of economic production has replaced much of the textile industry, which is in the process of outsourcing after meeting WTO "standards." Its corporate-driven agendas and casualized labor policies have been praised as one of the leading models of the neoliberalization of research.

The university, as one of the main actors of the current economy, is completely embedded within the "real world out there." The university as such contributes to the production and reproduction of the same neoliberal world that many of us had been fighting on the "outside." Thus, activism—commonly thought of in the US as having little to do with academia—was more necessary than ever at the heart of the university, in order to explore the shortcomings and possibilities of the system's reproduction machines.

After looking into some of these questions, new activist research experiments, and debates on precarity, a working group emerged on campus focused on the cartographic strategies that movements were developing to interact with the changing economic situation. This group—under the temporary name of Counter-Cartographies Collective—has been meeting at 3 Cups, a slow-food business in town, since April 2005. The idea is to appropriate some of those techniques to trace out some of the economic shifts within our local area. One of 3C's current projects focuses on mapping/drifting/intervening in the university machine. This project was inaugurated with the intervention on Labor Day.

As mentioned before, the examples of Bureau d'études and Precarias a la Deriva have fueled our imagination to start a cartographic activist research project at UNC-CH. These are some of the *translations* of the methodological contributions by both projects for mapping the university.

Drifting through the circuits of a post-Fordist factory

Among the university's main taboo subjects, are the labor and life conditions of its workers. The university erases the bodies and the materiality involved in knowledge production. Service and infrastructural sectors, as well as academic work itself, are going through parallel processes of outsourcing, temporary contracting, self-managerial approaches, and other "treats" of flexible labor markets. Precarity—manifested in multiple forms—presented itself at home. The post-Fordist regime of the knowledge economy was waiting to be researched and intervened in, and the methodological tools developed by Precarias a la Deriva fascinated us with their possibilities.

Feminist drifting as TAs, undergraduates, cafeteria workers, professors, janitors, adjuncts, ground keepers, etc. allows us to mark the territory of knowledge production as the object of examination, the object upon which to produce knowledge. Our everyday lives as university inhabitants have become our temporary field sites, appropriating our research skills to investigate our own labor/life conditions and explore the possibilities of struggle. The university always expects researchers to examine the outside, the real world out there, the far away, the other, the heterotopia. That very same university is made into our object of examination because of its important role in the making of economic, political, and cultural processes and their intense connections with the supposedly "real world." Our drifting will be made through the circuits of a post-Fordist/precarious university. Just as the Situationists found the city fascinating for its power of capturing contemporary processes, we, as temporary inhabitants of the university system, find our academic territory to be an incredible source of information on current production modes in the knowledge economy. Following the itineraries or circuits of each of our drifts would allow us to uncover the conditions for the university's production of neoliberal subjects.

Drifting through the everyday circuits of labor at the university (knowledge, manual, and everything in between) opens the possibility to draw connections between individual experiences and larger processes in the current political economy. In addition to exposing these connections, it becomes a tool to explore the potential articulations within a situation of total fragmentation among the labor force of a changing US academy, overcoming radical occupational differences through common language—the knowledge factory—and hopefully opening a new terrain of struggle. Feminist drifting on campus would encompass collective field tours. Each drift can involve different recording devices (notebooks, video camera, audio tape). It is a kind of collective interview in motion, led by one/two/three guides through their everyday-life itineraries. The recorded drift may involve diary entries, interviews, discussions, etc. Afterward the material could be discussed in internal workshops. Some of the possible drifts identified by 3Cs are:

- drift 1: wandering through different TAships in order to understand the intersection/continuum of "student" and "worker";
- drift 2: engaging the military presence on campus by conducting interviews and having collective discussions with combat veterans and soldiers on the political economy of the military/academic/industrial complex;
- drift 3: the world of the adjunct (temporary contracts, health insurance, and second jobs) is it possible to raise a family?;
- drift 4: drift through the world of outsourced food and corporate cafeteria construction;
- drift 5: cleaning your room, and the campus, as a way to highlight existing conditions of housekeepers and grounds crews (withheld pay, temp contracts, racialized hiring, etc.).

Mapping the networks of the knowledge machine

One of the main myths about the academy is the independent ivory tower, which reinforces its exclusivist role of knowledge-making, untouched by historical dynamics and free from possible turmoil. Contrary to this well-established myth, we can see the university as a gridded space crisscrossed by intense relations of power: instead of a privileged, bounded ghetto, we see an interlocking system with multiple power and counterpower networks flowing through it. Both the conditions of current academic knowledge production and the possibilities of resistance within it relay into broader networks.

The maps á la Tangente—post-representational flow charts of both power and resistance—present themselves as a counter-device that enables us to denounce some of the university connections, and also to explore some of its hidden possibilities for struggle and articulation.

Mapping the university would require a series of cartographic representations to visualize each structural layer that traverses the knowledge machine. In a brainstorming session about the different networks of the university involved, 3Cs came up with a series of issues to be researched and mapped out: 1) employment numbers, kinds of contracts, and labor casualties; 2) links to the knowledge economy's development poles; 3) construction, urban restructuring, and gentrification effects; 4) diversity numbers and racialized spaces; 5) connections with the military industrial complex, including defense industry and foreign policy; 6) links to corporate power in research agendas and service industries on campus; 7) activist efforts and their targets; 8) links to immigration and security agencies; 9) loans, credit, and the connections with the world of credit as the basis for the American middle-class.

The Untrodden path

Through these various models of researching the university, the group is hoping to produce a multi-layered cartography in which several maps and itineraries would be superimposed and intertwined, exploring sites of contradiction and possible interventions.

These initial sketches of our as-of-yet uncharted interventions into the foundations of the post-Fordist knowledge economy bear the marks of influence from inspiring militant research projects. The irony is that these same projects, often developed at the edge of, or in antagonism with, the university, are now permeating its borders and contaminating its canons. The border between school and the "real world" must be breached since the ivory tower nowadays is only a metaphor for the defenses of these development poles of neoliberalism. The ivory towers are used as citadels in the newly conquered territories of the global economy, dotting our landscapes with sentinels/centurions of empire. They must be laid siege to, they must be infiltrated. As any good barbarian horde knows, a proper siege requires blueprints, and infiltration requires lived experience and adaptation.

But let us not fall solely into the militaristic metaphor. Inside the ivory tower lay tools of empowerment and communication amongst antagonistic subjects of the future; inside the tower lay the archives of the same system that gave it birth, often including all sorts of critical analyses, all the better to empower the struggles of the horde; inside the tower lay their excess material, secret treasure rooms, their darkened corners, all sites where the barbarian infiltrators might spin a counter-web that will wrap itself around and overgrow the "tower," replacing it with a new, as yet unmapped, territory.

Notes

1. For a complete account of the Labor Day action, see http://www.unc.edu/~macasas/labor_day_presentation_with_map.ppt.

2. For many activists (whether working at a university or not) academia is seen solely as a "site of privilege" (as opposed to seeing it as a knowledge factory) and a place to get some individual resources (instead of collectively reappropriating its productive tools).

3. For some other examples of activist research that we have participated in, particularly from the US, see "Rebellious Research: Itinerarios por la investigación activista en EEUU" at *www.euromovements.info*. We wrote this piece for the *Activist Research Newsletter* in reaction to the absence of US experiences in some of the current debates on activist research. It includes examples like Chicago DAN, Mexico Solidarity Network, Participatory Action Research, the Coalition of Immokalee Workers, and the University of the Poor.

4. See Desobediencia Global at http://www.sindominio.net/unomada/desglobal for more information about the Spanish presidency of the European Union in 2002, and the campaign against it.

5. For activist references on debates about precarity in Europe see www.precarity.info or www.euromayday.org.

6. Precarias a la Deriva, *A la Deriva por los Circuitos de la Precariedad Femenina* (Madrid: Traficantes de Suenos, 2004), 48.

7. Lavapiés is a downtown neighborhood that has recently become well known for the confluence of youth, working-class, and immigrant populations.

8. Precarias a la Deriva, *A la Deriva por los Circuitos de la Precariedad Femenina*, 21–22.

9. The translation of this term is very tricky: "feminine casualization," "contingent women," and "flexible girls" don't capture it. In order to be consistent to the original meaning, then, we would like the reader to get acquainted to the Spanish terms.

10. Precarias a la Deriva, *A la Deriva por los Circuitos de la Precariedad Femenina*, 17.

11. Some of the work we engage with here come from neo-Marxist notions of affective labor, feminist debates on reproduction, postcolonial insights

on taken-for-granted supremacies, poststructuralist theories of power, and Deleuzian understandings of subjectivity.

12. For example, an undocumented domestic worker and a freelance journalist are both flexible, temporary, part-time, and self-employed workers—however there are huge differences in social status, salary, rights, risks, etc.

13. See cartographic representations of their drifts in Precarias' publication (2004).

14. See Brian Holmes at http://utangente.free.fr.

15. Some of the Bureau's theoretical background seems to jive well with Foucault and Deleuze and Guattari. If interested, see examples of work by Brian Holmes.

16. Bureau d'études/Université Tangente, "Autonomous Knowledge and Power in a Society without Affects," at the Université Tangente: www.utangente. free.fr.

17. See John Pickles, *A History of Spaces: Cartographic Reason, Mapping and the Geo-Coded world* (London and New York: Routledge, 2004).

18. See the action-map "People's Guide to the National Republican Convention," (NYC, August–September 2004).

Autonomy, Recognition, Movement

Angela Mitropoulos

In 1964, Mario Tronti began putting forward an analysis of working class autonomy that would come to be identified—and not always accurately—with an entire period and millieu of radical politics in Italy. The argument went something like this: while capitalists must necessarily equip themselves with the state so as to enter the field of class struggle, working class struggles can occur independently of any given form and level of representation. In "Lenin in England," he dismissed claims of any "inexorable necessity of working class mediation," insisting that, to the contrary, the state amounted to capitalist subjectivity *as such*.[1] Put otherwise: the subjectivation of capital consists of law as well as necessity accounted for through law and the state, whereas working-class struggles imply an indeterminacy but not, for all that, a haphazardness.

Moreover, for Tronti, "the beginning is the class struggle of the working class. At the level of socially developed capital, capitalist development becomes subordinated to working class struggles; it follows behind them, and they set the pace to which the political mechanisms of capital's own reproduction must be tuned." As an instance of this, Tronti argued that the unification of the world market was imposed on capital by the unity of movement of the working class at the world level. He would later characterise this unity of the movement of the working class as the "strategy of refusal."[2] In the rejection of work, widespread non-cooperation, and the desertion of traditional forms of working class representation (such as unions and parties) that characterised the 1960s in Europe and elsewhere, Tronti (and others) discerned not the end of class struggle—as the optic of socialist orthodoxy would have it—but *a different strategy*. In retrospect, and with a nod to historically parallel theoretical discussions in a French idiom, Franco Berardi described these insights as "the emancipation from the Hegelian concept of subject." For him, the distinct innovation of class composition analysis developed through Potere Operaio and Autonomia consisted of a reappraisal of the understanding of class, seen not as an "ontological concept, but rather as a vectoral" one.[3] Therefore, there was no essential form of organisation or struggle that was valid for all time but, instead, movements and compositions.

More recently and well beyond Europe, the theme of autonomy has become pivotal to discussions of migration, border policing, and global capital. There it has come to imply—in view of the intervening conjuncture of debates over "globalisation"—an emphasis on the strategic-analytical priority of the movements of people over those of capital.[4] As the so-called "anti-globalisation" protests began to circulate in the late 1990s, so too debates over the analysis of globalisation became more acute. By 1999, what had become apparent was the dominance—both presupposed and disseminated by the designation of the anti-summit protests as anti-globalisation campaigns—of a perspective in which the "unification" of the world market was accomplished at the expense of nation-states, in turn regarded as the necessary condition for the defense (and/or representation) of the working class against capital. Though, to be more precise, the concept of class had long receded behind or been redefined as that of "the people" and, in so doing, counterposed nation-states to global capital in a move that was as historically forgetful as it was analytically untenable.

In other words, the reverse of Tronti's argument as noted above, which is also to say: the standard social democratic account prevailed as both a condition and the result of the mediation of those protests as a substantively homogenous campaign. The stakes and implications, therefore, were by no means hypothetical. *De Fabel van de Illegaal*, a Dutch anti-racist organisation, was among the first to raise the alarm at the presence of nationalist and, in some cases, explicitly xenophobic groups and perspectives around the anti-summit protests.[5] In the USA, an unflinching alliance between Pat Buchanan and Ralph Nader ferried stacks of paper, photocopiers, and fax machines to Seattle for the protests against the World Trade Organisation (WTO) in 1999, while ATTAC similarly concentrated on capital's movements, and lobbied for a Tobin Tax throughout Europe. But if, in the US and Europe at this point, this displayed a typical distance between lobbyists and protesters that was also a difference of orientation toward the state, by 2000, the demarcations were starkly posed as riots and mass escapes occurred in Australian internment camps, just days before the protests against the World Economic Forum in Melbourne.[6]

And so, if one aspect of the radical response to the nationalist figuration of anticapitalist protests was to argue for the organisational decentralisation of the anti-summit protests—against the recurrent demands for unity and mediation and for the political creativity of irreconcilable differences—the other, and not unrelated, response was to insist that the globalisation of finance and trade was historically preceded by the globalisation of labour. Only this could account for the apparently paradoxical circumstances of the post-1989 period that consisted of *both* the deregulation of capital and trade flows *and* the re-regulation of the movements of people. The first as a catching-up measure, the second as a means to reinstate control and manage the flows. The analyses that located deterritorialisation on the side of capital and, more or less implicitly, territorialisation on the side of labour, were obliged to erase an entire history of struggles against the enclosures just as they were inclined to proffer an argument for their fortification.

The calibrations of capital flight are *always* premised on the organisation of differential and segmented markets. To put this another way, and to echo Tronti's initial formulations: capital's global unification—globalisation—was imposed on it by a widespread refusal and flight of people. This flight took shape not only as an exodus from the factory and the unions that the writings of Potere Operaio sought to analyse, but as a simultaneous exodus from what has usually been referred to as the "Third World," the poorhouses and workhouses of 18th-and 19th-century Europe which had been exported across the world as the very meaning of its partitioning as "first," "second," and "third." The attempted global reorganisations of finance and trade of the late 20th century, as well as the post-1989 border regimes introduced in the US, Australia, Europe and Canada, postdate the movements of people from "periphery" to "core." This is in no way to suggest that there has not been a world market prior to this, which is as absurd as the suggestion that the world market has not always been an *inter*-national system. Rather, it is to note that what has been called globalisation of late can only be explained with regard to the recent history of movements that were an attempt to escape the specific conditions of exploitation of the post-WWII period. Those conditions being, in short: a Fordist production system divested of its early resort to a relatively higher wage and "Third World" nationalisms increasingly, and in the least violent moments, operating as Bantustans. It might be worth noting here that it is precisely the failure of that attempt to secure the movements of people, to accomplish a repartitioning of the world into spaces of exception and norms that was once constitutive of the distinction between "First" and "Third" Worlds, that has precipitated the more recent resort to a seemingly permanent global war.

In a more specific sense then, in discussions of migration the notion of autonomy comes to imply both an analytical proposition and a political disposition. First, it not only suggests the political-strategic precedence of the movements of people over those of capital and, not least, the state's policies which give strategic and subjective form to capital, as outlined above. It also involves an insistence that migration is a *strategy*—a strategy that is undertaken in and against the cramped spaces of the global political economies of work, gender, and desire, among other things, but also a strategy for all that.[7] Of the terms of such an approach, and echoing Sergio Bologna's earlier work on class composition, Yann Moulier-Boutang noted that it is not only important to "look only to the tip of the iceberg: the institutionalized forms, or the word of the people, the way in which they speak, supposing that, as soon as they aren't saying anything, they aren't acting." It is important to heed "the silences, the refusals, and the flight as something active."[8]

Secondly, what is at stake in this attentiveness to a subterranean analytic becomes apparent if one considers the ways in which migration policy is crucial to the organisation of differential and segmented labour markets, on national, regional, and global scales, and not least through the creation of illegalised strata of workers. Therefore, migration, particularly that which is undocumented and criminalised, means movements in the face of global divisions that are as biopolitical and affective as they are legal, economic, and military. In one sense, then, the flight from devastation can be akin to a strike for higher pay, the withdrawal of one's labour from impoverished layers of the market, in which destitution is routinely deemed to be an ecological and/or biological condition, inherent to those regions and/or the bodies of those who inhabit them. What often comes into play here—not only in the organisation of state policy, but also in ostensibly "progressive" responses to it—is racism, sovereignty, the entire terrain upon which it becomes possible, habitual even, to depict migrants as bereft of political action, indeed of activism.

In the Australian context, the concept of the autonomy of migration came to imply a more explicit opposition to racism, perhaps because here it requires a good deal more effort than usual to distinguish the nation-state from colonial, missionary, and carceral undertakings. As Brett Neilson argues, "to oppose racism...one first needs to question the constituted power of the Australian state and its correlate forms of identity and subjectivity." In this discussion with Neilson on Australian and European borders, Sandro Mezzadra noted a tendency to "depict those who suffer the effects of globalisation in the global south as mere victims, denying them a position as protagonists or active social subjects in contemporary processes of global transformation. From this perspective, migration becomes just one in a long line of catastrophes occasioned by neoliberalism."[9] This is also why the path of an assumed political expediency at work in "mainstream" defenses of migration so often involves the re-victimisation of those whose movements have been criminalised by the state. Consider here the preference among many NGOs for depictions of migrants as mute victims who, in the very spectacle of this inability to speak or act, invite the observer to assume the task of representation.

At issue here is not simply the objectification of migrants, but also a very particular form of subjectivation of the non-migrant that is assembled by implication. Namely, the construction of a more or less furtive bond between "activist" and "state," in which political subjectivity is invoked on condition of assuming the perspective of the state—or being, literally, a subject of it. Moreover, in the absence of manifestoes, programmes, and spokespeople, much of the Left is all too ready to assume that migration implies the absence of political decision and action; thus reserving for itself the semblance and definition of political struggle, movement, and representation. In this way, the form of the political decision—what it means to be and to enact the political—is made synonymous with the structure of the sovereign decision. In the wake of the Australian military's seizure of the Norwegian freighter that had rescued over 300 undocumented migrants from drowning, the Prime Minister pithily summarised the conceit of the sovereign decision in the form of an election slogan: "We will decide who comes here and the circumstances under which they come." The prevalent and ostensible counter-slogan of "Refugees are welcome here" not only repeated the classificatory machinery of migration policy that obliges the other to beg, but positions the "we" as the one who must be persuaded by such pleading, who has the authority to welcome, or not. The affective economy of migration policy involves a resignation to the state as the model behind which political action and thinking always lurks and—perhaps more captivating than this—the wish to hold fast to the right to decide the exception that is bestowed by rights-based politics. Or as Hannah Arendt put it, the right to decide who does and does not have rights and, it should be added, the processes through which the sovereign state and its exceptions are constituted.[10]

At stake in every politics of border control is control over the border of the political. In presenting the act of migration as something outside the field of politics, the very definition of what a movement and politics is remains tied to the organisation of democratic representation in a very precise sense, and so, *in turn*, the terrain in which migration occurs appears as that which must be controlled, regulated, and mediated. For if democracy means the rule of the *demos* (the people), then the formal emptiness of the proposition of who the people are is nevertheless constantly played out along both anthropological and racialised axes of differentiation that are as eager to make of humanity the beginning and end of the sense of the world as they are to adjudicate upon the non-human.[11]

In this regard, the concept of the autonomy of migration is not a claim about the absence of economic or other pressures around migration and migratory flows, as Nicholas Bell from the European Civic Forum supposed.[12] Nor is it, similarly but in a philosophical register, the proposition of an autonomous or unconditioned subject as it appears in the works of Immanuel Kant or John Locke, where autonomy is defined as *self-possession*. Even less does it mark the contours of an identity that calls out for recognition. As Maurizio Ricciardi and Fabio Raimondi have argued, viewing "migrants as

subjects deprived of rights and citizenship" means that they are presented
as indicators of a political lack and a sign of the inexorable necessity of the
nation-state.[13] Above all, the concept of autonomy, as a way to orient oneself
around the issue of migration, means that one does *not* concern oneself with
the reasons why another wishes to move across borders; it insists that the
other is autonomous, particularly where one's *self* is most liable to assume
the pose of deciding on such matters for an other, either because one's own
belonging is not in question or as a means to prove that it should not be.
The concept of the autonomy of migration is an insistence that politics does
not need to be the property of the state and those who—however implicitly
and by dint of a claim to belong to it, as the subject that is *proper to it* (its
property)—can claim to reserve for themselves the thought and action that
is deemed to be properly political. Therefore, it amounts to a challenge to the
sovereign and representational dispositions within what passes for the Left,
to the very construction of what it means to be an activist, to do politics, and
to recognise movements and struggles as such.

One of the questions that arises, then, is of the relation between cognitive labour and movements, particularly as this gives form to the question of the relationship between recognition and autonomy. Throughout its
recent history in radical politics, the concept of autonomy has not simply
indicated a distance from the state, forms of mediation, and representational
politics. More specifically, it has called into question the role of recognition
and, thereby, the particular role that has been assigned to cognitive labour
since Fordism of managing as well as representing the figure of the working class.[14] For while it would be more than plausible to read Tronti's early
account of the autonomy of working class struggles as pointing toward its
more recent appearance in discussions of migration in almost every respect,
for Tronti the explicit sense of autonomy remains that of an autonomy which
admits no heteronomy—save for that of the work to be done by research.
This research, Tronti argued, was necessary to "work out the form that will
be taken by a future dictatorship of the workers organised as a ruling class."
Therefore, while he insisted that the existence of working class struggles
was independent of its formal organisations, that working class struggles
menaced every category of political-economy, every policy of the state and
economic reorganisation, the means by which this could be *recognised* and
translated into organisational forms remained the province of "theory."

However problematised the role of cognitive labour was by Tronti, it
nevertheless came to assume the task of recognition and, thereby, the terrain upon which the autonomy of the working class is not simply identified
but, in a very specific sense, constituted. Yet if what survives from Tronti's
early analysis is less the explicit "project to research a new Marxist practice
of the working class party" than the concept of autonomy, this is in part
because the presumed externality of "theory" to the "working class" was

undergoing a significant shift that has, likewise, become a significant theme in post-*autonomia* writings. Indeed, such a shift was already more than apparent, even in its ambivalence. In "The Strategy of the Refusal," Tronti also argued that culture is "always a relation between intellectuals and society, between intellectuals and the people, between intellectuals and class; in this way it is always a mediation of conflicts and their resolution in something else." The reformulation of the question of the role of the "intellectual" was part of the importance which Tronti and others assigned to the shift from formal to real subsumption: "now that capital itself is calling them back into the world of production, they arrive as objective mediators between science and industry: and this is the new form that is being taken by the traditional relationship between intellectuals and the party." He argued, therefore, that it was necessary to refuse to be intellectuals. In posing the question of the shift from formal to real subsumption, the very understanding of cognitive workers as a distinct and managerial strata was, subsequently and in its most interesting aspects, transformed into a question of the forms of exploitation of cognitive work (and immaterial labour).[15]

But if the writings of Paolo Virno, Maurizio Lazzarato, Antonio Negri, and others have focused more recently on the theme of immaterial labour, there is a sense in which the reception of such writings, if not always the analyses themselves, have retained an impression of cognitive work as a privileged site for the recognition—or, perhaps, the very constitution—of a revolutionary subject. Some of this is due to the uninterrupted transfer of political models from Leninism to so-called "autonomist Marxism," in which Leninist organisational forms are deemed to have been adequate for an earlier epoch but not for the present or, at the very least, where the task of analysis is one of discerning the presence of a revolutionary subject. Yet, this is also due to a continuing reluctance to treat cognitive labour *as labour*—that is to say: as labour with its particular forms of exploitation, subjectivation, and command that must, as a question of habit, shape an approach toward other kinds of labour. And here it becomes crucial to restate a critical understanding of the philosophical concept of autonomy given that, in the specific context of cognitive work, autonomy is intimately bound up with exploitation. In other words, it is precisely through a degree of self-management that cognitive labour is mobilised as labour and made available for exploitation.

As Augusto Illuminati warned some time ago, the "movement of the exodus is ambiguously marked by the opposition to dominant ideas and their molecular renewal." The terrain of autonomy might well be "the practical beginnings of communism," but for others it amounts to the "liberalism of the market."[16] In retracing the history of the concept of autonomy from the early writings of Tronti to its more recent appearance in discussions of migration, the very ambivalence of this notion might be emphasised by mentioning another theme prevalent in the early writings of Potere Operaio and Autonomia, that of self-valorisation. Insofar as autonomy means something like "to give oneself one's own law," self-valorisation means "to determine one's own value." There is a deep ambivalence in both the question of law and value. Radical notions of value may well manifest a refusal of the determinations of value *as established* or presently recognised by capital, but it can also exhibit a striving for self-possession. The latter articulation retains distinctly capitalist aspects of valorisation which function as a prelude to— or aspiration of a future—exchange.[17] But they can also indicate a bid for autonomy from the world that is also, in another sense, a kind of enclosure: the attempt to seek a cognitive shelter from the impact, whether troubling or invigorating, of the touch of the world.

The question of the internalisation of law as habit remains to be more fully examined than I can do on this occasion, as this might be illustrated through the relation between the ostensible contractual freedom of the wage and the persistence of slavery, or as this inflects associations between, say, "chainworkers" and "brainworkers," given that the latter are compelled (as Lazzarato would say) to present themselves as subjects and, to a degree at least, self-manage their exploitation.[18] More broadly, it is perhaps not necessary to reiterate here the banality of a cognitive labour, given over to calculation and exchange, which sees in movements not the potential for the world to be otherwise, but the capacity for accruing value, to recall that capitalism remains characterised by expropriation.

The question at this juncture is more precise than this. It is important to consider the extent to which a subaltern analytic adopts the demeanour of "making the invisible visible," of conceding, in other words, to the role of representation that has been regarded as the province of intellectual labour and the gesture of its managerial rank.[19] Here, it becomes apparent that while the concept of autonomy assumed something of the character of a self-sufficient subject in its earlier *Operaisti* manifestations—autonomous *viz* the state and capital—as it has passed through to a discussion of migration it has undergone a significant modification. In other words, the question that has been thereby posed is of the relation to the other, whose difference is irreducible to, even while it is conditioned by, understandings and compositions of the working class, or more broadly of who "we" are and the world is.

Autonomy is not the proposition of a self-sufficient working class but of the discrepancy between a labouring on the sense of the world and the sensory impacts of movements on the world. The autonomy, if you will, of an aleatory materialism from any given representations of it, which is by no means confined to a discussion of struggles against migration controls.[20] Nevertheless, the concept of the autonomy of migration has emphatically posed the question of the association—and breach—between a state-bound definition of movements and their kinetic existence. From that point it marks the space not of an accomplishment, nor a substantive political identity in which the presence of a revolutionary subject might be recognised, but an ongoing tension in which mediation always risks positioning itself as an instance of capture. This is the question that arises for cognitive labour—for research, reading or simply thinking on the sense of the world—each and every time.

Notes

1. "Lenin in England," first published in *Classe Operaia*, January 1964 and republished in *Operai e Capitale*, (Turin: Einaudi, 1966), 89–95, under the heading "A New Style of Political Experiment."
2. "The Strategy of the Refusal." This essay was written in 1965 as part of the "Initial Theses" in Tronti's *Operai e Capitale* (Einaudi: Turin, 1966), 234–252. The whole of *Operai e Capitale* has yet to be translated into English.
3. "What is the Meaning of Autonomy Today? Subjectivation, Social Composition, Refusal of Work." Available at http://info.interactivist.net/print.pl?sid=04/01/16/1733237.
4. Angela Mitropoulos, "Virtual is Preamble: The Movements Against the Enclosures." Available at http://www.makeworlds.org/node/133 (Orig. 1999.) More recently, see the conversation between Manuela Bojadÿzijev, Serhat Karakayalõ and Vassilis Tsianos (Kanak Attak) and Thomas Atzert and Jost Müller (Subtropen) on migration and autonomy, and "Speaking of Autonomy of Migration," available at http://www.kanak-attak.de/ka/text/conver.html and http://www.kanak-attak.de/ka/text/esf04.html, respectively.
5. Merijn Schoenmaker and Eric Krebbers, "Seattle '99, Marriage Party of the Left and the Right?" Available at: http://www.gebladerte.nl/30016v02.htm.
6. See http://antimedia.net/xborder.
7. See Sabine Hesse, "I am not willing to return home at this time." Available at http://www.makeworlds.org/node/19.
8. "The Art of Flight" Interviewer, Stanley Grelet. Available at http://slash.autonomedia.org/article.pl?sid=03/02/07/1350202.
9. Sandro Mezzadra and Brett Neilson, "Né qui, né altrove—Migration, Detention, Desertion: A Dialogue," *Borderlands* 2, no. 1 (2003). Available at http://www.borderlandsejournal.adelaide.edu.au/vol2no1_2003/mezzadra_neilson.html.
10. See Mitropoulos, "The Barbed End of Human Rights." (Orig. 2000). Available at http://www.borderlandsejournal.adelaide.edu.au/vol2no1_2003/mitropoulos_barbed.html.
11. See Giorgio Agamben, *The Open: Man and Animal*, trans. Kevin Attel (Stanford: Stanford University Press, 2004).
12. "Migration, Autonomy, Exploitation: Questions and Contradictions." Available

at http://thistuesday.org/node/91.

13. Maurizio Ricciardi and Fabio Raimondi, "Migrant Labour." Available at http://thistuesday.org/node/72.

14. It is not necessary here to reiterate the managerialist parallels between Fordist production methods and, say, Leninist understandings of the relation between the party (conceived as a gathering of radicalised bourgeois intellectuals) and the masses. Suffice to note that the more interesting question is of the post-Fordist arrangement of this relationship—for instance, Maurizio Lazzarato's discussion of the reorganisation of the relationship between command and autonomy, in "Immaterial Labor," available at http://www.generation-online.org/c/fcimmateriallabour3.htm.

15. See Jason Read, *The Micro-Politics of Capital* (New York: SUNY Press, 2003) for a discussion of formal and real subsumption and some of its implications.

16. A. Illuminati, "Unrepresentable Citizenship" in *Radical Thought in Italy: A Potential Politics,* eds. Paolo Virno and Michael Hardt, (Minnesota: University of Minnesota Press, 1996), 166–85.

17. For a brief discussion of this in relation to the university and the militarisation of the intellect, see B. Neilson and A. Mitropoulos, "Polemos, Universitas" in *Borderlands* 4, no. 1 (2005).

18. For the first, see George Caffentzis; for the second, Mitropoulos, "Precarius?" *Mute* 29 (February 2005). Also, see Barchiesi for an English-language review of Moulier-Boutang's work. Available at http://www.generation-online.org/t/imprisonedbodies.htm.

19. For a longer discussion of the ways in which the task of "making the invisible visible" played itself out in the no-border networks, see Mitropoulos, "The micro-physics of theoretical production and border crossings," *Borderlands* 3, no. 2 (2004). Available at http://www.borderlandsejournal.adelaide.edu.au/vol3no2_2004/mitropoulos_microphysics.htm.

20. See edition of *Multitudes* on aleatory materialism, as well as *Borderlands*, forthcoming.

Fragments on Machinic Intellectuals

Jack Bratich

There is a common complaint leveled at intellectuals today, lobbed from both Left and Right, which says intellectuals are holed up in the ivory tower. They are accused of being either elitist or reformist liberals, out-of-touch Marxists, or armchair activists. In each case, intellectuals are assumed to be isolated from everyday life. Over recent decades, this charge has been thrown by the Left against that all-purpose brand: theory. Charges of obscurantism, jargonism, and armchair strategizing were leveled at "posties" (postmodernists, poststructuralists, postcolonialists), yet this specter of irrelevance obscures a larger trend taking place in the US academy: the growing corporatization of the university.[1] According to Maribel Casas-Cortés and Sebastián Cobarrubias in this volume, the ivory tower itself has a mythic function—erasing the university's immersion in historical processes. The increasing dependence of universities on corporate and federal funding has created a set of interlocking institutions that, if anything, makes intellectual work extremely relevant to and integrated with pragmatic interests. Put simply, we are in an era of *embedded intellectuals*.[2] What can we make of this new condition?

I address this question by evaluating recent tendencies in the academy, especially in the field of communications studies. Using the theoretical lens of autonomist Marxism, I examine intellectual labor, the working of the general intellect, as a means to think through these conditions and offer some conceptual devices for understanding new potentials for radical subjectivity. Given the prominence accorded by autonomists to communication, media, and information technologies in the new landscape of labor, I will highlight the academic disciplines where these processes are being studied and developed. Given the significance of communications both as growing academic field and infrastructure for the general intellect (GI), as well as my own immersion in it, I concentrate on that circuit.

Embedded Intellectuals

Let's begin with a recent public face of the embedded figure: the now almost forgotten practice of embedded journalism. Brainchild of Victoria Clarke, then Assistant Secretary of Defense for Public Affairs, embedded journalism involved integrating reporters into the very machinery of the military (living with troops, going out with them on missions, wearing military gear) during the 2003 invasion of Iraq. While a few journalists wrung their hands in disapproval, mainstream media welcomed this innovation in wartime reporting. This new propaganda involved the state merging with private sector consultants (the Rendon group, Burston-Marstellar, the Bell Pottinger group) and professional journalism to form a nexus that Guy Debord once called "networks of influence, persuasion, and control."[3]

As a mix of publicity and secrecy, this form of journalism recalls another, older definition of embedded. It has a very specific meaning in subliminal psychology research. Embedded refers to the hidden symbols, voices, or messages buried in a text. The word "SEX" in the Ritz cracker or the skull in the ice cubes of a Smirnoff print ad were embedded, according to Wilson Bryan Key (author of those 1970s mass market paperbacks on subliminal seduction in advertising). Even today, if you take a Neuro-Linguistic Programming course or order a subliminal message CD, you too can learn to drop embedded commands into your speech patterns. But this Tony Robbins spectacle of war journalism originally got it backwards: rather than have the signifier disappear into the background (à la the hidden penis in the Camel cigarette pack), the embedded journalists took center stage, making their military handlers vanish and exert hidden influence. Only now, as the very practice of embedded journalism has become normalized, do we see it disappearing as object of scrutiny.

Another definition of embedded comes from electrical engineering and computer architecture, where embedded systems refer to special-purpose microprocessors that reside in other devices (like wristwatches, antilock brakes, microwaves, and cell phones). These are the applications that are producing smart appliances, e.g., refrigerators that will tell you when your milk is spoiled or when you are running low on beer.

Combining these notions of embedded, we can think of journalism as being embedded into an integrated circuit, where it becomes a component of a strategic assemblage of vision machines, programmed info-flows, and material PSYOPS. One does not have to be in a desert to be embedded: it can just as easily occur in the White House briefing room or at one's own news desk. Modifying Baudrillard's assessment of Disney and Watergate, we can say that embedded journalism arose to make us think that the rest of mainstream journalism is not embedded.

From smart appliances to smart bombs to smart news, the ultimate dream here is to have *embedded audiences* who appear to speak freely, without a background of handlers. These would be smart audiences, capable of interacting continuously via cybernetic feedback loops and integrating smoothly in a war/media machine.

But why limit such a rich concept like embeddedness to journalism? As an image of institutions interlocking via their knowledge producers, embeddedness can easily translate to the academic world. We could say that journalists themselves are embedded intellectuals, and by extension embedded intellectuals exist in many fields and disciplines.

The Academy

As mentioned before, there is an increasing tendency for "network university" scholars to be embedded in a host of institutions, policies, and organizations.[4] Among these academic embeds are the following:

1. Funding. Namely, outside grants to study policy issues and corporate strategies.
2. Swinging door relations between university faculty and outside institutions (e.g., corporations, government agencies, public relations firms). Examples include partnership agreements in which corporations fund research budgets in exchange for exclusive access to raw data (and often the right to delay publication, or to review and change manuscripts before publication).
3. Semi-autonomous mechanisms that establish and maintain these links. Examples include lablets, leadership training institutes, entire degree granting units, and industry-university cooperative research centers, even whole industrial parks.
4. Media relations units (linking scholars to media outlets). A double function: It works as PR for the particular university and contributes to a wider circulation of knowledge that shapes public opinion.

University faculty are increasingly interlocking with other institutions. With all of these recent developments, intellectuals are less and less housed solely in the academy. More importantly, intellectual work is not necessarily even being primarily produced in the academy.

Scholars who still wish to link themselves to progressive struggles are finding themselves in a bind. For many, interlocking the institutions of knowledge-power signals a corruption of thought, as it undermines the essential autonomy of research. And there is much to be concerned about here.

Links between academia and other institutions are not open connections. These pathways are highly circumscribed, routed tightly to a range of legitimate (and legitimizing) discourses.

More than that, these interlocks influence the *standard* for scholarly work. In other words, instrumental thought and research is gaining currency. The criteria for what counts as legitimate research is now closely tied to the utility of the results. The *fundability* of research is becoming a standard of judgment (explicitly acknowledged or not), and career advancement (and security) is dependent on the ability of the researcher to obtain external funding.

Take the case of professional associations (e.g., the Modern Language Association, the American Sociological Association, the American History Association): while professional associations have historically functioned as gatekeepers within their respective fields, now they gate-keep between the field and state/corporate institutions. Publishing in association-affiliated journals enhances professional status, especially in contrast to the proliferation of non-association journals (where more experimental and critical work can take place). The invocation of standards in the field has the potential to further marginalize innovative and critical work. It is not that cutting-edge work can't appear in the association-sponsored journals; it often does. But more and more the assumption is that the only innovative work that matters appears in the official organs. This fetishizes the field's own filters, which is by definition a conservative maneuver.

The subtle interlocks above are part of how academic intellectuals are embedded in other institutions. There are much more explicit, long-standing ties worth mentioning. Obviously, large grants are given to the hard sciences by state agencies for weapons development. During the Cold War, scholars were funded, published, and promoted by US clandestine services in order to foster a dominant consensus in fields like political science, sociology, and history. Anthropology has publicly confronted its legacy of studying the Other as a kind of knowledge-gathering to make colonialism and neocolonialism persist. Communication studies has recently begun to outpace these disciplines in terms of funding and administrative expansion. With this in mind, I want to explore the current state of the field, as it crystallizes the new evolution in embedded intellectuals.

Communication Scholars as Embedded Intellectuals

In the Fall of 2005, the National Communication Association (NCA) announced that the keynote speaker for their annual convention would be Judee Burgoon, and her talk titled "Truth, Deception, and Virtual Worlds." Burgoon, it was noted, "has received funding in excess of $6 million from several federal agencies, including the Department of Defense, the

Department of Homeland Security, and intelligence agencies to study human deception, nonverbal communication, and detection technologies."[6] In a time of Terror/War, NCA had selected someone who was actively engaged in research explicitly funded by, and supporting, the state's war machine.[7] The major disciplinary association was making public its declaration that the new research agenda is a solidly statist one.[8]

The history of communication studies is bound up with state and corporate interests. It is no accident that communication studies originated in public universities.[9] Ronald Greene and Darren Hicks have convincingly argued that the field of rhetoric and public speaking was a part of the domestic "civilizing" mission.[10] Fashioning well-spoken and articulate citizens, especially in the early 20th-century rural Midwest and South, was a governing strategy whereby subjects would be trained to become functioning members of the emergent mass society.

In the case of mass communications, the relation to the state is more explicit. Christopher Simpson's *Science of Coercion* details this history, noting that the field of mass communications essentially arose in the aftermath of World War I.[11] Wartime use and study of propaganda needed further development. The upsurge of university mass communications departments in the interwar period became the home for this research, with plenty of federal funding. Armand Mattelart adds to this critical historical analysis by placing communications in the context of cold war social science.[12] The mission of mass communications was to manage the multitudes, developing informational weapons to use against official enemies as well as discipline the US populace. Communications was developed through counterinsurgency analysis, whereby war planners understood the importance of studying guerrilla innovations in information warfare. As late as 1973, the explicit naming of PSYOPS in relation to communication was in effect, evidenced by the collection "Art and Science of Psychological Operations." This US Army pamphlet contains analysis by Pentagon PSYOPS specialists, advertising professors, filmmakers, etc.[13]

This history can be summed up in the social science distinction between administrative research and critical research. The difference refers to a split between Paul Lazarsfeld and Theodor Adorno in the 1930s. As Lazarsfeld defined it, administrative research is "carried through in the service of some kind of administrative agency of public or private character."[14] Whether or not explicitly commissioned by a specific agency the research is instrumentalized within the established parameters of already existing institutions. Critical research sought to question the very foundation and power relations that infused those institutions, connecting them to larger political and economic contexts. This tradition is associated with the Frankfurt School.

Administrative research seeks to make Western institutions run more smoothly while critical research challenges the very legitimacy of those institutions. Even today, communication studies finds itself embedded in this legacy.

This history is important to remember as the field of communication studies is propelled into a conspicuous future. While some disciplines are waning, even disappearing, others are increasing their dominion. The placement of communications PhDs into tenure-track jobs is high compared to other fields within the social sciences and the humanities.

This growth is a double-edged sword. On the one hand, for those in the academy there are new opportunities for a secure future. I encourage grad students that I know in traditional disciplines (e.g., sociology, history, even English) to add media or new information technologies to their projects as a way of expanding their chances of getting an academic position. On the other hand, the quality of the future of the discipline is not heartening. The hard science model is gaining dominance in determining the field's standards. One need only look at the simultaneous growth of telecommunications with the diminution of humanities-oriented communication.

If you ask subscribers to this model why, they'll say it's because it produces the most methodologically rigorous research. But they forget their own legacy in the administrative vs. critical debate. Their scholarship is valued because it produces easily digestible and usable results as administrative research. In other words, the growth of communication studies research is tied to fundable research. Grad students, for example, are not always funded internally by a university; many are expected to get funding by latching onto a faculty member's external grant money. "Growth," then, moves through particularly constrained avenues.

Embedded intellectuals seem to be holding sway in the field of communications. What does this mean for critical and politically inflected communications studies? Should we think of academics as embedded in universities? Is being employed somewhere the same as being embedded? It is certainly the case that the professionalization of research has occurred, and in the US that means being housed in the academy, or, when non-academic, being embedded in think-tanks or public policy institutions.

So what is a potential counter-practice to the embedded intellectual? The independent thinker? This is too individualistic, and would of course confirm the criticisms against the ivory tower intellectual. But the embedded intellectual does not need to be greeted with dystopic surrender. These new conditions create both new intolerables and new potentials: antidotes "can be tracked down only in what for the moment appears to be poison."[15]

I want to argue here that the embedded intellectual is a figure not to be denounced, but *reappropriated*. At first this may seem regressive. But while what most intellectuals are embedded in needs challenging, the very fact of being integrated into social circuits and knowledge-producing networks is a figure that can undergo elaboration and ultimately transmutation.

General Intellect and Communication

The general intellect is extracted from a single reference in Marx's "Fragment on Machines" within the *Grundrisse*. Essentially, it refers to the "general productive forces of the social brain."[17] For Marx, the GI was primarily concretized in machines and technology. It was a scientific, objective capacity. The technological fix here resulted in automation, as well as a socialized network of linkages (transportation and communication). The tradition of autonomist Marxism stressed the subjective side of the GI; namely that it involved above all the capacity of living labor.

GI ultimately addressed not just the classic point of production: it involves educational and cultural components.[18] Analyses moved from strictly economic spheres to the production and reproduction of the social, and the increasing merger of the two. Labor was increasingly becoming intellectualized in terms of: 1) the contents produced (information, symbols, affect); 2) the technologization of industrial forms and most importantly 3) the collaborative informational networks implemented to produce new and old commodities. This last component is most relevant here, as it begins to retool the traditional notion of the intellectual.

Intellectual work is therefore not a specialized erudition: it refers to the most generic aptitudes of the mind. As Paolo Virno puts it, the general intellect is less about the products of thought than the *faculty* of thought. It is this faculty that begins to connect diverse sectors through diffuse language.[19] Thought ceases to be an invisible, private activity and becomes something exterior, "public," as it breaks into the productive process.[20] The general intellect has communication as one of its key characteristics.[21] Immaterial labor, for instance, refers to work composed of the manipulation of symbols and knowledge production, and information transmissions. New information technologies have been indispensable to new configurations of capital. But to this more objective, mechanical side of communications in the GI we need to emphasize the subjective (affective) component.

Within the employ of a corporation, communication has a crucial place. Workers are given a certain amount of creative autonomy and self-direction in their operations, as long as they are directing their freedom toward the corporation's goals: "Participation schemes, wherein workers decide how to accomplish the businesses mission, but, crucially, not what the mission is."[22] Communication within the workplace (and across workplaces) thus becomes key to the socialized labor of GI. With a heavy concentration of capital into marketing, communication also becomes increasingly crucial for the management of social relationships with the consumer as well as within commodity production. Interaction, cooperation, communication: these are the material subjective processes composing networks of production and reproduction today. Communication and information transmission are constitutive of the general intellect.

Academia

Given this description of the general intellect, what is the place/role for the academy? As mentioned above, the intellect does not belong to the realm of the private or the individual. With the traditional intellectual, the ivory tower operated as an attempt at seclusion and segregation. Now, in order to remain viable as an institution, the academy cannot serve as the repository of private intellects. Perhaps no institution is more indicative of the changes in intellectual labor than the university. According to Negri and Lazzarato, "no site could be more vital to capital's harnessing of collective intelligence than academia."[23] As industry becomes more intellectualized, intellectual sites become more *industrialized*.[24] A brief look, then, at how academia operates in the general intellect is in order:

1. Knowledge. The most apparent thing that the academy produces is knowledge. Increasingly knowledge is produced in collaboration with state and corporate institutions. The research is then simultaneously used by those institutions in a varying range of proprietary claims, as well as published in academic journals to maintain its scholarly legitimacy (if not hegemony). In addition, the preferred forms of knowledge (quantitative, instrumental research) are geared towards use by these state and corporate interests. The recent controversies concerning the conversion of academic research into intellectual property is a key flashpoint here. For Dyer-Witheford, the virtual university is a key development in intellectual labor. As a labor-cutting measure, universities have increasingly looked into and developed online courses, even e-degrees. Students don't have to live on campus, or even leave their homes to get a degree. Pretty soon we may be seeing ghost campuses, monuments to an era of spatially socialized education. Among its many results, the virtual university produces a commodification of teaching itself: even non-research-based intellectual activity becomes intellectual property of the university, or of the course-management software companies.

2. Students. Perhaps the main product of universities is a student population trained for the future labor pool. The academy provides the skills needed for a new generation of general intellect. The ability to negotiate the fusion of work and leisure has been a part of the university for some time now. More attention has recently been paid to time-management and study skills (or as my university called their recent massive

overhaul of undergraduate curriculum, "Life and Learning"). These enterprises recognize the need to ensure students are able to juggle various obligations and desires. In addition, educational tools like collaborative projects, using new technologies (online communication, symbolic manipulation), social interaction (with each other in discussions, or with a supervisor), critical-thinking skills, life-long learning, creative problem solving, and independent work are all means of training future immaterial laborers. Even study abroad programs (now seemingly taken over by business schools) are ways of preparing the future global labor force in international social relations.

3. Academics. Finally, there is the question of how academic intellectuals are produced. In addition to communication scholars collaborating with state and private industry, even critical and cultural studies scholars have been encouraged to do so. This typically entails entering the media sphere, either as a public intellectual à la the 1960s New York "men of letters," or updated to TV news and popular culture appearances as "experts." Beyond this intellectual work outside of the university, academic characteristics of the general intellect include: being mobile and flexible (moving around to different positions, being able to teach a wide range of necessary courses) and time-managing work vs. leisure. The pedagogical re-skilling, self-governance, technological upgrading, and collaborative work that comprise academic labor puts them in common with other intellectual laborers.

Perhaps the most pernicious effect of the corporatization of academic subjects is the way its workers, along with many sectors of the labor force, have been *precaritized*. Precarity refers to the conditions of labor in post-Fordism; namely, as part-time or flex-time work, as insecure jobs without benefits, or as being easily replaced. Essentially, precarious labor is at the whim of capital. Within the academy, precariousness accurately describes most of the teaching force at universities. The increasing reliance on graduate student TAs (already a transient population) has put the burden on students to carry the bulk of teaching chores, while their attempts to unionize are blocked by employers. In addition, the swelling pool of adjunct teachers (hired on a course-by-course basis for low wages and given no benefits), often staffed by recently minted PhDs, has added to the multi-tier system of academic labor. Even the more secure faculty, the ones on tenure track, are often so filled with fear at the prospect of not getting tenure that they live in a continual state of anxiety and docility.

With all of these developments, it should be clear that what was once the ivory tower now becomes fully integrated into networks of production and reproduction. Given that the general intellect is so dependent on communication (or as Jodi Dean calls it, "communicative capitalism"), it seems appropriate to return to communication studies here.[27] The many strains of communication studies are relevant here, especially linguistic, techno-logical, organizational, and media. Currently the field is delirious with its own relevance and service to the state/corporate sector. Research on techno-competencies, life-long learning, mobile communications, public relations, and other topics prevail. Even the study of rhetoric plays a role in this field. Ronald W. Greene has powerfully argued that rhetorical studies, rather than continue to act as moral and political exemplar, would benefit from recog-nizing rhetorical agency as a component of living labor crucial to capital-ism.[28] Essentially, communication studies as a research area is making a denser and more self-reflexive web of connections.

Hegemonic communication studies also co-opts critical work for its own purposes. For example, there is much ado now in communication studies about dialogue and interaction. These concepts get defined as being related to freedom, being audience-centered, even being critical. But this two-way is contained within production imperatives. As Lazzarato argues, communi-cation is performed within narrow limits: it is the "relay of codification and decodification, within the context that has been completely normalized by the firm."[29] Instead of freedom, there is a totalitarian exhortation to express oneself, to communicate. A subject becomes a simple relayer of codification and decodification, whose transmitted messages must be "clear and free of ambiguity," within a communications context that has been completely nor-malized by management.[30] Dialogue is cybernetic feedback, as the means to increase productivity and reduce friction. Value within production is increased through more information and communication. Communication studies is poised to be this value-adding discipline.

The gleeful sentiments that fuel this kind of administrative research are as deluded as the corporations they shill for. The giddiness with which interaction and dialogic communication are applied assumes a set of com-municators who are all too eager to be included in the process, to feel like they matter. This hoodwinked approach depends on a deep, mystified work-er loyalty and docility. The cynicism of workers regarding their firm's PR babble is lost on these cheerleaders for global capitalism. The snickering mockery of, and outright hostility towards, corporate reaching out is a much more honest sentiment. Currently relegated to popular culture (*The Office*, for example), these sentiments are where critical communication studies can begin defining itself in an age of the general intellect.

Communicating Otherwise: The Machinic Intellectuals

The refusal of workers to comply with communication imperatives (even work itself) is a disembedding that produces new potentials for the general intellect. According to Virno, the general intellect becomes politicized when it detaches from its capitalist actualization and moves elsewhere: a radical break turning into a union with a political community.[31] For Virno, this new alliance of intellect/political action means civil disobedience and exodus. The GI defects in an autonomous withdrawal based on wealth: the exuberant and self-valorizing productive capacities of living labor.[32] What is needed is a circuit that moves as a "dramatic, autonomous, and affirmative expression of this surplus."[33] What are the potentials for intellectuals in interlocking with struggles and antagonisms, in producing new common bodies that refuse subordination to capital and seek out autonomous destinies?

What could this mean for academics and communication scholars? Given the conditions of the GI, the logical choice would be to become the general intellectual. However, this term might end up being too confusing and vague. In common parlance, "general" has associations with abstraction, transcendence, the ahistorical, isolation, and comprehensiveness. It also carries the connotations of a representative (think here of the "general will"). For these reasons we need a different figure for the general intellect.

Academia, as a site that embodies both the GI and its potential subversion, offers a possibility: not a representative, but *one intellectual circuit among many*. Circuit should be explained here: a circuit provides a path for electrical current to flow. In telecommunications, a circuit is a specific path between two or more points along which signals can be carried. Many believe the digital revolution was birthed from the invention of the *integrated circuit*, which essentially connects semiconductor devices. The valuable characteristics of the IC are its dense connections in a small space (chip), its reliability, fast switching speeds, low power consumption, mass production capability, and the ease with which it adds complexity. A circuit can be dedicated or application-specific, but can also be part of an emergent structure (a circuit of circuits, or network). For those who find this emphasis on circuitry too technophilic, let's remember that the properties of these circuits and networks have been found in bios as well, from brains to ant colonies.

This emphasis on circuitry should remind us of the opening discussion about embedded intellectuals. The academic's role in providing the factory of immaterial laborers and in developing new knowledges, skills, and competencies define its specificity in this general circuitry. Academics now can be reconfigured as embedded, but no longer within already existing institutions. A circuit, routing a flow-conduction, can just as easily be in an emergent network that *withdraws* from these institutions. To embed with an exodus and with antagonisms: how is this embedded intellectual possible?

Given the circumstances detailed above, I propose thinking of the embedded intellectual as a *machinic intellectual* (MI). This would dispel the romantic and overly humanistic notion of Gramsci's organic intellectual. It would also acknowledge the role of technology in the general intellect.

Unlike the passive connotations of "embedded," machinic has an active and productive sense. The Machinic Intellectual also does not represent: it is not an external synthesizing mechanism determining the true interests of a people. Rather it is more of an immanent translator, an *exchanger* as Foucault puts it, and attractor.[34] Keeping with the circuitry concept, we could also add: conductor, amplifier, resistor, insulator, capacitor, incapacitor, integrator, modulator, even *circuit breaker*. Finally, drawing from Guattari and Deleuze, machinic has an affective component that addresses the role of desire and transversals. Collectives are produced "not through representation but through affective contamination."[35]

According to Negri and Lazzarato, there are new conditions for relations between dissenting academics and oppositional social movements.[36] Academics get paid to think, analyze, teach, research, and write. The various disciplines each have their particular abilities and skills to offer: historians can give needed background on events, political philosophers can locate the nuanced arguments for various political projects, sociologists come equipped with detailed knowledge of social processes. Given their conditions of mobility and interconnectivity, academics are also in good position to form what Nicholas Dyer-Witheford calls "networks of counter-research and pools of shared experience."[37] One possible means is to think of academics as *conceptual technicians*. At least for the theoretically inclined machinic intellectuals, tinkering with concepts can open up new relations and imaginings.

Having the time and resource-access to fine-tune and develop concepts puts MIs in a position of communicating transversals. As David Graeber puts it, academics provide conceptual tools, "not as prescriptions, but as contributions, possibilities—as gifts."[38] For Guattari this means "intellectuals and artists have nothing to teach anyone…they produce toolkits composed of concepts, percepts, and affects, which diverse publics will use at their convenience."[39]

Once again, given media and communication's special role in the GI, the work of academics in this field should also be highlighted. The annual Union for Democratic Communications conference attempts to aggregate Leftist communication studies folks. More recently the Media Reform conferences sponsored by Free Press have brought together academics, activists, and media producers to collaboratively work on the major obstacles facing media justice. Supporting the radical components within professional conferences is an obvious strategy. Beyond the academy, there are also conferences like Allied Media, and various one-off grassroots and Indymedia-oriented gatherings that communications scholars can attend.

Faculty can conduct research on various streams of alternative communication culture and Indymedia, ranging from the topics chosen to the theoretical frameworks employed in communications studies (see Ronald

Greene, Nick Dyer-Witheford, Mark Cote, Alison Hearn, Ron Day, Enda Brophy, Stephen Kline, and Greig de Peuter).[40] Even critical communication studies is often fixated on the operations of dominant communications from corporate media consolidation to mainstream journalism's ideological machinations. While it is important to have evidence of how hegemony works, it is easy to fall victim to the seductive idea of how powerful these institutions are. Why not disembed from this symbolic dependency and re-embed with molecular communications and micro-media? A circuit of exit would involve breaking from the central concepts and assumptions about what counts as critical work.

Attending a variety of conferences and speaking to graduate students, one finds that the next generation of media scholars is tuning in to new political and social potentials (and not always relying on theory). Post-Seattle, a new crop of communications PhD students have emerged, with research projects involving independent and micro-media, virtual and cellular resistance, contestational robotics, network-centric activism, technologized collectives, and other experiments in the contemporary activist laboratory. These are not naïve technophiles seeking a cover shot on *Wired* magazine: they are apprentices in resistance-metallurgy, testing amalgams, doing trial runs on compounds, probing new syntheses, and assaying the results and potentials. To ignore (or worse yet, to misrecognize) these emergent networks of scholars-activists in favor of command centers, agenda-setting leaders, and recognizable institutions is akin to boarding up the exit door.

Communication scholars can be the media by writing for independent papers or producing alternative cultural products. More importantly, communication MI's can lend whatever skills and resources they have to media activism groups. As Jonathan Sterne argues, leftist scholars should perform academic pro bono work like other professions.[41] This would mean listening to the needs of activists, and offering services to concrete struggles. With these initial steps which are already occurring, we can see forming a "network of researchers engaged in the participatory study of emergent forms of struggle."[42]

And these new scholarly projects are not the only theoretical experimenters. This rich tapestry of activist research includes the drift-work of the 3 Cups Counter-Cartographies Collective at the University of North Carolina-Chapel Hill (see Casas-Cortés and Cobarrubias in this volume), and the research militancy projects of Colectivo Situaciones, Precarias a la Deriva, and Bureau d'études/Université Tangente. Maybe these innovators are in contact with some good theory translators, but maybe they just aren't relying so much on intermediaries. The future of critical media studies seems to be populated with machinic intellectuals who are already collaborating with nonacademic machinic intellectuals. Together, they are producing new circuits of exit.

Conclusion

The point here is that MI does not belong to the academy, but academics are a type of MI. The academic MI is an *interface*, embedded as a specific intellectual in its professional and disciplinarian skirmishes which themselves are now embedded in a larger circuit. These larger circuits are mostly state and corporate systems, but could also be lines of flight and circuits of exit. The academics, recognizing their positions as embedded intellectuals, must ask which to enhance and which to diminish: as machinic intellectuals, which circuits will they assist in immanentizing? When these circuits of escape and exuberant production coalesce, new historical subjects are not far behind. This subject's destiny is generated elsewhere, but the future of academy is bound to it.

The machinic intellectual as described here is admittedly optimistic, even too smooth. There are obviously bumps and short-circuits at work that hamper radical possibilities. Some involve external blockages, including reactionary counter-dissent on campuses that have taken the form of a crackdown on Left professors. Internally, the precariousness of academic labor detailed earlier can prevent transversals, as can the standardization of knowledge around instrumental research. Finally, there are still ivory tower-like effects where the machinic intellectual becomes more absorbed by the rewards and punishments of the academy proper, ultimately withdrawing into its sectoral demands. In other words, machinic intellectuals don't always work smoothly, but this is no reason to eliminate their potential, or worse yet, to retreat to the comfortable numbness of the tried and true paths. As an open source conceptual figure, the machinic intellectual needs collaborative retooling. As an experiment, the concept may even fail, but this would simply mean devising new ones!

In a world of symbolic and affective labor, machinic intellectuals become less a model than an experimental prototype. Regardless of their origins, machinic intellectuals produce relations and at the same time are seized by them. A kind of strange attractor, you might say—not visible as center or causal force, but nonetheless effective in gathering and distributing other forces. If this is still too self-important, we can abandon our own strangeness as attractors and become one of the forces drawn to a strange attractor we cannot even name yet.

Notes

1.   See Henry Giroux, *Impure Acts: The Practical Politics of Cultural Studies* (New York: Routledge, 2000); Jennifer Washburn, *University, Inc.: The*

Corporate Corruption of Higher Education (New York: Basic Books, 2005); Henry Giroux and Kostas Myrsiades, eds., *Beyond the Corporate University: Culture and Pedagogy in the New Millennium* (Boulder, CO: Rowman & Littlefield, 2001); Stanley Aronowitz, *The Knowledge Factory* (Boston: Beacon Press, 2000); Michael Gibbons, Camille Limoges, Helga Nowotny, Simon Schwartzman, Peter Scott, Martin Trow, *The New Production of Knowledge: The Dynamics of Science and Research in Contemporary Societies* (London: Sage, 1994); Robert Ovetz, "Turning Resistance into Rebellion: Student Movements and the Entrepreneurialization of the Universities," in *Capital and Class* 58 (1996), 113–152; Alan Liu, *The Laws of Cool: Knowledge Work and the Culture of Information*, (Chicago: University Chicago Press, 2004).

2.   The term is taken from "Empire's Embedded Intellectuals," a speech given by Professor Hatem Bazian of UC Berkeley in early 2005. He refers mainly to explicit academic supporters of US imperialism (like Samuel Huntington, Bernard Lewis, and Alan Dershowitz). As I retool it, it involves the very condition of being in the academy nowadays, regardless of one's direct ideological support. For a report on Bazian's speech, see http://amperspective. com/html/empire_s_embedded-i_.html.

3.   Guy Debord, *Comments on the Society of the Spectacle* (London: Verso, 1998).

4.   John Pruett and Nick Schwellenbach, "The Rise of the Network Universities: Higher Education in the Knowledge Economy." Available at http://www.ut-watch.org. Paper presented at the Education, Participation, and Globalization Conference, Prague 2004. The most succinct summary of the effects of this can be found in Jennifer Washburn's article "University Inc.: 10 Things you Should Know about Corporate Corruption on Campus." Available at http://www.campusprogress.org.

5.   See Frances Stonor Saunders, *The Cultural Cold War: The CIA and the World of Arts and Letters* (New York: New Press, 1999); Christopher Simpson, *Science of Coercion: Communication Research and Psychological Warfare 1945–1960* (New York: Oxford University Press, 1994); Christopher Simpson, ed., *Universities and Empire: Money and Politics in the Social Sciences During the Cold War* (New York: The New Press, 1998); Robin W. Winks, *Cloak and Gown: Scholars in the Secret War, 1939–1961* (New York: William Morrow, 1987).

6.   NCA is the major professional organization for US academic communication researchers, with convention attendance of approximately 5,000. Its choice of speaker (as for many conferences) indicates an exemplar in the field. From the NCA website: http://www.natcom.org.

7.   In addition, in my own School of Communication, Library, and Information Studies, Homeland Security Initiative money was regularly available, and faculty members were encouraged to apply for it. A former colleague of

mine received millions of dollars to develop digital deception detection technology. Also, the original poster on the cultstud listserv revealed that his department received large grants to monitor the effects of military recruitment games on players. A whole study is hopefully in the works right now that traces these funding sources and their impact on the communications field.

8.   The nonchalance of announcing this part of her research agenda caused a brief but intense controversy on the premiere listserv for international cultural studies. Message posted by Dr. Jeremy S. Packer, from the Dept. of Communications at Penn State University. ([cultstud-l] NCA and "Homeland Security?" June 7, 2005.) Within NCA, Critical/Cultural Studies is among the most popular divisions, with the fastest growing membership.

9.   While plenty of private schools have communications programs now, it was originally the provenance of major public universities. Even today the top programs are in the Big 10, while the Ivy Leagues are grumblingly beginning to even acknowledge communications as a scholarly pursuit.

10.   R.W. Greene and D. Hicks, "Lost Convictions: Debating Both Sides and the Ethical Self-Fashioning of Liberal Citizens," *Cultural Studies* 19.1 (January 2005), 100–126.

11.   Simpson, *Science of Coercion.*

12.   Armand Mattelart, *Mapping World Communication: War Progress Culture,* trans. Susan Emanuel and James Cohen (Minneapolis: University of Minnesota Press, 1994).

13.   This U.S. Army pamphlet (a two-volume, 1100-page hardbound set) contains analysis by Pentagon PSYOPS specialists, advertisers, political scientists, sociologists, theater professors, and filmmakers. *Art and Science of Psychological Operations.* United States Army Pamphlet, 1973.

14.   Paul Lazarsfeld, "Remarks on Administrative and Critical Communications Research," in *Studies in Philosophy and Social Science* 9 (1941), 2–16.

15.   Paolo Virno, *A Grammar of the Multitude* (Los Angeles, CA: Semiotext(e), 2004), 84.

16.   Critics have argued that the attempt to found entirely new historical analyses and materialist theories out of such a marginal moment is making mountains out of molehills. However, this "overproduction" is itself an autonomist performance, I would argue. The ability to elaborate and create new horizons with limited resources is an interpretive *vis viva*, demonstrating the abundant wealth that results from collaborative capacities.

17.   Cited in Nicholas Dyer-Witheford, *Cyber-Marx: Cycles and Circuits of Struggle in High Technology Capitalism* (Urbana: University of Illinois Press, 1999), 220.

18.   Dyer-Witheford, *Cyber-Marx,* 222.

19.   Virno, *A Grammar of the Multitude,* 108.

20.   Ibid., 64.

21.   Dyer-Witheford, *Cyber-Marx,* 227.

22. Chris Carlsson, "The Shape of Truth to Come," in *Resisting the Virtual Life*, eds. James Brook & Iain Boal (San Francisco: City Lights, 1995), 242; cited in Dyer-Witheford, *Cyber-Marx*, 228.

23. Dyer-Witheford, *Cyber-Marx*, 233.

24. This is not to say GI is universal, even within the university. Contrary to the typical notion that academic work is a disembodied endeavor, the bodies of academics matter (as one of my professors astutely observed, every academic gets a signature ailment). Universities also do not run without the symbolic and manual labor of its staff (from administrative assistants to maintenance operations).

25. Dyer-Witheford, *Cyber-Marx*, 233–235.

26. Interestingly, the annual *Renewing the Anarchist Tradition* conference takes place at such a ghost campus in Vermont. Having shifted much of their curriculum online, the campus is deserted except for a skeletal service staff. If these ghost campuses become home to swarms of radical conferences, then maybe this effect of GI isn't so bad!

27. Jodi Dean, "The Networked Empire: Communicative Capitalism and the Hope for Politics," in *Empire's New Clothes: Reading Hardt and Negri*, eds. Paul Passavant and Jodi Dean (New York: Routledge, 2004), 265–88.

28. Ronald Walter Greene, "Rhetoric and Capitalism: Rhetorical Agency as Communicative Labor," in *Philosophy and Rhetoric* 37, no. 3 (2004), 188–206.

29. Maurizio Lazzarato, "General Intellect: Towards an Inquiry into Immaterial Labour," in *Immaterial Labour: Mass Intellectuality, New Constitution, Post Fordism, and All That* (London: Red Notes, 1994), 1–14; cited in Dyer-Witheford, *Cyber-Marx*, 224.

30. Maurizio Lazzarato, "Immaterial Labor," in *Radical Thought in Italy: A Potential Politics*, eds. Paolo Virno and Michael Hardt (Minneapolis, MN: University of Minnesota Press), 133–147.

31. Virno, *A Grammar of the Multitude*, 68.

32. Ibid., 70.

33. Ibid., 71.

34. Michel Foucault, "Truth and Power," in *Power/Knowledge*, ed. C. Gordon (New York: Pantheon, 1980), 109–133.

35. Felix Guattari, *Chaosmosis* (Bloomington, IN: Indiana University Press, 1995), 92.

36. Dyer-Witheford, *Cyber-Marx*, 234.

37. Ibid., 227.

38. David Graeber, *Fragments of an Anarchist Anthropology* (Chicago, IL: Prickly Paradigm Press, 2004).

39. Felix Guattari, *Chaosmosis*, 129.

40. And this is just limited to the North American context. For a more global autonomist perspective on communications and media, see the work of

Bifo, Tiziana Terranova (*Network Culture: Politics and the Information Age* [London: Pluto Books, 2004]), Brian Holmes, and many of the researchers associated with Nettime (including the recent special issue of *Fibreculture* called *Multitudes, Creative Organisation and the Precarious Condition of New Media Labour.* Available at http://journal.fibreculture.org/issue5/index. html).

41. Jonathan Sterne, "Academic Pro Bono" in *Cultural Studies <=> Critical Methodologies* 4, no. 2 (2004), 219, 222.

42. Dyer-Witheford, *Cyber-Marx*, 233.

Reinventing Technology: Artificial Intelligence from the Top of a Sycamore Tree

Harry Halpin

I am a researcher in artificial intelligence and I live in a tree. To be more precise, a tree-sit where a motley band of poets, primitivists, hippies, and anarchists are making a last stand to save a beautiful Caledonian glen from being bulldozed to make yet another road. This is paradoxical: artificial intelligence (AI) seems diametrically opposed to the natural intelligence embodied by living ecosystems; it is the ultimate technologizing project. Technology seems to be the principal means by which global capitalism enslaves and encloses the world, regarding it as one giant standing reserve to be used to fuel its endless drive for ever more production. I find this paradox strange, but one does not learn by running away from paradoxes. Modern calculus came from a careful inspection of Zeno's paradox, and classical anarchism itself came from the seemingly paradoxical (at least to bourgeois ears) statement that "Property is theft." History has proven time and again that paradoxes are interesting places to begin. So here I am sitting on a branch high up in the tree that I am defending, contemplating the place of technology, and a question that is at the heart of the global justice movement. How do we use the master's tools—the computers and all other technology—to bring down the master's house, without sacrificing what we are trying to save in the process? To answer this, we should listen to both the silence of the sycamore and the nearly invisible buzz of our computers.

Just as in some readings of Marxism, capital itself inflicts suffering upon labor, for many latter-day anarchists, it seems that technology inherently opposes life, crushing nature in its terrifying gears. Yet, as countless hackers and activist websites have shown, technology is often used for distinctly revolutionary ends. From my tiny platform in one of Scotland's last remaining forests, technology seems not so far away. On the horizon, I can literally see the creeping concrete wasteland of an industrial estate. If I strain my ears, I can hear the infernal rumblings of hundreds of automobiles on a motorway that is just barely out of sight, if not out of mind. This motorway is going to be expanded. This expansion will involve the destruction of this little forest, and the beautiful, twisting sycamore I am sitting on will be cut down. It is almost enough to make one nauseous. I buckle up my harness and slide down the rope for a long hard day of chopping wood and programming computers.

The scene changes. Now I am in a cramped basement, a veritable hacker's delight, filled to the brim with half-functioning and nearly dead computers. This is the literal remains of the Indymedia Centre set up in Edinburgh to serve as the communications hub of the 2005 G8 summit mobilization. As one of the co-founders of Scotland Indymedia, I was astounded to see the ethereal Indymedia network materialize in my adopted hometown of Edinburgh, where it had formerly existed primarily as a website and scattered film showings. The abandoned church above the art café suddenly hosted hundreds of anarchists and other assorted radicals from across the world, busily checking their email, uploading pictures, editing video, and otherwise radically reappropriating technology. One cannot help but think how crucial technology is to the global justice movement. As I sit in this little basement that holds the computers left behind, a fellow resident of my tree-sit is busy designing a website for us. His eyes are fearsomely focused as he adds a picture of our triumphant little treehouse to Google Maps. A young Greek anarchist is busy moderating the listserv she established to help coordinate resistance to the G8 in Edinburgh. She's fighting off the spammers who threaten to turn our local communications hub into a cesspool of ads for better erections through chemicals. I get distracted by helping an elderly Scottish man make sure he's properly saved his hours of typing up photocopied UFO reports onto his diskette. He takes the Zapatista call for an Intergalactic very seriously. Who am I to argue that the G8 were not covering up the existence of aliens? I'm sure both the protesters and the capitalists appeared to be aliens to many of the Scottish people who wondered why the entire world suddenly focused its struggles here. As the bytes frenetically trace their electronic paths through cyberspace, carried by the GNU/Linux software designed through voluntary association by hackers determined to preserve my freedom, I can only wonder—what a weird world we live in. My earlier trepidation over the technological plague seems strangely naïve.

Beyond the Technological Image of Humanity

Artificial intelligence is itself the product of astounding naïveté. The essence of artificial intelligence is that the intelligence of humans, natural intelligence, can be replicated by a machine. In its stronger form, "The computer is not merely a tool in the study of the mind, rather the appropriately programmed computer really is a mind" (Searle 1980: 421). In AI's earliest formulation, researchers believed there was a limited, though large (perhaps numbering in the millions), number of building blocks of knowledge that constitute human intelligence (Lenat and Feigenbaum 1987). With help from a logical inference engine and a million commonsense facts encoded as logical propositions, we could create intelligence. This is a case of logical positivism taken to ridiculous proportions. If everything must be expressed in logic, "that of which one cannot speak, one must pass over in silence," and this leaves out most of the world (Wittgenstein 1961: 3).

Twenty years of research into the nature of intelligence have shown the picture drawn by classical AI to be dead wrong. The original Cartesian image of intelligence as rational deliberation far removed from engagement with the material world is a myth of the Enlightenment. Almost all the classic binary divisions that our culture teaches us have been proven wrong—not through clever application of critical theory, but through careful attention to scientific experiments on everything from reaction times to neuroscience. Emotion influences and guides our decisions (Damasio 1994). There is no mythical central executive that stands at the top of the hierarchy in the brain; instead, the brain's neurons are a decentralized network that produces behavior through coordination (Andres 2003). The mind relies not on perfect representation and deductive logic but on a series of shortcuts and heuristics based on exploiting the body and the environment (Clark 1997). Language is not a poor substitute for logic: logic is a poor substitute for the flexibility and analogical power of natural language whose very heart is poetic metaphor (Lakoff and Johnson 1999). We should not think of ourselves as rational disembodied intelligences, but as radically engaged with our world in all sorts of powerful but far from orderly ways. This view of humanity goes directly against modern neoliberalism, which pretends we all have access to perfect information and are perfectly rational.

At the same time this "philosophy of the flesh" misses the point: artificial intelligence was never really about humans, but is rather a celebration of computers: exploring and stretching their limits and demonstrating their possibilities (Bolter 1984: 206). The argument is that computers are not intelligent because they do not possess the characteristics of a human living through their five senses. Merleau-Ponty's concept of an "optimal grip" on the world is also dead wrong (Dreyfus 1972). Computers simply have a different grip on the world and are as physically embodied as humans. It should come as no surprise that computers, being constituted of transistors and plastic, and communicating with the world primarily through whatever we humans type into them, have little chance at being qualified as intelligent in the same way that humans are intelligent. All sorts of intelligent tasks are done easily by computers: they fly airplanes, play chess, make music, and search unprecedented volumes of text. We still don't really trust them with the full range of things humans do, such as taking care of children. Yet we trust them implicitly to help extend our capabilities. The most pertinent example is email, with which computers extend our ability to communicate. And this capability expands with texting, voice calls over the Internet, and more. It appears increasingly that humans are in love with digitizing our communication. And why not? Unlike snail mail, and the spoken word that slips into oblivion the moment we utter it, computers allow our communication to conquer time and space, providing communication at the speed of light. Increasingly, through the use of digital photos, blogs and music, we now trust computers with our vast collective memory. From Scotland Indymedia, to text-mobs at the Republican National Convention in 2004, to endless activist email listservs, we have shown ourselves equally if not more capable of using these digital networks of communication.

The All-too-Human Roots of Technology

So computers aren't special, and as the examples par excellence of technology aren't the replacement for humanity that Marx envisioned, supplanting "living labor with dead labor, replacing the variable capital of human workers with the fixed capital of machinery" (Dyer-Witheford 2000: 179). Computers highlight some of our characteristics, and compensate for some weaknesses. Computers are social corrections for our lack of a perfect memory, for the finite reach of our voice, for the limitations of our abilities to calculate and deduce. As Marshall McLuhan noticed, we extend ourselves through various artifacts. This is not a uniquely human characteristic. Tuna propel themselves by taking advantage of miniature eddies in currents. Very intelligently, tuna then re-create these eddies in order to make themselves swim faster (Triantafyllou et al 1995). In humans, this behavior is endemic. In order to lend precision to our ability to count things, our ancestors manipulated piles of pebbles, then made notches on sticks, and after millennia, created modern mathematics that reached its logical conclusion in the creation of computers (Logan 2000). Now when we need to calculate, we just press a few buttons. While some may lament the loss of the ability of humans to do large calculations in their heads, others may view this as liberatory; after all, now we can do other and possibly more interesting things with our memory. Whenever humans run into a limitation, we seem more than willing to create the solution ourselves in some artifact. Contrary to Zerzan, language and, by extension, communicative technology is a way of relaying exactly that which is difficult to communicate with mere gestures and pointing, and technology is inherently the most human of endeavors (Zerzan 1994). The general failure of Artificial Intelligence to create human intelligence should remind us to pay attention to the radical conclusion that humans manifest intelligence through the control and manipulation of their immediate physical environment, and this manifests itself in the creation of technology like computers (Clark 2003). Artificial intelligence got it backwards: all intelligence is artificial.

Technology For and Against Global Justice

The musings I had this morning in my tree do not leave me. We need to press deeper concerning our relationship with technology for "we shall never experience our relationship to the essence of technology so long as we merely conceive and push forward the technological, put up with it, or evade it" (Heidegger 1977: 4). The world around us has been shaped by generations of humans altering their physical environment. What has this left us with? With rising temperatures due to CO_2 emissions that are melting glaciers, and the rapid decomposition of the remaining rain forests, we may have literally destroyed these life support systems. Despite Bell's prophecies that the new postindustrial economy would somehow lift us from the grime and dirt of industrial production, this wild fantasy is simply not true (Bell 1973). As I learned in my days as a sweatshop protester in college, the world of seemingly abstract bytes is profoundly embodied in the extraction of copper, silicon, and other raw materials from the earth, and these demand a heavy toll in ecological and social devastation. The disposal of computers is an environmental nightmare as they are simply toxic to the core (Kuehr and Williams 2003). And, at the same time, with the inevitable depletion of oil reserves, new computers and parts for repairing existing computers will be unavailable, leading to social crisis in this computer-dependent world.

Technology can escape its bounds and be used to seize control of someone else's physical environment against their will. From the worker forced to assemble microchips in a factory to the programmer forced to program banking databases, everyone can be caught in the dehumanizing power of technology. We are part of an automatic system of machinery "consisting of numerous mechanical and intellectual organs, so that the workers themselves are cast merely as its conscious linkages" (Marx 1973: 692). Technology can be seen as a reified thing-in-itself, an external and dominating force that cruelly shapes humanity in its image. For every well-paid, white, male, white-collar computer programmer given free coffee and the ability to pop into the office whenever he pleases, there are hordes of mass workers from the global south employed in menial jobs assembling computer components under Taylorist sweatshop conditions. Where is the technological freedom to create and control the physical environment for the majority of the world's population, who seem ever more at the mercy of tyrannical capitalist forces beyond their control? For all the liberatory uses of computers to help organize demonstrations and provide knowledge, we cannot forget that their origins lie in computing ballistic missile trajectories. Even the toiling masses are slowly using technology. "Communication is to the socialized worker what the wage relationship was to the mass worker" of a generation ago (Negri 1989: 118), and the former are constantly subverting capitalism's use of computers for their own ends. Does this outweigh the fact that computers are the electronic nervous system of global capital, allowing stocks to be transferred at the speed of light, and directing missiles to murderously enforce its regime? Without computers, there might not be a global justice movement. Nor would there be all-encompassing capitalist globalization.

For the global justice movement, the Internet is the prime example of a decentralized network, which both embodies (even if ambivalently), and facilitates the new, primarily network-based forms of organization. It is not by chance that one of the most important international networks to emerge from the anti-globalization struggles is the Indymedia network, which exists almost exclusively as websites, and communicates primarily through digital means. One has the feeling that the use of networks as forms of organization and the rampant use of technology to communicate struggle in the global justice movement is only the tip of the iceberg. In one touching example provided by Arun Mehta, poor farmers in India write their questions to be searched on the Internet on postcards that are mailed to local radio stations. The local radio station then finds someone who speaks English and the local Indian language to search the Internet, translate the answer, and broadcast it over the radio. A simple, handheld radio receiver is the one piece of technology even the poor in India have access to. It is unclear what will happen once the excluded masses gain full access to global communications, but one could imagine that the first thing on their minds will be changing the global system that keeps them at the bottom. However, this technological eschatology does not bode well with my tree. Would it redeem technology if widespread computer usage did somehow end global capitalism? Yet what other hope do we have? Nineteenth century revolutionaries, from Kropotkin to Marx, did not clearly foresee two crucial things: the coming ecological collapse that may very well destroy any revolutionary social movement by destroying humanity itself, and the information technology that would allow unprecedented speed in the formation and coordination of revolutionary social movements.

The Ecology of Technology

Returning in the evening to the tree-sit, I see the dying light reflected off of her branches and I'm snapped out of my computational reverie. How blind I have been! The tree-sit has no computers. It doesn't even have electricity, and water has to be gathered by midnight missions to taps because industrial farm-waste and general pollution has rendered the waters that run through the tree-sit undrinkable. All around me I see the direct physical shaping of the environment. The houses that are set high off the ground with nothing but rope and some clever knots. A greywater system allows water to be disposed of and everything from food waste to human shit is composted. There are plans afoot to build a garden outside the woodlands in a nearby industrial wasteland. Everywhere in this tree-sit that exists to defend wild nature, there are signs of technology. Every activist might have a better chance of understanding the question of technology by looking away from computers to small-scale, low-tech, and sustainable forms of technology that exemplify, even more clearly than computers, humans seizing control of their own environment. Permaculture in general is a good example of this (Mollison 1997). It involves not only taking control of the environment, but working with it, not as stewards but as equals. It is the mundane and everyday use of technology, such as helping replant a forest that in twenty years time will produce enough fruit to feed a community, that may point the way to the meaning of technology and the possibilities therein.

This is not to put an inseparable gulf between computers and my tree-sit. Both the alluring glow of the computer screen and the simple act of lighting a fire are fundamentally technological. Both are the extension of one's ability to shape one's environment, not to conquer it but to establish some mutually beneficial way of interacting. Outside the digital Web, there is a worldwide web of plants, dirt, and bacteria that we are all part of. The digital Web is an outgrowth of this real world and not a replacement for it. When contemplating the Scotland Indymedia Centre, this small revolutionary node in the vast Internet, one is taken aback by the complexity of the global task in front of us. The global justice movement needs a space to communicate among and connect resistance movements. For this task carrier pigeons simply won't do: only computers have the ability to allow the global anticapitalist movement to connect and coordinate. Yet to save this precious little glen in Scotland, a different type of technology is needed: that of tree-sits, lock-ons, walkways. All the computers in the world are useless here without a stable source of electricity and global communication comes to nothing if there are no humans willing to put their bodies on the line between the bulldozers and these trees. And these people need a place to live far up in the branches of the tree, ways to get in and out of trees using harnesses and ropes, and ways to keep warm. Like all good uses of technology, the solution fits the problem at hand.

Technology For a World Worth Fighting For

Any technology worth fighting for is not just a choice between Coke and Pepsi, but the ability to create options that suit and improve not only your own environment, but all living things in it. We need technology that is both accessible and cheap, like tree-houses built out of locally available waste. Technology that is expensive and complex must be available to those who would otherwise be excluded, like the open computer access the Scotland Indymedia Centre allows. It will be difficult to tell the differences between, and long-term repercussions of, technologies and how they shape our character and reflect our values. We activists need to develop a discerning eye.

We must all be technologists, finding what computer jargon calls hacks: elegant and clever ways of solving our problems employing the materials at hand. And as much as technology affects our character, what computation requires—practical problem-solving and learning to deal with finite resources—is also what we need to confront the problems of global justice and ecological collapse (Bolter 1984).

I have never liked the saying "another world is possible." Another world is possible, but this world is ours. For all its beauty and horror, we must take this world seriously. It is this world that is worth fighting for. The original technologists were alchemists, and we latter-day alchemists, radical technologists of all backgrounds, must somehow overcome the ancient split between mind and matter, the world and humanity, and return a sense of wonder to this world. As I walk down the hill at night back towards the tree-sit, I hear the strange sounds of accordions and flutes drift towards me from the campfire in the distance. It is as if I have stepped into some enchanted world beyond the enclosures of capital, a tender shoot of the deep rhizomes of the global justice movements. Our task as theorists is to remind ourselves to wonder and puzzle over the subtle connections that are the hearts of these networks. As activists, we must fight to preserve these networks and expand them. As technologists, we have to provide solutions that respect the very human and ecological origins of these networks. To finally succeed in this task on a global level, we have to tear down artificial divisions between technology, action, and theory. In this way, we can heal the division between humanity and the wide world around us. Technology is no more neutral than we ourselves are neutral to the struggles of our day. As for the increasing number of technologists that are joining the struggle for global justice, the purpose of technology becomes clear at last: the re-enchantment of everyday life.

References

Andres Posada, "Frontal Cortex as the Central Executive of Working Memory: Time to Revise Our View," in *Cortex* 39, no. 4–5 (2003), 871–95.
Daniel Bell, *The Coming of Post-Industrial Society* (New York: Basic Books, 1973).

David Bolter, *Turing's Man: Western Culture in the Computer Age* (Chapel Hill, NC: University of Chapel Hill Press, 1984).

Andy Clark, *Being There: Putting Brain, Body and World Together Again* (Cambridge, MA: The MIT Press, 1997).

Andy Clark, *Natural-Born Cyborgs* (Oxford, UK: Oxford University Press, 2003).

Antonio Damasio, *Descartes' Error: Emotion, Reason, and the Human Brain* (New York: Avon Books, 1994).

Hubert Dreyfus, *What Computers Can't Do: A Critique of Artificial Reason* (New York: Harper and Row, 1972).

Nick Dyer-Witheford, *Cyber-Marx: Cycles and Circuits of Struggle in High Technology Capitalism* (Chicago: University of Illinois Press, 2000).

Martin Heidegger, *The Question Concerning Technology and Other Essays*, trans. William Lovitt (New York: Harper and Row, 1982).

Ruediger Kuehr and Eric Williams, eds., *Computers and the Environment: Understanding and Managing Their Impacts* (Boston: Kluwer Academic Publishers, 2003).

George Lakoff and Mark Johnson, *Philosophy In The Flesh: the Embodied Mind and Its Challenge to Western Thought* (New York: Basic Books, 1999).

Douglas Lenat and Edward Feigenbaum, "On the Thresholds of Knowledge," in *Proceedings of the International Joint Conference on Artificial Intelligence, 1987, Vol. 2*, 1173–1182.

Robert Logan, *The Sixth Language* (Toronto: Stoddart Publishing, 2000).

Karl Marx, *Grundrisse: Foundations of a Critique of Political Economy* (Harmondsworth, England: Penguin, 1973).

Bill Mollison, *Permaculture: A Designers' Manual* (Tyalgum, NSW: Tagari, 1997).

Antonio Negri, *The Politics of Subversion: A Manifesto for the 21st Century* (Cambridge, UK: Polity Press, 1989).

John Searle, "Minds, Brains, and Programs," *Behavioral and Brain Sciences* 3, (1980), 417–424.

Richard Stallman, *Free Software, Free Society* (Cambridge, MA: GNU Press, 2002).

M Triantafyllou and G Triantafyllou, "An Efficient Swimming Machine," *Scientific American* 272, no. 3 (1995), 64–72.

Ludwig Wittgenstein, *Tractatus Logico-Philosophicus* (London: Routledge & Kegan Paul, 1961).

John Zerzan, *Future Primitive and Other Essays* (Brooklyn, NY: Autonomedia, 1994).

Practicing Militant Ethnography with the Movement for Global Resistance in Barcelona

Jeffrey S. Juris

Since the first Global Days of Action against capitalism—including protests against the World Trade Organization summit meetings in Seattle on November 30, 1999—anti-corporate globalization movements have staged highly spectacular, mass direct actions against multilateral institutions, while generating innovative network-based organizational forms.[1] Activists have made particularly effective use of new digital technologies to communicate and coordinate at a distance, while grassroots media projects such as Indymedia have provided forums for creating and circulating alternative news and information. Indeed, contemporary anti-corporate globalization movements are uniquely self-reflexive, as activists produce and distribute their own analyses and reflections through global communications networks. Such practices break down the divide between participant and observer, constituting a significant challenge to traditional academic approaches to the study of social movements.

In what follows, I outline militant ethnography as an alternative research method and political praxis based on my experience as an activist and researcher with the Movement for Global Resistance (MRG) in Barcelona. What is the relationship between ethnography and political action? How can we make our work relevant to those with whom we study? Militant ethnography involves a politically engaged and collaborative form of participant observation carried out from within rather than outside grassroots movements. Classic objectivist paradigms fail to grasp the concrete logic of activist practice, leading to accounts and models that are not only inadequate, but are of little use to activists themselves. As activists increasingly generate and circulate their own analyses, the classic role of the organic intellectual is undermined.

Militant ethnography seeks to overcome the divide between research and practice. Rather than generating sweeping strategic and/or political directives, collaboratively produced ethnographic knowledge aims to facilitate ongoing activist (self-)reflection regarding movement goals, tactics, strategies, and organizational forms. At the same time, there is often a marked contradiction between the moment of research and the moments of writing, publishing, and distribution (Routledge 1996). The horizontal networking logics associated with anti-corporate globalization movements contradict the institutional logic of academia itself (cf. Juris 2004). Militant ethnographers thus have to constantly negotiate such dilemmas, while moving back and forth among different sites of writing, teaching, and research.

Grasping the Logic of Activist Practice

In his discussion of Bourdieu's reflexive sociology, Loïc Wacquant identifies the "intellectual bias," or how our position as an outside observer "entices us to construe the world as a spectacle, as a set of significations to be interpreted rather than as concrete problems to be solved practically" (1992: 39). This tendency to position oneself at a distance and treat social life as an object to decode, rather than entering into the flow and rhythm of ongoing social interaction, hinders our ability to understand social practice. As Bourdieu himself suggests:

> The anthropologist's particular relation to the object of his study contains the makings of a theoretical distortion inasmuch as his situation as an observer, excluded from the real play of social activities by the fact that he has no place...inclines him to a hermeneutic representation of practices (1977: 1).

Militant ethnography addresses these objectivist shortcomings. In order to grasp the concrete logic generating specific practices, researchers have to become active practitioners. With respect to social movements, this means helping to organize actions and workshops, facilitating meetings, weighing in during strategic and tactical debates, staking out political positions, and putting ones' body on the line during mass direct actions. Simply taking on the role of "circumstantial activist," as George Marcus (1995) puts it, is not sufficient. One has to build long-term relationships of mutual commitment and trust, become entangled with complex relations of power, and live the emotions associated with direct action organizing and activist networking. Such politically engaged ethnographic practice not only allows researchers to remain active political subjects, it also generates better interpretations and analyses. In her study of everyday violence in a poor shantytown in northeastern Brazil, Nancy Scheper-Hughes describes how she was coaxed into political organizing by her Bahian informants:

> The more my companhieras gently but firmly pulled me away from the "private" world of the wretched huts of the shantytown, where I felt most comfortable, and toward the "public" world of the Municipio of Bom Jesus da Mata, into the marketplace, the mayor's office and the judge's chambers, the police station and the public morgue, the mills and the rural union meetings, the more my understandings of the community were enriched and theoretical horizons were expanded (1995: 411).

Scheper-Hughes refers to such ethically grounded and politically committed research as militant anthropology, which captures the active and engaged style of ethnographic practice outlined here. She subsequently calls for a barefoot anthropology which involves a kind of witnessing, differing from active struggle *together* with the women of Bom Jesus she describes in the passage above. I thus refer to ethnographic research that is both politically engaged and collaborative in nature as militant ethnography.

This broader emphasis on ethnography transcends the exclusive realm of anthropology. Militant ethnography is relevant for a variety of disciplines and in many ways corresponds to methods practiced by activists themselves. Militant ethnography generates practical, embodied understanding. Indeed, mass direct actions generate extremely intense emotions involving alternating sensations of tension, anxiety, fear, terror, collective solidarity, expectation, celebration, and joy. In this sense, the militant ethnographer also uses her body as a concrete research tool (cf. Parr 2001).

Two Tales from the Field

My research explores the cultural practice and politics of transnational networking among anti-corporate globalization activists in Barcelona. I am particularly interested in how transnational networks like Peoples Global Action (PGA) or the World Social Forum (WSF) are constructed and how activists perform these networks through embodied praxis during mass actions. Specifically, I conducted participant observation with the international working group of the Movement for Global Resistance in Barcelona, a broad network involving militant squatters, Zapatista supporters, anti-debt campaigners, and radical ecologists.[2] I participated in mobilizations in Barcelona, Genoa, Brussels, Madrid, and Seville, and I had previously taken part in mass actions in Seattle, Los Angeles, and Prague.[3] Moreover, given that MRG was a co-convener of PGA in Europe and many activists were involved in the social forum process, I helped organize PGA and WSF-related events in Barcelona, Leiden, and Porto Alegre. By practicing militant ethnography, I aim to enhance our understanding of how social movement networks operate, thus helping activists build more effective and sustainable networks. The next section provides two concrete ethnographic examples.

Next Stop: Genoa!

At the end of a July 1 march against police brutality in Barcelona, a Milanese activist from the Tute Bianche took the microphone and announced the coming siege of the G8 summit. After describing the Genoa Social Forum and the pact that had been made with the city, he enthusiastically called on all Catalan and Spanish activists to make the trip, exclaiming in the spirit of the singer Manu Chao, "Next Stop: Genoa!" Ten days later, my friends and I were discussing our police evasion strategy on a regional train we had hopped through southern France. As we pulled into Genoa, the Italian police were out patrolling in force. Although we had done nothing wrong, our hearts began to pound. The paranoid feeling of being under constant surveillance would remain with us during our entire time in Italy. We spent our first few days sleeping in a squatted social center in the hills on the outskirts of town, where we met up with many PGA-inspired activists. Ricardo, a well-known solidarity activist and squatter was frustrated about how difficult it had been to coordinate with the Genoa Social Forum (GSF), the main body planning the protests in Genoa. He was extremely eager to fill us in and elicit more support for building a radical international contingent.

Ricardo was particularly troubled by the fact that the GSF had refused to create channels of communication with militant anarchists due to the Forum's strict "non-violence" stance. The dominant political forces within the GSF—Tute Bianche, NGOs, ATTAC, radical labor unions, and *Refundazione Comunista*—were characterized by autonomous Marxist, socialist, and social-democratic perspectives, and the use of strictly non-violent tactics. On the other hand, the guiding political ethos among decentralized grassroots networks like PGA or MRG is broadly anarchist, in the sense of horizontal networking and coordination among diverse autonomous groups. This networking logic also holds for the question of violence versus non-violence, where a diversity of tactical positions generally prevails. For radicals like Ricardo, even those who refuse to engage in violent tactics, it is important to establish dialogue with all groups regardless of the tactics they choose. The GSF's strict non-violent stance and unwillingness to communicate with groups outside their direct action guidelines was perceived by many grassroots anticapitalists as a major obstacle.

Over the next week, I became deeply embroiled in the complex discussions, debates, and negotiations that ultimately led to the creation of the

Pink & Silver bloc for the main action days, building on our experiences in Prague. Not only did we have to generate consensus regarding the wisdom of joining the militant squatters, whether self-defense constituted an acceptable response to police provocation and the specific protest route to follow, we also had to negotiate with the GSF and other international networks in order to carve out sufficient space within a crowded action terrain involving aggressive Tute Bianche, militant black bloc, festive pink bloc, and traditional Ghandian non-violent tactics.

There is insufficient time here for a full ethnographic account of the space of terror that subsequently emerged in Genoa (cf. Juris 2005a). Rather, I want to simply point out that it was only by becoming deeply involved in the direct action planning process, which at times meant positioning myself at the center of extremely intense and sometimes personal debates, that I could fully appreciate the complexity and logic of direct action planning and the accompanying fear, passion, and exhilaration. It was only through engaged participation that I began to realize how diverse activist networks physically express their contrasting political visions and identities through alternative forms of direct action. Tactical debates were thus about much more than logistical coordination: they embodied the broader cultural politics that are a crucial aspect of activist networking and movement building. Learning how to better negotiate such tactical differences can help activists build sustainable networks more generally.

At the same time, the overwhelming campaign of low-level terror unleashed by the Italian state also points to some of the potential limitations of the "diversity of tactics" logic. If, rather than dividing and conquering, the state pursues an indiscriminate strategy of physical repression, it becomes impossible to safely divide up the urban terrain. In particular contexts it makes sense to actively dissuade other activists from using militant tactics. However, blanket condemnations of protest "violence," including widely circulated statements by Susan George after Gothenburg and Genoa are not likely to produce the desired effect, as they violate the basic networking logic at the heart of contemporary anti-corporate globalization movements.[4] It is only through dialogue, and immanent critique based on solidarity and respect that such contentious issues can be resolved. At its best, militant ethnography can thus provide a mechanism for shedding light on contemporary networking logics and politics while also making effective interventions into ongoing activist debates.

Subverting the WSF International Council

Beyond mass direct actions, militant ethnography can also help activists negotiate more sustained forms of movement building, including the social forum process. First conceived as a singular event providing a space for reflection and debate regarding alternatives to neoliberal globalization,[5] the WSF has since morphed into a sustained process involving forums at local, regional, and global levels.[6] After three years in Porto Alegre, the WSF was held in Mumbai in 2004 before moving back to Porto Alegre the following year. Most recently, the 2006 WSF was "polycentric," held at three remote sites in Latin America, Asia, and North Africa.

The International Council (IC) was created shortly after the initial Forum in January 2001 to oversee the global expansion of the process. However, the relationship among the Brazilian Organizing Committee (OC), other local committees, and the IC has been somewhat contentious. In addition to the distribution of power and authority among these decision-making bodies, there has also been an ongoing debate about the nature of the process itself. Although the WSF Charter of Principles specifically defines the Forum as an open meeting space, others view it, at least potentially, as a political organization (cf. Patomäki and Teivainen 2004, Sen 2004, Whitaker 2004).[7] Such conflicts are rendered particularly visible during periodic IC gatherings, including the April 2002 meeting in Barcelona, where I was an active participant as a member of MRG's international working group (cf. Juris 2005b).

Shortly before the Barcelona meeting we learned that MRG had been invited to become a permanent member of the IC—most likely due to our reputation as an exemplar of an emerging mode of activism involving confrontational direct action and network-based forms. This unleashed a heated debate within MRG and among grassroots networks in Barcelona. How could a diffuse network with no formal membership, many of whose participants are deeply opposed to the Forum, participate in such a highly institutional representative structure? After a long discussion during an open assembly of social movements in Barcelona, MRG decided to offer its official delegate status to the larger assembly, including its right to speak during the IC meeting. Although MRG would ultimately refuse the Council's invitation to become a permanent member, radicals would at least have an opportunity to make their voices heard within the very heart of the Forum process.

This is where my own role in the meeting became more complicated. I was enthusiastic about attending the IC meeting not only as a delegate from MRG, but also as an ethnographer specifically studying transnational networking practices. The Barcelona IC meeting was a perfect opportunity to examine these processes first-hand. Although I initially wanted to simply observe, allowing others to intervene, I was quickly drawn into a more active role. The assembly of social movements had agreed to issue a statement during the meeting criticizing the IC for its vertical structure and lack of internal democracy. Since I spoke English and Spanish fluently, I was given the task of helping to draft and then present the declaration. So much for my role as neutral observer! By inserting myself into the flow and rhythm of such a contentious debate, I learned a great deal more about the social forum process than I otherwise would have.

The meeting agenda included the relationship between the WSF and the broader anti-corporate globalization movement, future challenges, regional social forums, methodology and architecture, and internal IC process. Throughout the three-day gathering, delegates debated critical issues such as whether the IC should continue to play a logistical and coordinating role or provide more active strategic and/or political direction. The autonomy of the local forums also generated significant disagreement, pitting those who wanted more central control against others who viewed the WSF as a kind of trademark, though freely available to anyone inspired by the Forum model and its ideals. It was only when I read the MRG declaration that I truly began to understand the diversity of positions represented within the IC, and what it actually felt like to be at the center of such hotly contested debates.

As soon as the session opened about internal procedures, delegates immediately brought up the issue of democracy and openness within the Council. Sensing that the right moment had finally arrived, I raised my hand, and after several long interventions, read the MRG declaration, which included the following text:

> We would like to thank the Council for the membership invitation, although we are not sure how it happened. MRG is part of a new political culture involving network-based organizational forms, direct democracy, open participation, and direct action. A top-down process, involving a closed, non-transparent, non-democratic, and highly institutional central committee will never attract collectives and networks searching for a new way of doing politics. This should be a space of participation, not representation.

Although we had expected to receive an extremely hostile response several delegates supported our contention. One member of the Brazilian OC tersely responded, "We have to clarify who wants to be a member, and who does not!" However, others were more receptive; as an important figure within the European forum process stressed, "We really have to figure out a way to include this new political culture despite their unique organizational form." Although he missed the point that our "new political culture" is specifically expressed—at least in part—through our innovative organizational forms and practices, he was generally supportive.[8] Perhaps not so incidentally the inaugural edition of the European Social Forum, ultimately held in Florence the following November, would be organized through an open assembly of social movements rather than a member-based organizational committee. Although our critique certainly ruffled a few feathers, we had more allies than originally anticipated.

Many radicals in Barcelona and elsewhere had assumed the IC and broader forum social process is dominated exclusively by reformists and Marxists. Although I suspected the reality was more nuanced, it was only after my active participation in the Barcelona IC meeting that I fully appreciated the complex internal dynamics *within* the Council. This understanding not only helped me conceive transnational networking as shaped by an intense cultural politics (cf. Juris 2005c), it also influenced my participation in subsequent debates about whether grassroots radicals should take part in the forum process more generally. My experience suggested that rather than boycott the forums, it perhaps made more sense to actively work together with those elements who shared our more libertarian goals and visions.

Specifying Militant Ethnography

Militant ethnography thus not only generates compelling analyses, it can also help inform concrete strategies and decision-making. If ethnographic methods driven by political commitment and guided by a theory of practice break down the distinction between researcher and activist during the moment of fieldwork, the same cannot be said for the moments of writing and distribution, where one has to confront vastly different systems of standards, awards, selection, and stylistic criteria. As Paul Routledge (1996) has suggested:

> When it comes to researching resistance, there has traditionally been what de Certeau (1984: 24–25) refers to as a gap between the time of solidarity and the time of writing. The former is marked by docility and gratitude toward one's hosts, while the latter reveals the institutional affiliations, and the intellectual, professional, and financial profit for which this hospitality is objectively the means (1996: 402).

A brief anecdote from my own experience illustrates some of the issues involved. In January 2004, my former MRG-based colleagues organized a conference in Barcelona to explore the theory and practice of activist research. The idea was to create an open space for reflection and debate among activists, those conducting research from within, and for social movements and others involved with self-managed political projects. During one session, a British activist mounted a harsh attack on academics studying movements from the outside. He was somewhat appeased when we explained we were using engaged methods, but he remained skeptical about how the research would be used, pointing out that, "You go back to the university and use collectively produced knowledge to earn your degrees and gain academic prestige. What's in it for the rest of us?"

For the militant ethnographer, the issue is not so much the kind of knowledge produced, which is always practically engaged and collaborative, but rather, how is it presented, for which audience, and where is it distributed? These questions go to the very heart of the alternative network-based cultural logics and political forms that more radical anti-corporate globalization activists are generating and putting into practice. Addressing them doesn't just respond to the issue of ethical responsibility toward one's informants, colleagues and friends, it also sheds light on the nature of contemporary movements themselves.

Part of the issue has to do with how we understand the nature of the intellectual. Barker and Cox (2002) have recently explored differences between academic and movement theorizing, criticizing traditional theories *about* rather than *for* movements. They explain the differences in terms of the distinction between "academic" and "movement" intellectuals corresponding to Gramsci's "traditional" and "organic" varieties: the former operate according to the interests of dominant classes, while the latter emerge from within and work on behalf of subaltern groups. However, not only does this distinction break down in practice, beyond that, it seems to me the relationship between activists and intellectuals within contemporary social movements is far more complex. When nearly everyone engages in theorizing, self-publishing, and instant distribution through global communication networks, the traditional function of the organic intellectual—providing strategic analysis and political direction—is undermined. In this sense, militant ethnography does not offer programmatic directives about what activists should or should not do. Rather, by providing critically engaged and theoretically informed analyses generated through collective practice, militant ethnography can provide tools for ongoing activist (self-)reflection and decision-making.

Several anthropologists have recently proposed strategies for making ethnography useful for activists that can be incorporated into a broader praxis for militant ethnography. Working with US-based, anti-corporate globalization activists, David Graeber has similarly noted the embattled position of the traditional vanguard intellectual, positing ethnography as an alternative, which would involve "teasing out the tacit logic or principles underlying certain forms of radical practice, and then, not only offering the analysis back to those communities, but using them to formulate new visions" (2004: 335). In this register, ethnography becomes a tool for collective reflection about activist practice and emerging utopian imaginaries.

Julia Paley (2001) enacts another kind of critically engaged ethnography working with urban community groups in Chile to analyze power relations and political processes that shape and constrain their strategic options at particular historical junctures. In this mode, ethnography becomes a tool for collective analysis about the outside world. In his study of gender, race, religion, and grassroots Afro-Brazilian movements, John Burdick (1998) suggests that ethnography can help movements represent themselves in order to understand the social and cultural heterogeneity within them. Militant ethnography can thus help activists carry out their own ethnographic research.

For Burdick, this means supporting movements in their efforts to reach out to a broader public. But it might also suggest working with activists to help them analyze different movement sectors, understand how they operate, their goals and visions, and how they can most effectively work together. In my own case I spent hours talking to MRG-based colleagues about diverse movement sectors in Barcelona and elsewhere, and how they might best coordinate. We held similar conversations about regional and global networking processes. In this sense, transnational activist networking always already involves a form of militant ethnography, while militant ethnography among contemporary local/global movements necessarily requires the practice of transnational networking.

In sum, militant ethnography involves at least three interrelated modes: 1) collective reflection and visioning about movement practices, logics, and emerging cultural and political models; 2) collective analysis of broader social processes and power relations that affect strategic and tactical decision-making; and 3) collective ethnographic reflection about diverse movement networks, how they interact, and how they might better relate to broader constituencies. Each of these levels involves engaged, practice-based, and politically committed research that is carried out in horizontal collaboration with social movements. Resulting accounts involve particular interpretations of events, produced with the practical and theoretical tools at the ethnographer's disposal and offered back to activists, scholars, and others for further reflection and debate.

The question remains as to the most appropriate context for practicing militant ethnography and how to distribute the results. One obvious place is the academy, which despite increasing corporate influence and institutional constraints, continues to offer a critical space for collective discussion, learning, and debate. As Scheper-Hughes (1995) suggests, those of us within the academy can use academic writing and publishing as a form of resistance, working within the system to generate alternative, politically engaged accounts. As Routledge suggests, there are no "pure" or "authentic" sites, as academia and activism both "constitute fluid fields of social action that are interwoven with other activity spaces." Routledge thus posits an alternative third space "where neither site, role, nor representation holds sway, where one continually subverts the other" (1996: 400). The more utopian alternative is suggested by the rise of multiple networks of autonomous research collectives and free university projects, including the activist research conference cited above, or the radical theory forums recently held during regional and world social forums. By exploring emerging cultural logics, networking activities, and utopian political imaginaries within contemporary anti-corporate globalization movements, militant ethnography can thus contribute to both academic and activist spheres.

Notes

1. The Seattle Protest was actually the third Global Day of Action inspired by the Peoples Global Action (PGA) network. The first took place on May 16, 1998, in conjunction with the G8 Summit in Birmingham and just two days before the WTO Ministerial in Geneva. The second was held on June 18, 1999, against major financial and business centers around the world during the G8 Summit in Cologne. Actions were carried out in more than 40 countries, including a 10,000 person strong "Carnival Against Capitalism" organized by Reclaim the Streets in London.

2. I refer to "anti-corporate globalization movements" in the plural to emphasize that activists do not oppose globalization per se but rather those forms of economic globalization that benefit transnational corporations, while recognizing the diversity of movement actors. Alternatively, many activists speak of the global justice or alternative globalization movements. However, these formulations are rarely used in Barcelona, the site of my own research. (Juris 2005).

3. MRG was founded during the mobilization against the World Bank and International Monetary Fund meetings in Prague in September 2000. The network ultimately dissolved itself in January 2003 in response to declining participation and as a broader political statement against the reproduction of rigid structures.

4. Barcelona-based research carried out from June 2001 to September 2002 was supported by a Dissertation Field Research Grant from the Wenner-Gren Foundation for Anthropological Research, Inc., and a Dissertation Field Research Fellowship from the Social Science Research Council with Andrew W. Mellon Foundation funding.

5. For example, see comments by Susan George regarding protest violence in Gothenburg ("I was at Gothenburg") and Genoa ("G8: Are You Happy?"). Archived at http://attac.org and http://www.corpwatch.org respectively.

6. Oded Grajew and Francisco Whitaker, two Brazilian civil society leaders initially proposed the World Social Forum idea to Bernard Cassen, President of ATTAC-France and Director of the *Le Monde Diplomatique*, in February 2000. The WSF would specifically coincide with the annual World Economic Forum (WEF) Summit in Davos.

7. The Charter defines the Forum as "an open meeting place for reflective thinking, democratic debate of ideas, formulation of proposals, free exchange of experiences, and interlinking for effective action." The WSF Charter of

Principles can be viewed at http://www.forumsocialmundial.org.br.

8. As I have argued elsewhere (cf. Juris 2005a/b), broader cultural ideals and political imaginaries are increasingly inscribed directly into emerging organizational architectures.

References

Colin Barker and Laurence Cox, "What Have the Romans Ever Done For Us?" Available at http://www.iol.ie/~mazzoldi/toolsforchange/afpp/afpp8.html.

Pierre Bourdieu, *Outline of a Theory of Practice* (Cambridge: Cambridge University Press, 1997).

John Burdick, *Blessed Anastacia* (New York: Routledge, 1998).

Michel De Certeau, *The Practice of Everyday Life* (Berkeley: University of California Press, 1984).

David Graeber, "The Twilight of Vanguardism" in *Challenging Empires*, eds. Jai Sen et al (New Delhi: The Viveka Foundation, 2004).

Ira Jacknis, "Margaret Mead and Gregory Bateson in Bali," in *Cultural Anthropology* 3, no. 2 (1988).

Jeffrey S. Juris, "The New Digital Media and Activist Networking within Anti-Corporate Globalization Movements," *The Annals of the American Academy of Political and Social Science* 597, no. 1, (2005), 189–208.

Jeffrey S. Juris, "Social Forums and their Margins: Networking Logics and the Cultural Politics of Autonomous Space," *ephemera: theory & politics in organization* 5, no. 2 (2005b), 253–272. Available at http://www.ephemeraweb.org.

Jeffrey S. Juris, "Networked Social Movements: Global Movements for Global Justice," in *The Network Society: a Cross-Cultural Perspective*, Manuel Castells (London: Edward Elgar, 2004a).

Jeffrey S. Juris, *Digital Age Activism: Anti-Corporate Globalization and the Cultural Politics of Transnational Networking*, PhD Dissertation, (Berkeley: University of California, 2004b).

George E. Marcus, "Ethnography In/Of The World System," in *Annual Review of Anthropology* 24, (1995), 95–117.

Julia Paley, *Marketing Democracy* (Berkeley: University of California Press, 2001).

Hestor Parr, "Feeling, Reading, and Making Bodies in Space," in *The Geographical Review* 91, no. 1–2 (2001), 158–167.

Heikki Patomäki and Teivo Teivainen, "The World Social Forum: An Open Space or a Movement of Movements?" in *Theory, Culture, and Society* 21, no. 6 (2004), 145–154.

Paul Routledge, "Critical Geopolitics and Terrains of Resistance," in *Political Geography* 15, no. 6/7 (1996), 509–531.

Nancy Scheper-Hughes, "The Primacy of the Ethical," in *Current Anthropology* 36, no. 3 (1995), 409–420.

Jai Sen, "How Open? The Forum as Logo, the Forum as Religion: Skepticism of the Intellect, Optimism of the Will," in *Challenging Empires*.

Loïc J.D. Wacquant, "Toward a Social Praxeology: the Structure and Logic of Bourdieu's Sociology," in *An Invitation to Reflexive Sociology*, eds. Pierre Bourdieu and Loïc J.D. Wacquant (Chicago: University of Chicago Press, 1992).

Francisco Whitaker, "The WSF as an Open Space," in *Challenging Empires*.

:: Communities of/in Resistance ::

:: Communities of/in Resistance ::

> We must believe that it is the darkest before the dawn of a beautiful
> new world. We will see it when we believe it. —Saul Alinsky

Between circulating moments of rupture, through circuits and cycles of
struggle, we find the processes through which communities are formed in
resistance. By confronting and overcoming exploitation and oppression,
new affective bonds and solidarities grow, turning collections of people who
occupy the same physical space or time into arrangements united in understanding their position and how it can be overcome. Whether building and
reclaiming new forms of commons through the planting of food or demand-
ing that housing be a right for one and all, common demands and victories
create new forms of common experience and connection generated through
and by resistance.

Based on struggles that do not make demands upon the state, the tactics
and politics of direct action are important in these experiences. Solutions
for common problems are found without recourse to state intercession; action is founded upon the notion that the authority of the state is illegitimate.
Direct action becomes a strategy and tactic that is not just about attaining
particular goals, but about the process through which this happens. It is not
just about putting our bodies on the line to oppose any number of question-
able financial institutions or state structures (as important as that might be),
but also about finding solutions to problems through common struggle and
creativity.

The formation of communities of/in resistance is about being open to
the possibility that opportunities often come from unexpected tactics and
places. New social bonds can be woven while crafting resistance in front of
a chain-link fence or in the warmth of a shared meal. It can be grown in a
community garden or over coffee shared during a boycott. Far from exclud-
ing people who are not able to participate, direct action is not so much about
the particular tactics used, as it is about the strategies that are based upon the
common social wealth of human capacities found within our communities.
This wealth does not need the state to exist: it simply does. Moving between
providing resources that people need to survive and the campaigns to secure
them, collectively reclaiming the materials of life is both a form of political
action and shared joy.

Eating in Public

Gaye Chan + Nandita Sharma

Part 1: Autumn

In November of 2003, we planted twenty papaya seedlings on public land near our house in Kailua, Hawai'i. In doing so, we broke the existing state laws that delineate this space as "public" and thereby set the terms for its use. Our act had two major purposes: one was to grow and share food; the other was to problematize the concept of "public" within public space.

Our questioning of public space may at first glance seem odd, perhaps even reckless. Many progressives see the defense of all things public as a necessary response to neoliberal assaults on state-funded spaces and services. The maintenance of resources as "public" is seen as working against processes of privatization. These sentiments are based upon two assumptions: that public space is the antithesis of private property, and that the existence of public space represents a victory of the people over nefarious special interests. The concept of the "public" is a corollary of nationalist ideologies of state power that legitimate and sustain unjust social relationships, particularly those organized through private property rights. The liberal-democratic national state is camouflaged as a political apparatus, indeed *the* political apparatus, designed specifically to serve "the people." The legitimacy of modern state power within liberal democracies, such as those of Canada and the United States, is widely regarded as being derived from popular, public consent. The "public" is touted as holding the power to revoke this legitimacy through their votes or their participation in the state's daily operations. The idea that the national state exists because of the will of "the people" conflates the existence of the national state with the actions of political rulers/administrators of the moment and promotes the assumption that all have equal access or say in making decisions. It also obfuscates how the historic formation of national states is rooted in the struggle over land, labor, and life—a struggle *lost* by those who fought against capitalism and for common, rather than private or state (i.e. "public") property. The conflation of the state and "public will" conceals that the "public" is never the sum of all those who are born, live, work, and die in any given space, but is limited to members of an always gendered and racialized discourse of citizenry.

Historically, the creation of "public" spaces came at the expense of "commonly" owned property, and alongside efforts to annihilate multifaceted, broad social movements mobilized to protect a communal way of organizing life in spaces simultaneously local and global. Contrary to contemporary popular belief, common land was not only reorganized as "private" property, but also as "public" space. Nascent national states expropriated common lands as *their* newfound property. The violent enclosure of common lands preceded the formation of both the national state and global capitalist markets for labor and for trade. Everywhere, public spaces that had been known as the commons, were converted into sites of either private/capitalist or public/state power. Thus, while public land is said to exist as the goodly opposite to the theft that is private property, the two different ways of relating to space are actually mutually constitutive.

Private property laws legislated by national states secure the personal investments of those with capital. Public property serves a host of purposes (although it too is often used as a resource-rich haven for capitalists). Perhaps most importantly, property owned by the public serves the *ideological* purpose of assuaging people who otherwise are exploited and oppressed into believing that the territorial nation state is indeed *theirs*—even as it is the main regulatory mechanism for ensuring the rights of private property owners.

To this day, public land use is narrowly defined by the state within the confines of leisure activities, such as soccer, picnicking, admiring the view, walking a dog, and being edified by the display of commissioned artworks. In this way, the public comes to be understood as the group that *already* has access to private property where they can conduct all the other activities that life demands: sleeping, working, having sex, growing food. All those things that are banned from public space. For those without private homes or reliable access to food, or for those performing activities prohibited in public, "public space" becomes a zone of criminality. Like us, the planters of prohibited papaya seedlings, all such trespassers can be charged with being a nuisance to the public, thereby eradicating them from this supposedly all-encompassing category and making them legitimate targets for coercive state force.

In planting the papaya seedlings, we invoked the name of another group who were maligned simultaneously as insignificant *and* as a massive threat to the security of the public: the Diggers.

The first Diggers organized in the seventeenth century, in one part of the space reorganized as England during this time. Their movement rose in defense of the commons' that were being systematically destroyed by the violent land reforms, privatizations, and thefts characteristic of the formative period of industrial capitalism and the consolidation of European colonialism. We see our planting of papayas in public space as a continuation of their struggle. By making many of the same points, we are trying to recall and revamp their methods of resistance. Common land belonged in perpetuity to the community as a whole. Self-sustenance was dependent on the ability of people *to common* (i.e., to hunt, graze, forage, fish, and farm). *Commoning* was well understood as the only way of life in which people could remain free from complete bondage. The Diggers knew that the continued existence of the commons was vital to the independence of individuals and collectivities from the arbitrary demands of rulers. The retention of lands as a commons was equally essential to their freedom from hunger and desperation. The liberatory politics of the Diggers thus integrated a politics of eating. The Diggers came together to fight against the expropriation and transformation of their common lands into either parcels of private property or into the public property of the nascent national state. The Diggers and their allies (the Levellers, the Ranters, the urban rioters, the rural commoners, the fishers, market women, weavers, and many others) waged a battle that was about the preservation and maintenance of a communal life. The Diggers therefore raged against the drive to entrap displaced people as either slave or wage labour in the factories, or on the plantations and ships of the emerging nascent capitalist system.

The Diggers movement organized itself on behalf of *all* people—not only one subsection of an increasingly parceled portion of humanity. They seemed subtly aware that during the early seventeenth century, the nascent idea of what was "European" was integrally related to the ongoing appropriation and parceling of land characteristic of colonization. The Diggers were thus equally concerned with the dispossessed of "Europe" as they were with the diverse people of Africa, Asia, and the Americas being dispossessed and enslaved through colonial expansion. Theirs was neither a prototypical version of Eurocentric universalism, nor simply charitable humanitarianism. Instead, the movement articulated the radical call for self-determination for all people, and the recognition of their increasingly global interconnections. The Diggers were as much opposed to the project of making "Europe" as were those who would be colonized by it in the centuries to come.

One of the signature actions of the Diggers was to sow the ground with edible seedlings, such as parsnips, carrots, and beans. A simple gesture, no doubt, but their goal was no less than global justice, freedom for all, and the self-sufficiency of all producers. By planting on land previously stolen from commoners, the Diggers gave notice that the battle over what kind of property laws would prevail was far from over. In taking direct action to reclaim their stolen land, the Diggers came up against some of the most powerful forces in society at the time: merchants, lesser gentry, and early industrialists. These groups were eager to overturn the existing ruling structure and bring about their new world order.

The new elites backed the leaders of the emerging parliamentary movement against the King. Led by Oliver Cromwell and his militant Puritans, the aim of the parliamentarians was to create a liberal democratic state with the respectable citizen-worker as its national subject. The new parliamentary democracy created the conditions of "national" security and the rule of law much desired by the ascendant bourgeoisie.

The Diggers, and their attempt to repossess the commons, were seen as a threat to the new Parliament. The new Council of State belittled the Diggers as "ridiculous," yet it declared: "that conflux of people may be a beginning whence things of a greater and more dangerous consequence may grow." Unsurprisingly, one of the first actions taken by the new English parliament was the military suppression of the Diggers. Under the command of the new parliamentarians, soldiers destroyed the Diggers' spades, trampled the crops they had carefully planted and tended, flattened their homes and drove them from the land. This was no small loss. The defeat of the Diggers and groups like them around the world assured the centrality of the market economy, the further entrenchment—and later racialization—of slavery, and the hegemony of both global capitalism and the national state.

Currently in Hawai'i, as in most parts of the world, practices of commoning have been more or less eradicated. Commoning is now practically impossible due to the imposition of private and state/public property laws including patents on life issued by the state, the ecological destruction wrought by cash crops (sandalwood, sugar, pineapple, etc.), the engineering of water canals, and the ongoing effects of both industrialization and tourism. The site where we planted the papaya seedlings is evidence of such destruction. The seedlings grow on a narrow strip of public land upon which only grass and a few weeds grow. A chain-link fence separates this slip of land from what was previously known as Kaelepulu Pond (renamed Enchanted Lake by developers).

The fence was erected by Kamehameha Schools (formerly the Bishop Estate), the most recent in a long line of state-recognized owner/developers, that parceled out parts of the land surrounding the lake to be sold to individual homeowners. The Enchanted Lake Residents Association, made up of these homeowners, was established as the authority that oversees the lake. With the complicated bureaucracy enacted through both the state and Kamehameha Schools the latter still has the right to determine what happens on the six feet of land on either side of the fence.

Kaelepulu Pond was once a thriving fish cultivation area. Its corollary streams fed taro and rice crops. It is now part of a fetid lake in which the water can no longer flow freely to the ocean. Those with homes abutting the lake create their own community entitled to gaze, boat, and occasionally haul garbage out of its now murky depths. The fence serves the dual purpose of protecting Kamehameha Schools from injury claims as well as the Lake Residents Association who wish to keep out what they identify as trespassers who poach now polluted fish from their lake.

In responding to these contemporary developments, we find that we have to contend with something that was less of a problem for the first Diggers. During their time, it was fairly clear to people that their land was being stolen, their labor was being exploited and that nationalism, racism, and sexism were being used to sow dissent amongst the motley crew of commoners, peasants, artisans, and the emerging proletariat throughout the world. Today, many of the things that the Diggers fought against—private property and the nation state with its public lands—are so hegemonic that to merely question them is to open yourself up to ridicule and perhaps much worse.

As Audre Lorde pointed out long ago, we live in a time when we are enthralled by the very instruments used to oppress and exploit us. The enclosure of common lands has been accompanied by the enclosure of our imaginations. The notion of the goodly public space is one such instrument of colonization. The global system of national states, with its legalization of the expropriating practices of capitalists, has been and continues to be an integral feature of capitalist colonization. The fostering of national identities, particularly those of oppressed nations, is seen as a sign of empowerment, and eventual liberation instead of seeing such identities as the prison in which to contain us in the service of capitalist globalization. This is evident in the progressive rhetoric that complains about the loss of citizen's rights while remaining largely mute about the exploitation of non-citizens and/or that of people living in other nations—an outcome that Oliver Cromwell himself had hoped for so many centuries ago. This is evident in both mainstream and progressive versions of nationalism around the world.

The goal of our papaya planting is to stir desires of self-sustenance that *are not* based on the self-righteous desires of national entitlements for citizens. We erected a sign next to the papaya seedlings. It says:

> These papaya plants have been planted here for everyone. When they bear fruit, in about a year, you are welcome to pick them as you need. We will return to feed the plants with organic fertilizer once a month. Please feel free to water and weed. Do not use chemical weed killers as this will poison the fruits and those that eat them—The Diggers

By associating our planting with the Diggers movement, we are reiterating the legitimacy of the commons as an alternative way to relate to the land. We are reasserting the authority of a community built upon a politics of communal eating and needs over the needs of capitalist ideology and expansion. By doing so, we hope to fuel the recognition of the global interdependence of all those struggling for control of their communal lands. Such a politics of communal eating and land use instigates the shared dreams of freedom from capitalists and national states that, at best, sell us the notion of the public in place of our freedom from rulers. An old man walked by while we planted and said, "Oh good, I can have free papayas later." Exactly.

Part 2: Winter

Our project met with two predators within three months. First were joggers engaging in accepted public acts. Moving too fast to read the sign and unprepared to imagine another use for this land, the joggers reduced the number of plants by half in the first month. Trampled and torn by the new year the remaining ten nonetheless grew to a hefty three feet.

The second predator showed up in January as scrawls on the corner of our sign:

> Dear Diggers, Sorry, I've been instructed to remove papaya plants by March 2004. Please transplant.

We were intrigued by the tension revealed in the message—the apologetic tone, the writer's attempt to distance her/himself from her/his boss, the effort made to save the plants. We decided to utilize the writer's empathy with the Diggers' project to elucidate the power distinction between those who determine land usage and those who are charged with carrying it out. We put up a second sign:

> Thanks for the notice but we can't think of any other place better than here where everyone has easy access to the free papayas. If your bosses have a better use for this spot I guess they will have to kill the plants. We are anxious to see what they have planned —The Diggers

One week later a note was wedged into the fence behind the papaya trees. The note was crafted by taping together two postcards. On both the postcards were aerial views—one of a beautiful stream on the island of Hawai'i and the other of the eastern shore of Oahu's coastline. On the back was a note addressed to the Diggers in the same handwriting as the earlier scrawls. Almost entirely smeared by rain, we could barely make out its suggestion—that we seek out the help of a mediator.

We chose not to respond or to seek out a mediator. The Diggers project must be considered in two separate ways—whether we succeeded in providing the stuff of life for free and whether we succeeded in shifting consciousness regarding community, resources, and authority. While there was a remote chance that we may have convinced the state and/or Kamehameha Schools to allow the plants to grow, it was much more important to simply not acknowledge the legitimacy of their state and market-mandated authority. Instead of well-lobbied pleas for tolerance or the co-optation of our action by Kamehameha Schools to ensure its own continued existence, we chose to hold our ground. Knowing ours was a small gesture with great potential, we waited and watched to see what those around us would do. From eavesdropping and our non-scientific observations, we believe that those who encountered the Diggers project were either ambivalent or supportive. Furthermore, some seemed to have followed the exchange that took place with interest. One neighbor, without knowing that she was speaking with a Digger, commented on the mean-spiritedness of the authorities in not allowing the papaya plants to grow.

Like the first Diggers, our project performed a David and Goliath story to decolonize imaginations about land and its usage by asserting a politics of communal eating, demonstrating how difficult it can be for community members to use land to develop communal practices of self-sustenance. Our action sought to re-present the figure of the activist as one engaged in more than symbolic protest. Since broad social relations such as those of class, race, and gender are shaped by how people struggle to make their lives viable, expanding our consciousness of what is possible can only occur in any meaningful way when we can imagine changing the everyday material reality of our lives. Put simply, change happens only when we change things.

Part 3: Spring

Almost one month later than forewarned, the plants were cut down. The entire fence that separated public land and the land owned by Kamehameha Schools was taken down and rebuilt two feet closer to the road right over the severed papaya stumps.

The authoritative repositioning of the fence is a poignant metaphor. While the lines drawn between public and private may shift, neither will, or is meant to, serve producers' interest of self-determination and self-sustenance. The private/public divide, long critiqued by feminists as ideological, is shown to be two halves of a globally encompassing system of capitalist colonization.

Part 4: Summer

On September 18, 2004, two blocks away from the papaya planting site, we opened Free Store, and a companion website Freebay (nomoola.com).

The term Free Store was used during the 1960s by a group calling them-selves the San Francisco Diggers. These Diggers were an anarchist, guerilla street theater group that formed to challenge the dominant US commodity system as well as the assumptions of the counterculture of the time. In one of their early leaflets, SF Diggers suggested, "All responsible citizens bring money to your local Digger for free distribution to all." Two of their most important initiatives were the Digger Bread (where free food was distrib-uted daily) and Free Store. Like their predecessors, this reconfiguration of the Diggers hoped that their actions would stir desires for radical change while showing how people's needs could be met outside of both the market-place and state disciplinary structures of miserly handouts to the "deserving poor."

Since the opening of our Free Store and Freebay, a bit over two weeks prior to the date of this writing, we have given away free plants and herbs, pipes, cinder blocks, and even free labor. On October 1, 2004 ten papaya seedlings were given out at Free Store. A "price tag" was attached to each plant:

ANOTHER FREE STORE SPECIAL
SUNRISE PAPAYA SEEDLING
Get 1 free, get another for the same price!
Suggestions from Free Store:
Papaya trees grow almost anywhere.
Plant in sunny spot in your yard,
vacant lots, or next to the sidewalk.
Try not to use chemical insecticide or fertilizer.
Trees will bear fruit in about a year.
Share your papayas.

All the plants were taken within two hours.

Part 5: Spring/Summer

Eighteen months since its inception, a following has developed for the Diggers site and Free Store. Regulars walk, jog, bike, skate, or drive by to either shop or restock the Free Store. The original Diggers site has been re-planted and expanded both in scale and range of food plants as a direct result of people's support and participation.

Both projects have succeeded in messing with the suburban obsession with security and propriety. Even many of the initially timid or those haunt-ed by middle-class decorum have become increasingly confident about tak-ing and leaving things at the Free Store as well as tending and harvesting from the Diggers garden. The projects inspire observers and participants to engage in surprising discussions on property, authority, self-sustenance, and collective responsibility. This growing interest and confidence has been accompanied by a growing understanding of how the Kamehameha Schools, the US, and the state of Hawai'i are part and parcel of the global capitalist market system and that this system is based on the theft of common property. This is an understanding based neither in unquestioning acceptance nor abstract objections to these systems, but on direct encounters with the Diggers Garden and Free Store. Both enthusiasts and detractors seemingly agree that neither capitalism nor state power have or ever will provide people with the stuff of life.

We expect that the projects will continue to change and shift with daily encounters. Like sweet potato vines, knowledge is rhizomatic and multi-directional. Among countless things we have learned is that sweet potato leaves are hardy little life forms that are heat resistant, look and taste good, and grow practically anywhere.

> *The gentry are all round,*
> *on each side they are found,*
> *This wisdom's so profound,*
> *to cheat us of our ground.*
> *Stand up now, stand up now.*
> *Glory here, Diggers all.*
> —The Diggers, 17th century

Bridging the Praxis Divide: From Direct Action to Direct Services and Back Again

Benjamin Shepard

In recent years, a new breed of organizing has ignited campaigns for peace and justice. Many of these campaigns utilize innovative approaches to organizing diverse communities against a broad range of local and transnational targets, including global corporations and organizations like the World Trade Organization (WTO) and the International Monetary Fund (IMF). According to the Institute for Policy Alternatives, the global justice movement (GJM) has had its greatest policy successes when matching the burlesque of protest with practical policy goals. While the movement has had policy successes in certain areas, such as slowing and shifting debates about "Fast Track" trade negotiations, compulsory licensing, debt cancellation, and through corporate campaigns like the Rainforest Action Network,[1] there are many areas in which the movement has failed to match its rhetorical goals with clearly outlined, achievable goals. While this limitation may result from challenging very large targets, it also results from ideological conflicts within this movement of many movements, herein referred to as movement of movements (MM).[2] Perhaps the MM's greatest strength is a focus on creative expression and praxis, rather than iron-clad ideological certainty.[3] Naomi Klein's now famous essay, "The Vision Thing," elaborates on this theme.[4] Anarchists have worked with liberals; queers have organized with environmentalists; and with respect for diversity of tactics, great things have happened through the savvy deployment of multiple approaches simultaneously. Once secretive policy meetings have become occasions for carnivalesque blockades, while the discussions inside become subject to newspaper accounts around the world. Yet work remains. While diverse groups have collaborated in direct action, not enough of them have worked to advance workable alternative proposals to neoliberalism, especially in the North American context. Tensions around the role of the welfare state, movement organizations, service provision, electoral politics, political compromises, and proximity to political power have emerged as sources of significant ideological tensions. Still the GJM churns forward.

What has been put forward is a "no" to neoliberalism and a prefigurative "yes" to community building. This elliptical disposition is embodied in the Zapatista call for "One No and 1,000 Yeses." At its core, this expression aims to create a new relationship to power and democracy. This new politics begins with a single "no," a *ya basta!* to the neoliberal economic trade and social policies embodied in the NAFTA accords in 1994. Refusal starts as a statement of rebellion and survival in the face of a future denied; it is then transformed into a series of yeses, encompassing encounters with new political spaces, strategies, dialogues, and a new political project creating a new kind of autonomy.[5] The movement's vitality is found in this open democratic call for a multiplicity of voices, grievances, approaches, and connections, all loosely coordinated within a democratic call to action.

Obstacles to the practical "winnable win," which organizer Saul Alinsky suggested is essential for group cohesion, are many.[6] Some argue that an era of corporate or "primitive" globalization has rendered efforts at local organizing obsolete.[7] Others suggest that the neighborhood is still a primary tactical site for movement attention.[8] As "convergence" actions against global summits, meetings, and conventions have increased; much of their suspense has diminished, especially in the North American context.[9] While the rhetoric of calling to "shut down the IMF" and "abolish capitalism" functioned as a broad critique, this framework was not matched with a set of strategies that produced results. As the War on Terror has translated into a war on dissent, the efficacy of broad convergence demonstrations has been vastly reduced in North America. Momentum and resources for social justice campaigns at home has dwindled.[10]

Along with these transformations, the link between a theory of action and practical tactics that helped create change became a chasm. As the refreshing spirit of engagement and problem-solving movements faded, the movement's praxis waned. The MM faces a praxis divide between its theory of action and political power capable of transforming lives. In response to this divide, a number of movement activists and theorists suggested that more dramatic, well-researched, tactical approaches to local targets could help infuse an ethos of success into campaigns for global justice in North America.[11] Such thinking harkens back to the notion that "all politics are local." The result is an organizing framework that involves identifying local needs, some of which involve transnational economic circumstances. Advocates suggest that translating movement goals into clearly identified manifestations of global problems is an effective approach to organizing for social change. After all, recent years have witnessed neighborhood actors in fields as diverse as urban housing, labor, gardening, anarchism, and public health, using both disciplined research and community organizing tools to create wins. The GJM has something to learn from them.

Burning Ambitions and a Praxis Divide

Many of the tensions within the GJM arise from a difficulty reconciling a series of lofty goals with the prerequisites of a system of global capitalism. This tension is complicated by dueling ideological conflicts between radical and liberal approaches to social change activism—the reform vs. revolution challenge that has long accompanied movements for change.[12] Yet few social movements are able to remain entirely outside a policy framework of the provision of services. The challenge for many in the Northern American GJM involves reconciling a struggle against unbridled capitalism and a practical need for immediate limited reforms necessary to make the rules of global capital more humanitarian. Much of the literature on the movement reveals an opposition to the work of nongovernmental organizations (NGOs).[13] This is understandable. The hierarchical nature of many organizations is worth addressing and improving. Yet these limitations do not preclude the need for both direct service organizations and grassroots groups to handle the short and long-term goals of movements. Dynamic movements need people in the streets, at the negotiating table, and providing services.[14] Each has a role in a movement built on respect for a diversity of tactics. After all, in these quiet days before the revolution, people get a little hungry. People need food, shelter, and medicine. Low-income people depend on NGOs and non-profit organizations to provide vital services, including clean needles, dental dams, stem kits, housing, food and healthcare. From the settlement house to the Civil Rights movement, progressive reforms and social programs only gain strength with the support of social movements.[15] Victories like Seattle set the stage for these forms of social change.[16]

Unfortunately, the North American GJM has had few such wins lately. One explanation is its lack of a coherent, overarching theoretical framework to propel itself forward.[17] According to this view, action is privileged over theoretical debate. Intellectuals don't play a coherent role in the MM. Critics of this view say that theory emerges from a coherent model of action, not vice versa.[18] Steve Duncombe suggests that it isn't a lack of theory as much as a lack of appreciation; that sometimes there is more to theory than talk. It may not be that theory is lacking, but that critics are looking at it too narrowly. "[P]erhaps a different type of theory is simultaneously being created, and importantly, employed by this new movement," Duncombe notes. "What I'm talking about here is praxis, or what I'll call, sans Greek, embodied theory. Embodied theory arises out of practice, the activity of engaging in the world, of coming up to solutions to problems and working out their resolutions."[19] Thus, "all successful theory is lived theory."[20]

ACT UP and LIVED Theory

In the case of ACT UP, its theory, "ACTION = LIFE" and "SILENCE = DEATH," propelled a generation of actors. For many, it involved a system of silences that allowed business as usual to create conditions for a deadly epidemic to progress unchecked. Many in the group assumed that participation within this system was tantamount to complicity. For others, this adherence to a notion of pure refusal smacked of social purity.[21] While members of the Treatment and Data affinity group advocated "drugs into bodies" regardless of the means, others suggested that negotiating access to experimental drugs for some but not all created another form of social and cultural apartheid. Long before the GJM calls for respecting a diversity of tactics, members of ACT UP went their separate ways over some members compromising with drug companies.[22] Yet the group continued, with some staying in the streets and others finding a place at the negotiating table. Members of the Treatment and Data Committee rejected the notion that the scientific establishment should be viewed simply as enemies. Mark Harrington, a founder of the Treatment Action Group, reflected on his first meetings with drug company representatives he had zapped in previous years: "At the time, I would just say that it was clear from the very beginning, as Maggie Thatcher said when she met Gorbachev, 'We can do business.'"[23] Rather than cower or scream, Harrington sought common ground when he met representatives of big science. The result was more rapprochement and dialogue.[24] Given the urgent need for results, many favored a pragmatic compromise rather than ideological purity.

Yet there was more to the group's work than difficult compromises. A second example is instructive. Jim Eigo, who was arrested during the first AIDS related civil disobedience in the US, recalls one of many occasions when ACT UP members advanced an effective alternative policy. Much of this work was based on a high level of research, a vital part of the group's approach. Initially, ACT UP's Treatment and Data Committee applied its work to local issues, by identifying local hospitals which received federal research funds for AIDS research and targeting them. From here, Eigo helped advance one of the group's greatest achievements. He explains:

> In February 1988, on behalf of my affinity group, I wrote a critique of AIDS research at New York University (NYU). We delivered copies to NYU's AIDS researchers. One suggestion of our (fairly primitive) critique was that the federal AIDS research effort initiate "parallel trials." A drug's major "clinical trials" gather data on a drug's effectiveness in

human subjects. They're very strictly limited to people who meet rigid criteria. We advocated parallel trials which would enroll anyone with HIV who had no available treatment options.

In 1988, an overwhelming number of people with AIDS were routinely excluded from trials due to gender, illness, or conflicting medications. Data collected from parallel trials, while not clean enough to secure a drug its final approval, would yield a wealth of data on how a drug worked in the target population. Our group sent our critique to Dr. Anthony Fauci, head of the federal AIDS effort. In a few weeks, in a speech in New York, Dr. Fauci was using several phrases that seemed lifted from ACT UP's critique. But one he rephrased: "parallel trials" had become "parallel track."[25]

As the story of parallel track suggests, ACT UP found much of its greatest success from advancing well-researched, practical working strategies. Parallel track was most certainly one of a thousand "yeses" the group would put forward. A large part of the group's influence on federal and state AIDS policy stemmed from its strength as a worldwide grassroots organization. Members were well aware that part of their power emerged from a consciousness that AIDS was an international problem; their local response addressed conditions of this larger problem. Much of this mobilization occurred within a 1001 local skirmishes—at hospitals, schools, boards of education, and even department stores—anywhere the homophobia, sex phobia, racism, and sexism that helps AIDS spread reared its head.

A Different Kind of Theoretical Framework

To bridge the GJM's praxis divide, many have come to look back at a number of classic community organizing approaches. According to Robert Fisher, US-based community organizing can be distinguished as social welfare, radical, and conservative approaches to social change practice.[26] For Jack Rothman, approaches to purposeful community change work within three distinct communities: urban, rural and international.[27]

These approaches are divided into three additional categories of practice: locality development, social planning/policy, and social action. Locality development assumes that social change takes place through active participation in local decision-making to determine goals, tactics and strategies for action. The style is deliberately inclusive and democratic.[28] Social planning/policy involves the process of identifying of social problems, assessment of their scope, data collection, and solutions on a governmental-policy level. This style is deliberately technocratic and rational. Community participation is often minimal. Professionals are thought to be best able to engage in this mode of social change practice. While community participation is not a core ingredient of this approach, differing circumstances and problems may require differing levels of community involvement. After all, garnering maximum civil involvement or successfully carrying out a protest demonstration against a carefully chosen target in the policy food chain requires a great deal of calculation. Thus, means are logically connected to intended ends.[29] In this respect, policy and planning are linked with the third category of community change work: social action-based practice. This type of community organizing assumes there is an aggrieved section or class of the population that needs to be organized in order to make its demands heard to the larger society. Classically stemming from the 1930s and 1960s, this involves a range of confrontational techniques, including: sit-ins, zaps, demonstrations, boycotts, marches, strikes, pickets, civil disobedience, teach-ins, and festive carnivals. The aim of these practices is for those with little financial power or access to use "people power" to apply pressure to or to disrupt carefully chosen targets. In this respect, even social action applies a rational theoretical analysis to its practice. Social action-based practice was first advanced by the settlement house movement. Saul Alinsky built on this model. His work was followed by the writings of Burghardt, Fisher, Piven and Cloward. In recent years, social action movements have moved beyond many of the traditional models to expand strategies and targets.[30]

Social Action from Housing to Direct Services

For activists involved in the AIDS housing movement in New York City, advocacy involves a healthy combination of locality development, social planning/policy, and social action constellations. Given the enormity of their tasks, these actors make use of every tool they can use. For the New York City AIDS housing and advocacy organization, Housing Works, like the Squatters of Amsterdam and the Sem Terra land occupants in Brazil, a single sentiment drives their work: everyone deserves a roof over their head. Housing is a human right. Housing Works locates itself within this ethos. According to their mission, "The purpose of Housing Works is to ensure that adequate housing, food, social services, harm reduction and other drug treatment services, medical and mental health care, and employment opportunities are available to homeless persons living with AIDS and HIV and to their families." The group is committed to reaching its ends through: "Advocacy that aggressively challenges perceptions about homeless people living with AIDS and HIV, both within their indigenous communities and in the larger society," and "Direct provision of innovative models of housing and services." Thus a diversity of tactics for Housing Works bridges a range of tactics from direct action to direct services.

In New York City, where gentrification has put housing costs beyond the reach of many working people, the AIDS crisis compounded the problem as people who were once able to house themselves fell ill, lost their jobs, faced eviction, entered the homeless population, and gridlocked the hospitals. Keith Cylar, co-founder of Housing Works, described the challenges faced by social workers as the AIDS crisis emerged:

There was a gridlock in the hospital system.... For me working in the hospital...I couldn't get people out of the hospital because they didn't have a place to live. We'd get 'em well from whatever brought them in; but then they wouldn't have a place to live. They'd stay in the hospitals and they'd pick up another thing and then they'd die. Remember, '88, '90, '91, '92—New York City literally had hospital gridlock. That was when they were keeping people on hospital gurneys out in the hallways. That was when people were not being fed, bathed, or touched. It was horrendous. You can't imagine what it was like to be black, gay, a drug user, or transgender, and dying from AIDS. So housing all of a sudden became this issue. ACT UP recognized it and formed the Housing Committee.[31]

Here service delivery became a necessary goal to save the lives of people with HIV/AIDS in NYC. Charles King, another co-founder of Housing Works recalls:

You know, there were several of us in ACT UP, somewhat separately who had been passing homeless people in the streets. And in the late '80s was when you started seeing the cardboard signs that said, "Homeless with AIDS Please Help." I was a poor student so when I passed someone who was homeless on the street, I would given them a quarter. When I passed someone and they had a sign that said they had AIDS, I gave them a buck. But really hadn't figured what to do with that. And it sort of crystallized when we attended the Republican Convention in New Orleans in 1988. And those of us that went spent the week hell-raising there and organized a New Orleans ACT UP while we were there. And some of the folks who were there became very, very involved in what we were doing, demonstrating with us all day, every day. As it turns out, they were two homeless men. And when we got ready to leave, they asked if they could come back with us. And we were very cavalier about it; yeah, things were better in New York. When we got back here and tried to help these guys get things together, we realized that things were much better for people with AIDS who were housed but if you were undomiciled you might as well still be in Louisiana.

And so we organized the Housing Committee of ACT UP. We spent the next year and a half very aggressively challenging the city around homelessness and AIDS and its responsibility. Ginny Shubert had filed a lawsuit, Mixon vs. Grinker, to establish the right to housing. I like to think of it as the best lawsuit we ever lost.... We won it all the way up to the state court of appeals. We lost it there but basically it forced the production of almost all of the AIDS housing that now exists in New York City.

Anyway, Ginny had started that lawsuit at the Coalition for the Homeless. And the Housing Committee of ACT UP actually did its first direct action in support of a plaintiff in that lawsuit to get the city to file an injunction to take this person out of the shelter. So, to fast forward, we saw Dinkins as our great hope. Ginny had actually drafted his position paper on homelessness and AIDS. And as soon as he was elected, he repudiated his position and adopted a modified version of the Koch plan which was literally to create segregated units in the armory shelters, indeed running a curtain down the middle of the shelter, with people with AIDS on one side and other people on the other. No one would do anything. At one point in the struggle over Mixon vs. Grinker, a gay man with AIDS actually testified that homeless people with AIDS were actually better off in the shelters. And it was sort of devastating to hear this.

I actually remember a meeting on a Wednesday night the day or the day after his testimony. We met in an apartment on Eighth Avenue and 23rd street. And people were just so discouraged. And we started talking about it and decided that if the people that we cared about were going to be housed then we'd have to do it ourselves. And the only thing that we agreed upon was that we were going to start this new organization. And that it was going to be called Housing Works.

From their beginning, Housing Works approached their task with this sort of audacity. Keith Cylar recalled that the Housing Works took the approach that if no one else was going to house drug users with AIDS then they were going to do it:

To start off with, the Housing Committee of ACT UP was amazing fun. I remember when we were trying to get HASA [HIV/AIDS Services Administration] working—back then it was called the Division of AIDS Services. And they had a bunch of new hires, like sixty new employees, but hadn't given them any desks or workspace. So they were just spending their days sitting in a classroom. And so we organized this action. The union was picketing. We organized this action. Eric actually drove the truck where we brought a bunch of desks and chairs and phones into the middle of Church Street in front of HRA [the Human Resources Administration] and handcuffed ourselves to them. I loved the chant. It was probably one of the best that we ever created. It was: "The check is in the desk and the desk is in the mail." (Laughs). Our HPD [Housing Preservation and Development] action was another amazing one. On Gold Street they have revolving doors. We went around on a Sunday night and picked up a bunch of abandoned furniture on the Lower East Side and Monday morning took it down to Gold Street and stuffed the revolving doors with furniture trying to deliver it to furnish housing for people living with AIDS.

So, the actions were fun. The actions were creative. We saw success at the margins. But at the end of the day, the truth of the matter is that AIDS housing providers did not want drug users. Homeless providers didn't want people with AIDS. And so, even if the government had been willing to take on its part of the responsibility, there probably wouldn't have been providers who were willing to do it with people who we were trying to get housed.

And I think the way we brought that spirit of creative action into Housing Works was in how we designed the programs. Take our first scattered site program. Our housing contract around the country had some preclusion about drug use, requirements around being clean and sober. And we demanded and demonstrated for a contract that would allow us to take people who were still using drugs. What everybody else in the country was precluding, we decided we would fight for.

Cylar recalled the ways that the radical approach to social service work at Housing Works actually overlapped with a form of direct action. "Nobody knew how to treat an active drug user. No one knew how to deal with an active person who was dying from AIDS and HIV and they didn't want to confront that.... And here we were saying, 'Fine, everybody that you can't work with in your program, I want. I want to work with them and I'll find ways to move them.'" While other providers viewed drug users as problems, Cylar explains, "They were people. They were wonderful people and they had lots of stories. They had lots of life and they had lots of wisdom."[32] Since 1988, Housing Works has housed over 10,000 people. Yet many other homeless people have remained marginalized.

New York City AIDS Housing Network and Human Rights Watch

After Housing Works was born, the notion of housing homeless people with HIV/AIDS emerged as a social movement goal in itself. The core argument became "Housing is an AIDS Issue, Housing Equals Health." In linking housing and healthcare, AIDS housing activists linked the co-epidemics of homelessness and AIDS into a struggle to house homeless people with AIDS. Since the epidemic's earliest days, homeless people with HIV/AIDS in New York have been placed in Single Room Occupancy (SRO) hotel rooms. Yet even this remained a battle.

To guarantee a right to shelter for homeless people with HIV/AIDS, housing activists fought for the creation of the New York City Department of AIDS Services (DASIS) within the city's Human Resources Administration (later renamed HASA) in 1995. They also fought for a law passed in 1997, referred to as Local Law 49, that guaranteed people with HIV/AIDS the legal right to be housed by the city within a day of a request for housing placement. Yet the fact that the law was on the books did not ensure its implementation. The spirit of the local law would not find its full expression for another five years. Integral to this was the work of the New York City AIDS Housing Network (NYCAHN), whose watchdog role brought their volunteers into the streets outside New York City's welfare centers for nearly two years. NYCAHN members ensured that either people with AIDS got placed that day, or else lawyers, politicians, and newscasters would be notified that the city was violating the law.

In a campaign reminiscent of the 1960s National Welfare Rights Organization campaigns, NYCAHN workers spent well over two years monitoring the city's compliance with this local law.[33] The core organizing principle remained the demand that the City of New York obey its own law. By the end of the campaign in 2001, the city was compelled to do just that—some four years after the local law's passage. In the following interview, NYCAHN co-founder Jennifer Flynn is accompanied by homeless advocate Bob Kohler. They explain how they forced the city, mayor, and welfare offices to obey the letter and spirit of Local Law 49. The campaign involves elements of legal research into the workings of the cumbersome public welfare bureaucracy and the determination to make it work; it included the willingness to be there through cold winter nights and hot summer days. Activists had to be smart about a media strategy that highlighted these wrongs: they had to build support on the grassroots level as well as with policy makers, and had to be willing to make use of direct action. Much of the interview begins where Charles King and Keith Cylar leave off. I began the interview by asking Flynn what the conditions were like for people with HIV/AIDS ten years ago. She explained:

> Well, prior to the early 1990s, people with AIDS (PWAs) lived in the shelters like homeless people in New York do. In New York State, we have an interpretation in our constitution that gives us a right to shelter. However, there was a tuberculosis outbreak in the shelters. People living with compromised immune systems in the shelters were dying. So there was a court case, Mixon vs. Grinker. That court case said that shelters are not medically appropriate housing for people with compromised immune systems. As result of that, the city really did start to send

people to single occupancy hotels, the same hotel system we use now.

So throughout the 1990s, PWAs, when they identified themselves, were being sent to these hotels. But from there, there really wasn't anywhere else to send them until 1993. Bailey Holt House was really the first AIDS housing residence that was created [on the East Coast]. Housing Works was started in 1990. And then a few other organizations were created. There was an initiative that was created through HRA/Welfare in New York, the Department of Health, specifically to provide housing for people with HIV/AIDS who were suffering from tuberculosis.... And a lot of this housing now started as a result of those funding streams.

Then in 1994, when [Mayor Rudolph] Giuliani came into office... it was the first time that social services across the board were cut.... Straight up, every single social service program was being cut. That led, in 1995, to this kind of unified cry out for attention to fight back against those cuts. And that led to the 1995 Bridges and Tunnels action.[34]

It happened because all social services were being slashed. There were also a few high-profile police brutality cases. And people really thought that was result of the policies of the Republican mayor, which they were. It was also that he was talking about cutting welfare in a way that predated federal welfare reform. He talked about changing welfare. One of the first things he did when he came into office was try to shut down the city agency that provided welfare benefits, including housing for PWAs, the Division of AIDS Services. There was an enormous outpouring of anger over that, and he was stopped in a number of different ways. First he was stopped because of the publicity. ACT UP had been doing a lot of organizing against Giuliani around his attempts to dismantle DASIS, which would have resulted in homeless PWAs going back to the shelters.

So some members of ACT UP made calls to other organizers throughout the city. I think that the first call that they made was to Richie Perez, who was at the National Congress for Puerto Rican Rights. He'd been organizing this coalition of parents whose kids had been killed by the police, and had looked at some changes in policing that were resulting in increased cases of police brutality in New York City.... ACT UP had a history of doing Richie Perez type of direct action.... Then they brought in some other groups, such as Committee Against Anti-Asian Violence, the Coalition for the Homeless, and surprisingly, the Urban Justice Center. At the time, there also were huge cuts to public education. So CUNY [City University of New York] students were organizing. In the months before April 25th, 1995, they had had ten thousand students descending on City Hall. New York City hadn't seen such numbers in a few years. It was pretty remarkable. So they brought in the

CUNY students.... Then those groups kind of morphed into SLAM.

So there was a complete shut down of the East Side of Manhattan. ACT UP and Housing Works had about 145 people arrested at the Midtown Tunnel, the one that goes to Queens. And Committee Against Anti-Asian Violence and the National Congress for Puerto Rican Rights took the Manhattan Bridge. The CUNY students took the Brooklyn Bridge. The Coalition for the Homeless and Urban Justice Center actually had homeless people getting arrested, I guess on the Williamsburg or the Manhattan Bridge. And the entire East Side was tied up for a good two or three hours as a result of that... We beat back a lot of those cuts that year but never really got back to the point before. The other thing he kept doing in every budget was to do away with the Department of AIDS Services. He really hated it.... He was always trying to weaken the welfare system, anyway. And he hated that there was this separate agency that served PWAs.

To buttress DASIS, ACT UP partnered with a broad-based coalition to help pass the Local Law 49. Flynn explains:

It was like he decided to dismantle DASIS as soon as he came into office. City Council members, particularly Tom Duane, and his then chief of staff who was Christine Quinn, and Drew Cramer, started to write the legislation. And they really worked to pass that legislation in the next two years. I think they have a lot to do with it but I think, I mean Tom Duane was essentially a member of ACT UP, so it kind of came from ACT UP. People say that it was an insider strategy, but Tom Duane really was not an insider kind of guy at that point. His power really came from ACT UP. It was a grassroots strategy. He was able to say to other council members "If you don't sign onto this, I will have 1,000 people at your door in the middle of the night." They knew that this was possible. They were people who had money and resources that they should be afraid of. By that point, there were AIDS service organizations who came to the table.

There was this huge march across the Brooklyn Bridge in 1996, the year before the law was passed. It was organized by ACT UP and Housing Works. About 1,000 people marched across the bridge. About 300 people stood outside of the gates of City Hall waiting to get in. And they were really sick people with AIDS. I guess it was early 1996 so people were looking sick. I think there was the contempt case. There was a ruling on Hannah vs. Turner in 1999. We felt that the city had violated the ruling, which meant providing same day—meaning 9 AM to 5 PM—emergency housing placements to everyone who qualified, and everyone who requested it. A lot of AIDS service organizations had started to get tired of it.... It wasn't playing well anymore.

We needed to do something so we begged Armen Mergen, who was the lawyer from Housing Works. He had this whole theory of why it was a difficult case. It went through the court of appeals and he was very concerned about it. But finally, he took the seventeen people that we gave him. We sent more. [T]hat legal strategy alone could not have worked. It worked purely as the perfect storm of an organizing strategy, having the testimonies of people who were affected, and having your [Kohler's] testimony.

And it was also using everything together. It was sort of targeting Giuliani, directly, trying to make policy changes. Also, everybody wanted to be the one who solved it. At some point, there were insider lobbyists, who were hired by these big AIDS service organizations, who kept telling me they had met with someone in Giuliani's office and they were going to fix it tomorrow. I think that probably helped. And I think the legal strategy helped. The leadership development and organizing helped. The monitoring—just standing there with a moral purpose. It's also one case where it was so clear that we were right. There just isn't any gray area about that.

The wins would build on each other. "Other people could just go to a welfare center and track complaints. And it always fixed something. Even if the whole problem wasn't getting fixed, you got the doors on the bathrooms stalls," Flynn explains.

"But once you get one win," Bob Kohler recalls, "then you want more. Once you got a water cooler and doors then you keep going. And it shows you: we got that."

Community Gardens and a Struggle for Healthier Neighborhoods

Throughout the years of Housing Works and NYCAHN's work, a community garden movement gained steam in New York City, its aim to make streets and neighborhoods healthy places for joy and connection. I came into the gardens direct action movement in March of 1999, during the organizing to stop the auction of 114 community gardens. Throughout that spring, garden activists from the More Gardens Coalition and the Lower East Side Collective Public Space Group had been engaging in a theatrical brand of protest, which included activists dressing like tomatoes and climbing into a tree in City Hall Park, and lobbying dressed as giant vegetables. The state Attorney General even noted that the reason he put a temporary restraining order on the development of the garden lots was because, "A giant tomato told me to." All these actions seemed to compel neighborhood members to participate in a process of creating change. Faced with a gentrification and globalization process that was homogenizing and privatizing public spaces at an astounding rate, garden activists dug in to defend their neighborhoods through a wide range of tactics. As with Housing Works and NYCAHN, their campaign involved a savvy use of research with an engaging model of protest.

Michael Shenker, a long time Lower East Side squatter and garden activist, recalls four tactics used in the garden struggle in NYC. These included: direct action, a judicial strategy, fundraising, and a legislative approach.[35] Direct action combined with a joyous approach played out through tactic including a "sing out" disrupting a public hearing, as well as an ecstatic theatrical model of organizing that compelled countless actors to participate in the story themselves. The aim was to convey their messages and engage an audience without being excessively didactic. Thus, groups made use of a range of crafty approaches, engaging audiences in playful ways with stories that seduced rather than hammered. This theatrical mode of civil disobedience had a way of disarming people and shifting the terms of debate. More Gardens Coalition organizer Aresh Javadi explained this successful approach to bridging the looming praxis divide facing the group:[36]

> Theater has always been a method, going back to Iran, where troupes, singers, and theatre people would come and do the performance of Hussein, where he is martyred. When they did that they came from village to village to village, they would tell the real stories behind what was going on through theatre that was also interactive. The whole village would be singing and dancing with it backwards and forwards. So you were absolutely ingrained in it. There was no one person to see, and the other person to act. It opens you to all sorts of possibilities. Again, when you see a plant or a vegetable, you automatically come back to a world of childhood, cartoons, something that is not like the "this is a protest and they are against us" response. Rather the reaction is, "That's so magical. That's so amazing and concrete." It brings you a recognition of why it is that people care so much about green space when you can't actually take them to the garden. Did you see this over here—what it meant to this woman, to this grandfather, this granddaughter, how much it's improved their health, their life? You can do that by having a flower dancing with a giant tomato, and then there is the action of someone trying to take that away from people and people are willing to step up and change that. It allows people to really engage and question their own intents. It's a very, very powerful thing that Bread and Puppet and other groups have utilized. But Bread and Puppet tends to be a little bit darker. We are just like, this is fun, it's loving, and you are going to see how passionate we are about it. The other aspect was that even during

the civil disobediences, we would have hats and colorful things. The police sometimes didn't even know what to do with the puppets. And they would be like, "We can't arrest a flower." [Laughs] "That's not a person that we can arrest."

As with AIDS activists, the garden struggle is about life and community. Aresh explains how he planted those seeds within his campaigns:

> To me it was just like, how can we be a "yes group." Yes, we agreed that this needs to be approved. We never said, "No, you suck." We said, "Yes, you can do the right thing, like the flowers, like the fruits, like the yeses that have been created and brought forth in visual and even in food." This is what we're visioning and this is what we want—a celebration, a bringing together of the spirits, and having the politicians just follow what was right. And putting facts out. When we did a banner hang, the visual enhanced the words. We didn't try and overstate it or get wordy, saying, "Oh well, housing vs. the sunflower. Do you want a house or do you want homeless children?" We said, "There it is: 10,000 vacant lots and they are being given away to rich developers, while the community gardens that could be there next to real housing, are being bulldozed." We were not against real housing. Why not have these two balanced? And keep both of them. We want both—real housing as well as real green spaces. I think any time anyone builds over a piece of land, he or she should automatically be adding community gardens with their money for the community. The point is to open spaces that are communal and cultural. To me, that's what needs to be pushed forward.
>
> The strategy was always to advance images of a healthier community. Sustainable healthier communities. From the Romans to the Greeks to the Persians to the Chinese—they've always had spaces where people can gather and be part of nature. And realize that we are nature—no matter how much steel and concrete break us away from that.
>
> During the organizing to save the 114 gardens, we had moments where we were in the gardens that were a week away from being destroyed or given away to some developer. And the children came and took the puppets and automatically told the story. They would tell the story of the garden. And they would say, "So why do you think we shouldn't have housing right there?" And the other kids would say, "Look at that house across the street. That's not for us." And I had nothing to do with that scene. Yet, these kids represent a future of why New York is going to be such an amazing space. The end result of this organizing was a compromise, which helped preserve the community gardens in New York City.[37]

Art, Creativity, and Victory in an Anti-Corporate Campaign

The final case in this essay offers another example of the use of creative direct action and community organizing, yet in a strikingly different context: the successful campaign by the Coalition of Immokalee Workers (CIW) for better pay from Taco Bell. Like the garden activists, this campaign made use of a prefigurative organizing model. Long-time organizer David Solnit, who worked on the campaign, elaborates on this form of organizing: "I think its essential to think below the surface, from the gut, if we don't learn to articulate the core roots of the problems we face, we'll always be on the defensive."[38]

For some three years, Taco Bell neglected the CIW's simple request: an increase of one penny per pound of tomatoes picked for their tacos. And it's no wonder, small wages translate into large profits. The demands of migrant and immigrant workers—such as the mostly Haitian, Latino, and Mayan Indian immigrants subsisting on poverty wages who constitute the CIW coalition—are a low priority for companies like Taco Bell. Poverty among migrant farm workers saves consumers some $50 a year.[39] Thus, campaigns for higher wages faces an uphill challenge. At first Taco Bell refused to even acknowledge the CIW requests. Yet the company reached out after the CIW's staged a guerilla performance/production of the mock marriage of a ten-foot-tall Queen Cheap Tomato and King Taco Bell in the street facing their corporate headquarters in Irvine, California.[40]

Fast forward five years. Facing a mounting boycott and pressures from workers, students, and activists around the world, Taco Bell agreed to the core demands advanced by the CIW on March 8, 2005. The CIW could thus celebrate what amounted to a complete victory against one of the largest fast food corporations in the world.[41] David Solnit suggests the campaign be understood as a best-practice example for a GJM facing a praxis divide. Through its use of highly theatrical guerilla theater, organizers involved in the campaign successfully bridged the movement's broad critique with an effective organizing strategy and messaging. This also helped bring new workers into the campaign.[42] After all, Solnit suggests: "People join campaigns that are fun and hopeful. It's always been there—in the Civil Rights movement, and art helped shut down the WTO." This creativity helped highlight the social and economic issues involved in their campaigns in countless engaging ways.[43] It involved combinations of art, research, well-targeted theatrics, and grassroots, non-hierarchical organizing utilized by the CIW.[44]

A vital part of this consciousness-raising included an engagement between arts, playfulness, and creativity capable of inspiring action. The CIW explain: "By looking at the roots of the agricultural industry's problem, we were able to come up with a strategy to change the problems that we face in our community. We do this through popular education: flyers, drawings, theater, videos, weekly meetings, and visits to the camps. We draw on the innate leader that exists in every worker."[45]

Community building was also a vital element of the success of the campaign. The CIW worked from their local bases to expand a series of networks that allowed coalition allies to feel part of this community. These networks helped transform an isolated struggle of one of the least visible communities in the world into one of the most connected struggles in North America. The CIW began by building an effective neighborhood campaign and expanding from this base. As with ACT UP and countless other labor struggles, consciousness of the global dynamics of the struggle helped cultivate a solidarity that invigorated the campaign—"[W]hen we came to understand that the root of our problem was located at a much higher level, we knew we would have to get our voices heard all across the nation"—and momentum steamrolled.[46] In many respects, the boycott built on the vitality of the pre-9/11-backlash global justice movement's political agenda. In the summer of 2001, before the terror attacks, the Harvard Living Wage campaign galvanized the nation. US senators, student activists, anti-racism, and poverty activists found common ground and worked together to fight for a social and political agenda that challenged the idea that it is acceptable for workers to live in subpoverty conditions.[47] The CIW began their work in this same milieu.[48] In the same way that the Zapatista movement built an ethos that allowed anyone with a computer to become part of their community, the CIW invited citizens from around the world to participate and feel part of their struggle. In this way, leadership and community emerged in bountiful ways. "Our network spread and grew like wildfire. And suddenly, wherever we would go and mention that we were from Immokalee, it would elicit the reaction, 'Oh, the tomato pickers' or '*yo no quiero* Taco Bell.'"[49] Yet, for the campaign to sustain itself through the years, as much of the vitality of the global justice struggle was overtaken by a push for permawar, the CIW built on an approach that broke down the struggle into a series of Alinsky-like winnable goals.

Certainly art and culture helped this coalition stay engaged and move forward. The CIW explain: "The corporations who we are fighting have multi-million dollar advertising budgets, we the farm workers from a small and resource-poor community don't have the same kind of access to the media."[50] What the CIW had was a conscious appreciation of the intoxicating possibilities of creative play. Combined with a willingness to make use of the tools of popular education, storytelling, art, and joy, this spirit helped advance a viable winning approach to organizing strategy. "We have to be creative about communicating our story. Art, images, and theater played a very important role. We were able to show through their use what the reality of our lives is really like. We were able to catch people's attention by making our marches and protests colorful and fun. And through the images and signs we were able to more effectively communicate our message to anyone who might have driven by or seen us on the news or in the newspapers."[51]

The result of the work was a successful, prefigurative yes to community and the rights of workers. The result is an inspiration and a future best-practice model for those involved within campaigns for global peace and justice.[52] In many respects, the CIW, Housing Works, NYCAHN, and the Community Garden Movement operate within the same ethos. They show people social change is possible through community building. Here, social change is activism in process, not a theoretical promise.

Notes

1. John Cavanagh and Sarah Anderson, "What is the Global Justice Movement? What Does it Want? What is in It? What has it Won?" in *Institute for Policy Studies*, Washington, DC, 2002.

2. For an elaboration, see Tom Mertes, ed., *The Movement of Movements: Is Another World Really Possible?* (New York: Verso, 2003).

3. For an example of the movement's creative expression, see Notes From Nowhere, eds., *We Are Everywhere: The Irresistible Rise of Global Anticapitalism* (London and New York: Verso, 2003).

4. Naomi Klein, "The Vision Thing," in *From ACT UP to the WTO: Urban Protest and Community Building in the Era of Globalization,* eds. Benjamin Shepard and Ron Hayduk (New York: Verso Press, 2002).

5. David Solnit, ed., *Globalize Liberation: How to Uproot the System and Build a Better World (*San Francisco: City Lights Press, 2004), 215–20.

6. Saul Alinsky, *Rules for Radicals* (New York: Vintage Books, 1971).

7. William Sites, *Remaking New York: Primitive Globalization and the Politics of Urban Community* (Minneapolis: University of Minnesota Press, 2003)

8. Benjamin Shepard, "Review of *Remaking New York*," *Urban Affairs Review* 41, no. 1 (September 2005), 106–8.

9. Certainly, the protests in Cancún in the fall of 2003 were profoundly effective—far more so than the police crackdown in Miami during the FTAA meetings. In many ways, the militarization of police has shifted the ways we understand social protest.

10. See Benjamin Shepard, "Movement of Movements Toward a Democratic Globalization," in *New Political Science: A Journal of Politics and Culture* 26, no. 4 *(*December 2004).

11. Eddie Yuen elaborated on this theme during the Spring 2002 release party for *The Battle of Seattle* (New York: Soft Skull Press, 2002).

12. For a review of these ideological conflicts, see Robert Mullaly, *Structural Social Work* (Toronto: McClelland and Stewart, 1993).

13. James Davis, "This Is What Bureaucracy Looks Like: NGOs and Anti-Capitalism," in *Confronting Capitalism: Dispatches from a global movement,* eds. Eddie Yuen, Daniel Burton-Rose, and George Katsiaficas (New York: Soft Skull Press, 2004).

14. Martin Luther King "Letter from a Birmingham Jail," in *Why We Can't Wait* (New York: American Library, 1964). King suggests the point of civil disobedience is to get policy makers to the negotiating table.

15. See J. Addams, *Twenty Years at Hull House* (New York: Penguin and King, 1910/1998).

16. See Benjamin Shepard, "Review of *The Battle of Seattle: The New Challenge to Capitalist Globalization*," in *Socialism and Democracy* 18, no. 1 (January–June 2004), 258–65.

17. Liza Featherstone, Doug Henwood and Christian Parenti, "Activistism: Left Anti-Intellectualism and Its Discontents," in *Confronting Capitalism.*

18. Certainly, intellectuals and academics, including Douglas Crimp, Michael Warner, Kendall Thomas, and others helped infuse a critical theory into the work of ACT UP and SexPanic!; others, including Hall (2003: 80) suggest they borrowed from ACT UP's work to infuse its vitality into the academic field of queer theory—see *Queer Theories,* Donald E. Hall (New York: Palgrave Macmillan, 2003). Many activists suggest these theorists retreated to the academy when things got tough with organizing. Certainly, intellectuals including Jeremy Veron, David Graeber, Steve Duncombe, Kelly Moore, and countless others are frequent players in GJM activist circles here in New York City. Some suggest the movement was legitimized when former World Bank head, Columbia economist, and Nobel laureate Joseph Stiglitz seemed to endorse many of its claims in *Globalization and Its Discontents* (WW Norton: New York, 2002).

19. Stephen Duncombe, "The Poverty of Theory: Anti-Intellectualism and the Value of Action," in *Radical Society* 30, no. 1 (April 2003).

20. Ibid.

21. Stanley Aronowitz elaborates on Marcuse's principal of "repressive tolerance" in *The Death and Rebirth of American Radicalism* (Routledge: New York, 1996), 206.

22. For Sara Schulman, this period represented a fundamental Rubicon, which resulted in a split among the group. See "From the Women's Movement to ACT UP: An Interview with Sara Schulman" in *From ACT UP to the WTO.*

23. Steven Epstein, "Democracy, Expertise, and AIDS Treatment Activism," *in Perspectives in Medical Sociology,* ed. Phil Brown (Long Grove, Illinois: Waveland Press, 2000), 614.

24. Ibid.

25. Ibid. ACT UP members would eventually testify to Congress on the issue of parallel track. For a review of the 1989 Congressional hearings in which Eigo spoke on this issue, see "Congressional Hearing on Parallel Track, JULY

20," in *AIDS Treatment News*, July 28, 1989.

26. Jack Rothman, "Approaches to Community Intervention," in *Strategies of Community Intervention Macro Practice,* eds. Jack Rothman, John L. Erlich, and John E. Tropman (Itasca, IL: FE Peacock Publishers, 1995).

27. Robert Fisher, *Let the People Decide: Neighborhood Organizing in America*, Updated Edition, (New York: Twayne Publishers, 1994).

28. Ibid, 28.

29. Ibid, 30–35.

30. Lesley J. Wood and Kelly Moore, "Target Practice – Community Activism in a Global Era," in *From ACT UP to the WTO*.

31. Keith Cylar, "Building a Healing Community from ACT UP to Housing Works: An Interview with Keith Cylar," by Benjamin Shepard in *From ACT UP to the WTO*.

32. Ibid.

33. See Frances Fox Piven and Richard Cloward, *Poor People's Movement: Why They Succeed, How They Fail* (New York: Vintage, 1977), 264–362.

34. See Ester Kaplan, "This City is Ours," in *From ACT UP to the WTO*.

35. Interview with the author, August 22, 2005.

36. Interview with the author, August 23, 2005.

37. See Elliot Spitzer, "Memorandum of Agreement between Attorney General and Community Gardeners, " 2002. Available at http://www.oag.state.ny.us.

38. Interview with the author, August 24, 2005.

39. Eric Schlosser *Reefer Madness: Sex, Drugs, and Cheap Labor in the American Black Market* (New York: Houghton Mifflin, 2003), 102–3.

40. Katie Renz, "People Power: An Interview With David Solnit," *Mother Jones Magazine,* March 22, 2005.

41. Ibid.

42. David Solnit "The New Face of the Global Justice Movement: Taco Bell Boycott Victory—A Model of Strategic Organizing. An interview with the Coalition of Immokalee Workers," in *truthout | Perspective*, August 24, 2005.

43. Interview with the author, August 24, 2005.

44. See Solnit, "The New Face of the Global Justice Movement."

45. Ibid.

46. Ibid.

47. See Benjamin Shepard, review of "The Betrayal of Work: How Low Wage Jobs Fail 30 Million Americans," in *WorkingUSA: A Journal of Labor and Society* (Spring 2004).

48. See Solnit, "The New Face of the Global Justice Movement."

49. Ibid.

50. Ibid.

51. Ibid.

52. Ibid.

The Revolution Will Wear a Sweater: Knitting and Global Justice Activism

Kirsty Robertson

It is April 2001 and more than 50,000 protesters have gathered in the streets outside the Summit of the Americas in Québec City to oppose the signing of the Free Trade Area of the Americas (FTAA). Québec City, replete with the history of a divided nation, has never seen, smelt, or felt anything like it. A concrete-enforced chain-link fence has been built around the UNESCO-protected old city, now protecting the leaders and negotiators from thirty-four nations in the Western Hemisphere. The streets are lined with provincial and national police clad in post-apocalyptic riot gear and armed with the weapons of a new global order. The protesters surge towards the fence and are pushed back repeatedly with tear gas, rubber bullets, pepper spray, and water guns. The ground is littered with torn posters, burnt gas canisters, and small fires.[1]

Imagine the helicopters overhead, the sound of thousands of people beating rocks on the flagpoles and barricades, mingled with the rhythmic marching of the police and the crack of their batons beating on plexiglass riot shields. Imagine the chants, the singing, the tear gas canisters hissing into the crowds. Downtown Québec City is a ghost town, the entire eerie center wrapped in a thick stinging fog, the buildings obscured, and everyone in gas masks. Imagine the arrests, some violent, some frustrated, some sympathetic. Imagine the buses crowded with arrested activists, the tear gas everywhere, the city boarded up, the fence wrapped in posters, the riot police on guard, eyes hidden behind helmets. And then focus in. In the middle, the tear gas rising around them, a group of people sit in a circle, knitting.

It is the productivity of this seemingly inappropriate gesture that interests me here. The incongruity of seeing knitters at a protest, that at least according to mainstream news sources, was violent and chaotic is for me a moment of potential. It is this potential that I would like to explore, analyzing both the success and potential failure of revolutionary knitting as a mode of protest and daily activism. Generally constructed as a feminine and domestic craft, knitting enjoys a symbolic potency in its sheer out-of-placeness at recent protests, undermining accepted ideas of protesters as violent, and offering what is seen, at least to many knitters, as a constructive approach to activism that encourages interpersonal interaction and everyday resistance. Perhaps, however, revolutionary knitting has not been pushed far enough, and the links between revolutionary knitting circles, knitting as contemporary art, and a resurgence in feminine/feminist crafting thus remain largely unexplored. Without exploring these links, the revolutionary aspect of knitting is based largely on the element of surprise, rather than on the nurturing of systemic change.

The knit-in mentioned above was organized by the Ithaca, New York-based Activist Knitting Troupe in response to government legislation proposing a ban on the wearing of scarves and masks in Québec City and the nearby Ste. Foy during the summit weekend. It was part of a larger response called Weaving a Web of Solidarity, a series of actions designed by women's groups to celebrate a coming together of global feminisms while also bearing witness to the disproportionately negative effects of corporate globalization on women. In their call to action, Weaving a Web organizers noted:

> We are taking action because we will no longer tolerate the web of corporate control that binds us down and constricts our lives. We will not allow this system to continue. We have taken its measure: its time is done. Instead, we will become spiders, spinning a new web of connection, of solidarity out of our rage, out of our love.

In the heady language of manifesto, the call to action continues for several pages, combining a radical (if broadly essentializing) feminism with metaphors of weaving, connectivity, and knitting:

> We will, as women, weave together our hopes and dreams, our aspirations, our indictments, our testimony, our witnessing, our demands, our visions. We will write on ribbons, on strips of cloth, on rags. We will draw, paint, knot cords, braid yarn, whisper into pieces of string. And from these materials we will weave our web.

An important aspect of the action was both to demonstrate the global solidarity of women and to foreground the handmade as inherently anticapitalist. Conflating the feminine with the feminist, the project at least in part brought the domestic to the public realm of activist politics, including a parade with an oversized goddess puppet, an action wherein ribbons, bras, and flowers were woven into the fence, and a collective weaving project in which participants made, in wool, the material manifestation of the symbolic webs of connection. The actions were entirely non-violent, and given the concerns of some of the participants, had been largely cleared by the organizers, Toile Femme Québec, with the police beforehand.

Held on April 19, 2001, two days before the main demonstration, the Weaving the Web action received relatively little coverage in the mainstream news. Though it foreshadowed a number of subsequent media-successful knitting actions at the 2003 anti-G8 and anti-Republican protests in Calgary, Canada and Washington D.C., in Québec City media attention was focused almost entirely on the perceived violence of protesters (Langlois 2004). It could be argued that mainstream, and to a certain extent independent, media only focused on the knitting and women's actions when an absence of expected violence forced searches for new editorial content.

At the center of such discussions is the Revolutionary Knitting Circle, a group started in Calgary in 2001 in an effort to "create soft barriers of knitted yarn to reclaim spaces from the elite to the common good. As the community is knitted together, corporate commerce is slowed or halted and the community can prosper." The knitting circles, which have now spread to cities throughout the Americas and Europe, meet regularly in both real and virtual space, creating projects both as groups and individuals, thereby acting out the double purpose of withdrawing from capitalism and building up grassroots initiatives. Designed to cross age and gender barriers, knit-ins staged by the Calgary Group combine individual work with group projects, including the now well-known Peace Knits banner, a large knitted banner made of colorful squares spelling out the words "PEACE KNITS." Each knitter was given the assignment of knitting several squares as a part of the puzzle that could only be put together once everyone had completed their piece. The banner also played on the outdated hippie label/insult "peaceniks" often used in the conservative province of Alberta to dismiss protesters.

More than five years later, the Calgary circle is still going strong, organizing a series of events including the knitting of peace armbands, black flags to represent Iraqi civilians killed, and socks with intarsia lettering calling for peace in Arabic and Hebrew. The question remains, however: are the revolutionary knitters just another largely forgettable affinity group, or does the embodied act of knitting, combined with the collective atmosphere of the knitting circle and the links to wider methods of communication, make it a potential form of resistance that could create connections across lines of age, gender, ethnicity, and class? Could the links forged between knitters create a wide support network at protests, in the community, and in movement building that takes place between actions? Could radical knitting offer an alternative to activist burnout—a way of healing that remains, in its essence, subversive?[2]

When faced with what communications theorist Andy Opel calls the postmodern weapon of tear gas (a weapon that destroys the empathetic relationship between spectator and victim) and the more recent introduction of tasers, caged protest areas, the refusal of marching permits, arrests, characterizations of activists as terrorists, and an ongoing media unwillingness to record anything but violence, protesters have had to devise new strategies of engagement (Opel 2003). In large part, these new strategies have involved moving away from spectacular protest toward daily actions that perhaps more effectively engage the diffuse systems of control in contemporary society. In the case of knitting, why not engage in a way that also draws in other arguments, building, so to speak, webs on top of webs?

Writing in 1998, Montréal artist Ingrid Bachmann noted the frontier mentality regarding the landscape and vocabulary of cyberspace, and observed that visions of the future are often predicated on structures of the past. Contrasting the material and physical conditions of daily life with the promise of the immateriality and the transcendence offered through emerging technologies, Bachmann notes that technology is always already a product of economic, political, and cultural structures. "Why is weaving considered antiquated, artisanal, slow, gendered female?" she asks. "And conversely, why are computers considered fast, new, state of the art, virtual, gendered male?" (Bachmann 1998: 25–27).[3]

Bachmann argues that this socially constructed binary plays a key role in maintaining unequal relations that construct textile art and weaving as feminine crafts located in domestic space, and redolent of a technologically obsolete past.[4] Even as knitting and other craftwork is reclaimed by a youthful audience, a language of stereotype and obsolescence remains. As Charlotte Higgins writes of a recent British exhibition of radical knitting, "An exhibition at the Crafts Council Gallery in London next month will show that knitting—long belittled as the preserve of elderly ladies declining towards senility—has become a politically engaged, radical art form." It could, in fact, be argued that the use of textiles has always been both technologically and politically engaged. Textile production played a seminal role in both the industrial and digital revolutions, and the romanticized nostalgia that often accompanies descriptions of textile work is undermined by contemporary textile production and the enduring presence of sweatshops for clothing manufacture. Tracing the industrial revolution through textile production, from the home to the factory, through surplus economies, capitalism, and the consolidation of workers under the watchful eye of disciplinary management, it is perhaps ironic that the forerunners of the first computing machines were based on early nineteenth century Jacquard looms with their system of punch cards to store and process information. Weaving is after all a process of information storage, a binary system of interlocking threads, mirroring the 0s and 1s of computer programming (Bachmann 1998: 25– 27). Knitting patterns are much like a computer code—the P and K of purl and knit following a logical and binary order to a finished product.

Knitting and weaving are hence linked to the coding of the new technologies of communication that surround us. British artist Freddie Robins' recent art project and website *Bugbear*, for example, allow online users to choose a knitting pattern that highlights the similarities between new technologies (computer language, pixellation, computer viruses, etc.) and knitting. Once they're chosen, the user/viewer can print out the pattern and knit the object in three dimensions. The patterns from *Bugbear* include one in moth/moss stitch, highlighting the problem of "bugs" to both computer users and knitters, and a pattern called "it's all gobbledygook to me," stressing the similarities between computer and knitting languages. Robins, who embraces what she calls an anarchist style of knitting, uses the familiarity of wool garments to engage with the politics of genetic engineering (she knits sweaters for "genetic mutants"), with the loss of feelings of personal safety in contemporary society (showcased in miniature knitted versions of the houses where crimes have been committed), and with the possibilities of radical knitting in public (she is an active participant in Cast Off, a British knitting group that strives to make knitting both accessible and resistant).

That artists like Robins are participating in a much wider resurgence of knitting is perhaps not surprising—crafting has become a subgenre of both the capitalist and alternative economies (as shown by articles in *Vogue* and *Bust Magazine*, innumerable websites, newspaper articles, and even a few academic forays). Certainly, the Internet has played an extremely important role in popularizing craft through the huge number of websites, pattern exchanges, discussion boards, and online lessons. In this aspect, the links between digital technologies and knitting and weaving remain strong. Making a slightly different interpretation, however, knitter and activist Betsy Greer argues that the resurgence of knitting is a response to the destruction of community wrought by these same technologies of communication. Describing her knitting experiences, which found her knitting with "punks…goths…aging hippies…people who spoke no English…my really old Aunt Gene…children, friends, and strangers," Greer describes an experience of connection across social lines fragmented through capitalism. "It's not about clothing people out of necessity," she writes, "it's about clothing people out of love" (Greer 2004: 8–9). She notes how she re-engaged with people after spending too much time away from face-to-face communication and how she developed a number of lasting friendships with people with whom she shared little other than knitting.

Greer continues, noting how, for her, the coming together of domestic craft and feminism was in itself subversive. Arguing that her history as a riot grrl had resulted in political burn-out, she suggests that knitting and crafting offer a way to live in a subversive manner, while avoiding the exhausting and all-encompassing anger of earlier movements. Defending herself against critiques of co-option and selling-out, Greer argues that her approach to making her own garments is actually more subversive than her earlier, louder, angrier feminism. But, I wonder if this reclaimed domesticity is not so much reneging on the goals of second-wave feminism as believing those goals have been achieved. The denigration of second-wave feminism as mere anger is, however, an unfortunate misreading. As knitting and crafting are increasingly co-opted into the mainstream, the writing over of feminist history into newer, more easily commodified, feminine-feminism will be palatable for the denizens of post-Fordist capitalism. As Susan J. Douglas writes:

> Of all the social movements of the 1960s and '70s, none was more explicitly anti-consumerist than the women's movement. Feminists had attacked the ad campaigns for products like Pristeen and Silva Thins, and by rejecting makeup, fashion and the need for spotless floors, repudiated the very need to buy certain products at all (1995: 227).

This is an important insight when it comes to analyzing the role of knitting in the recent global justice movement. To overlook the anti-consumerism of 1970s feminism is to write over women's history with a masculine tale of anticapitalist genesis. Further, as Debbie Stoller writes, "The very fact that knitting, sewing, crocheting, and other skills of the happy homemaker have been considered too girly to be done in public is proof that these crafts need to be reclaimed by the same feminist movement that initially rejected them." Unlike increased consumption, this is progress.

Rachael Matthews, who runs the London-based guerilla knitting club Cast Off (infamous for their knit-ins on the London Underground), notes: "It seemed odd that you were allowed to read a book on the tube, but knitting was abnormal." As public space becomes increasingly privatized, these small moments of subversion are also moments of reclamation. To knit in public is to be truly visible and oddly subversive. "It seemed almost as transgressive as breastfeeding in public twenty years ago," notes another member of the group. Like the broken windows left by black bloc protesters, knitting in public acts as a caesura in the capitalist screen, a brief interruption in the smooth face of neoliberal conformity.

The knitters of Cast Off argue that knitting is more than a consumer choice, although this does not always come through in popular writing on the topic, for example in the following quote from salon.com writer Janelle Brown: "Since cookie-cutter consumerism makes it difficult to be unique when everyone is buying the same Pottery Barn place mats, the new craft-ies have found a way to express individuality, showcase personal design sensibilities, *and* make a small statement against conspicuous consumption by taking production into their own hands." (Brown) There is an idea that there is something more going on here. Shoshana Berger, editor of the craft magazine *ReadyMade*, is quoted in Brown's article as saying: "There's a real yearning for slowing down the pace of our culture, which is running amok. I think in this age of mechanical reproduction people are intrigued by the aura of the original." Another member of Cast Off writes that not only is knitting "very meditative" but "when you are knitting you are ready to listen."

I love this quote. I love the way that it dreams of a tactile and aural subversiveness: for at the center of neoliberalism is vision—the (re)visioning of life as perceivable, obtainable, and material. Art historian Jonathan Crary has set out the most useful analysis of the links between perception, capitalism, and modernity. Crary situates his argument not simply in an ocularcentric bias in Western society, but also in what he terms "a capacity for paying attention" (1999: 1). For Crary, vision has been constructed as a privileged sense of truth, conflating knowledge with the ability to see, and adding to it through the visionary prosthetics of millennial culture (cameras, surveillance, and so on) (1992: 67). He suggests that to cut visuality off from the embodied subject is to cut off the embodied subject's relation to systems of power and also to the potential for resistance (1999: 3). Thus, in spite of the fact that systems of modernization and capitalism rely on the attentive and perceiving body (that is, in terms of requiring attention to aid production, and also to create interest in new products), at the same time, the individual and embodied movement of each subject consistently and continuously undermines any totalitarian logic of perception. It is a flickering gaze, unwilling to pay complete attention, rapidly flitting from one thing to another, and accentuating the accelerated circulation of capitalism that, according to Crary, produces this perceptual fluidity: "a regime of reciprocal attentiveness and distraction" (1992: 29–30).

Crary writes of Sir David Ferrier, a doctor in the 1870s who noted that attention often depends upon the physiological *suppression* of movement. Thus, an attentive observer might appear motionless, but their very lack of motor activity belies the ferment of physiological and motor occurrences upon which that relative "stasis" depends (1999: 41). This idea can also be found in Rozsika Parker's earlier work in the *Subversive Stitch*, where she argues that the attentive downcast head of the knitting woman represents not submission, but the thoughts of private reverie, uncontrollable and potentially threatening to a patriarchal status quo (1989: 10). Attention can thus be subversive, and attention combined with the act of listening, contemplation, and interaction can be construed as a radical act. "I really do believe," writes knitter and artist Shane Waltener, "If more people knitted, the world would be a more peaceful place."

Not all, however, are in agreement. Taking on the feminine/feminist resurgence of knitting, as well as its slow and quiet qualities, Tonya Jameson argues that the resurgence of knitting in the United Stated after 9/11 echoes a sort of cocooning inimical to radical feminism. Jameson argues, "Too many sisters fought to free women from aprons and mops for me to voluntarily become Aunt Bee and pretend it's by choice." For Jameson, the return to knitting is simply an underscoring of the conservative turn of American politics—social peer pressure that encourages hiding from reality, isolationism, and depoliticization. "Instead of reconnecting with traditions," she writes, "it seems like we're knitting, cooking and hiding in our homes because we're scared. Creating something with our hands gives us a false sense of control at a time when we have little." (Jameson)

For Jameson, knitting and crafting require a distancing from politics, a move away from political engagement. "Instead of fighting for real control, like lobbying legislators for patients' rights," she argues, "we're playing Holly Homemaker."[5] While Greer dismisses Jameson out of hand, arguing that knitting is political, Jameson's argument is not incorrect—there is a deeply conservative edge to knitting—there are strong ties to the military and feminine participation in war tied up in knitting resurgences. Knitting certainly can be about containment, tradition, and unequal gender relations. But what if the conservatism of knitting was seen instead as a point of potential and connection? Knitting as a radical act depends upon the conservatism of its history, and as such, is able to occupy spaces often closed to more radical political manifestations. Though this should not be seen as a critique of protest, nor of other life choices, knitting is productive in its ability to cross lines, to start conversation, to form connections from the strangest of bedfellows—it is tactile, affective, and attentive.[6]

I like how all these ideas fit together—a digital information system based on weaving, a group of activists using knitting as a method of enabling cross-gender and age participation, all while echoing the metaphor of the web so beloved by global justice activists. The global justice movement has been dependent upon these webs of digital communication, and dependent upon affinity groups forming their own networks and bringing these networks together at various locales, community events, and social forums.

Radical knitting makes use of these networks of communication, and is often able to use the mainstream media to convey messages to viewers and readers who may not attend (or be interested in) protest. Though the Weaving the Web action went largely unnoticed in Québec City, this has not been the case for more recent protests. For the most part, reporters simply don't know what to do—a fair amount of the coverage is dismissive, "This will have you in stitches," writes one reporter, while others rely on a whole variety of witticisms—"a loosely knit bunch," of "dyed in the wool" activists. But as quickly as reporters come up with jokes, the knitters reclaim them—humor has always played an important role in the global justice movement. After all, because of all the stereotypes used to dismiss knitting, it's next to impossible to portray knitters as threatening: "Well, they needle the police," writes another reporter. More interesting to me is a rumor that haunts many of these articles—a story of an ill-defined protest held somewhere in Europe sometime around 2000, where a convoy of business and government leaders were driven each day to a meeting site outside of town. The story goes that knitters gathered at a main intersection through which the convoy had to pass, and by the end of the day formed a web of knitting to shut down the intersection and stop the convoy. No one seems to know which protest, where, or when, but the story has spread over listservs, through the media, by word of mouth, and across these webs of resistance. The actual web of wool was destroyed but a virtual web remains. And, in many cases, the knitted garments actually survive the action, marking with every stitch the presence of the body, and the inability to effect complete control.

"Knitting opens the door to talk to people," says Grant Neufeld, founding member of the Calgary Revolutionary Knitting Circle. It also re-genders the space of the city as feminine. In a recent action, Calgary knitters sat outside several financial institutions, knitting a series of 6-by-6 inch squares that were knitted first into a social safety net and then (after a game of volleyball with a paper mâché globe as a ball), into blankets and sweaters for the homeless. Breaking down a public/private barrier, reclaiming public space, softening the hard edges of corporate culture, and introducing a slow, hand-worked activity to the busy hubs of the downtown core—all of these elements challenge the smooth face of capitalist culture and the seeming inevitability of "progress."

Where radical knitting differs from many anticapitalist actions is in its use of bodily memory. Knitting is highly effective at exposing the invisible lines of global capitalism. Anyone who has actually hand—or even machine knitted—a garment will know that the $30 cost of a sweater in the store means that someone is being underpaid. Even machine-made knitwear has the same easily unraveled knitting codes and patterns, the same actions of knit, purl, intarsia, slipped stitches, and casts on and off—a language of sorts that links producers and consumers.

There is a potential intersection in the fact that textile production, cloth, and the wearing of fabrics cross the lines of global markets, diasporas, and protest movements. Textiles offer a text of sorts, reflecting the movement of people and the circulation of goods—the commodity fabrics and rugs made by child labor in India arrive in North America with tales of exploitation woven into the very threads. Word of the Zapatista rebellion in the Chiapas region of Mexico in 1994 was spread not only through the Internet, but also through the embroideries of the women's collective. It is this underlying knowledge—of clothing, of stitching—combined with the widespread acknowledgment of sweatshop production that allows textiles to seimotically bridge gaps that might otherwise remain chasms. Here, attention to products and attention to the system are one and the same thing.

One of the nodes where knitting is currently being used to cross political lines is in the art gallery. Susan Buck-Morss argues that the art world has been commodified in much the same way as the public spaces of the city under neoliberalism. She suggests that museums are tightly wound up in the politics of global capitalism and as such, political art is instantly consumed by the aestheticizing politics of the gallery, rendering political statement as mere aesthetic gesture (Buck-Morss 2003: 66–69). However, I'd argue that in a number of recent art world projects that combine political statements with knitting, a straightforward depoliticization is impossible.

Take, for example, the work of Canadian artist Barb Hunt. In her project *antipersonnel*, Hunt knits land mines, juxtaposing soft pink wool with the harshness of her subject. When I talked with her about this project, she mentioned a bodily response to her work, the way that people wanted to touch the wool, and to pick up the land mines. For her, something that is slowly and carefully made also slows down the viewer, causing him or her to stop and contemplate the knitted work as a space of difference within the museum. She writes, "The lowliness of hand-knitting really attracted me to its subversive potential. It is just about as far as you can get from the high-tech dangerous world of armaments (especially land mines which are so impersonal). And of course knitting is about love, built on the smallest of repetitive gestures. (Again, the opposite of a mine exploding all at once)."

Similarly, in Kelly Jenkins' large-scale, knitted, sex-industry calling cards, one is reminded that "everyone wears a piece of knitting every day"; that everyone is connected to the exploitation of women, and of labor (Higgins). Through a link between the garments on the viewer's body and a knowledge of knitting, the flickering gaze of the postmodern subject is stilled, at least for a minute. As Shane Waltener writes of his "Knitting Piece" performances, in which gallery viewers gather together to knit simple objects: "These performances are not just about knitting. They are about creating a space for social interaction, about conversations, stories told, memories recalled. The resulting knitted loops, with photographs of knitters attached, trace the history of the shared activity." "Each stitch," he continues, "contains a thought entered into a network that is passed around, like on an ancient form of the Internet."

For Walterner, "The comfort of repetition and the tactile nature of knitting encourages spontaneous exchanges between participants. An unspoken agreement is made between the knitters so that knitting speed and tension evens out, allowing the activity to go on uninterrupted. To knit, a craft seemingly outmoded in Western Europe, is to aim for greater self-sufficiency. In

a modest way, it is making a stand against the dictates of the fashion industry, and the globalization of markets." In this way, knitting is political.

Slowed down, the viewer pays attention, is stopped, and enters into a
space of criticality, a space represented by the surprising moment of seeing
knitters in the tear gas. Drawing on the tactile elements of knitting, this
space involves the "capacity to sustain sensation rather than highlight representation or communicate meaning" (Bennett 2005: 21).

Epilogue

I write this essay in part with the idea of analyzing my own experiences.
I have participated in the three elements brought together here—knitting at
protests, belonging to knitting circles, and engaging in knitting performances within the gallery/academic sphere. I will speak briefly here of the last,
in part because it is an ongoing participatory project. The Viral Knitting
Project grew out of a desire to bring together possibilities of viral communication over the Internet with the anti-war movement and revolutionary
knitting circles. The collaboration between art historians, communications
scholars, activists and artists, resulted in a project that took the binary code
of the Code Red Virus, a powerful computer virus that exploits a bug in the
indexing system of Microsoft Windows, and turned it into a knitting pattern.
The binary code was easily translated into the P (purl) and K (knit) stitches
of knitting patterns. Once knitted, the virus became a scarf, something that
was comforting, giftable, but intrinsically dangerous—a latent virus that
could be easily transported over borders, into restricted areas, and across
threatened territories. In turn, because it was a virus, we hoped that the pat-
tern/idea would spread, that people would pick up on the viral pattern and
begin to knit it, or would take the idea and translate it into other codes.

The Viral Knitting Project will hopefully mutate and travel over the
Internet, either through individual knitters using the pattern, or through the
performance of the project itself.[7] The performance consists of a download-
able video, any number of knitters, and re-claimed yarn, wound into balls
made from the unraveling of exhausted commodities—the used sweaters
that no longer play a role in the circulation of capital. Knitters gather in
front of the video, knitting the pattern of the virus in red, yellow, orange and
green, each color in proportion to the number of days since September 11th
that the United States has been under Code Red, Code Orange, Code Yellow,
and Code Green "security advisories." The idea is to bring together a number
of issues under one performance in a manner similar to the affinity groups at
global justice protests, but also to highlight some of the links between technology, culture, capitalism, and war. The Viral Knitting Project attempts to
push these ideas further, incorporating knitting-as-protest into the realm of

knitting-as-communication. As a collaborative and interactive project, the Viral Knitting Project changes with each performance, constantly accruing new interpretations and participants.

I don't think knitting will ever replace other forms of activism, nor do I think that it should. I do think that it is an important alternative or supplement to other forms of protest, lobbying, and daily choices. Where knitting succeeds is in crossing boundaries of age, gender, ethnicity, class and politics. Its fluidity and its community nature, its encouragement of interpersonal connection and conversation are all the basis of a quiet, slow, revolutionary movement. I always feel safer at a protest with knitting needles—they are the ultimate weapon, one of creativity rather than destruction.

Notes

1. This description draws on my experience in Québec City, and the diary-like entries of numerous protesters, compiled in publications like *RESIST!* (2001), *Counter Productive* (2002), and *Fish Piss Zine*; documentaries such as *A View from the Summit* (2001), *Tear Gas Holiday* (2001); and websites such as www.indymedia.org and www.stoptheftaa.org, among others.

2. I would like to thank Lindsay Leitch for bringing this idea to my attention. Leitch is writing her MA thesis at Queen's University (Canada) on quilting and activism.

3. Many of the ideas linking technology and knitting on which Bachmann draws, are found in Sadie Plant, *Zeros and Ones: Digital Women and the New Technoculture*, (London: Fourth Estate, 1997).

4. See also Rozsika Parker, *The Subversive Stitch: Embroidery and the Making of the Feminine*, (Routledge: New York, 1989).

5. An even further to the right reply from Government Shrinker (re-posted on the conservative Free Republic website): The author goes a bit overboard, but I thinks she's right that knitting and similar activities can often be an unhealthy habit used to block out serious matters that the woman ought to be addressing. Repetitive, nervous activities engaged in compulsively for no good reason, are unhealthy, whether it's women knitting constantly or kids spending hours at video games while their schoolwork and social development go untended. As for "traditional," our grandmothers knitted because it was the most cost and time-effective way to produce items that were actually needed, or to produce occasional nice little gift items. Very different from many of the compulsive knitters of today, whose kids are dumped in public schools and parked in front of the TV or a video game, while mom obsesses over her latest knitting project and spends gobs of time and money at craft stores.

6. The last resurgence of knitting took place during the Second World War, and indeed knitting played a vital role in most wars of the nineteenth and twentieth centuries. Knitting gave women a participatory role: knitting socks, mittens, hats and bandages for the troops.

7. There were other aspects to the Viral Knitting Project, including a culture jam, a soundtrack, and a video, all of which can be accessed from www. pixelvision.org.

References

Afghans for Afghans, see Afghansforafghans.org

Liz Armstrong, "The Crafty Protester," in *The Chicago Reader*, October 22, 2004, np. Available at www.microrevolt.org

Ingrid Bachmann, "Material and the Promise of Immaterial," in *Material Matters: The Art and Culture of Contemporary Textiles.* Ingrid Bachmann and Ruth Scheuing, eds. (YYZ Books: Toronto, 1998), 23–34.

Jill Bennett, *Empathetic Vision: Affect, Trauma and Contemporary Art* (Stanford, CA: Stanford University Press, 2004).

Janelle Brown, "Do It Yourself," in *Salon Magazine,* May 21, 2001. Available at www.salon.com

Susan Buck-Morss, *Thinking Past Terror: Islamism and Critical Theory on the Left* (London and New York: Verso, 2003).

Crafts Council of England, "Knit 2 Together." Available at http://www. craftscouncil.org.uk

J. Chang, B. Or, E. Tharmendran, E. Tsumara, S. Daniels, and D. Leroux, eds., *RESIST! A Grassroots Collection of Stories, Poetry, Photos and Analysis from the Québec City FTAA Protests and Beyond* (Halifax: Fernwood, 2001).

Susan J. Douglas, *Where the Girls Are: Growing Up Female with the Mass Media* (New York: Three Rivers Press, 1995).

Jill Freidberg and Rick Rowley (directors), *This is What Democracy Looks Like,* (Seattle: Seattle Independent Media Center and Big Noise Films, 1999).

Anne Galloway, "Resonances and Everyday Life: Ubiquitous Computing and the City," 2003. Available at http://www.purselipsquarejaw.org/mobile/cult_studies_draft.pdf.

Betsy Greer, *Taking Back the Knit: Creating Communities Via Needlecraft.* MA Thesis (London: Goldsmiths College, 2004). Available at www.craftivism.com.

Elizabeth Grosz, "Woman, *Chora*, Dwelling," in *Space, Time and Perversion: Essays on the Politics of Bodies* (London: Routledge, 1995), 111–24.

Charlotte Higgins, "Political Protest Turns to the Radical Art of Knitting," in *The Guardian* January 31, 2005. Available at http://www.guardian.co.uk

Magnus Isacsson (director), *A View From the Summit* (Ottawa: National Film Board of Canada, 2001).

Tonya Jameson, "Nesting Urge Won't Remove Cause of Fears," in the *Charlotte Observer*, March 23, 2003. Re-posted at http://freerepublic.com.

Andrea Langlois, *Mediating Transgressions: The Global Justice Movement and Canadian News Media*, MA Thesis, (Montréal: Concordia University, 2004).

Claudette Lauzon, *Whose Streets? The Visual Culture of Resistance During the 2001 Mass Demonstrations Against the Free Trade Area of the Americas in Québec City*, MA Thesis (Ottawa: Carleton University, 2003).

Anne MacDonald, *No Idle Hands: The Social History of American Knitting* (New York: Ballantine Books, 1990).

Andy Opel, "Punishment Before Prosecution: Pepper Spray as Postmodern Repression," in *Representing Resistance: Media, Civil Disobedience, and the Global Justice Movement*, eds. Andy Opel and Donnalyn Pompper (London and Westport, CT: Praeger, 2003), 44–60.

Luca Palladino and David Widgington, *Counter Productive: Québec City Convergence Surrounding the Summit of the Americas* (Montréal: Cumulus Press, 2002).

Rozsika Parker, *The Subversive Stitch: Embroidery and the Making of the Feminine* (New York: Routledge, 1989).

Sadie Plant, *Zeros and Ones: Digital Women and the New Technoculture* (London: Fourth Estate, 1997).

Project Linus. See Projectlinus.org

Revolutionary Knitting Circle. See www.knitting.activist.ca

Shane Waltener. See www.shanewaltener.com

Toronto Video Activist Collective (director), *Tear Gas Holiday: Québec City Summit 2001* (Toronto: TVAC, 2003).

Weaving a Web of Solidarity: A Feminist Action Against Globalisation Summit of the Americas FTAA, Québec City, April 2001.

Hard Livin': Bare Life, Autoethnography, and the Homeless Body

BRE

On the streets there's no forgetting your body. Its hunger gnaws at you constantly. Tired bones offer regular reminders that pavement makes a rotten mattress. Skin burns from the heat of sun and lash of wind. The wet cold of rain…the entire body shivers from the marrow outward.

My homeless body is the low-end site of biopolitics. It is the low-rent district in which postmodern struggles are engaged. The street is perhaps the prime example of what Mary Louise Pratt calls a contact zone, those spaces in which cultures meet, clash, and wrestle with each other. Despite the postmodern emphasis on playful encounter these contacts are quite often brutal and vicious.

Poor people are subjected to ongoing violence simply because of the poverty that we embody.

> "Those cheaters on welfare are useless,"
> the young man says. "The best thing
> to do is set up a machine gun
> at Hastings and Main
> and open fire.
> They're gonna die anyway, so it
> might as well be sooner as later." (Cameron 1995)

Sandy Cameron's poem expresses a view that I have overheard many times from "respectable citizens"—my life is not worth living. My body is expendable.

My body is viewed as garbage. In a popular series of ads for a local Toronto radio station, a homeless person is shown sitting on a garbage can. Emblazoned on the photo is the word "PEST."

A middle-class tourist is overheard saying, about those of us who rest outside his hotel: "The kindest thing would be to get them all drunk and just put them to sleep. Nobody would know the difference. Nobody knows them. They'd never be missed." Graffiti screaming, "Kill the poor" has appeared around town over the last few years.

The threatened violence is too often played out for real. There has been an increase recently in the number of physical attacks on homeless people by neo-Nazi gangs. We are reminded of the vulnerability of our bodies when a friend is killed while sleeping in a park, or dies from the cold of a winter night, or her body turns up in an alley near the streets where she worked.

Not long ago, I was physically attacked by a self-styled street vigilante screaming at me that he was "cleaning the garbage off the streets." The intersection of inferiorized subject positions was clear in his thinking as he identified me as a "faggot" and my partner as a "whore" simply by virtue of our being on the streets.

As Jean Swanson suggests: "The poor in Canada are not yet being murdered by government bullets, although some of them are being murdered when they try to supplement inadequate welfare rates with prostitution." Swanson also points out that "the contempt, the lies, the innuendo, and the stereotypes of the media and the politicians are the first manipulating steps to the hatred that must be necessary before killing seems acceptable" (2001: 104–105).

When I'm living on the streets, my body is painfully exposed. I have no shelter and few defenses. Our life expectancy in Canada is six-and-a-half years shorter than wealthier people. My body simply stands less of a chance of being around for a while, less than the likely reader of this book. Mine is an ephemeral body, even in the mortal human terms of life expectancy; a term that exists for others with the time to sit around and worry about it.

This is bare life. As Giorgio Agamben (2000) notes in his discussion of naked life, we are the ones whose lives are considered worthless. We are the exception to the human subject of modern sovereignty: the citizen. We are the naked lives, and there are many, including indigenous people and non-status immigrants, who are deemed not to be part of the decision-making body: the citizenry.

Being labeled criminals, deviants, even "thugs" and "pests" as homeless people too often are, erases my humanity; it places me in a postmodern realm, the realm of the post-human. I was human once, but that was before I "chose" to abandon the civil society and its work ethic and became the despised street youth, the mere echo of a person, a post-human. Naked life. A condition of violence.

This politics of exclusion removes our poor bodies from civil society and the realm of citizenship. Exclusion, being rendered invisible, immaterial, is a common bodily experience. Governments don't invite us to take part in discussions on issues that affect our lives. The comfortable chairs at summits on living and working opportunities are not filled by poor people. We are not asked to tell our own stories and we do not get many opportunities. We are treated as objects rather than subjects. "Poor people have as much control over government experiments or think-tank theorizing about their future as lab rats have in a cancer experiment" (Swanson 2001: 77–78). We don't ask which questions to address. We don't design the experiment and we are not invited to present the findings.

bell hooks argues that while it is now fashionable to talk about overcoming racism and sexism, class remains "the uncool subject" that makes people tense. Despite being such a pressing issue, class is not talked about in a society in which the poor have no public voice. As hooks (2000: vii) notes, "We are afraid to have a dialogue about class even though the ever-widening gap between rich and poor has already set the stage for ongoing and sustained class warfare." Breaking this silence is crucial.

So we must present it ourselves. We must do autoethnography. We don't have much access to computers and we have even less access to publications that will relay our stories, so our autoethnography is expressed in more direct, one might say, traditional means. Oral traditions are strong among us, and we can spin yarns all afternoon under the right circumstances.

Autoethnography: Sociology and an Emergent Methodology

Postmodern research has questioned dominant research methodologies for obtaining social knowledge. This includes a critique of traditional qualitative research practices. In response, new research practices have recently been developed. Specifically an emergent ethnographic practice, autoethnography, which involves personalized accounts of authors' experiences, has emerged as a tool to give greater attention to the ways in which the ethnographer interacts with the culture being researched. Autoethnography is a form of research that connects the personal with the cultural, situating the researching subject within specific social contexts. Autoethnograpers' texts, which vary in their emphasis on self (*auto*), culture (*ethnos*), and process (*graphy*), offer means to closely examine self/other interactions.

Autoethnography finds its roots in the postmodern crisis of representation in anthropology. It poses a response to realist agendas in ethnography and sociology "which privilege the researcher over the subject, method over subject matter" (Denzin quoted in Spry 2001: 710). As described by Ellis (1999) the work of the autoethnographer involves moving back and forth between a wide ethnographic lens focusing on social and cultural aspects of experience, and a more personal lens exposing a researching self that moves by and through cultural interpretations that are often resisted.

By placing themselves clearly in the story—as agents from specific locations in processes of social and cultural production—autoethnographers have openly challenged accepted views about silent authorship. Indeed the "living body/subjective self of the researcher is recognized as a salient part of the research process, and sociohistorical implications of the researcher are reflected upon" (Spry 2001: 711). In autoethnography, the researcher is firmly in the picture, in context, interacting with others.

By altering how researchers are expected to write, autoethnographies have allowed some researchers to avoid the constraints of dominant "realist" modes of ethnography while opening new options regarding what ethnographers might write about. Autoethnographic texts have been presented in forms including poetry, photographic essays and journals, as well as more customary social science essays (Ellis 1999). Within these texts, autoethnographers "identify zones of contact, conquest, and the contested meanings of self and culture that accompany the exercise of representational authority" (Neuman 1996: 191). In these writings, actions, emotions, and ideas are featured as relational and institutional stories influenced by history and social structures that are themselves engaged in dialectical relations with actions, thoughts and feelings (Ellis 1999).

Autoethnographies offer explanations of othering practices in research, and analyses of difference from the inside. They encourage practical rethinking of terms like validity, reliability, and objectivity. Autoethnographers offer a critique of representation and legitimation within social science disciplines. These are perhaps some of the reasons that this emergent methodology remains controversial within social sciences such as sociology. I suggest that autoethnography offers critical researchers a useful new tool for understanding complex social relations in contemporary contexts.

While autoethnography has received growing attention within academic disciplines like anthropology, literature, and history, sociologists have been left on the sidelines of discussion around this emergent methodology. I view that as unfortunate, since autoethnography offers a potentially useful methodological alternative as sociologists grapple with questions of community, identity, values, and structure within the current context. It might also take sociological discussions of autobiography and biography beyond viewing these texts as resources or data, toward discussing them as topics for investigation in their own right. The lack of comment from sociologists is particularly curious if one remembers C. Wright Mills' insistence that "unless sociology works at the level of biography it does not and cannot work at the level of structure" (Stanley 1993: 51).

In a work that predates most of the writing on autoethnography by several years, Liz Stanley argues that sociological discussions of what she terms auto/biography rather than autoethnography have two parallel origins. The first is the feminist concern with reflexivity within sociological research processes. The second is Merton's discussion of sociological autobiography. Through his investigation of the dynamics of sociological autobiography, Merton draws "analytic attention to the way that insider and outsider positions systematically influence what kind of knowledge is produced" (Stanley 1993: 42). These differently located and produced knowledges raise crucial issues for the sociology of knowledge, notably affirming that reality is not singular. Stanley (1993: 41) suggests that auto/biography "disrupts conventional taxonomies of life writing, disputing its divisions of self/other, public/private, and immediacy/memory." In her view (1993: 41), "the auto/biographical I signals the active inquiring presence of sociologists in constructing, rather than discovering, knowledge."

Crucial in this movement are processes of reflexivity, a key component of feminist praxis. Reflexivity treats the researching self as a subject for intellectual inquiry "and it encapsulates the socialized, non-unitary and changing self posited in feminist thought" (Stanley 1993: 44). In feminist praxis, conventional dichotomies that separate the social and the individual, the personal and the political, are refused. Academic feminist work has focused on women's autobiographies in part because "feminism as a social movement is concerned with the re/making of lives, of inscribing them as gendered (and raced, and classed, with sexualities), and also with inscribing a wider range of possibilities for women's lives by providing contrasting exemplars" (Stanley, 1993: 46). These have also been the concerns of critical sociological work.

Some of the sociological silence over autoethnographic practice might be the result of loudly negative responses that have been leveled by gatekeepers of sociological methodology. Perhaps the most vocal opponent in sociology, Herbert J. Gans (1999: 540) asserts that autoethnography is "the product of a postmodern but asocial theory of knowledge that argues the impossibility of knowing anything beyond the self." In light of the numerous examples cited above, this appears as a rather unfair caricature of autoethnography. What most autoethnographers argue is the need for practices that actively and directly situate the researcher within social relations beyond the self in which the self is engaged and developed, and to which the self contributes. Instead of a self/other dichotomy, autoethnographers recognize the mutual constitution of self and other as relational concepts and seek to understand and express the processes by which they are composed and, significantly, might be re-composed or de-composed. What is presented is a re-evaluation of the dialectics of self and culture.

Gans argues that autoethnography abdicates sociology's main roles in, and for, helping people understand their society. It is precisely this sort of patronizing approach, in which only (or mostly) sociologists understand society and the (other) people who live it must be helped, that has spurred some autoethnographic writing. Instead, autoethnographers insist that members of marginalized communities have great insights into their society and the mechanisms by which marginalization is constituted and reproduced, including through academic elitism. Autoethnography seeks to situate the sociologists as the ones in need of understanding.

Gans (1999: 542–543) bemoans the loss of "researcher detachment" and "distancing" and contends that this leads to a loss of reliability, validity, and possibly funding. He then tries to disparage autoethnography by comparing it to social movements, as if they are negative aspects of society. Finally Gans (1999: 543) dismisses autoethnography as being "too ordinary to become part of any sociological canon." To that the autoethnographer might say: "Hear, hear!"

While I agree with some of the cautions put forward by Gans, and indeed all methodologies should be approached with caution, overall his presentation of autoethnography is so distorted that it borders on caricature. Whether this rather one-sided reading suggests a specific agenda more than an open attempt at understanding is open for debate.

While Gans argues that autoethnography is inherently non-sociological, one gets a decidedly different perspective from Robert K. Merton's description of sociological autobiography: "The sociological autobiography utilizes sociological perspectives, ideas, concepts, findings, and analytical procedures to construct and interpret a narrative text that purports to tell one's own history within the larger history of one's times" (Merton 1988: 18). He goes on to suggest that "autobiographers are the ultimate participants in a dual participant-observer role, having privileged access—in some cases, monopolistic access—to their own inner experience" (Merton 1988: 43). Autoethnography has its sociological interest "within the epistemological problematics concerning how we understand 'the self' and 'a life,' how we 'describe' ourselves and other people and events, how we justify the knowledge-claims we make in the name of the discipline, in particular through the processes of textual production" (Stanley 1993: 50). Doane (2001) suggests that autoethnography juxtaposes memory and social theory, extending and embodying theoretical conflicts.

Stanley (1993: 45) asserts that "focusing on 'the sociologist' and their intellectual practices and labour processes does *not* mean that we focus on one person and exclude all else," as Gans claims. Rather, these practices and contexts can reveal much about the history of sociology, divisions within society, social networks and the social production of ideas (Stanley 1993). Autoethnography doesn't imply a shift of sociology towards individualism.

Autoethnographers suggest that sociologists situate themselves materially within a specific labor process and be accountable for the products of their intellectual labor. This also means acknowledging the situational and contextual production of knowledge and the sociologist's position within a social division of labor. The positionality of the sociologist is important for understanding each research activity. The autoethnographer is involved in the active construction of social reality and sociological knowledge rather than discovering it. For Merton, good sociological autobiography "is analytically concerned with relating its product to the epistemological conditions of its own production" (Stanley 1993: 43).

Autoethnography replaces the "power over" of scholarly authority, offering instead a "power with" the researching self and others. An autoethnographic text reflects a space in which "truth and reality are not fixed categories, where self-reflexive critique is sanctioned, and where heresy is viewed as liberatory" (Spry 2001: 721). It situates itself personally and politically: it interrogates the realities it represents. It invokes the teller's story in the history that is told (Trihn 1991).

Spry (2001: 721) offers an account of some of the benefits for research that she identifies with autoethnography: "I am better able to engage the lived experience of myself with others. I am more comfortable in the often conflictual and unfamiliar spaces one inhabits in ethnographic research. I am more comfortable with myself as other." While Gans argues that autoethnography will cause readers to lose interest in sociological texts, for autoethnographers a "self-reflexive critique upon one's positionality as researcher inspires readers to reflect critically upon their own life experience, their constructions of self, and their interactions with others within sociohistorical contexts" (Spry 2001: 711).

Still there are obstacles faced by practitioners of autoethnography in their attempts to develop alternative methodological practices. As Spry (2001: 722) notes: "An autoethnographic voice can interrogate the politics that structure the personal, yet it must still struggle within the language that represents dominant politics." In particular, "[s]peaking and embodying the politically transgressive through experimental linguistic forms (i.e., autoethnography, sociopoetics, performance scripts) can result in a lack of publications." Thus, autoethnographers must often become advocates for the multivocality of form and content in academic journals, against the academic preference for impersonal and nonemotional modes of representation.

The defensive reactions of disciplinary gatekeepers, what some autoethnographers call a "backlash" (Rinehart 1998), has had the effect of silencing larger sociological debate over the emergence and development of new methodological practices. It may also explain why some autoethnographies have been written recently on experiences with the gatekeepers of academic journals and attempts to publish autoethnographic works. As Sparkes (2000: 30) suggests, charges of individualism or subjectivism "function as regulatory charges against certain forms of sociology and act to re-inscribe ethnographic orthodoxy."

I would much rather see an open and honest engagement with auto-ethnography in sociology. Such an engagement would not shy away from critique, but would at the same time address the challenges to sociological practice posed by autoethnography.

As Spry (2001: 727) writes, understanding human experience requires "a pluralism of discursive and interpretive methods that critically turn texts back upon themselves in the constant emancipation of meanings." Researchers in anthropology, history, and literature have turned to autoethnography as one means to address this. I would suggest that not only would sociologists benefit from this emerging method, but we might also contribute to its critical development. Rather than reacting against the experimental and the personal in autoethnography, sociologists might do well to see this as a method suited to what Mills once called (unscientifically it seems now) the "sociological imagination." We must question how sociologists can live up to Mills' crucial challenge to connect personal issues with public problems if we continue to disavow methodological practices that have no time for the personal experiences, concerns, and contexts of the sociologist.

Act 1: Of Safe Streets and the New Poor Laws

It's another tough year in Toronto for those of us who have already suffered years of vicious attacks by various levels of government. On February 1, 2005, Toronto city council voted to accept a proposal to ban homeless people from sleeping in Nathan Phillips Square. The amendment to Bylaw 1994-0784 specifically says "no person can camp" (which includes sleeping in the square during the day or night, whether or not a tent or temporary abode of any kind is used) in the square. Incredibly, the council went even further and decided to extend the ban to all city property.

This move to ban homeless people from sleeping in public spaces like Nathan Phillips Square is only part of a city staff report "From the Street into Homes: A Strategy to Assist Homeless Persons to Find Permanent Housing." In discussing ways to address street homelessness the report also suggests enhanced legal and legislative frameworks and more enforcement of current provincial laws and city bylaws. The report also recommends that the Toronto police service be requested to participate in the work of the Street Outreach Steering Committee. Behind the report's velvety language of "outreach," one finds the iron fist of the Toronto police.

This is no way to address homelessness in the city and is an open invitation for more attacks by cops on homeless people. It offers little more than an excuse to expand the already bloated Toronto police budget that, at around $690 million, already gobbles up 22% of Toronto's property tax dollars.

These proposed policies are a throwback to the brutal days of former Mayor Mel Lastman's regime. Lastman had long engaged in an open campaign of class war against poor and homeless people (whom he labels as thugs). Adding to this chorus, the Ontario crime commissioner (charged with overseeing crime policy for the entire province) declared in an interview with the Canadian Broadcasting Corporation (CBC) that squeegeers were the province's top concern.

In 1999, with much fanfare and plenty of snarling, spitting, growling, and gnashing of teeth, Lastman and the City Council launched a so-called Community Action Policing (CAP) program backed by $2 million of public funds. The following year the city managed to find another $1 million in a supposedly tight budget. Following the model of Rudolph Giuliani's rampage in New York City, the money was spent to pays cops overtime to harass, intimidate, and threaten poor people in targeted areas of the city. Each year the cops have kept up their campaign until well into the fall. After that they hope Mother Nature will put in the overtime for them. As the Inspector in charge of the operation stated at its launch: "The best crime-fighting tool we have is minus-30 in February" (*Globe and Mail*, July 26, 1999, A10). So having no home is now a crime. Given that several homeless people have frozen to death on the streets of Toronto during the past two winters, it would appear that capital punishment is being practiced in Canada after all; but only if your crime is poverty.

Around the same time, the provincial Tory government, with much prodding from Lastman and right-wingers on Toronto City Council changed the Ontario Highway Act to make squeegeeing and so-called "aggressive" panhandling illegal. The resulting legislation, "The Safe Streets Act," makes it illegal to give any reasonable citizen "cause for concern" (whatever that might be). In sentiment and in practice, this law has given cops, local vigilantes, and business improvement associations great leeway to continue or expand their harassment of the poor and homeless. Yet the current "From the Street into Homes Report" only recommends that this brutal legislation be enforced more systematically.

Many Torontonians had hoped for more under the new Council headed by the supposedly progressive mayor Miller. Unfortunately, the current Council is showing that, like the one before, it favours criminalizing homeless people rather than developing real solutions such as affordable housing. Last year, Miller's office sent bulldozers under the Bathurst Street Bridge to destroy the homes of a community of teenage street youth. This attack was accompanied by a heightened police presence on the streets. The corners of Queen and Spadina and Queen and Bathurst have been hardest hit. Homeless people who access services at these corners are targeted by police, harassed, ticketed, and arrested.

Ticketing and arrests under anti-poor law infractions such as the Safe Streets Act have already been stepped up. Young people have found themselves being held in jail for minor infractions and released on stringent bail conditions: not to possess cups and cleaning equipment, and prohibiting access to parts of the city. Along with the massive ticketing, cops have used pepper spray to awaken youth sleeping on the streets.

The city has also revitalized a park ambassador program to move and harass homeless people in city parks. Along with their efforts to drive squeegeers out of the city, the cops have been busy chasing homeless people out of public parks. Poverty's okay, just keep it out of sight.

Of course, a very real and vicious crackdown has been in effect for some time now. Cops have routinely ticketed us for anything, be it trespassing, loitering, or littering. Likewise some store-owners make it a hobby to verbally or physically attack panhandlers, or get the cops to do it for them.

Cops claim that they're not trying to rid the city of homeless kids, they're just trying to keep people from stepping into the roadway. So far there's been little demonizing rhetoric or physical harassment related to the jaywalking scourge.

It is important to consider the recent and ongoing history of the city's preference for criminalizing homeless people, rather than addressing root social and economic causes of homelessness, such as the lack of affordable housing, availability of social services, and access to jobs with a living wage. The Council's proposed plans only serve to distort these "lacks" as criminal matters.

People sleep at City Hall because the shelters are full and conditions in many of them are dreadful. People sleep outside because there's not enough affordable housing. By removing the homeless from the Square, the politicians hope to remove a major political embarrassment from under their noses. They will also send a message to every cop, city official, and narrow-minded vigilante in Toronto that it's open season on the homeless.

While the CAP was touted as "all of the forces' best and latest thinking on community-based policing" (*Globe and Mail*, July 26, 1999, A10), none of this is new at all. These are the same tactics the bosses have hit us with for centuries (they called them poor laws in 17th century England). The names change but the intentions remain the same. Along with programs like workfare and the reduction or elimination of social services, criminalization is about driving the poor, unemployed, and homeless, into wage slavery or death. Serve capital or go away!

In case this point is missed, the "soft cops" in social services launched a "Squeegee Work Youth Mobilization" program to teach squeegeers to get jobs repairing bikes ($250,000 from the City Council and $395,000 from the federal government). What was not reported was that this program was a complement to the CAP, with cops involved in its implementation and decision-making.

Despite the great career prospects for budding bike repairers, the City Commissioner of Community and Social Services has admitted the program faces some obstacles: "The challenge is this is a group of kids that does not fit into the system. They are very wary of any kind of authority—police, schools *and even social agencies.*" (*Globe and Mail*, July 27, 1999, A9, emphasis added).

Naturalizing Poverty Violence: Practices of Poor Bashing

Jean Swanson identifies such practices as poor-bashing: the widespread discursive attacks on poor people. She suggests that "poor-bashing is when people who are poor are humiliated, stereotyped, discriminated against, shunned, despised, pitied, patronized, ignored, blamed and falsely accused of being lazy, drunk, stupid, uneducated, having large families, and not looking for work" (Swanson 2001: 2). It also involves unequal power, threats, beatings, and murder. Simply because we are poor.

Swanson situates poor-bashing among other practices of inferiorization, such as racism, sexism, and homophobia, by which the subaltern others are constituted and maintained. Robert Miles argues that the model for racialist inferiorization began in 16th century Europe as discrimination against the poor, especially beggars. This was part of civilizing projects designed to establish and legitimize a social system of emerging power differentials. Feudal rulers changed their behaviors initially by making their bodily functions more private. This behavioral shift allowed them to contrast their refined activities with those of the inferior people whom they ruled (Miles 1993: 90–97). People in the business and industrial classes imitated this civilized behaviour, presenting their prudent values as inherited rather than socially constructed. Miles suggests that this civilizing project encompassed forms of domestic racism in Europe, in which privileged Europeans portrayed themselves as superior to the people they ruled, providing the foundation for colonial racism.

> Since feudalism changed to capitalism in Europe the elite have defended their wealth in the midst of poverty with myths, language, and patterns of thinking that justified treating Aboriginal people and women as cattle, people of colour as savages, the poor as "vicious" and lazy, and themselves as "civilized" and "virtuous." A huge part of justifying personal wealth is treating the people who don't have it, or the people it's taken from, as lesser human beings (Swanson 2001: 186).

This inheritance was presented in biological or bodily terms. The word "breeding" suggested that the unequal social stations of the rich and poor resulted from biology rather than from circumstances. Breeding is defined both as civility, culture, good manners and refinement, and as biological reproduction. My poverty is inscribed in my physiognomy; it is part of my body.

> The people of property were secure in their belief that they were a superior "race" and that the poor in England, as well as the indigenous peoples of other continents, were somehow less human and deserved their poverty. For them, low wages for the poor, slavery and colonization became legitimate, even preferred, elements in the continuing quest for accumulation of wealth (Swanson 2001: 42).

Police reformer Dr. Patrick Colquhon wrote in 1806 that poverty "is the source of wealth, since without poverty there could be no labour; there could be no riches, no refinement, no comfort, and no benefit to those who may be possessed of wealth." He continued: "Poverty is therefore a most necessary and indispensable ingredient in a society, without which nations and communities could not exist in a state of civilization" (Webb and Webb 1963: 6–9). In the 1990s, corporations and governments imposed trade deals to expand global capital's attacks on poor people, which seem to imply that the degradation of large sectors of the world's population is a natural phenomenon that cannot be avoided.

As in 16th century England, contemporary poor-bashing suggests that we deserve the conditions we endure on the streets as in the poor houses. These views are internalized. Poor-bashing is so embedded in our thinking, in politics, in the media, in organizations, and communities, that it's often difficult to identify it and challenge it. I constantly have to challenge language, myths, and assumptions about poverty and poor-bashing.

Opposing poor-bashing is a good way to confront the internalized messages of shame and blame over our situation. It can stop the bashers, deconstruct the messages about poverty and causes of poverty, and provide a starting point for organizing with other poor people to fight poverty.

Act 2: Bodies in Struggle

On Thursday June 15, 2000, I joined two thousand people in Toronto for a protest called by the Ontario Coalition Against Poverty (OCAP), involving fifty-eight allied groups, including the Canadian Union of Postal Workers, the Canadian Auto Workers, the Canadian Union of Public Employees, and the Industrial Workers of the World. People arrive from as far away as Montréal and Sudbury. We are poor, students, homeless, immigrants, youth, workers, First Nations, and the elderly.

Our reasons for coming together are many. Twenty-two homeless people dead in twenty-four weeks. Forced workfare labor. Olympic bids instead of affordable housing. Targeted policing. Squats torched by cops. Callous politicians blaming us for the poverty of their system.

Our demands are simple, straightforward and clearly stated:

1. Restore the 21.6% cut from social services by the Conservative (Tory) government, one of its earliest and most harmful acts.
2. Repeal the horribly misnamed "Tenant Protection Act" that has removed rent controls and allowed landlords to evict thousands of tenants in Toronto every month since its enactment.
3. Repeal the equally misnamed "Safe Streets Act" which outlaws panhandling and squeegeeing and makes streets much less safe for poor people.

We ask nothing more than that a delegation of people suffering from these vicious policies be allowed inside the Provincial Legislature to address the government. Their response is swift, violent, and cruel. Our request is arrogantly dismissed without consideration. Only heads of states allowed. We are determined to address the legislators and somewhat to our surprise, easily dismantle their first line of barricades.

Advancing, we take up a line in front of the row of riot cops standing behind the second barricade. A tense standoff ensues. Experience has taught us to expect blasts of pepper spray, now the first, not last, response of those protecting privilege. We are ready for it and well-prepared, wearing goggles, bandanas, and some gas masks.

Without warning, the municipal knights in their medieval armor begin clubbing and beating us with their batons and shields. People attempting to retreat are set upon by horses whose riders swing sticks and whips without restraint. I turn from the front line only to be jostled between charging horses. A hoof tramps on my foot momentarily pinning me in place. Shit! Already protesters have fallen or been knocked under the hooves of the enormous beasts. I watch a woman I recognize being desperately rescued by others, one lens of her swim goggles so full of blood I cannot see her eye.

On one side, people attempt to fend off seemingly crazed police who are targeting individual demonstrators for abuse. On the other, protesters protect themselves against the sluggers and their steeds. A woman to my left is smashed in the face with a riot shield. A gash opens under her eye. Blood runs down her cheek. She backs away, attempting to hold her position, but is driven to the ground and clubbed repeatedly. The cop doesn't let up even as it is clear she can no longer defend herself. Several of us manage to pull her away before she suffers grave injury. She is unable to walk to safety on her own.

By now it is clear: either we defend ourselves however we can, or suffer severe injuries. And defend ourselves we do. Rocks are plucked like an earlier generation's daisies from Legislature gardens, paving stones are torn up, broken and hurled skyward, shit is heaved back at its source, noisemakers rattle against shields and shoulders and picket signs fly like arrows. Their side has military training, space age armor, and an intimidating array of weapons. But our side has creativity, resilience, comradeship, and a relentless spirit. Unbelievably we hold our own in pitched battle, literally in hand-to-hand combat as one cop later calls it, for an hour.

We try to retreat to tend to our wounded. Still they come. Horses charge through our first-aid areas, threatening to trample medics and wounded alike. A street nurse desperately pleads with dispatchers to send ambulances. We have serious injuries, concussions, and broken bones. She implores, they refuse. All the while, several ambulances wait behind the Legislature, complete with armored personnel to transport any injured cops.

After more than an hour it is over. We disengage and march to a park several blocks away. As we attempt to disperse, individuals are swarmed and beaten. I see an elderly friend blasted to the ground as he attempts simply to cross the street. Another friend is chased and dragged down by several cops. He is beaten severely on the street and later at the station. Many of us know this violence: it is the same violence suffered by poor and homeless people every day in this city.

Almost immediately the corporate media declares it a historic day in Ontario. Never before has such a battle raged on the lawns of government, they tell us. This is one of the few things they get right. They call us "rampaging anarchists" for refusing to let ourselves be clubbed. They say that goggles and bandanas are proof of our intention to do violence. They deny that cuts to social services, loss of affordable housing, and the criminalization of begging deepen the pain of poverty. They say we are a fringe despite our diversity.

Poststructuralism in the Streets

Notions of objectivity and neutrality don't have much meaning on the streets. Not when you hear how objective observers like social workers and psychologists talk about you or you see how neutral agents like police respond when a shopkeeper accuses you of causing a disturbance or loitering. The context of objective and neutral practices in a capitalist, racist, patriarchal, and heteronormative context is always apparent.

Nowhere in official accounts are we portrayed as people with hopes, dreams, lives, and loves who are willing to stand up for ourselves: survivalists with a strong sense of self-preservation and dignity. Nowhere in corporate media accounts will you find that portrayal. It simply does not fit the essentialist depictions of poor people deployed in poor-bashing discourses.

Life on the street has made me see what I now know as essentialism, allowing for the exercise of various forms of power, and providing a unifying basis for various forms of authoritarianism. It appears directly in the capitalist notion that poor people are essentially lazy and must be coerced to work through mandatory workfare or retraining programs, or through the elimination of welfare programs and subsidized housing.

As one local politician and former food bank director put it after June 15, "I know poor people and these were not poor people. Poor people suffer in silence." Politicians expect us to go away without a fight, to take our bodies somewhere else. Where? And to do what, die? We are essentialized as thugs and criminals, and simultaneously as victims who suffer in silence.

At the same time, essentialist discourses accuse me of being driven by bodily urges, of being incapable of refusing my desires. I am poor because, in addition to being lazy or immature, I cannot delay gratifying my immediate desires for sex, booze, or a leisurely life.

Poor-bashing, as a form of dehumanization, doesn't necessarily ask about the basis of humanity or ask what is the essence of being human. It simply denies us a place in the category "human" itself.

Other modernist categories of gender, race, and sexual preference are blurred as our clothing, appearance, and demeanor stamp us with an unavoidable class mark. The words used by mayors, chamber of commerce leaders, crime commissioners, and city councilors make little distinction for race, age, gender, or sexuality. We are thugs, criminals, garbage, waste. We are simply poor, lumpenproletarians for the more learned sectors.

This class position is supposedly marked on our bodies as popular class stereotypes claim we are "easily spotted by skin ailments, bad dental hygiene, and hair texture" (hooks 2000: 111). Gumball machines in local malls, frequented predominantly by middle-income consumers, sell "Jimmy-Bob Teeth," a variety of grotesque fake teeth and gums filled with cavities, abscesses, and lesions. The teeth of the poor, available for purchase by those with Colgate smiles. Of course, there is some truth in this since all of "these things are affected by diet" and poor people often suffer from malnutrition (hooks 2000: 112).

In response, I can't adopt either the positive essentialism of Kropotkin (human nature as good) or the negative essentialism of Hobbes (human nature as bad). On the streets you see both, often in quick succession. So-called human nature as I have experienced it is in conflict with itself.

As one interesting approach, Gayatri Spivak speaks of the notion of strategic essentialism. Being poor makes you practice strategic essentialism or, indeed, anti-essentialism. You know that what people with positions of authority and respect are saying about you is inaccurate, ideological, and wrong. Spivak advocates strategically speaking from the place of the subaltern, not too hard when you actually are in that position—while recognizing how this place is itself constructed by power.

Experiencing poverty, having the view of the subaltern because I am subaltern, encourages a poststructuralist sensibility. We come to see, in experiential rather than theoretical terms, the necessity of ending "the kind of thinking that puts people into groups like, 'the poor,' or those 'on welfare,' or 'immigrants' or 'Third-World people,' or 'Indians' to justify treating them badly and/or blame them for poverty" (Swanson 2001: 8).

Poststructuralist critiques of essentialism open new possibilities for the assertion of agency, and as such resonate with the experiences of oppressed and marginalized people, even if distances exist between them. We always have to fight off attempts to force fixed and false essences upon us. We have to fight to tell our own versions of things.

Act 3: Bodies in the Courts

Despite the images conjured by names like vagabond, drifter, or hobo, being homeless is an experience of bodily and spatial confinement. "Poor-bashing is being told you aren't free to go where you choose" (Swanson 2001: 19). More and more, poor bodies are constrained, immobile bodies. If I wander into the wrong neighborhood I have private security officers, who are bound by no regulations on conduct, hassling me.

We cannot avoid each other's bodies the way middle-class suburbanites can. Our notions of property and privacy are vastly different from those who have plenty of room and living space. In hostels and shelters, our bodies are crammed together in small spaces under conditions that don't even meet United Nations guidelines for refugee camps.

Going to shelters can leave us beaten up, having our few belongings stolen or contracting tuberculosis, supposedly a disease of the past but rampant in contemporary shelters. Ironically, given our immobility, our bodies are time travelers picking up ancient illnesses that the rest of the population only reads about in history books.

The ticket to mobility is the capacity to spend, to be a consumer. As hooks (2000: 82) notes: "No matter your class, no matter your race, if you have access to credit, to cash, every store is open to you." If you lack such access, the possibility of adopting the consumer subject-position, all doors are slammed in your face. Nowhere is this clearer than in the criminalization of poverty, when the body ends up in cells and courtrooms.

At least forty-two arrests were made relating to the events of June 15. Thirty-four cases have actually been sent to trial, beginning in February, with some charges being dropped and people in vulnerable situations compelled to take pleas.

Outstanding charges include a wide variety of things such as obstructing (falling in front of) or assaulting (being attacked by) peace officers (baton-wielding, shield-carrying maniacs), or possessing weapons (a picket sign or water bottle). The state has even dug out an old charge that has not been used since the 1960s called: participating in a riot. They have not made clear whether a police riot in which one is caught standing one's ground constitutes such participation.

Trials continued for three years after the riot. Immediately it became clear that the courts would go after the most vulnerable people the hardest. People who are homeless, who have other charges or records, and people with addictions have received the most severe treatment.

On June 15th, the police played out their roles as the strong arm of Ontario's neoliberal government. We do not want the Tories to succeed in passing further legislation against working people, students and the poor, just because their paid goons try to use court charges and outrageous bail conditions as a deterrent. People cannot start avoiding protests, strikes, or other forms of resistance out of fear of police repression, because that will only strengthen the Tories' resolve.

People should not feel they have to stand alone or feel alienated by surveillance and images of riot shields and batons. It is crucial to recognize that some people are more vulnerable than others. We need to establish networks of defense not only to defend those arrested, but also in order to demystify the state's legal processes and to work to bolster confidence that people can fight to win. Most of us certainly do not want to go to jail, but we know that the city's prisons have become warehouses for poor people under Tory rule and this must never be forgotten as part of our solidarity work. If people go down because they took a stand, then we must stand by them and their families. We must organize funds and social support so that people do not feel abandoned to the merciless court and jail system. Jail visits and donations to canteens are aspects of this.

Court solidarity for June 15 defendants has been strong, with thirty or more people regularly showing up to fill courtrooms and hallways. There is no way for judges and bailiffs to miss the fact that the defendants have tremendous community support. As people show up at court to do solidarity work, they also gain insights into the system. The extent of attacks on the working class that take place everyday, literally behind closed doors, tells everyone of the need to take our work inside the institutions. Visits to the courts, housing tribunals, and immigration offices almost uniformly show poor people being worked over by the state.

Those of us who experienced it know that the police violence that took place on June 15th, 2000 is the same violence that is meted out routinely against poor people in Ontario. That violence is not simply delivered through baton blows and fists, but through lengthy court proceedings, bail conditions, demeaning legal aid applications and of course, jail time. And that is why we stress the political nature of our trials.

Street Body Politics

Despite its high-sounding name, autoethnography is a street idiom. Almost every other street kid I know keeps some kind of journal. We record our lives, often as poems, sometimes as detailed comics and graphic novels that would put *Spawn* to shame. And it's not simply personal rants either. We seem to have an almost instinctive understanding of Marx even if we've never read him. Often the ideas that most excite us, though, come from the anarchists. As one of my partners says, "When you live on the streets anarchism isn't an abstract theory, it's the story of our lives."

Suffering the almost constant abuses of authority figures, from police and social workers to shelter staff and psychologists, means that an anarchist, anti-authoritarian perspective resonates very deeply with my own lived experiences. It doesn't share the distance of some Marxist approaches with their talk of political parties, vanguards, and transitional programs (a phrase remarkably similar to the ones used by cops and social workers).

Of course, some poststructuralists, most notably Todd May and Saul Newman, have outlined the family resemblance between poststructuralism and anarchism. Both anarchist and poststructuralist approaches emphasize the decenteredness of power relations and an appreciation of the extensive character of power. They also share a critique of representational politics and a strong do-it-yourself practice that rejects deference to would-be experts. When you're poor you experience micro-power and you survive through micro-politics. Squats, graffiti, zines all sustain us and help us continue the fight to survive.

Academic leftists or poststructuralists writing about class are often trapped within specialist jargon that prevents them from communicating with those of us whose perspectives are developed and expressed in experiential terms. Hopefully this small piece will help to bridge that gap: to open channels of communication, understanding, and solidarity. Poststructuralist writings on the body, and the embodiment of power relations—some instances of which I discuss here—have something to offer struggles against poverty.

Poststructuralists are dead on target when they identify the body as a site of struggle, a matter of great contest. My poor body is beaten by police and would-be vigilantes cleaning up the streets, insulted by professionals, dragged into courts. It endures days in welfare and legal aid offices.

Still my body is also a site of strength, standing strong, withstanding blows. When you've lived on the streets and dealt with various abuses the body becomes resilient. To survive I must struggle over perceptions of my body and the meanings attached to it.

Part of this struggle involves recounting our stories, providing glimpses into the many contact zones, streets, struggles, and courts, in which our bodies live. Sometimes telling our stories, raising our voices enough to be heard beyond the streets, requires a good old-fashioned bread riot. We are hungry, let us eat. We are weary, let us rest.

References

Giorgio Agamben, *Means Without End: Notes on Politics* (Minneapolis: University of Minnesota Press, 2000).

Randal Doane, "Exhuming and Slaying Adorno," in *Qualitative Inquiry* 7, no. 3 (2001), 274–278.

C. Ellis, "Heartful Autoethnography," in *Qualitative Health Research* 9, no. 5 (1999), 669–683.

Herbert J. Gans, "Participant Observation in the Era of Ethnography," in *Journal of Contemporary Ethnography* 28, no.5 (1999), 540–548.

Carlo Ginzburg, *The Judge and Historian* (London: Verso, 1999).

bell hooks, *Where We Stand: Class Matters* (New York: Routledge, 2000).

Robert Merton, "Some Thoughts on the Concept of Sociological Autobiography," in *Sociological Lives,* ed. Martha White Riley (Newbury Park: Sage, 1988), 17–21.

A. Momigliano, *The Development of Greek Biography* (Cambridge, MA: Harvard University Press, 1993).

M. Neuman, "Collecting Ourselves at the End of the Century," in *Composing Ethnography: Alternative Forms of Qualitative Writing*, eds. C. Ellis and A. Bochner (London: Alta Mira Press, 1996).

R. Rinehart, "Fictional Methods in Ethnography: Believability, Specks of Glass, and Chekhov," in *Qualitative Inquiry* 4, no. 2 (1998), 200–224.

Andrew, C. Sparkes, "Autoethnography and Narratives of Self: Reflections on Criteria in Action," in *Sociology of Sport Journal* 17, no. 1 (2000), 21–43.

Tami Spry, "Performing Autoethnography: An Embodied Methodological Praxis," in *Qualitative Inquiry* 7, no. 6 (2001), 706–732.

Liz Stanley, "On Auto/Biography in Sociology," in *Sociology* 27, no. 1 (1993), 41–52.

Jean Swanson, *Poor Bashing: The Politics of Exclusion* (Toronto: Between the Lines, 2001).

Forging Spaces of Justice

Anita Lacey

It is the time for celebrating the joy of collectivity, the exhilaration
of creating something that snowballs into something much bigger,
and more amazing than previously imagined possible. It is a moment
when we can break free from the alienation that capitalism enforces
in so many ways —Notes from Nowhere

Images of activists protesting outside the summits of global political and
business elites have become commonplace in the mainstream media in the
last five years. As activists dance and chant, march and shout outside the
meetings, states respond with increasing force—armed police barricade the
buildings, temporary physical walls are erected, and zones of exclusion are
drawn to shut out opposition. Yet, rather than be discouraged and dispersed,
thousands of alternative globalization activists continue to gather outside
these summits. These activists are doing more than enacting a simple response to the assemblage of power brokers: alternative globalization activists are creating spaces of inclusion in opposition to the injustices generated
and exacerbated by bodies like the International Monetary Fund, the World
Trade Organization, the G8, and the World Bank. These spaces, the physical sites of resistance that develop to counter the exclusive meetings and
the dominance of neoliberal capitalism, are temporary expressions of what
alternative globalization activists are striving towards. They are expressions
of the social divine, a sense of being together in a self-directed and shaped
environment.

Spatial negotiations of justice and militant particularisms

Through the dialogues and practices of social justice in contested spaces, new spaces are forged in opposition to the dominant spaces of injustice. People continuously operate in opposition to the dominant mode of

being—they do not resist only in deliberately forged protest spaces. The protest space is both temporal and continuous: it can be interrupted and disseminated in multiple forms with no termination date. The spaces forged by activists opposing the institutions of neoliberal globalization can be temporary physical or emotional spaces. Ideas and practices of social justice are negotiated and played out in spaces that are then dismantled and reassembled at another physical location, continued virtually, or at face-to-face meetings. Each time, new sets of dialogues and practices are established, partially dissolved, and re-established in new configurations. There are, however, constant themes—particularly the desire for an end to the dominance and dominations of neoliberalism and for greater social justice.

Establishing temporal zones of social justice enables activists to elude the shackles of identity and place: "In clinging, often of necessity, to a place-bound identity—oppositional movements become a part of the very fragmentation which a mobile capitalism and flexible accumulation can feed upon" (Harvey 1989: 303). Many alternative globalization activists have embraced an organisational mode that is as multidimensional as contemporary global capital, overcoming what Arjun Appadurai describes as the inability of many transnational advocacy networks to combat global capital (2000: 16). Rather than relying on face-to-face meetings alone, alternative globalization activists plan actions against global neoliberal institutions through various communication technologies as well as at small, local-based collectives (Lacey 2005, Wright and Lacey 2004, Routledge 2004). Ongoing experimentation with rhizomatic forms of organization and with the self-production and distribution of media are two of the key characteristics of alternative globalization struggles in the last decade.

The organizational characteristics described above are common features of what Mertes describes as a diverse movement of movements (2004). These characteristics enable global activist networks to remain outside of state-based, hierarchically organized political circles, and to act independently of neoliberal news media. Most importantly, they are able to challenge the assumed irrevocability of global capital and the current manifestations of globalization. As a mode of interaction and organization, networks allow activists multiple voices, divergent ideas, and disparate visions, yet still enable them to interact and act collectively. Contextualizing activist networks as forms of community allows us to understand the potential—and perceived—strength of activists organizing rhizomatically, while at the same time highlighting the emotional bonds that they share (Arquilla and Ronfeldt 2001).

Michel Maffesoli provides a particularly apt conceptual framework with which to examine the emotional space encircling protest: the idea of the social divine (1996). He adopts the term from Emile Durkheim, who uses it to describe the essence of religious collectivity, while Maffesoli uses it to describe the aggregate force at the base of any society or association (1996: 38, Durkheim 1965: 58–63). For Maffesoli, shared proximity, customs, and rituals give meaning to the social divine, which "allows us to recreate the cenacles that keep us warm and provide social spaces in the heart of the cold, inhuman metropolis" (Maffesoli 1996: 42).

The social divine implies a conscious desire to dissolve into the collective, to lose oneself in a greater whole, in a micro-group or tribe. This would seem to overstate the anonymity of collectivism; for activists who are part of these global networks, there is perhaps a sense of acting as part of a greater whole rather than losing one's individuality through a desire to connect with others. The sense of belonging that Maffesoli describes drives people to act within micro-groups does not subsume difference. Participation in activist networks is one of many layers of social identification. The notion of the social divine as the intangible feeling that encompasses people within a shared emotional space facilitates understanding of why people are increasingly acting within network frameworks.

Alternative globalization activists act within and move among rhizomatically organized and informally connected activist networks. Demands for global justice, for greater autonomy—and therefore freedoms and inclusion in democratic processes—motivate activists, as do more specific local struggles. Nevertheless, there is a perceptible overriding sense of connection between local and global struggles. David Harvey argues that the concept of militant particularism recognizes the embeddedness of ways of life and structures of feeling particular to places and communities (Harvey 1989: 193). Militant particularist movements for social change play a mediating role between individuals and local solidarities, reaching beyond the local and across space and time. The coalescence of activists from disparate locations and backgrounds in one locale with local activists thus facilitates militant particularism. The constant re-formation of activist networks at protest sites allows for a continual adoption of local issues and circumstances into alternative globalization activists' agendas, practices, and discourses.

This process was reported in Mumbai at the 2004 World Social Forum. Janet Conway details the move of the 2004 Forum from Porto Alegre to Mumbai and the ramifications this move had on the nature of the 80,000-strong gathering (2004). Caste-based injustices in India were brought to the immediate attention of delegates from some 132 countries by the presence of *dalit*, or "untouchable" movements, who transformed the political culture of the WSF. Hundreds of poor people's organizations, like the *dalit* and *Adivasis* (or tribals) movements, and many others historically marginalized by the Left—like people with disabilities, people with AIDS, sex trade workers, and sexual minority groups—participated in the WSF at Mumbai (Conway 2004, Sargeant and Albert 2004).

Questions of gendered justice were voiced there as well. Among many feminist spaces created at the forum, the World March of Women organized a workshop titled "Religious Fundamentalism, Communalism, Casteism, and Racism: Actually a Globalization Agenda." America Vera-Zavala describes how, although the workshop was packed, few participants were Western women—which undermines the stereotype of alternative globalization activism as the domain of primarily privileged young white students (2004).

Women's voices took center stage at Mumbai, and this happened because women activists demanded a space that represented their dominant numbers. The official organization of the World Social Forum 2004 continued to have men dominating the star panels, echoing wider patriarchal relations. This is just one of many points of criticism leveled against organizers by participants in ongoing evaluations of the form and content of the WSF. Nevertheless, women forged spaces of justice for themselves in Mumbai: they decided to occupy more space than they had been officially given and they moved women's rights onto center stage.

Taking space: the street as site of justice

Accounts of women's actions at the WSF continually emphasize the idea of actively creating spaces and the links between patriarchy and neoliberalism. These spaces took the form of planned physical meeting spaces and shared emotional spaces of resistance. Countless other spaces were and are created spontaneously, very often on the street. The street is a key site for the expression of dissent in the face of injustice. Taking to the street, gathering and communicating a desire for change, is a vital form of political discourse that isn't reliant on formal access to power. By forming en masse outside the meeting sites of the institutions of neoliberal globalization, activists who oppose their practices are able to form a visually and physically tangible statement of opposition.

Not simply an act of negation, street protest can also work as *détournement*. This Situationist term aptly encapsulates the way activists alter and subvert existing images or acts of dominant power. Rachel Neumann writes of one such act of *détournement* on the streets of Seattle during the anti-WTO protests in November 1999:

> It is dishonest not to talk about the intangibles: the feeling in the air and the smiles on people's faces as the Nike sign was being dismantled in Seattle. It wasn't so much the rage of the people destroying the sign—they were calm and focused. It was the reflection, and the release, of the crowd's rage, and a symbol of how it could be transformed into action. Without the sign, the place felt different; as if it belonged to us, the people in the streets and not the police (2000).

The street thus becomes a site of vital refusal of injustices wrought by the primacy of capital and neoliberal globalization.

The street can act simultaneously as a protest space and a site of community. Activists coalesce on the street and form emotional communities where desires for social justice act as a link or inexplicable glue between diverse peoples. Militant particularism forges space for difference and also for commonalities to emerge from difference.

It is vital to note the non-instrumental elements, the social divine, that binds activists on the streets and in forums. Social relations are established at actions we have witnessed in recent years in cities across the globe. These relations are often built upon pre-existing ones whereby local collectives and/or friendship circles travel together to the site of an alternative globalization demonstration. New relations also emerge at the protest sites themselves:

> I came to Genoa to be with people, who like me, felt that intense rage against inequality and injustice.... I wanted to feel that solidarity, that warmth of people like me, and I also wanted some outlet for my anger, and they [the G8 leaders] as the most powerful politicians in the world seemed a justifiable target.... The atmosphere was great. I, and the people I was with, got to know people from all over the world there, in the few days before the demos, we ate together, laughed together and all shared the same sleeping space (Jones 2001: 9).

The spaces described by Jones are referred to as "convergence spaces." The notion of a convergence space offers a way to contextualize the spatial relations of loose or contested coalitions of divergent site-specific social movements that together constitute global networks. Convergence spaces can also embody both the militant particularisms of a physical location and diverse spaces or flows of planning and shared ideas. Routledge argues that it is the ability to conceptualize and value difference that makes the notion of convergence spaces such a valuable tool when looking at alternative globalization activist networks (2004: 14–15). This difference is expressed in the composition of groups outside the meetings and summits. It is expressed in the multiple modes of communication and rhizomatic organizational styles, in the celebration of diverse voices and views: it is expressed in the way alternative globalization activists carry out globalized local actions and localized global actions.

The idea of alternative globalization protests as convergence spaces allows for a more complete recognition of the sense of emotional community that supports and evolves from collective dissent. The spaces of justice that emerge from alternative globalization activists' gatherings are generated in part by the act of being together physically or symbolically. Ideas of social justice are discussed, debated, and practiced by activists in shared physical and emotional convergence spaces that are constituted equally in the planning of actions and their execution. Rather than acting simply as a political slogan, "solidarity" describes the bonds felt amongst activists.

Another world is possible: an ongoing conclusion

The protest spaces formed in response to neoliberal globalization are simultaneously tangible, albeit fleeting, physical protest spaces, but also rhetorical and emotional spaces. Doreen Massey argues that there is a need to rethink *place* as something beyond physical location, to explore it as a locale of social interactions. What defines a place is not only its physical location—the ability to articulate where it is on a map—but also the web of "social relations, social processes, experiences, and understandings" that occur there (1993: 66). The protest spaces generated by alternative globalization activists are fluid and open; signed-up, paid-up membership is not required to participate, there are no physical barriers to involvement and the actual physical space changes tactically. Considering the sites of alternative globalization protest as both physical and emotional protest spaces where the social divine is created and practiced allows for an understanding of the connections between activists across physical space and time—that there is simultaneous fragmentation and fluidity in their coming together. The WSF can itself be seen as a temporal place—a physical space that reconstitutes itself in multiple arenas—and also as an open space of dialogue and relationships in direct opposition to the workings of neoliberalism.

There is a sense of camaraderie in the accounts above. To overlook the debates that often rage between activists would be a mistake. The spaces of social justice that are forged in opposition to the current dominance of neoliberalism are heterogeneous: difference is celebrated. *On Fire*, a collection of activist accounts of the G8 protests in Genoa in 2001, celebrates solidarity, but is also largely a reflection of the ongoing debate amongst activist networks about tactics and directions (One Off Press: 2001).

At such events, activists coalesce and create participatory, open, and inclusive protest spaces that convey not only their dissatisfaction with global injustices perpetrated by transnational neoliberal agencies, but also positive alternatives. Diffuse activists continue to come together to collectively to express that another world is possible. Both this shared expression and the act of being together, in person or across distance, continue to provide a feeling of belonging amongst diverse alternative globalization networks and simultaneously fuels the resistance to neoliberalism.

References

Arjun Appadurai, "Grassroots Globalization and the Research Imagination," in *Public Culture* 12, no. 1 (2000), 1–19.

John Arquilla and David Ronfeldt, "The Advent of Netwar (Revisited)," in *Networks and Netwars: The Future of Terror, Crime and Militancy*, ed. John Arquilla and David Ronfeldt (Washington: RAND, 2001).

Janet Conway, "Brazil to Mumbai: A Controversial Move," in *Rabble News*, February 11, 2004. Available at http://www.rabble.ca

Emile Durkheim, *The Elementary Forms of the Religious Life*, trans. J. W. Swain (New York: The Free Press, 2005).

David Harvey, *The Urban Experience* (Oxford: Basil Blackwell, 1989).

Diego Jones, "Shooting Blanks?" in *On Fire: The Battle of Genoa and the Anti-Capitalist Movement* (London: One Off Press, 2001), 7–16.

Anita Lacey, "Networked Communities: Social Centres and Activist Spaces in Contemporary Britain," in *Space and Culture* 8, no. 3 (2005), 286–99.

Anita Lacey and Steve Wright, "Inform/azione e informatica tra attivisti anti-capitalisti australiani," in *DeriveApprodi* 24, (Winter 2003–Spring, 2004), 107–112.

Michel Maffesoli, *The Time of the Tribes: The Decline of Individualism in Mass Society*, trans. D. Smith (London: Sage, 1996).

Doreen Massey, "Power-Geometry and a Progressive Sense of Place," in *Mapping the Futures: Local Cultures, Global Change*, eds. J. Bird, B. Curtis, T. Putnam, G. Robertson and L. Tickner (London: Routledge, 1993), 56–69.

Tom Mertes, "Introduction," in *A Movement of Movements: Is Another World Really Possible?*, ed. T. Mertes (London: Verso, 2004), vii–xii.

Rachel Neumann, "A Place for Rage," in *Dissent* 47, no. 2 (Spring 2000), 89–96.

On Fire: The Battle of Genoa and the Anti-Capitalist Movement (London: One-Off Press, 2001).

Jamie Peck and Adam Tickell, "Neoliberalizing Space," in *Antipode,* Vol. 34, 2002: 380–404.

Paul Routledge, "Convergence of Commons: Process Geographies of People's Global Action," in *The Commoner* 8, (Autumn/Winter 2004).

America Vera-Zavala, "A Space of Freedom: The World Women's Forum," 2004. Available at http://www.zmag.org

:: EDUCATION & ETHICS ::

:: EDUCATION & ETHICS ::

> Our critique of "The Scientific Method" skips "Science"…skips "Method"…but finds "The" guilty of a crime. The tyranny of "The" is a part of language that attempts to unify the menagerie of human curiosity and struggle into just one investigative technique and in doing so fails both science and humanity. —Frederick Markatos Dixon, from "This is Folk Science!"

Many who read this book will have some relationship, however ambivalent, with the university—as a student, as faculty, as an employee, or as a resident in the community around the university. The university, far from being removed from the workings of the economy and the state, plays different roles in the various fields of power in which it operates. Ivory tower no more, if it ever was. The question is how the space of the university can be used for something else, for a purpose that goes beyond and undermines its current role in reproducing the social order. As Noam Chomsky comments, "It would be criminal to overlook the serious flaws and inadequacies in our institutions, or to fail to utilize the substantial degree of freedom that most of us enjoy, within the framework of these flawed institutions, to modify or even replace them by a better social order."

How can we create, to quote Osterweil and Chesters, a space, ethic, and practice that uses the space of the university to go beyond itself to create something else? How can we open the university to use its resources for the benefit of movements and organizing? How can we use it to create a forum for collective reflection, to re-imagine the world from wherever we find ourselves? It is through this constituent process of collectively shared and embodied imagination that the boundaries of the classroom, of where knowledge is created and struggles occur, start to break down.

Where might we go from this space? It's hard to say. This is a question that only can be answered from the particular situations in which it is asked. Just as the vanguardist notion of a cadre providing strategies from on high is deeply problematic, the idea that one could know from where and how to go about forging such new spaces would also be deeply flawed. We can say that it is more likely to resemble what Frederick Markatos Dixon describes above as a folk science. That is, in a direction not motivated by some quest for universal knowledge, or to fill the ever-revered gap in the literature, but rather to explore problems and curiosities as they arise, to find new, hidden passageways and lines of flight. It becomes a question of inheritance and transformation, of repetition, resistance, and creation. Inheriting the forms of knowledge and practices developed by current organizing efforts, along with the historical experiences and concepts of movements and struggles.

Global Uprisings: Towards a Politics of the Artisan

Michal Osterweil + Graeme Chesters

In this way, thought takes on a creative, affirmative function, in order for us to cease to simply make mere reproductions of the present...there are no global knowledges, but rather situational ones. And because of this, struggles don't depend so much on techniques and concrete knowledge as on the possibilities to produce your own situated knowledges. —Colectivo Situaciones

The urgency of today...is the potential force of theoretical practice, an ongoing research that does not look either to linearly prefigure remote futures, or to simply review irreplicable pasts, but rather, to interrogate the present in order to transform it. —*DeriveApprodi*

There are no shortcuts and, if there are, they are only "table tricks." There is only experimentation as method and substance of the becoming-movement. —Global Project

Our Project (Space)(Ethic)(Practice)

We are part of the editorial collective producing *Global Uprisings: A Journal of Ideas & Action*—a new journal that seeks to contribute to the emergent alternative globalization movement (AGM) by creating a *space, ethic,* and *practice* in which the politics of alternative globalization movements can be articulated, debated, and cultivated.[1] Each of these—*practice, space,* and *ethic*—is a key term to understanding our project.

Practice—from the theoretical to the everyday

Central to this project, and perhaps contrary to more common-sense activist and academic notions of the political, is the belief that how we think and narrate has everything to do with how we live and change politics. Similarly, how we live our everyday lives has everything to do with the projects we aspire to create and enact. Theory, analysis, and narration are a central part of our daily actions, and these daily actions are, by definition, the materiality of politics. We are working on this journal not to create yet another isolated academic or intellectual analysis of what social movements and groups do, or ought to do, but rather because we believe that *theory, analysis, and narration are critical and inseparable parts of our actions.*

Ethic

At the same time, our project goes beyond the political and practical nature of theory, analysis, and narration. We aspire to co-create and develop a form of theory that is not only deeply informed by action, but that *constitutes a critical and ethical practice in and of itself.* In this vein, we avoid classical political labels or definitions of our project as socialist, progressive, anarchist, or ecological—although each of these terms defines some aspect of our politics—and argue strongly for an understanding of politics as cultural, based on creating new modes of being and relating, which are based on the idea that self-making and ethics are at the core of any effective and radical political project.

We also use the term "ethics" in a different sense, one inspired by Foucault's *Ethic of/Care of the Self.* We see *Global Uprisings* as an ethical attempt to humanize activist and academic practice—to consider human bodies, desires, endurance, affects, quirks—to create a new activist and intellectual ethic. Our journal is meant to serve as a corrective not only to detached academic research *on* movements, but also to the rigid dogmatisms that often characterize activist practice—the kind of activism that leaves certain things unquestioned and consequently unchallengeable. We see "critical praxis" as an instantiation of the Zapatista call to *caminar preguntando*, to walk while questioning.[2] Rather than beginning from a totalizing program, ethical practice develops its political interventions processually and conjecturally. As such, complexity and contingency are not perceived as obstacles or setbacks, but as the very things that constitute political action.

Space

Related to this ethical practice is the importance of space as both a concept and relation. Discussions about the concept of space have proliferated

in both academic and activist milieus. Popular concepts like "temporary autonomous zones," "convergence centers," and "open spaces" are indicative
of spatial imaginaries.[3] Our understanding of our project as creating a space
(rather than manifesto, movement, or utopia) has come via our direct experiences of the alternative globalization and social forum movements. That is
to say, among the hundreds of thousands at a social forum, we would all find
ourselves at the same workshops, in the same alternative spaces, interested
in and frustrated by very similar aspects of the larger spaces and movements
of which they were a part. We realized that, while the spaces at various
social forums, conferences, and protests were phenomenal, they were also
extremely temporary and intense. A great deal of energy and many connections are generated, but they have not achieved their goals. That is, they have
not directly produced anything that could be clearly or linearly linked back
to the hopes and plans of those involved. Whether this is good or bad is not
the issue here. These experiences have nevertheless pointed out the political
importance of spaces—specifically spaces of encounters—because of their
open and not fully directed or oriented natures. *Global Uprisings* is our attempt to create a critical public space, one that exists for sustained periods of
time and in various physical and virtual places. We believe that the creation
of such a space will allow us to include more people and different ideas, as
well as make possible wisdom that only comes with reflection; reflection
and iteration that in turn only come with time. The content of our politics is
more precisely that of engagement, culture, and encounter than of programs,
campaigns, and building institutions.

Like many of the groups that comprise the AGM, there is no clear or
simple way to define our we-ness, our existence as a group. We do not have
what social movement theorists and social psychologists term a "collective
identity"—even though we identify as a collective. We do not share this
space because of a particular political campaign, or structural position vis-
à-vis capital.[4] We do not necessarily share a primary political label like socialist, feminist, libertarian, environmentalist, or even anarchist. We are this
collective because of something akin to a compulsion, an affinity—a shared
set of not-easy-to-articulate frustrations and, more importantly, hopes and
beliefs about the politics of our times, as well as a sense of connection to one
another. This sense of connection is closer to the love of friendship than the
rationality of a political stance.

Background

Many of us who grew up in the late-twentieth century—especially in
the English-speaking world—are used to presuming and/or living with a
sort of enmity, or at least a very notable tension, between activism and academia or rather, between what is understood to be "properly activist" versus

"properly intellectual" *practice*. We could provide caricatures of both sides of this stereotype. The point is that commonplace understandings of activism and politics have been separated from, and pitted against, definitions of knowledge and thought, as well as knowledge and theory production.

For those of us who came together to create *Global Uprisings,* this division has impinged upon our everyday lives and passions, and goes against our very understanding of political practice. In fact, most of us can describe our own biographies as a series of collisions with this divide, collisions that have in turn led us to oscillate ad infinitum between spaces and work that are defined as either "activist," or "intellectual." Sometimes this oscillation simply has meant changing which passions and skills we focus on at any given time.[5] But now we have reached a point where we are dizzy and tired of constantly moving back and forth between two distinct realms. So we are starting *Global Uprisings* as an attempt to find both a resting point for our perpetual oscillations and a tangible form to our politics, both as a sustainable space and an ethical practice.

Global Uprisings is a collaborative project. It is a product of our schizophrenic biographies, on the one hand, and a belief in the political significance of this intersection of knowledge and politics—what we call critical praxis. In this sense, the journal is the positive outcome of a particular political analysis that not only values critique, reflexivity, creativity, and analysis, but sees all of these as essential to producing the kind of subjectivities, social relations and institutions that can reinvent politics in a way that might really be able to remake the world.

The uniqueness of theoretical practice today

Global Uprisings is part of a growing network and tendency among organizations, collectives, and informal groups that are doing a good deal of their activism explicitly at this nexus of thought and politics. These projects have been variously characterized as activist research, action research, hacktivism, theoretical-practice, *conricerca* (co-research), situational praxis, and radical theory.[6] Our aim in this piece is to explain why so many groups, collectives, and practices are emerging now and what the political implications and possibilities of this flurry of critical praxis might be.

At one level, all movements throughout history have worked at this nexus, for there are no social or political projects without ideas, analysis, communication, culture, and what Gramsci referred to as intellectual work. What we see as notable in these groups is the centrality of intellectual, critical, thought-based practice. It is not simply that these groups do intellectual and analytical work in order to further their more central *political* agendas, but rather that many define themselves and their core sets of actions and practices *as* intellectual and investigative.[7] In other words intellectual work is considered part of the ongoing day-to-day work of activism.

This suggests that such practice can no longer be considered the exclusive and superstructural terrain of a vanguard.[8] Some of the AGM's most diffuse and widespread concepts and practices, including its architectures and imaginaries, also emphasize the need for thought, reflection, and experimentation. Consider, for example, terms and concepts like *caminar preguntando*, network(ing), open space, the forum and the *encuentro*.[9] Each involves an understanding of politics as open, non-formulaic, non-linear, and not necessarily concerned with ends. This is a politics that values communication and the exchange of ideas, *not* in order to come to an agreement on one plan or solution, but for the unpredictable, often subtle, affective effects of the process of critical engagement and encounters. This includes the production of different critical subjectivities and relations.

Each of the terms contains an understanding that thought, dialogue, analysis, and critique are central parts of transformative and radical political action. By radical, we should clarify, we do not mean the most extreme or the most violent, but rather, something that gets to the roots—the radices—of the problems and systems we oppose.[10] These critical practices are as much about producing and creating subjectivities and mechanisms capable of coping with constant uncertainty, than they are about producing accurate theories, or building new macro-systems and institutions.

So why now?

The centrality and visibility of these various forms of critical praxis are in part a result of the fact that today, following the failures of state-sponsored communism, it has become "common-sense" that there are no *meta*-models, narratives, or theories of social change. This does not deny that people— even those who claim to avoid them—assert universalizing metatheories all the time. A growing number of movements around the world have come to recognize the need for different theories for specific times and places, each of which needs to be partial, continuously interrogated, and revised. This is why the World Social Forum, the International Encuentros for Humanity and other gatherings have come to be recognized as important even when they do not produce clear-cut campaigns.[11] Each contributes to this new understanding of radical and effective politics, an understanding based on the recognition of politics as a sort of non-directed, critical space and capacity rather than something necessarily directed at the institutional level. This does not mean ignoring or neglecting more traditional political levels, but rather taking seriously how these forms of criticality might be articulated to traditional spaces and institutions.

Today the particular forms of theoretical practice this network and our collective are developing embody a particular type of politics: a politics that is quite distinct from what traditionally gets included under that rubric, as well as from how mainstream political actors affiliated with the AGM and contemporary oppositional politics define the term. It is a cultural politics: a politics based as much on creating and producing critical subjectivities— on creating carnival and joy, on recombining cultural codes—as it is about changing current laws and institutions.[12] This form of politics corresponds to *a particular mode of theorizing and ultimately of being* that is more ethical because it recognizes the limits and partiality of all knowledge claims.

Simon Tormey makes an interesting distinction between two areas of the AGM. He differentiates between the imaginary of "utopian worlds" and the proliferation of "utopian spaces." One of the key characteristics of working to build utopian *worlds,* he argues, is the "creation of a fixed and determinate social reality"—in other words, the need to base political practice on predetermined understandings of reality before the act of engagement.[13] This form of theorization necessarily presupposes the political and social primacy of certain aspects of social reality—i.e. categories such as labor and class. A politics based on this ideological structuring tends towards a practice with no space for questions, experiments, or uncertainty. This fixity, he argues, is (also) the very mode of political philosophy—or, we would claim, political philosophy as it is traditionally defined. While not everything called political philosophy is necessarily so rigid, the importance is the connection of a form of thought to a form of politics. In contrast, a politics engaged in the proliferation of utopian *spaces*, eschews imposing one master-narrative or vision of reality, opting instead to create and provide spaces: for encounter, discussion, experimentation, and affinity.[14] One form of politics and theory-making is open-ended, creative, and inherently multiplicitous. The other is constrained by a teleological and universalizing mode of thought, one that subordinates desire and spontaneity to a rational and future-oriented schema. Ultimately, this difference refers back to a different ontology corresponding to a different understanding of the political.

We see *Global Uprisings* as directly related to the segment of the AGM that openly articulates a desire to elaborate *new* forms of politics. The politics of *Global Uprisings* and this diffuse network must be understood as a way of engaging with the world and practicing the political. This engagement is partial and reflexive, enacting an ethical criticality that not only avoids creating universalizing programs, but also refuses rigid categorizations and judgments of political actions as "reformist" or "radical" outside of particular contexts and circumstances.

"New" Politics!?

The question of newness is an interesting one. We do not want to claim that these are *new* political practices. The form of intellectual praxis and

ethics we are discussing and developing, as well as the definition of the political they are based on, has existed in various instantiations and levels of
visibility for a long time. More often than not, these have remained subterranean or at the margins, excluded by more mainstream political actors and
discourses for being *merely* cultural. They have been rendered marginal and
invisible, which has resulted in dominant theories and strategies that leave
much of the fundamental political and economic system in place. We can
call these marginal politics the minoritarian strain of politics.[15]

Today, the invisibility and marginality of the minoritarian can no longer
be maintained. So, while these politics have existed before, today the historical awareness and self-reflexiveness of these practices are of a quantitatively
denser nature. This increasing visibility leads to a qualitative shift, a shift to
a qualitatively different form and potentiality for politics. Notably this is not
simply within and among the traditionally minoritarian actors, but within
the terrain of the political overall.

It is even more important to point out that these new politics have only
been made possible by their direct relationships with movements and political theories of the past. The historical specificity of this moment and the diffuse, distributed emergence of a set of practices that emphasize critique, reflexivity, and analysis—whether formally or informally—has only occurred
as a result of many years of collective learning and capacity-building within
movements[16] and among the "submerged networks" that linger in periods
when collective action is less visible.[17]

From architects to artisans?

Given the growing visibility of the minoritarian trajectories, the question remains: Where do we go from here? Of course we don't have *the* answer to this question, but we are fond of posing the question in another
way, as a means of giving life to the critical praxis we have outlined. Our
question, courtesy of Deleuze, concerns whether we understand ourselves
to be architects or artisans. The architect is a designer of utopian worlds,
a would-be "master" of the material, who attempts to impose, through her
practice, a grand design, a design that is "other-worldly" in that it comes
from the outside as an imposition of the will. The architect uses blueprints
and plans, the product of a "great revolutionary imagination." The artisan,
however, is someone who works at the cusp of the imaginary and the material, whose imagination is directed by the self-organizing tendencies of social and material systems. The artisan is the under-laborer of utopian spaces,
an individual or collective who responds to and cajoles, who traces, shapes,
and sharpens, but who cannot direct or determine. In this sense, we see
Global Uprisings as an artisanal project, something that we are struggling
to follow and realize—*Zapatismo, autonomy, carnival*—yet something that

simultaneously eludes us, that diverges, reiterates, and re-emerges. We are excited and nervous about the work to be done. More importantly, we invite others to join us in our artisanal theoretical practice, by contributing to and utilizing the space we are creating.

Notes

1. The AGM can be understood as the movements against neoliberal corporate globalization that became known through the Zapatistas, protests in Seattle, Genoa, and Prague, as well as more recently through the various Social Fora. However, when scrutinized more closely, the term "movement" is itself too narrow to capture the rich and varied events and practices that make up what is called the AGM.

2. For an excellent description of the political implications of this phrase, see Holloway, 2004.

3. For the prevalence of the term in political and academic debates, see Bey, Lefebvre, Massey, Pickles, Teivainen, Tormey, Whitaker, as well as Sen and Keraghel.

4. Although one could argue that we do have the latter, we simply need to re-define what we mean by capitalism, as well as our structural relationships to it.

5. While some of us are currently situated (sustained economically, profession-ally, institutionally) in the academy, others are located within social-centers, towns, cooperatives, DIY movement groups, or are just working to make a living and living out our politics.

6. For activist-research, see www.investigaccio.org. For action research, see www.euromovements.info. For hacktivism, see www.rekombinant.org. For theoretical-practice, see www.deriveapprodi.org. For situational praxis, see www.situaciones.org. And for radical theory, see http//www.indymedia.org. uk/en/2005/06/314299.html.

7. This centrality has, at times, become quite controversial. At the last World Social Forum, several groups were worried that the research-activist themes were taking up too much time and discussion, and deflecting attention from more urgent issues and goals.

8. Unless we use the Zapatista definition of "vanguard" which means peo-ple who go forward to chart and get to know an unknown terrain. See Al Giordano "Marcos to Launch Six-Month Tour of All of Mexico Beginning January 1," at http//www.narconews.com, September 19, 2005.

9. The International Encuentros For Humanity called by the Zapatistas in the mid-1990s, and the Social Forums begun in 2000.

10. This, of course, requires that we refine traditional definitions of capitalism as being simply an economic system, and recognize that it is a system that is

present and premised on the minutiae of our everyday lives.

11. There is a lot of debate, especially within the Social Forums, about whether the WSF should aspire to be more like a movement with clearly articulated goals and objectives around which everyone should unite, or whether to remain an open space. For more, see Whitaker and Teivainen's pieces in Sen, J., Anand, A., Escobar, A. & Waterman, P. (eds) (2004).

12. For a better explanation of these cultural politics, see Osterweil.

13. Simon Tormey (2005), 398.

14. Ibid. 404.

15. See Chesters and Welsh (2006) and Nicholas Thoburn (2003).

16. By "direct" we mean either very concretely that the same people have always been present and learned from the practices and analyses of their past experiences and reflections, or when new people have come into organizations or networks that have been formed and informed by this type of collective and social learning processes. What Welsh (2000) calls "capacity building." See also Plows (2002), and Eyerman and Jamison (1991).

17. See Melucci (1989).

References

Sonia Alvarez, *Contentious Feminisms: Critical Readings of Social Movements, NGOs, and Transnational Organizing in Latin America* (Durham, NC: Duke University Press, forthcoming).

Hakim Bey, *Temporary Autonomous Zone* (Brooklyn, NY: Autonomedia, 1985).

P. Bourdieu and L. Wacquant, *An Invitation to Reflexive Sociology* (Chicago: University of Chicago Press, 1992).

Graeme Chesters and Ian Welsh, *Complexity and Social Movements: Multitudes at the Edge of Chaos* (London: Routledge, forthcoming).

R. Eyerman and A. Jamison, *Social Movements: A Cognitive Approach* (University Park, PA: Pennsylvania State University Press, 1991).

Al Giordano, "Marcos to Launch Six Month Tour of All of Mexico Beginning January 1." Available at http//www.narconews.com

John Holloway, "*Zapatismo Urbano*" in *Humbold Journal of Social Relations* 29, no. 1 (2004), 168–179.

Henri Lefebvre, *The Production of Space*, trans. Donald Nicholson-Smith (Oxford: Blackwell Publishing, 1974).

Doreen Massey, *For Space* (London: Sage Publications, 2005).

Alberto Melucci, *Nomads of the Present: Social Movements and Individual Needs in Contemporary Society* (Philadelphia: Temple University Press, 1989)

Michal Osterweil, "A Cultural-Political Approach to Reinventing the Political," in *International Social Science Journal* 56, no. 182 (December 2004).

John Pickles, *A History of Spaces: Cartographic Reason, Mapping, and the Geo-Coded world* (London: Routledge, 2004).

Alexandra Plows, *Praxis and Practice: The "What, How and Why" of the UK Environmental Direct Action (EDA) Movement in the 1990's,* Dissertation Thesis (Bangor: University of Wales, 2002).

R. Ray, *Fields of Protest: Women's Movements in India* (Minneapolis: University of Minnesota Press, 1999).

Jai Sen and Chloe Keraghel, eds., "Explorations in Open Space: The World Social Forum and Cultures of Politics," in *International Social Science Journal*, 56 no. 182 (December 2004).

Jai Sen, Arturo Escobar, Peter Waterman and Anita Anand, eds., *World Social Forum: Challenging Empires* (New Delhi: The Viveka Foundation, 2004).

Teivo Teivainen, "The WSF: Arena or Actor?" in *World Social Forum: Challenging Empires*, 122–129

Simon Tormey, "From Utopian Worlds to Utopian Spaces: Reflections on the Contemporary Radical Imaginary and the Social Forum Process" in *ephemera: theory, politics and organization* 5, no. 2 (2005), 394–408.

Nicholas Thoburn, *Deleuze, Marx and Politics* (London: Routledge, 2004).

Ian Welsh, *Mobilising Modernity: The Nuclear Moment* (London: Routledge, 2000).

Chico Whitaker, "The WSF As Open Space" in *World Social Forum: Challenging Empires*, 111–121.

Black Sails in the Corridor: Treasonous Minds and the Desire for Mutiny

Dave Eden

On December 2, 2005, *The Australian* reported that the federal government would be holding back five percent of promised funding increases for universities until compliance teams could verify that individual universities were in accordance with the government's industrial relations agenda.[1] This agenda is based on the increased application of individual contracts resulting in intensification of wage disparity and job casualization. This is just one plank in the current offensive against conditions for staff and students on campus. Both face intensified state meddling in their ability to organize on campus, withdrawal of funding for controversial research, and intensified market pressure. Universities, like all of Australian society, are engulfed in wave after wave of neoliberal reform that intensifies work discipline and encloses the few radical moments of the commons that were won through (and often despite) the social democratic forces of Australian capitalism.

This is not remarkable. What is troubling is the lack of any serious and liberatory resistance. The most vocal voices of opposition such as the National Tertiary Education Union position their arguments on a firmly liberal terrain. The defense is based on an ideology of liberal meritocracy and various inherited notions of the university as a place of excellence unsullied by the direct machinations of government or money, yet contributing to the general health of civil society. These arguments are palatable in the official spaces that manufacture public opinion. They will be debated in editorials and on the floor of parliament, a polite campaign of public rallies is in the works—in this sense they reaffirm the illusions of parliamentary democracy; they will have little to no effect on the actual administration of these applications.[2]

The mood on campus is a mixture of despair and self-deception. With the absence of collective and transformative struggle on campus—a struggle that could disrupt the normality of academic knowledge-work—many of my colleagues seem to try to escape the current enclosures by further investing in the structures of the university. It is thus in the interest of those of us who see no future in either the university as it currently exists, or as it is being reformed, to attempt projects of critical analysis of ourselves and our labor in hopes of fleshing out the ruptures and short-circuits that could lead to an (anti)politics of joy and desire, and a liberation of life.

There are multiple reasons why resistance has not manifested itself on campus. One could be a question of self-image. For self-professed revolutionaries, the image of the academic knowledge-worker is one that is denied radical and destabilizing potential. Most often the academic is seen as analogous to the figure of the intellectual. In classic radical thought, the intellectual is seen as a distinct and separate category from the proletariat proper.[3] The usual image of the academic knowledge-worker as intellectual robs the academic of rebellious potential in two profound ways: one, that the work they do is seen as being peripheral to the functions of capital, and as such their revolt lacks power; and secondly, that the contribution of the intellectual to revolutionary struggle is one of allying with those who are engaged in the negation of capital and of themselves. This process of alliance is one that *reaffirms* rather than transcends the category of the intellectual. The above analysis is not only unfortunate, but also incorrect. Perhaps an investigation of how the role of universities in contemporary capitalism has changed could also unearth the potential for our own revolt and allow us to dream new forms of defiance into being.

Thinking about/as work

A useful and fertile tool for this investigation is Marx's idea of *real subsumption*. Marx argues that in its early period(s) capitalism does "not at first affect the actual mode of production" but rather imposes its control over what it has inherited (formal subsumption).[4] It is only later with the "production of relative surplus-value [that] the entire real form of production is altered and a *specifically capitalist form of production* comes into being."[5] Real subsumption involves at least two interrelated phenomenon. What goes on in the process of production increasingly involves the social, and the social increasingly becomes a moment in the general process of production. The clear distinctions between work and what is outside work begins to crumble under a general logic of capitalism—*even if they maintain an illusionary appearance of separation*. In "real subsumption...every act of production incorporates knowledge, instruments, discoveries, and social relations that are not present in the limited space or time of the factory. The factory becomes a social factory."[6] Camatte describes this process as capital coming to constitute the "material community."[7] On one hand, most human existence now takes place as commodified and alienated activity, and, on the other, the general social conditions become increasingly crucial to the process of work/commodification. It becomes almost impossible to find human interactions that are not stamped or formed by capitalist modes of production/exchange/consumption. If some spaces can be found that are not directly under capitalist logics, they seem to be *generally* motivated by them. In this sense, we can talk about the proletarianization of humanity. This arises partly through increasing amounts of human activity being organized via alienating wage-labor, but also through the tasks of social reproduction outside that wage (housework, study, etc.), that are "work" (activity commanded by capital that serves its regime of accumulation) in the period of real subsumption. In a sense, this is a process of homogenization, but it has not produced the homogenized proletariat beloved by classical Marxism.

Marx asserts that, in the process of real subsumption, there is the development of the "productive forces of *socialised labor*" coupled with "the use of *science* (the *general* product of social development) in the *immediate process of production*."[8] Both these processes involve the emergence and development of the collective intellectual powers of the population and their application in the now society-wide matrix of production. In the *Grundrisse*, Marx writes that "the development of fixed capital indicates to what degree general social knowledge has become a *direct force of production*, and to what degree, hence, the conditions of the process of social life itself have come under the control of the general intellect and been transformed in accordance with it."[9] Both socialized labor and the productive apparatus (which now encompasses society) are increasingly characterized by the application of this general intellect. The old figure of the intellectual has no place in this. The realm of thought does not live outside capitalism but rather becomes a crucial component to it. The role of the academic has to be seen then in this light of the production and application of knowledge as a crucial ingredient in the general re/creation of the social relations of capital. The figure of the intellectual as a member of a minority that holds some kind of unique access to knowledge is replaced with the development of *mass intellectuality*.

In the work of the post-*autonomia* theorists, an immanent critique of Marx's idea of the general intellect has lead to its useful applications to contemporary conditions.[10] Lazzarato argues that immaterial labor has risen in contemporary capitalism both from the increased application of communicative skills in the work process and through activity not typically conceived of as work, yet that creates the "cultural content of the commodity."[11] The vast expansion of cybernetics/info-tech, the mobilizing of nuanced identities in the production of commodity fetishism, the application of micro-management, all require mass intellectuality. This manifests in overlapping ways:

the need to display certain emotions in the work place, investing cultural understandings in what is being produced, relating to others in particular ways, and so on. For this to function, a certain type of individual must be created to function in this work place. To quote Lazzarato:

> If production today is directly the production of a social relationship, the "raw material" of immaterial labor is subjectivity and the "ideological" environment in which this subjectivity lives and reproduces. The production of subjectivity ceases to be only an instrument of social control (for the reproduction of mercantile relationships) and becomes directly productive, because the goal of our postindustrial society is to construct the consumer/communicator—and to construct it as "active."[12]

It is, then, in people—in the collective life of the population that works in the context of post-Fordism—that the general intellect is located. This is a break from Marx. Virno argues that Marx locates the general intellect in "fixed capital, with the 'objective scientific capacity' inherent in the system of machines."[13] Virno sees the general intellect present itself as "living labor."[14] The general intellect then involves all the cognitive-linguistic functions of the population put to work. He contests that even in the classic manufacturing industries, the bastion of work associated with the mass worker, this is the case. Lazzarato has previously argued that, in large-scale industry, production has already become geared to what goes on outside the factory—"sales and relationship with the consumer"—a process that requires the application of mass intellectuality in the entire circuit of conception and promotion.[15] Virno complements this by arguing that, within the process of production, it is the communicative skills of the workers with each other that become crucial.[16] The modern workplace involves putting the entire "team" into motion (to use a keystone of the modern management lexicon). Hence the centrality of human relations to capitalism and, more disturbing, the defining of human relations by capital.

There are a number of criticisms one could raise to this. While sometimes post-*autonomia* theorists of the general intellect make their observations site-specific, there is an often louder tendency to overemphasize the importance of the general intellect. Virno is careful enough to locate his analysis in the work done in the "post-Fordist metropolis."[17] Negri on the other hand makes the figure of mass intellectuality—called, in turn, the socialized worker and the cyborg—the hegemonic figure of struggle. George Caffentzis makes an important critique of this, observing that this entire line of thinking conforms to the old Marxist paradigm of emphasizing the activity of the most productive workers, often resulting in blindness to the rebellions and self-activity of the vast majority of the world proletarianized population.[18] Indeed these formulations do not fit with the actual patterns of revolt in which those who appear to be engaged the least in immaterial labor—indigenous peasants in Chiapas, the miners of Bolivia—are also those the seem to be having the most success in destabilizing the order of capital.

This investigation leads us to an interesting vantage point to understand, sublate, critique, and/or negate the academic. It is quite simple now to see the university as a node (and probably not the most important) in the general chain of the application of immaterial labor, the creation of mass intellectuality, and the development of the general intellect. Some academics' work (especially that which sees direct results in industrial development—biotech, informatics, etc.) appears as more obviously related to the advancement of the productive apparatuses. Teaching might be less obvious, though its role is still apparent. A process of training students is one of creating the boundaries for thought to function in the social machine. The emphasis is on developing students' abilities to ingest past knowledge and relate it in a group form—all under the disciplinary function of the grade. Even if study appears to have no direct relationship to later wage-labor it still works to create mass intellectuality; it produces the linguistic-cognitive abilities of the student in a way that is *generally* copacetic with the functions of capital. The process of study is one element in the creation of the subjectivities necessary for this post-Fordist metropolis to function.

The labor of teaching shares similarities with contemporary service work in that it is what Hardt and Negri call affective labor: "Affective labor, then is the labor that produces or manipulates affects such as feelings of ease, well-being, satisfaction, excitement, or passion. One can recognize affective labor, for example, in the work of legal assistances, flight attendants, and fast food workers (service with a smile)."[19] The difficulty with understanding affective labor is the contradictory nature of generating pleasurable experiences that are part of the world of alienation. Teaching has a sense of reward and joy to it—yet this joy works in affect to reinforce the process of reification that places human experience into fetishized forms. It would be a mistake however to see the more positive moments of teachings as being *unreal*: as a manifestation of false needs that trample over deeper needs that arise from our species-being. Rather it is a question of what invests desire into the social machinery that negates a more liberating possibility, and how we can invest desire in negations of said machinery.

There is one element of academic work that deserves specific attention: *research*. In broad terms, academic research is a process in which elements of the world are made intelligible to the society of capital. It is the process of the fetishization of phenomena, their transformation into things, into a form that can be linked into and reaffirm the general intellect. Luce Irigaray makes a savage and nuanced critique of this (ultimately gendered) process. Research is still, almost without exception, conceived within the parameters

of scientific discourse. The activity of science is the activity of "[i]mposing
a model on the universe so as to take possession of it, an abstract, invisible, intangible model that is *thrown over* the universe like an encasing garment."[20] Thus, the gaze of the university constructs and imposes. It is a part
of the broader matrix that codifies flows of desire. This codification normal-
izes what is studied to the patterns of the social conformity of capital. They
become invested in its symbolic economy. The object of study is now spoken
about with the voice of authority and is "taught" to society. Again this might
seem more obvious in those disciplines with an apparently directly techno-
rationalist application: sciences that involve the subjecting of natural forces
to economic imperatives. It is also the case for the more intangible subjects.
What goes under the name "humanities" or "arts" are often the disciplines
that still cling the hardest to notion of intellectual exceptionalism, that still
wish to define themselves as outside the tawdry world of the state and the
dollar. Some attempt to define themselves as inherently subversive. They
often bring to light histories and stories that have been almost erased by the
trajectories of colonialism. This bringing to light still carries on the work of
transformation/assimilation. Their discoveries become commodities in the
general marketplace of ideas. All the standard conditions of the commodity
apply: a process of reification, most often into an ideology, imbues the product of research with potentialities that were previously human. So too the
academic in the process of research reifies their labor into a fetishized form
and cements their own misery. The university then is a moment of both the
application and the re/production of the general intellect in way that makes
these two tasks difficult to distinguish with any confidence.

What does this mean for the revolt of the academic? Post-*autonomia*
writers generally describe the application of the general intellect optimis-
tically. Capitalism has had to move towards this particular régime of accumulation because of struggle—and libertarian social relations exist already in this communicative multitude. Important to this, is the idea that
the shift from Fordism to post-Fordism was driven by the struggle of the
proletariat. The worker then is the inheritor of those previous struggles' victories. The work that takes place under post-Fordism then is the product of
these struggles—it is liberation, upon which capital is a parasite. To quote
Negri: "The socialized worker is a kind of actualization of communism,
its developed condition."[21] If this is the case then the task is quite easy. All
that is needed is to overthrow the axiomatics that capital imposes and let
communism speak its own name. What is needed is the "reappropriation of
administration" through "the soviets of mass intellectuality."[22] The struggle
of academics is essentially one of struggling for autonomy—the delinking
of their work—from the pressures of the state and market, and the creation
of new truly democratic bodies of social organization. Indeed, this is how
Bifo typifies recent social struggles—a struggle to "reclaim the autonomy

of their brain from profit."[23] Thus it would only be possible as part of a society-wide revolt and would involve much turmoil and confrontation with the baggage of history, and yet...

Problem 1

What if a more separate, more autonomous workforce, does not accompany the rise of mass intellectuality? What if the application of the general intellect rather than create a more antagonistic social subject has done the reverse? What if the continual development of technology actually produces increased domestication? In the schema above, the development of productive forces (both that of "actual" machinery—fixed capital—and the "social" machinery of the general intellect) is seen as progress. Indeed, the continual constitution of life with a techno-scientific framework—as cyborgs—is seen as liberatory. Hardt and Negri assert that the process of exodus—of rebelling against /leaving from empire—is a machinic exodus, that part of the process of liberation is the actual "hybridization of humans and machines."[24] Here we hit a wall. While the development of information technologies involved moments of rebellious activity—from the hacker to computer piracy—it seems impossible that this world of cyber-tech can exist *without* capitalism. How can the actual physical structures of the cyborg exist without the manufacturing of its parts in sweatshops, without the soldier-miner of the Congo, without vast toxic pollution? Indeed, does not the development and application of mass intellectuality exist in a world of increasing fracture, incorporation, biopolitical domination, and social atomization?

Working against the technological determinism of orthodox Marxism, Camatte writes: "[C]apitalism imposes its despotism on human beings by means of objects and things that are invested with new modes of being appropriate to capital's new requirements."[25] The continual subsumption of existence by capital is facilitated, in part, by the continual application of techno-scientific rationality throughout the social body. Mass intellectuality is in a constant state of surveillance, construction, and guidance, much of this facilitated by information technology. This continual application of techno-scientific rationality also results in escalating specialization and division of labor—a fracturing of the human population. Camatte continues that in this condition, this despotism of capital, "it is things that are the real subjects. They impose their own rhythm of life and ensure that people are confined to the level of their own single existences."[26] Post-Fordism is the further erasing of wild and unplanned behavior from human bodies and the world through the continual application of the will of capital congealed into the bio/cyber/industrial-technological apparatus.

In this sense, the post-*autonomia* authors still hold too much of a debt to the past, believing that the world of work can be taken over, freed from capital and made liberating. But to really be rid of alienation must not we completely destroy the proletarian condition? The general intellect and mass intellectuality—as moments of proletarianization—are not to be liberated from the control of capital, but destroyed as part of the world of capital.

Problem 2

It is common for academics (especially in art/humanities) with "radical" politics to make rebellion their study, to write on critical theory, uprisings, social movements, etc. It is what I'm doing right now. What does this mean if it is through research that the university, in part, fits into the productive machinery of capital? If academic work is alienating, then is the study of rebellion the process of its recuperation? One of the privileges of being an academic is the ability to often choose what one studies. But is this really a privilege? It is only allowed because the process of research nullifies the radical potential of what is studied. Contemporary capital thrives on its ability to ingest previously radical moments and reintegrate them through commodification and social management. Zizek asserts that the modern freedom of thought "does not undermine actual social servitude, it positively sustains it."[27] The contemporary academic can study *anything* as long as they study, as long as the production of "ideas" continues. Conferences and journals can be on any topic as long as they work to reproduce the world of conferences and journals. You may work on anything as long as you work. All this means is that academic labor is consistent with labor generally—it reproduces the conditions of our alienation. The university, however, functions under certain ideological mystifications that obscure this and generate a certain kind of semi-autonomous servitude that is necessary for academic work to take place. This is even more horrific when you consider that academics often bring movements and rebellions they have been involved with—and are deeply invested in—this process of recuperation. All the little rebellions that make life livable are encouraged to enter the spotlight of legitimate research. Through building a career as an academic we built monuments of our accumulated alienation. When do you stop being a punk and start theorizing about punk? When do you stop being a feminist and become a theorizer of feminism? Is not the pleasure of reading searing critique nullified by the process of grading it? Is not the joy of creative labor drained by its entrapment in forms that slot into the larger productive matrix? The result of this process is the draining of radical content from both the object of study and our very lives.

It might be possible to reverse the polarity. Rather than struggle entering the terrain of the university as an object of study, the process of academic work could be subverted by our own immersion in struggles. The more we rebel the more we can ally with the rebellion of others. These alliances, spiraling conspiracies, open up the terrain of our lives, allowing us to de-invest from the dominant order and built radical subjectivities of our own. This itself would be the beginning of the formation of another world, a collective dreaming, a group fantasy that could help us unplug our investments in the social machine and offer fragmentary glimpses of other ways of being. These conspiracies of fantasy and support are what Deleuze and Guattari call "agents of the real productivity of desire."[28] This is *not* the movement of the intellectual going to the people, bringing knowledge and receiving authenticity. It is collective exodus and the mingling of desire and autonomy, based on both what we share and what we hold uniquely.

There are, of course, moral panics over certain academics and certain works; for example, the media attack on a conference at Sydney University where Negri was going to speak.[29] But what is crucial here is who is being attacked, the academic going beyond the boundaries of study. It was Negri's relationship to *revolutionary praxis* that was the issue—not philosophical anticapitalism. The study of an idea becomes a problem for capital when it stops being the study of an idea. This perhaps is our point of rupture.

Conspiracy & Treason

Academic labor can be subverted. On any given day it probably is. The same tactics of auto-valorization are carried out in the university as much as they are anywhere. People slack off, fudge deadlines, email friends endlessly, steal office supplies. Students and staff form other dynamics, they hang out together, fall in love, have sex, get drunk, etc. Even with the pressure to produce we can often weasel out little parts of our day which we can dedicate to labor that actually brings us joy. This is all hidden; it exists as a special little secret world that we try to escape into as much as possible. Our precarity often makes us the ones who hide this. People talk of how hard they work because of the presence of discipline. And this discipline functions largely because of our atomization—both the atomization amongst academics and also the general atomization of the multitude (that continues despite/because of capital's reliance on general social cooperation in post-Fordism). Increasingly proletarianization has only homogenized the population in the *broadest* sense. Our daily lives still find us alone in a crowd. Federici identifies that the process of proletarianization has historically been the production of difference *within* the proletariat.[30] This is part of the condition of precarity—there is always someone worse and better off than you.

This same precariousness forces humiliating compromises. I intellectually critique grading, but still grade: I need the tutoring money. In honesty, this article will contribute to my CV. Lying in bed in the middle of the night, worrying about my future, with the only real solution—revolution—seeming so far away, I would like to get an academic job. The only other work I can get without cutting my hair, and taking out my piercings (a humiliation that I as yet refuse to accept) is in call centers—and I'll be fucked if I am ever going back there.

What are the possibilities? In the short term it seems that conspiracy is the most obvious form of dissent. This could consist of loose networks that weave across and beyond the university, forming links of trust and mutual aid, involving us, not through our roles allotted by capital, but against them. These could work to provide social solidarity to weather the storms of wage-labor and provide material comfort that makes the prospect of outright rebellion less daunting. They would work to generalize our experiences, help develop revolutionary self-theory, and overcome, in practical ways, the divisions of labor and specialization that cripple us. Indeed most of us already form such conspiracies with family and friends as a defense mechanism. But we can push them to more aggressive footings and also open them up to other similar networks.

Doing this would allow the *possibility* of acts of treason. These acts would be any that defy the application of our labor towards the re/creation of capital. In the daily work of an academic—teaching, marking, administration, research, etc.—there could be numerous opportunities for sabotage. What simple acts could just fuck things up a little and create/reclaim moments of joy? What would be the more public and confrontational ones? Refusal to grade, perhaps, or strikes on research? If social struggle intensified, what possibilities would open up? Objectively, the power of academics to disrupt the functioning of capital has never been more potent. If mass intellectuality is crucial to the functioning of capital, then we are in a prime position to sabotage its development.

The figure of the revolting knowledge-worker has not yet truly made its presence known. Cyber-punk seems to have been overly optimistic. I prefer to think in terms of pirates. The pirate is a representation of the triumph of previously contained and repressed desire. Think of the sailor: uniformed, codified, and slotted into a hierarchy. The sailor press-ganged for matters of state, is a cog in a greater national, mercantile, and military project. Any sense of individual subjectivity is broken by harsh discipline. Yet it is the sailor who transforms into the pirate—in an explosion of color, rage, desire, and violence through a collective process of reappropriation. The loyal subject who participates in the internal functioning of power becomes the outsider, becomes barbaric. While the pirate world is one of rich symbols and its own egalitarian cosmology, the pirate's life no longer fits into a reified cause that demands their supplication. The mercantile naval apparatus, built by their alienated labor, is turned upon—not to be taken wholesale, but broken up, destroyed, and consumed to increase their enjoyment and liberty. Piracy weakens a key imperial apparatus and opens up the possibilities for freedom for all those who face the machinery. And in doing so, the pirate takes part in the creation of a new world of the commons and of anarchy.[31] Is it possible to dream of black flags on our horizon?

Ultimately, humanity will only be in any sense free when the totality of global capitalism is destroyed through conscious revolution. This involves the destruction of the university as part of the destruction of all concretized moments of the division of labor. We can only really dream about what this would look like, drawing on the tumultuous history of revolt and our own experience of struggle for sustenance. Yet the potential to turn the world upside down is not some gift in the future but an immanent and imminent possibility. This possibility, at least in Australian society, has not been picked up. Rather, contemporary conditions are typified by a numbing social peace. Molecular forms of disobedience seem to be the only ones really open to us. Though this could change—just one really serious moment of struggle could suddenly make everything appear combustible.

It seems facile to suggest some kind of platform for a way forward. Struggles on campus, are at this point, still locked in Leftism. There are some brief and beautiful exceptions. Recently, leaflets entitled *Destructivist Position on Militarism and Higher Education* appeared around the Australian National University. They contained beautiful and lucid calls for students and soldiers to join together, and with the aid of "powerful weaponry...partake in the enjoyable exercise of absolutely smashing all the current ivory towers and ivy-covered halls, all the sandstone monuments to elitism, business, and boredom."[32] Its surreal "madness" expressed so well the very manifestation of desire and the schizing out of normality that is needed in the here and now. As such, it simply does not compute with the standard and repressive consciousness of the academic, the paranoid and self-righteous fantasies that lead so many of us into a defense of our own alienation. Like so many of the subjects of capital in the post-Fordist metropolis, we find ourselves constantly reinvesting in the machinery, apparatus, practices, and technologies that encage us. The way out is unclear, but a critical understanding of our condition and lucid dreams of revolt glimmer like spider webs in the moonlight.

Notes

1.   B. O'Keefe, "Canberra to Suspend University Funds Over IR Guidelines" *The Australian*, December 2, 2005. Available at http//www.theaustralian. news.com.au.

2.   For updates on both government legislation and the official union response see http//www.nteu.org.au.

3.   For a further examination of the ideologies of the Left that have constructed a role for the intellectual, see an earlier version of this article, "Treasonous

Minds: Capital and Universities, The Ideology of the Intellectual and the Desire for Mutiny" in *ephemera: theory & politics in organization* 5, no. 4 (November 2005). Available at http//www.ephemeraweb.org.

4. Karl Marx, *Capital: A Critique of Political Economy Volume 1* (London: Penguin Classics, 1990), 1010.

5. Ibid., 1024. This raises a host of questions: When did this happen? And where? Marx writes as if this moment of real subsumption is emerging or has emerged as he writes. Yet capitalism has changed massively since then, and its development is uneven. We can look at the modern metropolis and say that life is subsumed by the relations of capital—the commodity, wage-labor, (cyber)-industrialization etc.—but what about in the peripheries, that is if they even still exist? Is there something beyond real subsumption—a total subsumption for instance? These questions need answers. Yet we can still use the idea of real subsumption as a broad abstraction to help us understand the role of the academic in capitalism.

6. Jason Read, *The Micro-Politics of Capital: Marx and the Prehistory of the Present* (Albany: State University of New York Press, 2003), 122.

7. Jacques Camatte, *This World We Must Leave and Other Essays* (Brooklyn, NY: Autonomedia, 2005), 39.

8. Marx, *Capital: A Critique of Political Economy* Volume 1, 1024.

9. Karl Marx, *Grundrisse: Foundations of the Critique of Political Economy* (London: Penguin Classics, 1993), 706.

10. For those unfamiliar with the various trajectories that came out of the Italian *operaismo* and *autonomia*, I recommend Nick Dyer-Witheford's *Cyber-Marx: Cycles and Circuits of Struggle in High-Technology Capitalism* (Urbana, IL: University of Illinois Press, 1999).

11. Maurizio Lazzarato, "Immaterial Labour," in *Radical Thought in Italy: A Potential Politics*, eds. Michael Hardt and Paolo Virno (Minneapolis: University of Minnesota Press, 1996), 132.

12. Ibid., 142.

13. Paolo Virno, *A Grammar of the Multitude: For an Analysis of the Contemporary Forms of Life* (New York: Semiotext(e), 2004), 106.

14. Ibid.

15. Lazzarato, "Immaterial Labour," 140–141.

16. Virno, *A Grammar of the Multitude*, 106.

17. Paolo Virno "Labour & Language," (2003). Available at http//www.generation-online.org.

18. George Caffentzis, "The End of Work or The Renaissance of Slavery," in *Revolutionary Writing: Common Sense Essays is Post-Political Politics,* ed. Werner Bonefeld (Brooklyn, NY: Autonomedia, 2003), 129–130.

19. Michael Hardt and Antonio Negri, *Multitude: War and Democracy in the Age of Empire* (New York: Penguin Press, 2004), 108.

20. Luce Irigaray, *An Ethics of Sexual Difference* (London: Continuum, 2004), 103.

21. Antonio Negri, *The Politics of Subversion: A Manifesto for the Twenty-First Century* (Cambridge: Polity Press, 1989), 81.

22. Antonio Negri, "Constituent Republic," in *Revolutionary Writing: Common Sense Essays is Post-Political Politics,* ed. Werner Bonefeld (Brooklyn, NY: Autonomedia, 2003), 252.

23. Bifo, "The Warrior, the Merchant and the Sage" (2004). Available at http//www.generation-online.org.

24. Hardt and Negri, *Multitude*, 108.

25. Camatte, *This World We Must Leave*, 39.

26. Ibid.

27. Slavoj Zizek, *Welcome to the Desert of the Real!* (London: Verso, 2002), 3.

28. Gilles Deleuze and Felix Guattari, *Anti-Oedipus: Capitalism and Schizophrenia* (London: Continuum, 2004), 33.

29. Keith Windschuttle "Tutorials in Terrorism," *The Australian*, 16 March, 2005.

30. Silvia Federici, *Caliban and The Witch: Women: The Body and Primitive Accumulation* (Brooklyn, NY: Autonomedia, 2004).

31. Peter Linebaugh and Marcus Rediker, *The Many-Headed Hydra: Sailors, Slaves, Commoners, and the Hidden History of the Revolutionary Atlantic* (Boston: Beacon Press, 2000).

32. Temporary Bureau of Destructivist Activity, *Destructivist Position on Militarism and Higher Education* (Leaflet).

Practising Anarchist Theory: Towards a Participatory Political Philosophy

Uri Gordon

In contrast to the empirical thrust of most contemporary activist research, this essay explores the possibility of a participatory and embedded approach to political philosophy. Specifically at stake are the concerns, dilemmas, and controversies encountered by anarchists in their self-critical reflection. Prominent among these are debates around internal hierarchies or leadership in the movement; around the definition, justification, and effectiveness of violence; and around anarchist attitudes towards technology and modernity. These debates represent the evolving, polyphonic thinking of a re-emergent social movement. What does it mean to be an anarchist philosopher/activist? Is this a role open to anyone? What tensions arise in the attempt to carry out such an enterprise among one's comrades? And most importantly, what concrete tools and methods can be offered for facilitating the collective production of reflective political philosophy within anarchist movement networks?

By anarchism, I mean primarily what is by now a relatively well-defined political culture at work within sections of the global justice movement, primarily in Europe and North America. This political culture, or set of common orientations towards political action and speech, manifests itself in the combination of: (a) shared forms of organisation (networked, decentralised, horizontal, consensus-based); (b) a shared repertoire of political expression (direct action, constructing alternatives, community outreach, confrontation); (c) a shared political language, including a distinct commitment to resisting all forms of domination, from which is derived resistance to capitalism, the state, patriarchy, and so on; (d) shared narratives and mythologies invoking the Zapatista uprising, the Seattle protests, etc.; and (e) shared features of dress, music, and diet, primarily those associated with the punk and hippie subcultures. Historically speaking, contemporary anarchism is largely discontinuous with the nineteenth and early-twentieth century workers' and peasants' movements bearing the same name. It is a political culture that has fused in the intersection of other movements such as radical ecology, feminism, black and indigenous liberation, anti-nuclear, anticapitalist, and anti-war movements. Many people associated with this political culture would prefer to call themselves anti-authoritarian or autonomous.

Here we begin with a look at the social role of the philosopher and move on to consider the growing tradition of Participatory Action Research and its relevance to philosophy. From there one can spell out procedures that can be applied to a participatory philosophical engagement and consider their importance in relation to issues of access, interpretation, and scholarly distance.

The philosopher as facilitator

As a communicative praxis, political philosophy consists in the argumentation of values, principles, and the appropriate use of concepts in different contexts. The idea is to integrate inclusive and cooperative research techniques into conscious engagement in these debates, specifically regarding topics of controversy within anarchism. There is another sense of anarchist political philosophy that seeks to convince its audience of the general validity or applicability of anarchist positions. This is anarchism as social analysis or as core argumentation, which I do not deal with here. The case for anarchism has been presented exhaustively in two centuries of anarchist literature, and has also been the theme of several works in academic political philosophy (Wolff 1971, Taylor 1976, Ritter 1980, Taylor 1982, Brown 1993, Carter 2000) that many anarchists have most likely never heard of. The area on which I focus here is less developed: anarchist political philosophy as an intramural debate. While points like the generalised resistance to domination or the politics of direct action represent a consensus at the back of anarchist organising, the movement has also been the site of a great deal of introspective debates, dilemmas, and controversies. These debates take place on the basis of certain shared assumptions such as: generalised resistance to domination or the politics of direct action. The assumptions are necessary because it makes no sense to ask whether anarchists should ever use violence to achieve their ends if the ends themselves are not justified. One cannot ask whether some forms of leadership in the anarchist movement are more problematic than others if one does not endorse some ethos of horizontal organising to begin with. In other words, there are debates that only come into being on the basis of such assumptions. The anarchist activist/philosopher would seek to facilitate such debates.

Recently, David Graeber has described an approach to anarchist social theory with a similar agenda. In addition to endorsing the initial assumption that another world is possible, he argues, "any anarchist social theory would have to self-consciously reject any trace of vanguardism." What this means is that the role of the anarchist theorist is not to arrive at the correct strategic analyses and then lead the masses to follow. The point is to answer the needs of anarchists for theoretical expression on the issues that concern them and "offer those ideas back, not as prescriptions, but as contributions, possibilities—as gifts" (2004: 10–12).

The recognition of the importance of an activist-grounded approach for doing political theory or philosophy extends beyond the specific interest in anarchism. Writing about environmental political philosophy, Avner De-Shalit has recently argued for essentially the same type of enterprise. He argues a political philosophy or theory should "start with the activists and their dilemmas.... It is therefore a theory that reflects the actual philosophical needs of the activist seeking to convince by appealing to practical issues." Although s/he may side with the broad agenda of environmental activists, "the philosopher should not take the value of the activists' claims for granted; their intuitions, arguments, claims, and theories should also be scrutinised. However, the fact that they need to be critically examined does not affect the main point: that the activists' intuitions, claims, and theories ought to be the starting point for a philosophy aimed at policy change." Procedurally, this means that the philosopher "studies the intuitions and theories that exist within the given society and analyses 'popular' theories with a view to refining them" (De-Shalit 2000: 29–31). By bringing the often conflicting views of activists to a conceptual level, the philosopher can construct a discussion where the activists' debates can be undertaken in a more precise and clear way, with attention to detail and a coherent thread of argument. The role of the philosopher is to partake in and facilitate the reflexive process of theorising among activists, functioning as a clarifier, organiser, and articulator of ideas, an activity that takes place with and for activists. Her or his goal is to address in theoretical form the issues that activists face in their everyday organising, to assemble ideas so that they can be discussed carefully, to lay open hidden assumptions and contradictory statements, and in general to advance activists' thinking by transposing it from the fragmented terrain of brief and informal debate to a dimension where a more structured and "high-definition" discussion can be undertaken: on the written page.

While the gist of this approach is very close to the type of theorising activity proposed here, one aspect of it is not sustainable for application to the present context. Clearly anarchist philosophy is not geared towards underpinning policy change, which inevitably means change through the state. Rather, the goal is to underpin various forms of grassroots action that take place outside and against the state. This observation does not invalidate De-Shalit's basic approach. What it does do, however, is shift our understanding of what these needs may be. The anarchist philosopher's engagement with the popular argumentation is not intended to help anarchists articulate better arguments they can use to influence the electoral process, but to improve their understanding of the issues that guide them in the project of transforming society without recourse to the state.

This aspect of De-Shalit's metatheory can be criticised along more general lines. In essence, he seems to be embracing, quite uncritically, some very naïve assumptions about the way in which politics actually functions. The rationale that underlies his account is that the purpose of theory is to equip activists with arguments which they then enter into a presumably open and free arena of public debate. Here, success in convincing other members of the public is understood as automatically translating into policy changes. This can only be if this public has a deciding influence over what the state does. Such an orientation seems to inhabit, along with much of contemporary political theory, some kind of dreamland in which there are no such things as systematic collusion and revolving doors between political and corporate elites, professional lobbyists and millionaire donors, manipulative news channels, and governments that lie to the public about anything from the dangers of GM crops to the existence of weapons of mass destruction in oil-rich countries. If a political theory really wants to have an impact, it should at least consider empirically what the world actually looks like, instead of assuming that the philosopher is embedded in a well-functioning democratic polity. This assumption is not very widely shared among De-Shalit's own audience of environmental activists.

It could also be asked whether it is really the province of theory to convince the public of the appropriateness or viability of a political position, whether anarchism or De-Shalit's democratic and socialist environmentalism. What convinces people much more effectively than theory is ideological communication: propaganda, slogans, cartoons, and, perhaps more than anything, the living practice of activists, which most directly inspires people by way of example. It is doubtful whether anyone has ever been won over to a political position on the strength of a well-constructed argument or appealing theory. It is likely that people come into their positions on the basis of a personal process that takes place not only on an intellectual/theoretical level, but also on the basis of emotion, conviction, and belief.

Philosophy and participation

Such an approach requires concrete tools for accessing the theories of activists. How is the philosopher supposed to know what activists are saying? Who does s/he reach out to in order to source the popular theories, arguments, and debates that form the basis for discussion? Although he continuously emphasises the need to do so, De-Shalit never actually spells out how. What I would like to suggest here is a strategy in which the philosopher more fully participates in the movement being theorised—or wherein the philosopher begins with an anarchist activist who decides to apply structured, systematic thinking to debates of political significance. A participatory strategy provides the most adequate and enriching access to (fellow) activists' ideas, codes, theories, and debates.

This type of theorising activity recalls Antonio Gramsci's idea of the "organic intellectual." According to Gramsci, each social group that comes into existence creates within itself one or more strata of intellectuals that give it meaning, that help it bind together and function. These intellectuals can be attached to the ruling class—as managers, civil servants, clergy, teachers, technicians, and lawyers—but may also rise out of the oppositional sections of society. Gramsci maintains that not only should a significant number of traditional intellectuals come over to the revolutionary cause (Marx, Lenin, and Gramsci himself were examples of this), but also that the working class movement should produce its own organic intellectuals. He goes on to point out that "there is no human activity from which every form of intellectual participation can be excluded," and that everyone, outside their particular activity, "carries on some form of intellectual activity...participates in a particular conception of the world, has a conscious line of moral conduct, and therefore contributes to sustain a conception of the world or to modify it, that is, to bring into being new modes of thought" (Gramsci 1971).

What is relevant here is not Gramsci's reified notion of social classes, nor his integration of the organic intellectual into an authoritarian Marxist framework. Rather, what can be stressed here is the embeddedness of the organic intellectual in a particular liberatory milieu towards which s/he remains responsive. Hence, the process of generating anarchist theory itself has to be dialogical in the sense that both the people whose ideas and practices are examined and the people who are formulating theory on their basis must be involved in the process of theorising. Only from this dialogical connectedness can the anarchist philosopher draw the confidence to speak. The voice of the intellectual should no longer come "from above, but from within" (Gullestad 1999; Cf. Jeppesen 2004b).

It is not surprising that the bulk of recognised anarchist philosophers were anarchist militants who were deeply involved in the social struggles of their day and whose theorising work was inseparable from their engagement in action. Bakunin was a permanent fixture at almost every European uprising and insurrection of the mid-nineteenth century. Kropotkin, who wrote about the practical realisation of anarchist social forms, was also a tireless organiser in mutual aid groups, working with the revolutionary Jura federation and closely involved in workers' movements and publications. Emma

Goldman not only made theoretical contributions to feminism and anti-militarism, but also campaigned for birth control and set up anti-conscription leagues. Rudolf Rocker helped sweatshop workers organise in London and New York, was a founder of the German *Freie Arbeiter* Union and the first secretary of the International Workers Association. The major exceptions in the cynosure of anarchist philosophers—William Godwin, Leo Tolstoy, perhaps Max Stirner—were labeled anarchists only in hindsight; Godwin and Stirner never used the word, whereas Tolstoy expressed sympathy with the anarchists, but not identification.

This approach allows us to elaborate themes in anarchist theory that reflect more genuinely the debates, mentalities, and language of the contemporary anarchist movement that are found in everyday actions and utterances. Following on from these considerations, we may posit three stages of theoretical research that can be offered as a structure for initiating and engaging in a collaborative inquiry. These remarks assume that an individual activist/philosopher is at work, but they are equally relevant for undertaking the same enterprise in a small group.

The first stage or initial condition is that of immersion. In order to have access to the theories and arguments that anarchists employ and which will become the initial building-blocks for analysis, the philosopher either begins from the position of being native to the anarchist movement or undergoes a process of going native—in any case the result is that s/he is situated seamlessly within its networks.

The second stage is that of absorption: the philosopher continuously participates in actions, meetings, and discussions, closely following the process of political articulation, which has by now become a frame of reference with which s/he has a greater degree of intimacy. This stage can be expected to be the most protracted one, with a constant influx of ideas into the philosopher's emerging framework, and a continuous process of refining the way in which ideas are positioned and connected in the researcher's own mind. The process can happen initially in an unstructured manner, from the position of observation and non-intervention. What can also be expected from this stage is that the philosopher will eventually encounter a number of recalcitrant debates continuously returned to, thus identifying what are the most valuable and relevant topics of theoretical inquiry. This can also take the form of the philosopher initiating focused discussions on a particular topic among activists—whether in personal dialogue with numerous activists, or at seminars and workshops (at activist gatherings or in the run-up to mass mobilisations, for example). To all of this is added an informed and contextualised discussion of relevant arguments and approaches using provided anarchist texts.

The third stage is that of integration, which parallels the writing process of the philosophical output. Here the activist/philosopher takes a step back from the process of absorption and undertakes their own exercise of arranging the ideas that they have encountered in a more structured manner. This stage can take place when the philosopher feels that s/he has reached a certain point of saturation, or when further discussions that s/he observes and participates in are yielding diminishing returns—the arguments and theories are now familiar and rarely is something new heard.

In the production of theoretical output, there are two major things that the activist/philosopher can do. The first is to give elaborate articulation to points that are judged to enjoy wide consensus in the anarchist movement; taking ideas and concepts in which there seems to be an intuitive agreement among activists and rendering more complex the ways in which they are understood. The philosopher can tease out the ways in which concepts are used in general free-form discussion, clarify the sources of agreement over them, and translate this consensus into a more comprehensive account. The consensus can, of course, also be challenged, or the philosopher may discover that it leads to some conclusions that activists have yet to consider.

A second function is to engage with particular areas of contention, mapping out the different arguments and spelling out the background of social action against which the controversy occurs. In addressing debates, then, the initial task is one of disentangling—differentiating between different aspects of a discussion, identifying patterns whereby speakers tend to argue at cross-purposes, pointing to confused uses of the same concept in different senses, and putting a finger on the questions that are the most relevant and debatable. From this follows the next task, which is to suggest directions for the reconstruction of certain debates, to formulate substantive arguments of one's own, and to ask whether and how the conclusions can be seen to filter back into cultural codes. In such a capacity, the theoretical intervention does not necessarily involve taking a position within the debate as it is currently structured—the goal can also be to intervene in the way in which the debate itself is structured, questioning the assumptions regarding its parameters and what we are having the debate for. Finally, the activist/philosopher may reach tentative judgements within a certain debate, offering a view that sees some positions as more attractive than others and making substantive arguments which are then fed back into the ongoing dialogue.

The role of the activist/philosopher is not simply that of an expert observer but primarily one of an enabler or facilitator, and the role of the participants is that of co-philosophers and co-activists.

There are strong parallels here to the emerging tradition of Participatory Action Research, which integrates diverse emancipatory and grassroots approaches to learning, including contributions of indigenous cultures, communities in the global south, radical pedagogues and philosophers, ecological practitioners and egalitarian, feminist, and anti-racist social movements (Freire 1970, Feyerabend 1970, Birnbaum 1971, Touraine et al 1983a, 1983b,

Rosaldo 1989). Reason and Bradbury provide a preliminary definition of PAR as "a participatory, democratic process concerned with developing practical knowing in the pursuit of worthwhile human purposes" (2001: 1). In such research strategies with a horizontal approach to the generation of knowledge, the rigid separation between researcher and researched is dissolved. These strategies emphasise the emancipatory potential of the collective generation of knowledge that legitimate and valorise a socially committed orientation in intellectual endeavours.

Proceeding in complete detachment from the realities of the anarchist movement creates interventions with no direct resonance with the actual debates that anarchists engage in. The explosive growth and deepening of discussion in anarchist circles recently, which has been touching on a multitude of issues and espousing original and sophisticated perspectives, has received little if any recognition from academic writers. Alan Ritter quite typically sees the gist of anarchism represented in the works of Godwin, Proudhon, Bakunin, and Kropotkin,

> whose contributions to anarchist theory are universally [sic] regarded as most seminal. These writers, who succeeded each other within the discretely bounded period between the French and Russian Revolutions, worked out a coherent set of original arguments, which, while continuing to be influential, have not developed much since Kropotkin's time. Hence, to comprehend anarchism as a political theory, the writings of more recent anarchists need not be considered (1980: 5).

Such an approach would have been hard to justify twenty-five years ago when anarchafeminism and ecological approaches to anarchism were already well developed. Today, it would be outrageous in light of the explosion of anarchist activity and reflection, readily available for sourcing and discussion if one knows where to look.

From texts to oral debate

The participatory approach is crucial when approaching issues of reliable witnesses and of valid documents and arguments, which come into play when carrying out theory from an engaged perspective. Consider the issue of texts. There is a great deal of anarchist literature out there—in books, pamphlets, and on the Web. A stroll through the yearly London Anarchist Bookfair uncovers four categories:

• Informational books, booklets, and pamphlets on contemporary issues and struggles, from the Zapatistas and climate change, to squatting

and campaigns against GMOs, including recent commentary from Chomsky, Zinn, Said, etc.
- Older literature—anarchist, Marxist, and libertarian-left classics.
- Underground music and printed material on cultural alternatives from punk to drugs to earth-based spirituality.
- Many self-published, photocopied, or cheaply printed booklets and zines. These include a mix of essays, action reports, comics, short stories, poetry, and do-it-yourself guides on anything from women's health to bicycle repair. Almost all pieces in these zines are undated and are written anonymously, collectively, or under a pseudonym.

This last class of materials is highly absorbing: it is the most grassroots expression of the contemporary anarchist movement, offering an intriguing vista into its political culture. But such materials do not lend themselves to straightforward selection—how is one to determine to what degree a text is relevant and influential? Also, a great deal of anarchist articulation takes place on the Web, with literally hundreds of websites dedicated to news, announcements and polemics from an anarchist perspective available for consideration to the engaged philosopher. Without any pre-set markers, we have no way of knowing whether a certain anarchist group, ideological configuration, or set of arguments that we encounter on the Web is in any way representative or influential. Since anyone with minimal Web-publishing skills and access to a server can set up a website and publish whatever they want on it, it is very easy to present a great deal of material in an attractive set up, that would give the impression of prominence and importance, where in fact the articulation is misleadingly louder on the Web than it is in reality.

Without an embedded presence in anarchist networks, the philosopher may be led to make vastly misguided judgments about the relative importance of various anarchist ideas and tendencies. This establishes the importance of the much richer orientation available to the observing participant who encounters the movement and its culture as a habitus rather than as an other mediated by, and limited to, the texts it produces. Judgments on relevance may be supported by their mutual consistency, by the reader's own interpretation of the cited source-material, and by other reports of participatory research undertaken in direct action movement networks (Plows 1998, Cox 1999, Wall 1999, Eguiarte 1999, Christensen 2001, Chesters and Welsh 2004/2005, Juris 2004). It also makes space for coping with issues of explanation and narrative building within social movements that escape other modes of validity (cf. Altheide and Johnson 1994).

Then there is the question of interpretation. In mainstream political philosophy, it would be reasonable to select some questions that other philosophers have already said something about and then to pick them apart to make one's own points. This would be easy because a text that is transparent and precise according to academic conventions provides rich pickings for criticism as long as the rules of the game are observed. Anarchist literature does not work in the same way. This literature may include rigorous argumentation, but it is always by definition polemical—very well structured, perhaps, but rarely of a philosophical nature. Anarchist essays are written with very particular audiences in mind, often other anarchists. Materials that are intended for the general public tend to be leaflets, posters, videos, and other creative media of propaganda, which address radical issues, but rarely anarchism itself.

Though there are many very insightful, calmly argued, and well thought-out essays out there, much of what one encounters in the polemical section of anarchist literature is just not very good. Polemical literature sometimes displays a lack of rigorous debate or careful attention to the complex and often conflicting meanings of concepts (like power or organisation), a reluctance to clarify one's arguments in a way open to challenge, and a failure to admit where there are gaps in one's knowledge and understanding. The reasons for this may gravitate between bad faith and what McQuinn (2003) calls, "inarticulate ignorance." McQuinn complains of the evasion of rational discussion in the anarchist milieu:

> It usually involves the refusal to reflect, self-critically evaluate and self-edit responses. The more unthinking, belligerent and vociferous participants tend to drive out the more thoughtful and considered opinions by making a never-ending stream of attacks, demands, and frivolous comments.... In other anarchist media, the evasion of discussion tends to be most obvious in the letters columns of periodicals...and in some of the rants that sometimes pass for personal, point-of-view articles. These are also formats that tend to lend themselves to those writers too irresponsible, unprepared and unself-critical to put together more coherent essays that would need to be more thoroughly thought through, more logically structured, and more self-critically examined in light of other perspectives.

McQuinn may be right, but only up to a point. To begin with, there are many well-constructed and careful arguments in anarchist polemical literature, even if they might not meet rigorous academic criteria. More importantly, McQuinn is casting his net of samples much too narrowly. The lack of rational discussion is far from the norm in the movement if we also count the everyday oral communication among anarchists, where the bulk of discussion within the movement takes place. These oral discussions, most often in the form of casual conversations among activists, tend to be of a far higher quality than what McQuinn is seeing in the narrow display box of anarchist print and Web-based media.

For this reason it is extremely important for whoever wants to write about anarchism to be attentive to these oral discussions and follow them in a consistent way. Such a position also allows the philosopher to witness the real-time vernacular discussions in which such concerns are expressed as well as the exposure to the shared narratives, beliefs, and practices that are loaded with significance for theory. By providing critically engaged and theoretically informed analyses generated through collective practice, participatory philosophy aims to provide tools for the ongoing reflection of anarchist activists while remaining interesting and relevant to a broader audience.

References

David Altheide and John M. Johnson, "Criteria for Assessing Interpretive Validity in Qualitative Research," in Norman Denzin and Yvonna Lincoln, eds., *Handbook of Qualitative Research* (Newbury Park: Sage Publications, 1994).

Norman Birnbaum, *Towards a Critical Sociology* (Oxford: Oxford University Press, 1971).

Susan L. Brown, *The Politics of Individualism: Liberalism, Liberal Feminism and Anarchism* (Montréal: Black Rose, 1993).

Alan Carter, "Analytical Anarchism: Some Conceptual Foundations," *Political Theory* 28, no. 2 (2000), 230–253.

Graeme Chesters and Ian Welsh, *Complexity, Multitudes and Movements: Acting on the Edge of Chaos*, International Library of Sociology Series (London: Routledge, 2005).

Graeme Chesters and Ian Welsh, "Rebel Colours: 'Framing' in Global Social Movement," *Sociological Review* 52, no. 3 (2004), 314–335.

Bolette Christensen, "From Social Movement to Network Culture: Collective Empowerment and Locality," in Colin Barker and Mike Tyldesley, eds., *Seventh International Conference on Alternative Futures and Popular Protest* (Manchester: Manchester University Press, 2001).

Laurence Cox, *Building Counter Cultures: The Radical Praxis of Social Movement Milieux,* PhD thesis, (Dublin: Trinity College, 1999).

Avner De-Shalit, (2000) *The Environment Between Theory and Practice* (Oxford: Oxford University Press).

Cristina Eguiarte, "Ideology and Culture Among Core Activists in the British Anti-Roads Movement" (1999). Available at http://sociology.berkeley.edu/faculty/EVANS/evans_pdf/eguiarte.pdf.

Paul Feyerabend, *Against Method* (Minneapolis, MN: University of Minnesota Press, 1970).

Paulo Freire, *Pedagogy of the Oppressed* (New York: Seabury Press, 1970).

Uri Gordon, *Anarchism and Political Theory—Contemporary problems*, Dphil Thesis (Oxford: University of Oxford, 2005). Available online at http://ephemer.al.cl.cam.ac.uk/~gd216/uri.

David Graeber, *Fragments of an Anarchist Anthropology* (Chicago: Prickly Paradigm Press, 2004).

Antonio Gramsci, "The Intellectuals," in *Selections from the Prison Notebooks* (New York: International Publishers, 1971), 3–23. Available online at the Marxists Internet Archive: http://www.marxists.org.

Gullestad, Marianne "The Politics of Knowledge," (1999). Available at http://culturemachine.tees.ac.uk.

Sandra Jeppesen, "Where Does Anarchist Theory Come From?" Institute for Anarchist Studies, (2004). Available at http://www.anarchist-studies.org.

Jason McQuinn, "Evasion of Rational Discussion in the Radical Milieu," in *Anarchy: A Journal of Desire Armed* 56, (2003). Available at http://www.anarchymag.org.

Alexandra Plows, *Practics and Praxis: The What, How, and Why of the UK Environmental Direct Action Movement in the 1990s.* PhD Thesis (Bangor: University of Wales, 1998). Available at http://www.iol.ie/~mazzoldi/tools-forchange/afpp/plowsphd.rtf.

Peter Reason and Hilary Bradbury, *Handbook of Action Research* (London: Sage, 2001).

Alan Ritter, *Anarchism: A Theoretical Analysis* (Cambridge: Cambridge U. Press, 1980).

Renato Rosaldo, *Culture and Truth: The Remaking of Social Analysis* (Boston: Beacon Press, 1989).

Michael Taylor, *Anarchy and Cooperation* (London: Wiley, 1976).

Michael Taylor, *Community, Anarchy and Liberty* (Cambridge: Cambridge University Press, 1982).

Alain Touraine, et al, *Solidarity: The Analysis of a Social Movement* (Cambridge: Cambridge University Press, 1983).

Alain Touraine, et al, *Anti-nuclear Protest: The Opposition to Nuclear Energy in France* (Cambridge: Cambridge University Press, 1983).

Derek Wall, *Earth First! and the Anti-Roads Movement: Radical Environmentalism and Comparative Social Movements* (London: Routledge, 1999).

Robert Paul Wolff, *In Defense of Anarchism* (New York: Harper and Row, 1971).

Toward an Anti-Authoritarian, Anti-Racist Pedagogy

Ashar Latif + Sandra Jeppesen

W hat follows is a collaborative work. There are two segments, the first from the perspective of a white academic anarchist using anecdotal evidence, the second from a more theoretical perspective of an anarchist of color. Together they form a cycle of thought. The ideas are mutually shared; the brainstorming and organization of this text were done collaboratively.

I. Beyond Critical Pedagogy: Anti-Authoritarian Activist Approaches to Anti-Racist Education

During a discussion of white privilege, several white male students walk out of the lecture hall. A black colleague tells me that on the first day of class, when white students see that she is black they withdraw from the course. When asked about racism in Canada students initially respond that it does not exist, that we have an ethnic mosaic, diversity, and multiculturalism. They have been schooled to believe that our society has no systemic racism. At the same time many students can see that this contradicts their experience. There is a struggle to be able to speak about racism as something we hold inside ourselves, when students and teachers might prefer the safer discourses of statistics or diversity. In this segment, anecdotal evidence from my experience as a white academic and anarchist organizer, and personal stories from anarchist anti-racist zines will be used to develop anti-authoritarian anti-racist pedagogical strategies.

In order to "see" racism, Joe Feagin argues, white people need to develop "empathy across the color line," which "requires a developed ability to routinely reject distancing stereotypes and a heightened and sustained capacity to see and feel some of the pain" that racism inflicts on non-white peoples (2000: 254). This is one of the first necessary steps toward an anti-racist pedagogy for white allies. When white people read anti-racist anarchist zines written by people of color we gain insight into their experiences and take responsibility ourselves for learning and unlearning racism.

In *evolution of a race riot*, Melissa explains how, as an "Indian," she is ashamed "when the teacher of [her] high school English class proceeds to tell his students how Indians today still live in teepees and trade with glass beads." She has spent a great deal of her life having "fought for acceptance in a white world that I've never had a place in, no matter how pale my skin—I fought because I had been told my Indian ways were dumb and inferior" (2000: 15). She spends her childhood and youth "passing" as white and hoping that when people like her English teacher make racist remarks about "Indians" that they don't realize that she is one. This is a strategy often used by people of color who can appear white. They still experience the racism, but it becomes internalized.

Vietnamese immigrant Helen Luu in *How to Stage a Coup* writes of her and her sister's experience of being called "Chink" on the playground by the white kids, an insult that she had never heard before: "It must have confused me as to why these children didn't like me. They didn't know me. They didn't even know my name. I guess they thought they knew enough. I had slanted eyes, yellow skin, almost black hair. I wasn't white like them" (2000: 12–13). Kristy Chan also writes of being called "Chink" in *evolution of a race riot*: "All my life I have basically divided myself into two parts: my Chinese self, which I always tried to bastardize in an attempt to be what everybody seemed to want, and my white self, which was synonymous with 'normal.' I was never allowed to be a whole person with one identity" (1997: 44). Shari Cooper-Cooper tells a similar story: "When I started this zine, I made the conscious decision that I…didn't want to be thought of as 'that Chinese girl.'…I didn't forget I was Chinese. It just wasn't part of my writing, my consciousness, or my written existence" (1997: 34–35).

Non-white people are expected to assimilate and "become American" or Canadian but at the same time they are never allowed to "forget" that they are not white, always asked where they come from, or told that their English is pretty good. They might be called "a 'spic' or a 'feminazi' by a punk…or called racist for dedicating a song to Latinos." When Taina Del Valle brings up racism, rather than acknowledging their own racist attitudes, white punks tell her variations of, "you are separating yourself from other people in the scene, thus creating barriers and alienating others" (1997: 83–84). Cooper-Cooper's initial response, similar to Melissa's, is an attempt to erase her own race by "passing" for white through writing, a space where racialized identities can be hidden.

Ricky Walker, Jr., who self-identifies as "eighteen; vegan, straight edge, African-American" writes:

> The same way I passively invalidated girls' complaints about sex-
> ism by laughing at jokes about feminists is the same way white kids
> invalidate me by dictating to me what is and is not racist, scoffing at
> my claims of racism and proposing to have all the answers to end-
> ing racism, often giving me a spiel that sounds like a fucking after
> school special. How absurd is that? (2000: 22–3)

The notion that people who are targets of racism should be the arbiters
of what racism is constitutes a crucial anti-authoritarian activist strategy
that needs to be taken up in anti-racist pedagogy.

The anger expressed in these zines is a powerful way for people of color
to struggle against racism and simultaneously reclaim individual and collective empowerment. As white allies, we need to support this. We can learn
about anti-racism through reading angry, empowered stories in zines, attempting to understand the source of non-white people's anger and power.
White people have internalized racialized stereotypes that we need to unlearn, nevertheless we like to insist that we are not racist. It is this contradiction that is at play when white people walk out of whiteness studies
classes. It is also at play in Walker's story when he says that a white person's
particular statement or behavior was racist, and the white person denies it,
effectively invalidating his experience and thus perpetuating the very racism they claimed did not take place. To develop transformative anti-racist
pedagogical strategies from the heart of this contradiction, white students
and educators must learn not just that systemic racism actually exists, but
also how to take responsibility for their own internalized racist thoughts and
related behaviors.

Internalized racism is also experienced by people of color. Shari Cooper-
Cooper, for example, does not want to think of herself as Chinese and even
changes her name from Wang to Cooper-Cooper. J., a non-white student,
told me that when he moved here from South Africa the kids at his predominantly white school teased him about his accent so he made a concerted effort to unlearn it, as he put it, to become more white.

Similarly, Assata Shakur describes her teaching experience: "i asked
everyone to draw themselves. When i looked at the drawings i felt faint.
All of the students were Black, yet the drawings depicted a lot of blond-
haired, blue-eyed little white children. i was horrified." This internalized
racism is equally destructive in whites and non-whites although in very different ways. Unacknowledged internalized racism among educators leads
to a white-dominated curriculum. To counter this Shakur "went home and
ransacked every magazine i could find with pictures of Black people...we
talked about the different kinds of beauty that people have and about the
beauty of Black people." What was at stake for Shakur was that "there was

a big contradiction between the intelligence they exhibited in class and their test scores" (1987: 187). This problem still exists, the result of curriculum that reinforces unequal, racialized power relations.

Anti-racist anarchist zines provide anti-authoritarian strategies for un-learning internalized racism. When people of color self-produce zines they find a safe space (unlike schools) to speak out against racism and become empowered through self-expression. Zines are also important pedagogical spaces for community and university-based, white, anti-racist allies to un-derstand and take action against racism. Joe Feagin suggests, "In the US case, the history of anti-racist action indicates that individual whites often begin the process of becoming activists by working on their own racist at-titudes, stereotypes, and proclivities." Unlearning racism is an important part of anti-racist education. "[L]earned approaches reinforcing systemic racism...can be unlearned and replaced" by a "new cognitive framework" (2000: 253-254) or system of beliefs and behaviors. Unlearning is a long-term project that must continue to be taken up by white and non-white aca-demics and activists alike.

Toward Transformative Anti-Authoritarian Anti-Racist Pedagogical Strategies

There is a track by hip-hop group Dead Prez called "They Schools" that I play for students when we are discussing the canon of so-called great works. Dead Prez suggests that "they schools can't teach us shit.... white man's lies pure bullshit."

White-dominated curriculum is clearly a problem in anti-racist peda-gogy. If we teach colonization using the discourse of pioneers and settlers, if we teach that Abraham Lincoln freed the slaves rather than that enslaved Africans rose up in struggle to achieve freedom, if we teach that everyone is equal in the eyes of the law when our legal system has a race and class bias, if we teach that our society is multicultural—meaning all cultures are equal—when the common conception is that "some are more equal than oth-ers," students can see through this. They know that it's "bullshit" and "white man's lies." Non-white students recognize that they are being taught their place in society, as are white students, and that these places for the most part are inherently different. Students of color seem to have two choices—be-come "white" as J. described, or assert their racialized identity and risk fail-ure, discipline and expulsion.

How can anti-authoritarian pedagogy intervene against racism in trans-formative ways? Lorenzo Komboa Ervin writes, "I believe that the history of the 20th century has been that of the struggles of people of color against colonial powers, and although we are in a postcolonial world, racism is still very much an essential ingredient of the capitalist world order" (2001: 12).

Black students challenging this racist "capitalist world order" by acting out against white teachers, principals or professors can be understood as an anti-authoritarian strategy on the part of students to bring anticolonialist, anti-racist struggles into the classroom. Rather than disciplining or expelling active students, teachers and administrators might consider the students' perspectives. They might ask non-white students what kind of curriculum would better engage them in their classes or encourage them to stay in school. Without spaces for addressing the complexities of racism, academic institutions will continue to perpetuate it. To transform universities from bastions of white privilege to anti-racist institutions, many white academics, professors, and administrators need to first become aware of, and then unlearn racism, a task that is difficult for authorities within the system. In other words, who will teach the teachers? Spaces to discuss and unlearn racism must be fostered, whether through discussion circles, anti-oppression workshops, or some other forum.

One strategy I use to make space for non-white students to take on the role of collective educators is to invite students to bring in their own material for discussion. Last year in a segment on hip-hop, B., a black student, brought in a friend of his, a black hip-hop artist called DJ Specs. He free-styled about growing up on welfare, describing how he had dreads because he couldn't afford a proper haircut, whereas other kids were paying money to have dreads put into their hair. This led into a discussion of cultural appropriation. A white student asked if he was going to produce his own music and have his own record label, but Specs said he wanted to get a big record label deal because basically he was tired of being poor. We discussed who controls the music industry and how hip-hop artists try to maintain control and power over their own music while also making sure they get wide distribution. A few white "indie kids" used Ani DiFranco and Fugazi as examples of musicians who have their own record labels. Specs acknowledged that it was a lot easier for them to be successful in the music industry because they are white. Another student suggested that as a white boy from the suburbs it might be easy for him to focus on self-expression rather than money because he would always have his place in the suburbs. This acknowledgement of white privilege opened up the classroom to a frank discussion of the intersections of race and class in the music industry, particularly in hip-hop.

This is a strategy I have learned through activist teach-ins. At an anti-globalization protest in Windsor in 2000 a group of two- or three-hundred activists were marching around a facility where some of the "world leaders" were expected for lunch. We wanted to block the driveway so after three laps around the perimeter, S., an activist of color and I started a spontaneous teach-in about globalization and the Free Trade Area of the Americas. S. talked about his work in Students Against Sweatshops, then I talked about Canada's inability under NAFTA to pass environmental law, and the corporate monopolies at York University. People sitting on the ground blocking the driveway put up their hands and asked questions. The first one or two questions S. and I answered but then there was a question about Colombia that we didn't know that much about, so we asked if anybody else did. Someone put up their hand and we passed the megaphone to him. From there the questions and answers came from every direction. S. and I blended back into the crowd. The blockade prevented the "world leaders" from attending their lunch for a period of time, so the action was effective in direct political terms, and knowledge was shared in an anti-authoritarian way among equals.

Activist Spaces: Learning Through Action

Helen Luu, in an interview with Mimi Nguyen, suggests that learning without taking action can be frustrating:

> I was sitting in one of my favorite classes in my final year of school and it suddenly dawned on me that I was really sick of that class and what it represented.... I thought about how far removed this all was from real people and real lives. I couldn't wait to graduate and get the hell out of there (2000: 37–8).

Academic theorizing about race and other social issues cannot happen in isolation from action. While struggling against racism within universities, another anti-authoritarian, anti-racist strategy is to delink anti-racist learning from the mainstream education system.

The location of learning is as important as the curriculum. In Canadian schools and universities, learning is turned into drudgery through authoritarian disciplinary practices, racist policing of students, and enforced attendance in classes that are uninteresting and that have little relation to students' lives. The education system can easily kill the students' desire to learn. According to Ivan Illich, a "major illusion on which the school system rests is that most learning is the result of teaching. Teaching, it is true, may contribute to certain kinds of learning under certain circumstances. But most people acquire most of their knowledge outside school" (1971: 9).

As a counterpoint to hierarchical university structures, Richard Day proposes "a non-profit, community-based 'third sector' which would operate outside of both the state and privately-funded educational systems. Activity of this sort is already becoming quite common, through teach-ins, conferences, and reading groups that are organized without any help or sanction from mainstream institutions" (2001: 337). Free schools such as the Toronto Anarchist Free University (AFU) are one example of this kind of community-based location. There are no designated teachers, students, curriculum, classrooms, assignments, or grades. Courses are proposed and, if there are people interested in them, they go ahead. Facilitators organize the space and reading material agreed upon by the participants. No fees are exchanged. Classes take place in people's living rooms or community spaces. Anti-racism is practiced by challenging hierarchies of curriculum, teachers, and modes of teaching, instead valuing anecdotal evidence, personal stories, zines, circular or non-linear thinking, questioning, and experimentation. Nonetheless, AFU is still a space designated for teaching and learning. Illich's notion of "deschooling society" suggests that learning takes place in our daily lives and that we are not dependent on spaces set up specifically for learning.

Robert Regnier suggests that learning can take place in the streets through community-based actions. "The liberation of aboriginal education, implicit in Chief Elijah Harper's opposition to the Meech Lake Accord and in the Mohawk warriors' confrontation at Oka, was acted out by many students in the summer of 1990, not by sitting in their desks bound to the standard curriculum but by helping to turn the streets of some Canadian cities into forums for anti-racist education" (1995: 85). The streets became a pedagogical space whereby students learned by participating in a social movement and simultaneously provided information about the political situation to the general populace, thus struggling toward indigenous self-determination by practicing a liberatory anti-authoritarian pedagogy of self-determination.

In actions such as this indigenous struggle and the anti-FTAA teach-in, learning took place when and where people needed it to. It also served a dual purpose—both to instruct and to accomplish a direct action protest. Anti-racist pedagogy is not something we can just do in the classroom. It is a lifetime commitment that includes a shift in our way of thinking and being in the world, the locations in which we teach and learn, the things we do every day, with whom we do them and how. It is not just schools and universities but society itself that needs to be deschooled. We need to challenge the organization of institutions that teach us that racism is bad, but that simultaneously enact racism. Those of us with white privilege need to empathize with non-white people's experiences of daily racism. This might involve taking a critical look at both our own internalized racism and our positions of authority to understand ways in which each of these might thwart rather than facilitate learning.

II. Anti-Racist Anti-Authoritarian Pedagogy

Academics have a paradoxical place in the system. While they are privileged by a racist system, they are also in a uniquely privileged position to go beyond merely speaking out, and actively engage in anti-racist struggle.

How does one go about engaging in anti-racist activism? Specifically, what can an academic do to help remedy not only the elevation of whiteness over color, but also the less acknowledged elevation of teacher over student?

The default pedagogic and epistemic modes of the academy are, by virtue of being the historically developed and promulgated modes of a Eurocentric and authoritarian institution, antagonistic to the aims of anti-racist education. Most blatant and evident is the appeal to the voice of authority, of expertise, of renown. Dissent is silenced as the hollow citadel of fossilized European thought amplifies the solitary figure at the lectern to near-deafening levels, and without access to this intellectual echo chamber there is no acceptance of our knowledge and no incorporation of our wisdom. This exclusion takes place in the guise of, among others, the use of systems of intellectual precedent and citation. Unless one cites existent institutional scholars to construct and buttress one's position, or has paid dues as a receptacle for knowledge, rising up through the system to the position of expert oneself, any contribution brought to the table is automatically and ruthlessly written off as amateur and irrelevant.

Knowledge is admitted to the pantheon by explaining, critiquing, agreeing with, or otherwise referencing existing inductees into the canon. And the touchstones of knowledge, old and new, are building on (and building up) the European tradition of knowledge: the primacy of the written word, the relegation of orality to the position of secondary evidence, the singular authoritative arbiter of truth and resultant marginalization of subjectivity, the strict separation between the spheres of learning and doing. The practical acquisition of knowledge is subordinated to abstract mechanics and linear thinking. By placing the intellectual developments and the methodology that those developments crystallized (and which in turn framed later thought) as the accepted body of thought, teaching entrenches the primacy of those developments and solidifies those modalities as the canon on which further learning, teaching, and scholarship is carried out.

Not only must we be familiar with foundational European thought in order to express our learning, we must also jump through the same methodological hoops to form critiques or to otherwise go against the grain. Thought is worthy only if it is somehow isomorphic to existent thinking, if it references the content or methodology of the academic edifice. The resultant thought has some inherent limitations, especially when it becomes self-reflexive. How can we critique a hegemonic system of thought using the very techniques it developed as the justification and vehicle for its own continuation? Looping back to negate and disprove a system with its own logic, through the rules it has developed and tweaked to its advantage, seems like an exercise destined to futility.

This is not to say that textual and didactic modes of promulgating information are inherently Eurocentric. What is Eurocentric is the reification of textuality, centralization of intellectual influence, and insistence on logical consistency above all else—those hallmarks of academic objectivity. It is not the use of authoritarian epistemology that defines Eurocentricity, rather it is the sole reliance on these modalities and the disparaging of all others that is truly offensive. This consistency is accomplished by silencing dissent and demeaning difference and subjectivity in the construction of thought systems and models.

Even as learning and teaching are organizationally combined and taken to be one didactic activity, the gulf between the binary poles of teacher as source of knowledge and student as receptacle grows ever larger. These movements are causally linked and central to the problem. As education is increasingly seen as a measured and rigidly codified body of hegemonic knowledge to be universally passed on, distilled, drilled, and instilled into partially willing minds, the experience and un-indoctrinated fearlessness of the non-expert is disregarded. The fearlessness I speak of is one stemming from the mind of a novice, the willingness to question the base assumptions of a body of knowledge, the ones left untouched by the institutionally initiated; although unfortunately this fearlessness does not always extend to expressions of inquiry. The flow of knowledge and thus influence is so tightly regulated and channeled that it becomes unidirectional. I christen thee curriculum: may you flow unhindered towards a regulated and productive generation of tomorrow.

Empowerment flows from the mouth of Authority (remember, knowledge is power) and the full repressive power of Authority is embodied in the person of the expert, going so far as to take on the title. The Authority's voice does not invite reply, does not tolerate dissent, and has no time for existential questions. It has idiomatically been equated with the final word on a topic. Without being a creator of knowledge, an Author, without having our subjectivity acknowledged as valid and equal, how can we be empowered? And, in the end, empowering ourselves to engage intellectual material on our own level and on our own terms; that is the purpose of education.

Schooling instills a sense of boundary to questioning, fencing off vast swaths of intellectual territory from prying minds. To have a say on a matter we must first be schooled in the niceties of inquiry. The schooled don't ask uncomfortable questions, they make the leaps of faith they are asked to, they certainly don't question the need for schooling in the first place.

Pedagogy, to be liberatory, needs to involve and provoke an empowered engagement with knowledge and the structures that govern and channel that knowledge. It is not enough to merely teach down to people. Self-avowed activism often consists in large part of education; however, again, the modes of engagement with the issue of racism take on the form of the monolith. Whether in the guise of workshops, panel discussions, or group discussion, the formats that anti-racist education takes fully embrace the idea of education that entails a separation from the practical locating of education within a hermetic environment, and signifying it as an area of expertise.

By forcing a crowbar between theory and praxis, and thereby distancing education from application and experience, anti-racist education in its current manifestation is self-defeating by virtue of its sterility and complete irrelevance to the practical. By focusing on the Other as the fount of knowledge and allowing the idea of education as a bounded social sphere to infect and sanitize the methodology, content, and form of anti-racist pedagogy, it can never perform its central function: that of passionate intellectual engagement, and thus empowerment. Panels are held, committees struck, conferences convened all with the purpose of spreading the word, reproducing the standard body of knowledge. But without external engagement, any education that happens in a classroom is ultimately of use only in the classroom.

The cycle proceeds in this manner: every so often a report is released studying youth of color in the education system (it doesn't matter which color—black, Latino, indigenous, etc.—the mechanics are identical) expressing concern at their inability (it may be unwillingness, although that generally isn't taken into consideration) to learn in the racist state's indoctrination machine. All the experts are paraded out to have their say: academics point out the problem and demand that someone else do something; community mouthpieces comment on neglect and socioeconomic imbalances; bureaucrats in charge of education complain about lack of funding and lack of passion on the part of the teachers, teachers bemoan student apathy and administration indifference; business panics at the thought of a drop in the supply of state-molded exploitable labor. A proposal is then put forward, ranging anywhere from the banal and routinely bureaucratic (shrinking classroom size) to radical pedagogical leaps (separate schools for black students with "Black curricula"). A strangled path is then followed to reach a ridiculously compromised decision, maybe some money is thrown at it, and then everyone marvels at how ineffective the solution turned out to be.

The entire process is compromised by an initial misstep. At no point is the base concept of schooling questioned. Do kids learn best in large inert (non-interacting) groups? Is being inside a classroom—by design, a non-distracting and therefore sealed, controlled, passive environment—the ideal environment for learning anything, let alone self-empowerment? Thirty-five years ago Ivan Illich pointed out the education establishment's propensity to "confuse teaching with learning," and that trend has only intensified ever since. Even if the curriculum was somehow overhauled and made more even-handed and culturally neutral (yes, I speak of honesty on the part of the establishment, however unlikely that seems), there remains a substantial personal distance from the material, stemming from the didactic nature of its delivery. Being told about a historical event even from a culturally balanced perspective (admitting, however grudgingly, that Western society is not the sole propeller of history, that history is a complex negotiation and interaction between many players) still bears the scars of the Great Man School of History, as all de-localized and curriculum-proscribed (textualized) information inevitably will. Schooled history is made by mythic larger-than-life individuals, dominatingly charismatic personalities who single-handedly subvert the forces of history. On top of that, all school-taught information is still a race to a singular point, to the right answer, to that magical 4.0. What is lost is the vibrancy, immediacy, and locality of the event, and with that any hope of engagement.

Much more is at stake when education is re-immersed into prosaic existence. Students would care much more about and therefore want to learn about something that affects them. A walk through the streets of a city is a much richer educational experience than any book, lecture, or workshop could ever hope to be. Surrounded by multiple intersections of historicity, lived authenticity, and contradictions, connections are made as issues rise to the surface in close proximity and are explored. Housing struggle next door to labor organizing down the street from racist policing incident; this not only produces more interest due to sheer proximity (not only spatial, but also in terms of content and integration with the everyday lives of students), but also instigates and induces more complex linkages in thought through exploring a continuum of intellectual material as opposed to a purposefully chosen and bounded curriculum.

This kind of epistemic plurality introduces dissonance, inconsistency, and dirtiness, rupturing the seamless surface of the dictated monolog(ue)ic to invite critical inquiry into its inner workings. Communicating with and truly connecting to events involving laborers and people of color, and to mass movements, throws into stark relief the image of white teachers in a white-run school (in a white-run country and world if we wish to proceed that far), who propagate the idea that white men marshaled the forces of change and progress.

The driving passion of lived experience may not speak for itself. It is permitted to be aired only when interpreted by and mediated through the methodology of the academy. And to be academicized and fit into a framework, turned into mere "secondary evidence" or an "anecdote" or, most tellingly, adding "color" to the story, is to have your voice fossilized and nullified.

The inactivity of the tenure-bound is legendary. To pontificate at length about racism and inequalities and unlearning internalized prejudices from behind the institutional protection of a racist and domineering institution is bad enough. But to then not do anything beyond speaking—to remain within the sterilized comfortable borders confining the podium, to extract education and action from the day-to-day to the safe remove of the academic cloister, to believe that merely speaking in (or from) rarefied air makes a difference—that is so disappointing it just straight-up hurts.

Even within the ostensibly activist interdisciplines (women's studies, black studies, queer studies), those potentially rich sites for renewed engagement with the structure of knowledge and for invigorated criticism and deconstruction of social and institutional hierarchies, this is only starting to take form. In terms of textual content, while the inclusion of the subaltern voice in ethnographies and other modes of social research is a first step towards obliterating hierarchies of meaning, the method of their inclusion perpetuates their subordination. Anecdotal evidence, the verbalization of concrete cultural and historical memory, is used as, at best, secondary supporting evidence, its essential orality and subjectivity judged as being inferior to the academy's dictated and contrived objectivity. Lived experience is a local aberration on the broad strokes approach that defines academic objectivity.

By allowing individuals to speak for themselves and of their experiences, to directly express their unmediated (immediate) thoughts and wisdom, we obtain rawer and more true-to-life, and therefore more infectiously educational, textual material. Bringing the explicitly personal into the textual makes the conditions ideal for introducing epistemic pluralism. Zines are a manifestation of almost unmediated personal and experiential communication.

Primary sources rubbing up together, the voices of the traditionally unprinted and definitely unheard, allows for a variety of subaltern voices to speak for themselves and together challenge the monolith of the accepted curriculum. Not only is the end result liberatory, but also the process of creation, of concrete authorship of ideas and subjective knowledge, presents a deeper engagement with the issues.

There is something fundamentally wrong about the idea of teaching anti-racism. Can non-discrimination and respect be taught? This is the starkest example of what Illich refers to as "confusing teaching with learning." Anti-authoritarian teaching must also include learning for all involved.

References

Ernesto Aguilar, ed., *Our Culture, Our Resistance.* Volume 1: *People of Color Speak Out on Anarchism, Race, Class and Gender.* Volume 2: *Further Conversations with People of Color on Anarchism, Race, Class and Gender,* (Austin: self-published, 2004).

Ian Angus, ed. *Anarcho-Modernism: Toward a New Critical Theory,* (Vancouver: Talon, 2001).

Kristy Chan, "I'm Half Chinese," in *Anti-Racism, Feminism, and Critical*

Approaches to Education, eds., Roxana Ng, Pat Staton and Joyce Scane (Westport CT: Bergin & Garvey, 1995), 44–45.

Colours of Resistance Collective, ed., *Colours of Resistance: Multiracial, Anti-Racist Revolt Against Global Capitalism* (Toronto: self-published, 2001).

Shari Cooper-Cooper, "slant eyes" in *Race Riot 2*, 34–35.

Richard Day, "The University as Anarcho-Community" in *Anarcho-Modernism: Toward a New Critical Theory*, ed. Ian Angus (Vancouver: Talon, 2001).

Dead Prez, *Let's Get Free* (New York: Loud Records, 2000)

Taina Del Valle, "Burning the Demographic" in *Race Riot 2*, ed. Mimi Nguyen (Berkeley: self-published, n.d.), 83–84.

Lorenzo Komboa Ervin, *Anarchism and the Black Revolution*. Available at http://lemming.mahost.org/abr/

Lorenzo Komboa Ervin, "untitled," in *Colours of Resistance*, 12.

Joe R. Feagin, *Racist America: Roots, Current Realities, and Future Reparations* (New York: Routledge, 2001).

Ivan Illich (1971) in *Deschooling Society*, (Toronto: Third Force, 2005).

Helen Luu, ed., *How to Stage a Coup: An Insurrection of the Underground Liberation Army* (Toronto: self-published, 2000).

Helen Luu. "How to Stage a Coup" in *Race Riot 2*, 36–40.

Melissa. "untitled" in *evolution of a race riot* (Berkeley: self-published, 1997), 15.

Roxana Ng, Pat Staton and Joyce Scane, eds., *Anti-Racism, Feminism, and Critical Approaches to Education* (Westport, CT: Bergin & Garvey, 1995).

Mimi Nguyen, ed., *evolution of a race riot*, (Berkeley: self-published, 1997).

Mimi Nguyen, ed., *Race Riot 2*. (Berkeley: self-published, n.d.).

Robert Regnier. "Warrior as Pedagogue, Pedagogue as Warrior: Reflections on Aboriginal Anti-Racist Pedagogy" in *Anti-Racism, Feminism, and Critical Approaches to Education*, 44–45.

Assata Shakur, *Assata: an Autobiography* (Chicago: Lawrence Hill, 2001).

Ricky Walker, Jr., "untitled" in *How to Stage a Coup*, 22–25.

Howard Zinn, *A People's History of the United States, 1492–Present* (New York: Harper Collins, 1995).

No Gods, No Masters Degrees

CrimethInc Ex-Workers' Collective

Can students and white-collar workers play roles in an uncompromising revolution for total liberation? The world has changed—it seems for the worse—since the high tide of revolts by unions and student radicals. Contemporary schools and universities in the United States are not exactly hotbeds of revolution. In fact, with the exception of some union organizing among graduate students and janitors, they are barely keeping the leftovers warm, in contrast to their contemporaries in France and Chile. This is a shocking state of affairs, given the once-respected position of students as igniters of global insurrection. What has become of the student mobs throwing teachers out of classrooms and lecture halls, the general assemblies in university auditoriums, the walkouts, the communiqués sent to presidents and prime ministers advising them of their coming demise?

And where are the masses of organized workers struggling for the destruction of capitalism? We need the second coming, the Wobblies of old, or the union organizers in West Virginia who were ready to take on the army itself at the Battle of Blair Mountain. Organized labor today seems barely able to combat the decline of wages and benefits, and is more terrified of strikes than capable of calling them. With people now feeling lucky to have a job, any job, it seems radicals have the impossible task of organizing a nation of phantoms: office workers, single mothers, the depressed and uninspired, the brokenhearted and overworked, all caught up in the system and unable get anywhere no matter what they do. What about the infamous dropouts? Has the composition of classes changed so much that revolution is now impossible beyond personal rebellion and individual revolt?

Meanwhile, the United States government and its allies seem to be hellbent on bringing about worldwide apocalypse, and an explosive revolutionary situation in the belly of the beast might be our only chance of survival. While students in the US have always been tamer than their comrades worldwide—research what students did in Mexico or did in the Vietnam area and prepare to have your paisley-colored glasses blown away—things are quieter than ever on the Western Front. Worse, those closest to the source of the problem—the middle-class, the "creative class," the white-collar workers, office managers, high school teachers—are living up to their reputation as mere drones.

Rather than complain about all the sectors of society that don't live up to our revolutionary ideals, however, we have combed the files of CrimethInc agents who made the ultimate sacrifice, who went to schools and workplaces with the explicit goal of undermining capitalism. In the course of several years in and out of high schools, universities, offices, and other psychiatric wards, these agents have formulated strategies and tactics for expropriating the white-collar world for revolutionary ends. Here follows the assembled notes of one such class mutineer.

Escaping the College-Industrial Complex

Education as we know it exists primarily to indoctrinate habits. It is designed to produce obedience and nurture a willingness to complete mindless and meaningless tasks without complaint. Since humans naturally prefer to have meaningful lives and do practical, useful things, this innate tendency must be repressed at all costs by authorities at the earliest possible age. Luckily, the educational system, given a number of years, can usually stamp out all traces of creativity and critical thinking. Indeed, now that the family, in former times the oppressive institution par excellence, is breaking down, only education can fill the gap it leaves. For children in school, every moment is regimented and controlled, every moment is devoted to some task—any task except actually pursuing their own desires.

Previously, keeping most workers until the end of high school was enough to ensure their domestication, not to mention provide them with the basic reading and writing skills necessary to pay taxes. With the advent of global capitalism and the subsequent specialization of work on a global scale, new and more intensive forms of education are increasingly required. Universities, formerly havens from reality for the spawn of the ruling class to network and mate with each other, have now been opened as holding cells for the children of the serfs.

Within the modern university, the sciences serve as convenient cover for state research into control techniques and methods of mass murder and exploitation. Likewise, the empire of machines requires people with mechanical backgrounds to fix cars, program computers, and balance the books of its various corporations. Since these require technical aptitude beyond basic arithmetic, schools offer everything from business and accounting classes to engineering and computer science programs. From time to time, the system needs apologists for the terrifying destruction caused by capitalism, so people are ushered into journalism schools and departments of economics. Departments of political science and international relations prepare others to join the minor bureaucracy of the state apparatus itself, where they can participate in repression and murder by relaying commands to soldiers and police themselves. Holdouts who still believe in romantic notions of education are directed to humanities curriculums or "art schools" where they waste years of their lives myopically burying their heads in books or other self-indulgent activities until they are humiliated enough to take up service industry jobs for which their high school diplomas would have qualified them. How many dishwashing philosophers does the world need?

The truly remarkable thing is that people subject themselves to these forms of "education" willingly. In a massive scam, capitalism convinces people to pay for the privileged of being "educated," and thus to go into debt from which they can never emerge, permanently yoking them to the system!

Let's focus in on my own experience here. Many of my comrades—hell, most of them—approached school solely for the sake of a career. A nice stable family. A job, respect in the community. Despite their punk bands and their activism, their causes and their marches, they still wanted fundamentally the same thing as their parents, or at least couldn't imagine anything else. Whatever their political commitments were, they seemed to regard them essentially as a hobby that would have to be given up sooner or later for the inevitable assimilation into working life; "politics" and "work" formed a dichotomy that could never be bridged or mixed.

I found all this incredibly disturbing. After all, the jobs they sought consisted for the most part of endless processions of paperwork, number-punching, and pointless meetings—and we're not talking about working class jobs, but privileged white-collar work! What joy could there be in that drudgery? Most of our parents were so busy they didn't even have time to play games with us as children, or to read us books. Instead, they put us in front of the television with a fast-food meal before collapsing in front of the television themselves. What community respected jobs like that, especially when most of them were involved one way or another in the pillaging of the world's remaining free resources and peoples? The most my parents had for "community" was a few friends from work unlucky enough to be in the same circle of hell as them, plus the people they saw at church. Did it matter if the job was selling organic food or working in a supermarket? Being part of the Social Security bureaucracy or killing people in the army? It all seemed like one big fucking scam.

In despair, I did what most people in that situation do. I began drinking heavily. I developed a taste for malt liquor, calculating that it was the cheapest way to obliterate consciousness. I started cooking bags of instant rice in malt liquor. I figured if life was a long and drawn-out suicide I might as well end it quickly and enjoy the trip down. Then one day, in the supermarket getting ready to buy my next forty-ounce, I met two lanky individuals who were in the process of stealing no small amount of food, the smiling woman running a distraction while the other escaped out with a bag full of groceries. Impressed by how easy it was and their suave confidence, I approached them outside. It ended up they were homeless, jobless...but they were also artists, anarchists, lovers, writers, and creators. As I sat talking to them, I realized that their lives had meaning. Their eyes shone with an energy I saw lacking in my all peers who had to drink themselves to bed just to wake up the next morning and face work. Impressed, I decided that at the next opportune moment I too would drop out of school, drop out of work, and never come back.

It didn't take long for my opportunity to come. Sitting among the ruins of our house with my friends, with a degree and no cash, I decided I was going to do it. I was going to drop out, go all the way in pursuit of my dreams. I know what we'll do: We'll do a CrimethInc tour! We won't even need a band! After criss-crossing the country, running countless scams, throwing donuts at cops in the middle of street fighting, making love underneath the canopies of ancient forests, and composing and performing a full-scale musical about anarchism, I felt something I hadn't felt in years, despite the fact there wasn't a cent in my pocket and my prospects for survival looked grim at best. I realized I was alive.

Reconsidering Dropping Out

Let's not lose sight of the obvious—no one is an island, including those who have dropped out. Like everyone else, dropouts depend on a whole network of people to keep them alive. Dropouts must learn survival skills such as dumpster diving and scamming, but it is the sympathetic cafeteria worker who turns a blind eye to the anarchists sneaking into the school cafeteria, the social worker who gives them food-stamps, the employee who knows that there is no way these people bought this multi-hundred dollar electrical tool but will let them return it for full cash—it is these people who create the holes in the system that dropouts need, in which an existence can be eked out with minimal work. These workers are crucial to the survival of the unemployed, even if some of them do their anticapitalist work almost unconsciously.

But how long can the unemployed anarchist, the prototypical dropout, survive off the kindness of strangers? When the last scam is shut down, when even the school cafeterias require retinal scans, when every store is crawling with armed security thugs and scrutinized from closed-circuit cameras, what then? Is our dropout doomed? And if capitalism ever undergoes a major economic collapse, when the oil is gone and the food has stopped coming to the shelves of the local supermarkets, what then? Is our dropout just on a more enjoyable trip to hell with the rest of us?

Let us return to the idea of the network of sympathizers and transform that into the network of revolutionaries. There is sometimes an unequal power distribution between dropouts and their sympathizers, with the former having no material ways forward and the sympathizers being stuck in some hellish corner of capitalism. In order to overcome this, we must go beyond this dichotomy of "dropouts" and "workers." Let us inspect the more interesting roles of "sympathizer" and "revolutionary." The difference between a sympathizer and a revolutionary is mainly a matter of commitment. In this regard, many dropouts are themselves just sympathizers. Sure, they may be contributing to revolution by not working, but the entirety of their activity is made up of just trying to survive. The main risk for revolutionary dropouts is that they become mere dropouts without adjectives, yet more homeless and jobless people secretly wanting cars, jobs, careers, heating, and a regular source of food instead of enjoying their opportunities and taking advantage of every moment to push for liberation. But if a dropout can indeed be a revolutionary, then an employed person can be more than a sympathizer too.

What would it entail to be a working revolutionary in this day and age? Would it involve organizing a union? Perhaps. Would it involve selling Marxist-Leninist papers to fellow workers who have not yet "Got Revolution?" Hopefully not. One of the most obvious tasks of the working revolutionary is simple: seize resources. Instead of feeling guilt about privileges, the working revolutionary does anything and everything to abuse those privileges, to cash them in for material resources needed by revolutionaries who lack access to them. This could mean anything from sneaking out photocopies to smuggling guns. Imagine the countless resources that are at the disposal of clever employees if they view work as one giant fucking scam that they milk as thoroughly as possible without getting caught. Revolutionaries need resources, need to eat, sleep, and have clothing. For people of color, unemployed people, people with families they can barely support, people brought up in generations of poverty, to be a full-time revolutionary without income is impossible. Yet if some of their friends and allies can work, can find jobs, they can make this easier. If the employed revolutionary is willing to live frugally, she can provide for dozens of her comrades—especially if she is absolutely merciless towards her superiors, always looking for a way to steal something, anything, from work to be put towards the revolution. No job but the inside job!

Even for the staunchest of politicized dropouts, the goal is not unemployment, but revolution. Both the unemployed and employed revolutionary—and all those in between, who take jobs when necessary and refuse to work when they can—face occupational hazards. The occupational hazard of the unemployed revolutionary is simply to become merely unemployed, indistinguishable from their grizzled peers who are just spanging for the next drink. The occupational hazard of employed revolutionaries is probably more dangerous—to begin to believe in their jobs and the system in which they play a part, or at least accept these as unchangeable elements of reality. To accept their positions in the economy and actually start following the rules, slowly adjusting to the idea that they are somehow different from, perhaps even superior to, all those unemployed people out there. To betray their dreams and begin living their death in life. It's a slippery road, and every employed anarchist should watch out.

Let us here resume the story begun above, taking up the thread some time after we left off. It was September 11, 2001, and we conceded that our careful preparations for the upcoming IMF/World Bank protests had been rendered moot by the terrorist attacks of the day. Two of us from various suburbs in the United States had converged in a sushi joint outside of Georgetown to reflect on our experiences as dropouts and plan for the years ahead. Our conversation was a heady mix of despair and tactics.

Both of us had similar "resumés"—we were hopelessly white anarchists from resolutely middle-class or upwardly mobile working class families. Both of us had been primarily concerned with destroying capitalism for several years, and had college degrees but no plans for utilizing them. In the course of our adventures, we had become so crusty as to be almost indistinguishable from many of the more well-to-do people in homeless shelters. We had hopped trains across the country, fed our friends and whoever else showed up at Food Not Bombs, and donned black masks to take to the streets. Yet after organizing protests, skill-shares, conferences and feeling closer and closer to revolution only to watch it all go up literally in flames, we felt strangely empty. Where to go next? Somewhere else, somewhere unimaginable...

What would we do? We both had families at this point—families not of blood, but of something stronger—families of life. People beside whom we had fought tooth and nail, with whom we had experienced the greatest joys and the bleakest hells. People we would take bullets for. It happened that by chance—or perhaps not—our comrades weren't from white, middle-class, college-educated families. Instead, they were high school dropouts, folks who had wised up before us or grown up in poor families. Our friends—and more recently, we as well—had been sent to jail. Been raped. Been hurt. Starved. Lived in tents in the cold, beneath concrete pillars underneath bridges. It seemed so unfair that the most noble and creative of our generation, people who either by force or by choice had forsaken the normal career path, were pushed to near death. We were always struggling for the next dollar, having to hustle just to get by. How the hell were we going to take down the entire fucking government, the global capitalist system, if we were always worried about our next meal and couldn't find a place to lay our heads? While this state of affairs kept us sharp, it was slowly having an effect on the less hardy of our comrades; one by one, those who could started settling down, getting jobs, having children, and becoming normal again. And why did having children force people to get jobs? If we were truly serious about a revolutionary future, we would have to find the resources to take care of children and the elderly in our communities.

Over sushi of all things, we cooked up a plan. It seemed crazy and morally wrong, but in our experience such plans were exactly the ones that worked. What did we have going for us at this point except our privilege? We had degrees. We could read and write. We could do the impossible. We could get jobs.

How I Became the Man and Lived to Tell the Tale

When one is shoplifting, a bizarre inverse logic operates; the inverse of the logic applied by the usual shopper. Since the punishment is always more or less the same, one steals the most expensive items as opposed to the cheapest ones. This inverse logic operates in a similar fashion in workplace scamming. Conventionally, people are accorded social status according to their rank in the workplace, but many revolutionaries get credit for their job in proportion to how low-paying their job is—for example, working at a organic health food store for slave wages—or how obviously their job relates to social justice—such as going door to door with petitions. Revolutionary union organizing is as laudable as ever, but the revolutionary who works for the primary purpose of seizing resources should aim for the job with the most resources that requires the least amount of commitment.

In this regard, the educational-industrial complex is especially ripe for looting. With the exception of recent events in the Sorbonne, most teachers and professors today seem to be in full support of the system, whether this manifests itself in papers about global macro-economics or in postmodern literary analysis. Even professors who oppose systems of oppression rarely make their voices heard beyond the world of papers and journals, let alone take action beyond it. If you look at the modern educational system not as a site for resistance but as a supply depot for looting, things brighten up quickly. While it is slowly being destroyed by neoliberal "reforms," the domain of the ivory tower is still notoriously slack and easy to take advantage of!

As a student, one qualifies for all sorts of loans and money. If one wants to, one can default on them and just keep the cash, as long as one is willing to commit oneself to a future free of state-sanctioned employment. After all, are banks even going to be here in twenty years? Also, one generally has little work to do as a student—if you can manage to read books outside of class, or impress the professor with your intelligence, you don't even have to attend classes regularly to get good grades. One can show up to a class, travel to another state to fight the minions of capital for a few weeks, come back, and often nobody even notices. Few jobs offer such flexibility.

Additionally, schools are known to give money to students for the flimsiest of reasons. If the locals of a heavily repressed country are calling for international assistance in the preparations for their next protest, say in Russia, what better time to go abroad for an immersion course in Russian? Or if you want to support revolutionary efforts to help people become self-sufficient in the wake of a disaster such as the one in New Orleans, why not just make it a school project? You can band together with like-minded students and form an organization to seize control of even more funding, with which to set up conferences for local anticapitalists and invite revolutionaries to speak at your school—in return for a fair bit of cash, which goes right back into the struggle.

There are all sorts of other resources in schools that are as good as gold to the revolutionary. Schools offer access to computers—and the free printing they sometimes include—which are hard to come by for most people. You could steal copies from the school to stock local infoshops or to make anarchist propaganda. Schools also have cafeterias, which are often unguarded. One could steal food from the cafeteria and bring it to deserving fellow revolutionaries, and if one has some sort of "meal card," one could always bring local homeless people and other hungry folks into the cafeteria for a meal at your—or preferably the school's—expense. Schools also feature strange locked closets, small rooms, and even entire abandoned buildings. There's no reason to pay for rent, even if you're working—that rent money can be spent on more exciting projects when squatting is an alternative! CrimethInc agents have inhabited broom closets in libraries, set up shop in empty rooms in philosophy departments, and even lived in tree-sits while being "in school." And for the clever revolutionary, not only is there a limitless supply of pencils and paper, there are countless other opportunities. One can walk in and steal just about everything from chalkboards to trashcans, and furnish a whole collective house!

If one is privileged enough, it is also possible to become a schoolteacher, or even a professor. Becoming a professor gives you a few more years of graduate school to live off of and continue the lackadaisical student life. Once one is a teacher of some type, one can also, as all great teachers since Socrates have done, corrupt the minds of the young. For example, one could focus on books like *1984* that have snuck into the curriculum of many schools when picking readings. You could have your students make zines as an assignment or more ambitiously, take on projects like building community gardens. If you are a professor and have enough leeway, you could teach classes on revolutionary theory or subjects like "Social Movements." A truly great teacher should be able to make even geometry a revolutionary discipline! Teachers can encourage students to organize everything from radical student unions to street demonstrations.

And so, once more, we'll return to my own experience, at another point in my life. The university where I had spent the last three years had become a hotbed of revolution. As a giant anti-globalization protest came to town, we few local hosting anarchists were overwhelmed. As former out-of-town shock troops against capital ourselves, we understood how important it was for the out-of-town black bloc to be able to meet safely and get a good night's sleep to be ready to riot in the morning. After the G8 protests in Genoa in 2001, we had the unhappy suspicion that the police would raid any private landowner that rented space to us. Indeed, the local police had already done their rounds, warning everyone to avoid suspicious characters that asked to rent large amounts of camping space.

It happened that a friend of a friend in our local Indymedia collective had attended high school with a left-leaning member of the local government. After nearly endless meetings ("But you realize we can't have peaceful protesters sleeping next to the black bloc!" Ah, if only he had known to whom he was speaking), the town government decided it was better to get all the anarchists in one place, instead of having to deal with them squatting all over town. They hadn't suspected that we'd prefer to have somewhere legal and safe to sleep rather than getting ourselves trapped by the police in a squat defense the day before the big action. Yet there was still no place for anarchists to meet and plan! I was morose, until one day a thought struck me. The police would never raid the Student Union at the oldest, most privileged university in town. It was a virtual historical monument!

With a little convincing, the head of the Democratic Student Union handed over the keys to the building, ostensibly to be used for a conference that happened to run the duration of the protest. As the big event approached, anarchists from all over the country showed up, and they all needed Internet access and photocopying machines. Almost overnight, my previously quiet little Department of Political and Social Studies metamorphosed into a full-scale office of revolutionary activity, and one anarchist even snuck in and got his own desk as a "Visiting Professor." I had managed to procure the keys from the night-guard, so when night came, we simply took out our sleeping bags and crashed in the office.

As the protest neared, it became clear this was no ordinary conference. There were direct action trainings, medical trainings, and videos shown of previous summits. A horde of black-clad miscreants occupied the Student Union. Shortly before the day of action, a huge anarchist assembly took place upstairs in the Union, where the forces of global insurrection decided to blockade by whatever means necessary the President and his cronies.

At this meeting, we had the horrible realization that no one knew the layout of the city. So under the cover of night, we snuck even more comrades into the Department of Political and Social Studies to mass-produce maps of the locations to be blockaded and research details of important centers of global capital. We turned on the departmental photocopier, and with a stolen password proceeded to make thousands of copies of blockade maps, while burning CDs with photos of important locations on the secretary's computer. We rushed the mysterious box of maps, ones that would surely doom us if we were caught with them, right out the department front door and to the cars waiting for us at the Indymedia Center. As I was leaving, I noticed that it was nearly nine in the morning, and to my horror I saw the head of the department, an ancient and respected professor, climbing up the stairs to the front door. He looked at me and smiled, "Up all night, eh? You won't believe it—those unwashed protesters just spray-painted an anarchy symbol on our building!" I just smiled and walked out with the secret plans.

Turning the White Collar Black

Let's take this story to its logical conclusion. After all, being a parasite and scamming money from a job is not the be-all end-all of revolutionary activity. If anything, anarchists invading the university is uncreative. It would be more creative for anarchists to invade everyday jobs at all walks of life, for the express purpose of causing trouble. As the surveillance state shuts down possible avenues of escape, strategically placed anarchists in the DMV and security agencies would be worth their weight in gold. If the state and corporations send infiltrators to our meetings, we should return the favor and place anarchist infiltrators in their offices! Anarchists often talk about getting our comrades out of jail. Why not get jobs as prison guards? Qualifying should be easy enough for those of us without arrest records. One could learn the ins and outs of a prison and plan the perfect escape route for prisoners. Anarchist librarians, anarchist carpenters, anarchist chefs, and anarchist bankers—there should be no job that we cannot subvert. If there is a job we cannot turn to the ends of anarchy, that attests to our lack of ingenuity, not to the strength of capital.

We anarchists need both material and human resources to fight the system successfully. Let us make no mistake about this: we're fighting a war, and in war, you have to make use of everything you can get.

The capitalist system seems to be doomed to collapse. Revolutionaries need urban social centers, both legally paid for and—if possible—squatted. Revolutionaries sometimes need jobs, so we may as well start up cooperative vegan cafés and similar ventures, so long as we channel all the resources we can into the struggle. To buy land and to buy buildings requires cash some anarchists can earn, while others with time instead of money can learn to farm and cook, and so on. These roles should never remain solid, though certain roles will be easier for some than others. If we take the idea of dual power seriously, we will develop counter-institutions that people can fall back on as the scanty remains of old social safety nets are destroyed by looting capitalists. If all anarchists do is travel from protest to protest, we'll never build the local strength, momentum, and roots we need for others to trust us and—more importantly—themselves when the system enters total collapse. A total collapse hopefully caused by us.

Yet the true test of anarchy is not whether we can push the system into collapse, but what we can do in the here and now, how we take advantage of any opportunity, including collapse, to spread anarchy. Let it never be misunderstood that the only path to revolution is for all anarchists to drop out. No, the important question is how we link the efforts and desires of those within the system to those without its assurances and controls. To this end, we need more analysis of how cross-class alliances have helped push forward the revolutionary struggle throughout history. Such a study could begin with the impoverished masses who let Russian princes such as Kropotkin and Bakunin throw their lot in with them, and extend up to the mixed-class groups cooking and serving Food Not Bombs today.

Revolution

Ultimately, we must not only use whatever resources we have to further revolution, we must also turn any and every situation to the ends of revolution, including white-collar jobs and university lecture halls. In this sense every revolutionary must be a situationist, an artist of situations.

If we are unyielding in our demand for world revolution not tomorrow, not after exams, not after the next book is written or after hours, but now, then we put you—dear reader—in a precarious position. We admit, we barely know you. You could be an embittered revolutionary, who has already spent all your money on countless hours of organizing, and is considering getting a job at the postal service. Perhaps, reading about academics attempting to walk their talk, you feel jealous of their privilege at not having to deal with the monotonous and endless nine-to-five grind. Where is the book composed by a collective of revolutionary postal workers, the book speaking of the lives and dreams of clerks and janitors? You swear to write that book.

Or maybe you are a student who recently stayed up all night reading the *Communist Manifesto* and, after a binge of underage drinking, proceeded to declare your dormitory a People's Republic. Confronted with the choice of endless classes ranging from Linear Algebra to Biological Anthropology, it all seems so meaningless, and the university no better than a vast factory of obfuscation and bureaucracy. Instead of deciding what you want to do with your life, which seems paramount to putting an end to your life then and there, you want life itself! Reading about academics trying to create that life in actuality, perhaps you may find it easier to feel that—even within the ivory tower—action can be taken, and you can take that action.

Or perhaps you are a professor, who has spent countless hours lecturing students on obscure postmodern philosophy. You dreamed as a young graduate student of changing the world, lighting it on fire with your ideas, writing famous books that would inspire the following generations to rise up and create a new one. Perhaps somewhere in the endless publish-or-perish cycle you lost that dream, and now you write endless articles for journals no one will ever read, much less find inspiring. Now, reading this book, you wonder if you could change things, if instead of just talking about revolution you could create it yourself. A dream has been rekindled. Who knows? These are just phantasms. We don't know anything about you!

Yet this we do know: everything depends on you. Your actions, over the next day, month, year, decade, lifetime, will determine whether or not you and the world itself survives. If you surrender to a life-in-death of obedience to the system, you will be fully complicit in its bloody end. However, within the deepest recesses of your being, you have the resources to do something beautiful, something that can change the world. You might think it is unfair for us to put all this weight on the shoulders of a stranger. After all, you're clearly not a revolutionary. Maybe you have a job that is counterrevolutionary to the core, and what type of revolution can be incited by someone with that type of job?

This is the crux of the argument: any job, anywhere, can be approached in a revolutionary manner. The less revolutionary potential you think a job has, the more likely that it will actually be radical to subvert it, if only you can find the courage!

On the other hand, perhaps your background's not right, you don't feel like a capable and sexy young revolutionary. You're too old, or too tired, or not confident, or deaf, or so on. Consider that this might be a hidden strength, that the very diversity of our lives is and must be the basis for a true revolution. A revolution brought about by only student revolutionaries, or for that matter any other demographic alone, would lead to disaster. Yet a revolution brought about by cunning alliances between the least likely of us will create exactly the type of situations we need, situations that can break us free from the chains of habit and separation.

What's stopping you? Here we find ourselves in an ironic situation, preaching revolutionary action from a book of words. No matter how they are arranged, words alone cannot create revolution. Likewise, despite our constant calls for action, neither can action without thought. Revolutionary situations arise when people bring their words and dreams into alignment with their actions on an everyday basis. No book, no matter how well written or insightful, can provide that last crucial step. That step involves closing the book, stepping back from it, and stepping forward into your own life.

So—go on—close this book. Confess your love, grab that gun, plant that seed, lay your body in front of that bulldozer. Seize your life by any and all means necessary.

Put down the book and take action. At that very moment, which we hope is just a few infinitesimal seconds away, the giant lie that has cast its shadow across human history will begin at long last to dissolve. What lies on the other side of history, no one knows. Yet we can promise you this—we'll see you on that other side.

Glossary

Artificial intelligence: A research program committed to making machines (in particular computers) more "intelligent," or as intelligent as human beings. However, there is not a solid working definition of intelligence.

Auto-valorization: See *self-valorization.*

Class composition analysis: Class composition analysis is a mode of intellectual practice that aims to both understand and intervene politically in the composition of the working class. There are two elements that make up the composition of the working class: the technical composition and the political composition, which roughly correspond to the distinctions of class-in-itself and class for-itself elsewhere in the Marxist tradition. The technical composition of the working class refers primarily to the organization of the labor process when it functions relatively normally in the production of surplus value. In this sense, technical composition includes machinery, the skills of workers, disciplinary practices in the workplace, everything that enters into how the spaces and times of work are distributed. The political composition of the working class refers to the organizations of workers, formal or informal, by which workers act in and against the labor process: the union, the party, the affinity group, the informal work group, etc. Political composition also includes the tactics or practices that workers make use of in conflicts in and against work: absenteeism, strikes of various types, mutual aid, marches, demonstrations, etc. Class composition analysis makes use of a range of types of inquiry that resemble social and oral history, ethnography, journalism, and others. See *Co-research, Militant research.*

Co-research: Co-research is a practice of intellectual production that does not accept a distinction between active researcher and passive research subjects. At its best, co-research aims for a productive cooperation that transforms both into active participants in producing knowledge and in transforming themselves. There is a long history of co-research in Italy and elsewhere, but not always under the name co-research. See *Militant research.*

Craftivism: Like radical knitting, craftivism combines crafting with radical purposes of withdrawing from capitalism, building communities, and often engaging in protest actions.

Eco-village: Eco-villages are urban or rural communities of people, who strive to integrate a supportive social environment with a low-impact way of life. One was set up in Stirling by the anticapitalist Dissent! network, during the mobilization against the G8, to serve as a base for activists.

Free software: Free software is a matter of the user's freedom to run, copy, distribute, study, change, and improve the software. This is further clarified by the Four Freedoms as defined by Richard Stallman and the Free Software Foundation: the freedom to run the program for any purpose; the freedom to study how the program works and adapt it to your needs (access to the source code is a precondition for this); the freedom to redistribute copies so you can help your neighbor; and the freedom to improve the program, and release your improvements to the public, so that the whole community benefits. This usually goes hand-in-hand with the GNU Project's GNU Public License. See the full definition at www.gnu.org.

General Intellect: General intellect is a term used by Marx in the *Grundrisse* in a section referred to as "The Fragment On Machines." In this section, Marx speculates on the role of intellect, specifically scientific knowledge and technical expertise, in present and possible future versions of capitalist production. For Marx, general intellect essentially resides in fixed capital, in machines and objective factors of production. Thinkers since the late 20th century have expanded the concept to refer to the role of intellect within variable capital, that is, skills and knowledges within the bodies and brains of workers, and how these capacities relate to capitalist production and radical possibilities. In some accounts, general intellect effectively means that the old Marxist project of seizing the means of production has already partially occurred: for workers such as graphic designers, translators, teachers, etc., important aspects of the material required for the performance of labor are owned by the worker in their own person.

Immaterial labor: Immaterial labor refers to the production of the immaterial content of commodities such as media and art, as well as the role of information and communication in sectors of material production and the production of affect in service work and elsewhere. Immaterial labor produces and/or manipulates signs and symbols, data, information, knowledges, affects, and biological life. Teachers, graphic designers, computer programmers, translators, retail clerks, prostitutes, nurses, nannies, and housewives are all examples of immaterial laborers. This labor occurs in and out of recognized workplaces in remunerated and unremunerated modes. Often, immaterial labor, particularly its more traditionally feminine forms, occurs in conditions of precarity. See *Precarity*.

Indymedia: The name of a loose network of individuals, independent and alternative media activists and organizations, offering grassroots, non-corporate, non-commercial coverage of current events. Founded during the 1999 protests against the WTO in Seattle. See www.indymedia.org for their global website.

Linux: The kernel, or master operator, of the open source computer operation system GNU/Linux, which incorporates many of the free software programs developed by the GNU Project in order to provide a free alternative to proprietary operating systems.

Militant research: Militant research has many meanings. It can be research carried out with the aim of producing knowledge useful for militant or activist ends. Militant research can also be research that is carried in a fashion in keeping with the aims and values of radical militants. In some parts of the Marxist tradition militant research is a moment of class composition analysis, and is sometimes referred to as workers' inquiry, after a document written by Marx in 1880. See *Co-research, Class composition analysis.*

Open source: A weaker version of free software that is more acceptable to some businesses as it allows them to copyright the results of an open source project, something that would be impossible using Free Software. See "Free Software" and the open source definition at www.opensource.org.

Precarity: Precarity is the subject of growing debate and political mobilization in Europe at the time of this writing, partly in response to changes in the regimes of labor and welfare policy as well as labor practices. Precarity has several related meanings. With regard to work, precarity refers to a variety of so-called "nonstandard" work arrangements: times of work (night and weekend work), quantities of work time (flexible or variable hours, part-time work, demands for overtime), and durations of work assignments (temporary work, non-contract work, freelance work). Precarity also refers to the legal status of work: whether work is legal or illegal, and which customary labor rights do and do not apply to which workers. Precarity also refers to instability of income, linked to precarious work arrangements, and to access to needed services such as healthcare and housing. All of these meanings of precarity indicate a general unpredictability of access to needed goods and services, whether via a welfare state or private sector, and a lack of control over work which in turn imposes less control over the rest of one's life. In this sense, precarity has historically been the general condition of the proletariat globally with moments of relatively less precarity being exceptions resulting from a number of political factors.

Primitivism: A radical current that poses an opposition to the totality of civilization. It rejects any ideology of progress and affirms the original primitive gatherer-hunter condition of humanity as one consummate to anarchy. In practice, it advances critiques of development, technology, and mass society as well as advocating an opposition to the Left as much as the Right. Influences are broad and include the French ultra-left (specifically Camatte and the Situationists), the Frankfurt School, iconoclasts such as Mumford, and radical elements of ecological and indigenous struggles. Prominent thinkers include Fredy Perlman, John Zerzan, and David Watson and publications associated with this perspective include *Green Anarchist, Green Anarchy,* and *Fifth Estate.* Watson and *Fifth Estate* have distanced themselves, in part, from some elements of this current.

Radical knitting: The name given to knitting with activist goals, which can include knitting at protests, knitting to withdraw from the system of capitalist production and distribution, and knitting to build communities across age, gender, ethnicity, and even political lines.

Real subsumption: Marx defined real subsumption of labor in "Results of the Immediate Process of Production," the so-called unpublished sixth chapter of *Capital: Vol. 1.* Real subsumption is defined in contrast to formal subsumption of labor. Formal subsumption occurs when capitalists take command of labor processes that originate outside of, or prior to, the capital relation via the imposition of the wage. In real subsumption, the labor process is internally reorganized to meet the dictates of capital. An example of these processes would be weaving by hand, which comes to be labor performed for a wage (formal subsumption) and which then comes to be performed via machine (real subsumption). Real subsumption in this sense is a process or technique that occurs at different points throughout the history of capitalism. For some thinkers, such as Antonio Negri, real subsumption of labor is transfigured into real subsumption of society, such that all of society becomes a moment of capitalist production. In this version, real subsumption is an epoch, a stage of capitalism within a historical periodization, analogous to postmodernity. This sense of real subsumption is very similar to the social factory when read as a historical periodization. See *Social factory.*

Reification: Marx's term, in *Capital,* for the alienation produced by capitalist commodity relations, where "social action takes the form of the action of objects, which rule the producers instead of being ruled by them."

Its application was later expanded by György Lukács in *History and Class Consciousness*, and by Guy Debord. See *Spectacle*.

Rhizome/rhizomatic: The stemless, bulbous root-mass of plants like potato or bamboo. Used by some writers as a metaphor for networks of power and knowledge based on connection, heterogeneity, multiplicity, and nonlinearity. See in particular Chapter 1 of Deleuze and Guttari's *A Thousand Plateaus: Capitalism and Schizophrenia*.

Self-valorization: Self-valorization, also translatable as auto-valorization, refers to the capacity of individuals and groups to autonomously produce different values other than that of capitalist value production and to produce social relationships and organizational forms in keeping with these values. Both self-valorization and auto-valorization are imperfect translations: the former connotes a type of individualism, and the latter connotes a mechanical, automatic, or predetermined process. In Italian and Spanish the phrase has neither of those connotations. For more on this concept, readers can consult the works of Antonio Negri and Harry Cleaver.

Social factory: The social factory is a term developed within the *operaismo* tradition of Marxism in Italy. There is an ambivalence in the term, between a conceptual optic and a narrative of historical periodization. The social factory as a conceptual optic argues that the techniques and practices of power deployed within the factory also impact life outside the factory, and vice versa. In other words, the walls of the factory are a semi-permeable membrane across which passages take place and across which lines of force operate. The basic point of the concept is that value production and resistance to value production do not occur only in determinate and recognized workplaces and in activity by waged workers. This concept of the social factory has a polemical force against the factory-ist political and organizational model that centers on workplaces and waged work. As a type of historical periodization, the social factory is a narrative in which the inside and the outside of the factory become contiguous over a period of time, such that capitalist command now comes to reach across the inside and outside of the factory. See *Real subsumption*.

Socialized worker: The socialized worker, also translated as social worker, appears in the work of Antonio Negri, among others. Negri has most recently begun to refer to the socialized worker using the term "multitude." The socialized worker is a figure in a history of changing class compositions that runs from the "professional worker" to the "mass worker" to the socialized worker. The socialized worker has the following general characteristics: work may occur at a number of different and sometimes varying sites within society rather than in one designated workplace; work may occur at different and sometimes varying times, and the work involves social capacities such as speaking, caring, writing, and so forth. The labor of the socialized worker is the set of activities that Negri and others refer to by the term "immaterial labor." See *Class composition, Immaterial labor.*

Spectacle: The Situationist International's term for the totality of capitalist social relations. It was most comprehensively explored in Guy Debord's 1967 text, *The Society of the Spectacle*, which developed from Marx's and Lukács' accounts of reification: "The first phase of the domination of the economy over social life brought into the definition of all human realisation the obvious degradation of being into having. The present phase of total occupation of social life by the accumulated results of the economy leads to a generalised sliding of having into appearing."

Tree-sit: The setting up of occupations in trees to prevent their destruction. This often involves platforms, walkways, and people physically living in the trees for a period of time. Often associated with the radical environmental group, Earth First!

Author Bios

Erika Biddle lives in NYC, is an active member of the Autonomedia editorial collective, a board member of the Institute for Anarchist Studies, and is trying to resuscitate the Artists in Dialogue (A.I.D.) collective. She writes, and makes videos and installations that address the concept of *zufall*.

Jack Z. Bratich is assistant professor of Journalism and Media Studies at Rutgers University. He has written articles that apply autonomist thought to such topics as audience studies, reality TV, secession, and popular secrecy. In Fall 2005, he co-taught (with Stevphen Shukaitis) "Strategies of Refusal: Explorations in Autonomist Marxism," the inaugural course in the Bluestockings Popular Education program. He is currently finishing his book on conspiracy panics and political rationality.

BRE is a Toronto-based organizer who has spent time on the streets and in school and is currently involved in the Toronto Anarchist Free Space and the Free Skool.

Maribel Casas-Cortés and Sebastián Cobarrubias (Producciones Translocales) are from Castilla and NYC respectively with rhizomatic roots. They are currently working and studying in the PhD programs of Anthropology and Geography at the University of North Carolina-Chapel Hill. They have been involved with different networks and organizations, engaging in direct action, popular education, and agit/prop production, including Chicago Direct Action Network, Mexico Solidarity Network, Intergalaktica Buenos Aires, the Coalition of Immokalee Workers, Universidad Rural–Paulo Freire, and People's Global Action. They are currently working on several projects translating the experiences of activist research to the current context of the US, including the "mapping the university" project with the 3Cs Counter-Cartographies Collective.

Gaye Chan is a visual artist and a professor of photography at the University of Hawai'i. Her work is primarily inspired by, and made from, found images and objects—mining their potential in making visible the invisible forces at work all around us. Chan is an exhibiting artist and a part of Nomoola and DownWind Productions.

Graeme Chesters is a writer and educator based in the Department of Peace Studies at the University of Bradford. His work focuses on complexity, participation, and social change.

Colectivo Situaciones is a collective of militant researchers based in Buenos Aires. They have participated in numerous grassroots co-research activities with unemployed workers, peasant movements, human rights groups, neighborhood assemblies, and alternative education experiments. The elaboration of their experience has resulted in many articles, a series of notebooks published under the title *Cuadernos de Situación*, and five books: *Genocida en el barrio: Mesa de Escrache Popular*; *La hipótesis 891: más allá de los piquetes* (with MTD of Solano); *Contrapoder: una introducción*; *19 y 20: apuntes para un nuevo protagonismo social*; and *Universidad Trashumante: Territorios, Redes, Lenguajes* (with Universidad Trashumante).

CrimethInc, sometimes known as the CrimethInc Workers' Collective or the CrimethInc Ex-Workers' Collective, is a non-hierarchical anarchist organization that publishes anti-authoritarian writings and videos, and leaves vague hints that it is committing non-violent crimes, most of which seem to involve leafleting. CrimethInc authors rarely sign their documents, but you can check out their webpage at CrimethInc.com.

Dave Eden is currently working on his PhD thesis, entitled *Insurrection & Exodus: a Contribution to Contemporary Anarchist Theory* at the Australian National University. His work generally involves an eclectic reading of divergent threads of anticapitalist praxis. He also writes under the pseudonym Dave Antagonism for multiple radical publications. He has been involved in anticapitalist struggle long enough to know better, most notably the collectives Revolutionary Action in Wollongong and Treason in Canberra.

Uri Gordon has spent the last five years as an activist and doctoral student in Oxford, UK. He now lives in his native Israel where he continues to be involved in radical initiatives for social justice and peace. His first book *Anarchist Anxieties: Contemporary Debates in Anti-Authoritarian Politics* is in preparation.

David Graeber is an Associate Professor of Anthropology recently fired from Yale University. He is the author of *Towards an Anthropological Theory of Value* and *Fragments of an Anarchist Anthropology*. For the last five years, he has worked within the anticapitalist and anarchist sections of the globalization movement including People's Global Action, the Direct Action Network, and the Planetary Alternatives Network.

Gavin Grindon is a PhD student at the University of Manchester, England, where he is studying the theoretical development of the concept of carnival as a form of radical activism. His publications include "Carnival Against Capital: A Comparison of Bakhtin, Vaneigem and Bey" in *Anarchist Studies*.

Harry Halpin is a post-graduate student at the University of Edinburgh, studying Informatics and the intersection between the Web, philosophy, and linguistics. He is also the co-founder of Scotland Indymedia and erstwhile resident of the Bilston Glen Anti-Road Bypass site. In former lives he has organized summits and protests around globalization, driven computers from Maine to Chiapas, and maintained various free software packages.

Nate Holdren is a teaching assistant and PhD candidate in Comparative Literature at the University of Minnesota. Nate has contributed numerous translations and other material to various electronic projects.

Brian Holmes is a cultural theorist, art critic, and a founder of Université Tangente. His publications include *Hieroglyphs of the Future: Art and Politics in a Networked Era* (Arkzin Communications, 2004) and *Unleashing the Collective Phantom* (forthcoming 2007, Autonomedia).

Ben Holtzman is an independent researcher and activist. He works as an editor in New York.

Craig Hughes is an activist and researcher who lives in Washington, DC. He holds a Masters degree in History and is a member of the Team Colors collective.

Sandra Jeppesen has a PhD in English from York University, Toronto. Her dissertation focused on Guerrilla Texts and anarchist cultural production. Her first published novel, *Kiss Painting* (Gutter Press, 2003), explores social relationships within the anarchist milieu. She has been a member of several anarchist collectives, including Who's Emma Records and Books, Uprising bookstore and infoshop, Resist (Toronto), the random anarchist group, the Toronto Anarchist Bookfair collective, and the Anarchist Free University.

Jeffrey S. Juris is an Assistant Professor of Anthropology in the Department of Social & Behavioral Sciences at Arizona State University. His research and teaching interests include globalization, social movements, transnational activism, new digital technologies, Spain, and Catalonia. Juris is dedicated to integrating research and practice by engaging in militant ethnography. He has also participated in several activist research networks, including the Open Space Collective, which emerged from the World Social Forum process. He is also developing a comparative ethnographic project exploring the use of new digital technologies and emerging forms of collaborative practice among media activists in the United States, Europe, and Latin America.

Anita Lacey is an activist and researcher living and working in Windsor, Canada. Her research fields and interests include global anticapitalist and justice movements, the idea and ideal of community and community spaces, particularly in regards to protest, and gendered development practices. She is passionate about activisms for social justice, and connections between people locally and globally who are in or seek communities that recognize and celebrate diversity and struggle to attain social justice in the current manifestation of globalization. This passion drives her research, writing, and teaching.

Ashar Latif was primarily molded by his childhood spent in Saudi Arabia, Pakistan, and the raging wilds of New Jersey. Currently residing in the frozen north, he still dreams of warmer climes.

Angela Mitropoulos lives in Melbourne, Australia. She has been involved in noborder campaigns and xborder. She has also written a number of essays on migration, labor, and the state for *Mute*, *Culture Machine*, and other publications.

Antonio Negri is an independent researcher, communist militant, and former professor at the University of Padua. Emerging from the heretical Marxist tendencies of the autonomous worker's movements of the 1960s, his work has been important in understanding the changing dynamics of capitalism and the possibilities of social resistance. He has written many books, including: *Marx Beyond Marx* (1979), *The Savage Anomaly* (1981), *Communists Like Us* (with Felix Guattari, 1985), and *Empire* and *Multitude* (with Michael Hardt, 2000/2004).

Michal Osterweil is a PhD student in Anthropology at the University of North Carolina-Chapel Hill. She has been involved in various activist research networks and projects, including Global Uprisings and Explorations in Open Space (a research project on Social Forums).

Kirsty Robertson recently finished her PhD, *Tear-Gas Epiphanies: New Economies of Protest, Vision, and Culture*, at Queen's University in Canada.

In Fall 2006, she will begin a postdoctoral fellowship at Goldsmiths College, University of London, on wearable technologies, textiles, and activism.

Nandita Sharma is an activist in transnational No Borders networks and an assistant professor in the School of Social Sciences at York University in Toronto, Canada. She is a part of Nomoola and DownWind Productions.

Benjamin Shepard is the author/editor of two books: *White Nights and Ascending Shadows: An Oral History of the San Francisco AIDS Epidemic* (1997) and *From ACT UP to the WTO: Urban Protest and Community Building in the Era of Globalization* (2002). Starting as a writer for the Bay Area Reporter in the early 1990s, he worked as an organizer with the AIDS Coalition to Unleash Power (ACT UP), SexPanic!, Reclaim the Streets, Times UP, the Clandestine Rebel Clown Army, the Absurd Response Team, and most recently with the Housing Works Campaign to End AIDS.

Stevphen Shukaitis is a research fellow at the University of London, Queen Mary. He is a member the Planetary Autonomist Network and the editorial collective of Autonomedia and *ephemera: theory & politics in organization*. He seeks to develop non-vanguardist forms of research as part of the global conspiracy against capitalism. For more on his writing and projects see http://stevphen.mahost.org.

Haduhi Szukis is a Lithuanian anti-fascist partisan, although he suffers from the historical irony of not having joined the resistance until after the Soviet occupation had formally ended. When not planning new insurrections against all forms of bureaucracy he enjoys long walks on the beach watching the smoldering remains of capitalism fall onto the boardwalk, and is currently the president of the Thomas Münzer Fan Club.

Sebastian Touza is a PhD candidate at the School of Communication of Simon Fraser University. His dissertation, *Antipedagogies for Liberation*, is a critique of the emancipatory potential of intellectual interventions seeking to expand intelligence, raise consciousness, and facilitate communication. In the late 1980s, Sebastian was involved in the Argentinean student movement. Recently he has collaborated with Nate Holdren in the translation of one book and several articles by Colectivo Situaciones.

Kevin Van Meter currently attends the Graduate Center of the City University of New York, studying political theory and everyday resistance. He is a member of Team Colors, a New York-based collective, which, in both workshops and articles, is seeking to address ways to explore strategic interventions in everyday life.

Resources

This is a far from complete list. More information and resources will continue to be compiled at http://www.constituentimagination.net.

Archives / Materials

Affinity Project: http://www.affinityproject.org
Anarchy Archives: http://dwardmac.pitzer.edu/Anarchist_Archives
Generation On-Line: http://www.generation-online.org
International Institute of Social History: http://www.iisg.nl
Kate Sharpley Library: http://www.katesharpleylibrary.net
Libertarian Communist Library: http://libcom.org
Nettime: http://www.nettime.org
Sarai: http://www.sarai.org
Situationist International Online: http://www.cddc.vt.edu/sionline
Zine Library: http://www.zinelibrary.net

Autonomous Learning

Anarchist University Toronto: http://www.anarchistu.org
Autonomous University Sydney: http://conway.cat.org.au/scooter/autouni
Copenhagen Free University: http://www.copenhagenfreeuniversity.dk
Institute for Social Ecology: http://www.social-ecology.org
Free University of Los Angeles: http://www.freeuniversityla.org
LASER: http://www.e-laser.org
Manoa Free University: http://manoafreeuniversity.org
Mobilised Investigation: http://manifestor.org/mi/en
Monochrom: http://www.monochrom.at
Plus-tôt Te Laat: http://www.pttl.be
Precarias a la Deriva: http://www.sindominio.net/karakola
Tangential University: http://utangente.free.fr

Universidad Nomada: http://www.sindominio.net/unomada
University of Openness: http://twenteenthcentury.com/uo

Books

Stanley Aronowitz, *The Knowledge Factory* (Boston: Beacon Press, 2000).
CrimethInc Ex-Workers Collective *Recipes for Disaster: An Anarchist Cookbook* (Atlanta: CrimethInc, 2005).
Eddie Yuen, Daniel Burton-Rose, and George Katsiaficas, *Confronting Capitalism Dispatches from a Global Movement* (Brooklyn: Soft Skull, 2005).
David Solnit, *Globalize Liberation: How to Uproot the System and Build a Better World.* (San Francisco: City Lights., 2003).
Subcomandante Marcos, *Ya Basta! Ten Years of the Zapatista Uprising* (Oakland: AK Press, 2004).
Notes from Nowhere Collective, *We Are Everywhere: The Irresistible Rise of Global Anticapitalism* (London: Verso Books, 2003).

Collectives / Projects

Chainworkers: http://www.chainworkers.org
Colectivo Situaciones: http://www.situaciones.org
CrimethInc Ex-Workers Collective: http://www.crimethinc.com/
Critical Art Ensemble: http://www.critical-art.net
Freebay: http://www.nomoola.com
Laboratory of Insurrectionary Imagination: http://www.labofii.net
RTMark: http://www.rtmark.com
Ontario Coalition Against Poverty: http://www.ocap.ca
Precarias a la Deriva: http://www.sindominio.net/karakola/precarias.htm
Wombles: http://www.wombles.org.uk
Yo Mango: http://www.yomango.net

Networks

Anarchist Yellow Pages: http://ayp.subvert.info
Dissent!: http://www.dissent.org.uk
Euromayday: http://www.euromayday.org
Euromovements: http://www.euromovements.info
Peoples Global Action: http://www.agp.org

Rhizome: http://rhizome.org
Video Activist Network: http://www.videoactivism.org

News / Information / Analysis

A-Infos: http://www.ainfos.ca
AlterNet: http://www.alternet.org
Anarchist News: http://anarchistnews.org
Common Dreams: http://www.commondreams.org
CounterPunch: http://www.counterpunch.org
In These Times: http://www.inthesetimes.com
Interactivist Info Exchange: http://info.interactivist.net
Infoshop: http://www.infoshop.org
Narco News Bulletin: http://www.narconews.com
The Nation: http://www.thenation.com
Schnews: http://www.schnews.org.uk
Slashdot: http://slashdot.org
Znet: http://www.zmag.org/weluser.htm

Publications

Anarchy: http://www.anarchymag.org
Aufheben: http://www.geocities.com/aufheben2
Borderlands: http://www.borderlandsjournal.adelaide.edu.au
the commoner: http://www.commoner.org
Culture Machine: http://culturemachine.tees.ac.uk
ephemera: http://www.ephemeraweb.org
fibreculture: http://www.fibreculture.org
Fifth Estate: http://www.fifthestate.org
Greenpepper: http://www.greenpeppermagazine.org
Journal of Aesthetics & Protest: http://www.journalofaestheticsandprotest.org
Mute: http://www.metamute.org
Social Anarchism: http://www.socialanarchism.org

Publishers

AK Press: http://www.akpress.org
Atlas Press: http://www.atlaspress.co.uk
Autonomedia: http://www.autonomedia.org
City Lights: http://www.citylights.com
DeriveApprodi: http://www.deriveapprodi.org
Exact Change: http://www.exactchange.com

Freedom Press: http://freedompress.org.uk
III Publishing: http://www.iiipublishing.com
See Sharp Press: http://www.seesharppress.com
South End Press:http://www.southendpress.org
Tinta Limon: http://www.nodo50.org/tintalimonediciones
Traficantes de Suenos: http://sindominio.net/traficantes

Radical Research

Anarchisms Research Group: http://www.anarchisms.org
Edinburgh Anarchist Studies Group: http://anarchist-studies.org.uk
Institute for Anarchist Studies: http://www.anarchist-studies.org
Institute for Distributed Creativity: http://www.distributedcreativity.org
Institute for Network Cultures: http://www.networkcultures.org
Mobilized Investigation: http://manifestor.org/mi
Research on Anarchism: http://raforum.apinc.org
Specialist Group for the Study of Anarchism: http://www.sgsa.org.uk

Index

ALSO AVAILABLE FROM AK PRESS

DWIGHT E. ABBOTT—I Cried, You Didn't Listen

MARTHA ACKELSBERG—Free Women of Spain

KATHY ACKER—Pussycat Fever

MICHAEL ALBERT—Moving Forward: Program for a Participatory Economy

JOEL ANDREAS—Addicted to War: Why the U.S. Can't Kick Militarism

JOEL ANDREAS—Adicto a la Guerra: Por qué EEUU no puede librarse del militarismo

ANONYMOUS —Test Card F

PAUL AVRICH—Anarchist Voices: An Oral History of Anarchism in America (Unabridged)

PAUL AVRICH—The Modern School Movement: Anarchism and Education in the United States

PAUL AVRICH—The Russian Anarchists

ALEXANDER BERKMAN—What is Anarchism?

ALEXANDER BERKMAN—The Blast: The Complete Collection

STEVEN BEST & ANTHONY NOCELLA, II—Igniting a Revolution: Voices in Defense of the Earth

HAKIM BEY—Immediatism

JANET BIEHL & PETER STAUDENMAIER—Ecofascism: Lessons From The German Experience

BIOTIC BAKING BRIGADE—Pie Any Means Necessary: The Biotic Baking Brigade Cookbook

JACK BLACK—You Can't Win

MURRAY BOOKCHIN—Anarchism, Marxism, and the Future of the Left

MURRAY BOOKCHIN—The Ecology of Freedom: The Emergence and Dissolution of Hierarchy

MURRAY BOOKCHIN—Post-Scarcity Anarchism

MURRAY BOOKCHIN—Social Anarchism or Lifestyle Anarchism: An Unbridgeable Chasm

MURRAY BOOKCHIN—Social Ecology and Communalism

MURRAY BOOKCHIN—The Spanish Anarchists: The Heroic Years 1868–1936

MURRAY BOOKCHIN—To Remember Spain: The Anarchist and Syndicalist Revolution of 1936

MURRAY BOOKCHIN—Which Way for the Ecology Movement?

MAURICE BRINTON—For Workers' Power

ARUNDHATI ROY—Come September

VARIOUS—Better Read Than Dead

VARIOUS—Less Rock, More Talk

VARIOUS—Mob Action Against the State: Collected Speeches from the Bay Area Anarchist Bookfair

VARIOUS—Monkeywrenching the New World Order

VARIOUS—Return of the Read Menace

HOWARD ZINN—Artists In A Time of War

HOWARD ZINN—Heroes and Martyrs: Emma Goldman, Sacco & Vanzetti, and the Revolutionary Struggle

HOWARD ZINN—A People's History of the United States: A Lecture at Reed

HOWARD ZINN—People's History Project Box Set

HOWARD ZINN—Stories Hollywood Never Tells

DVDs

NOAM CHOMSKY—Imperial Grand Strategy: The Conquest of Iraq and the Assault on Democracy

NOAM CHOMSKY—Distorted Morality

STEVEN FISCHLER & JOEL SUCHER—Anarchism in America/Free Voice of Labor

ARUNDHATI ROY—Instant-Mix Imperial Democracy

ROZ PAYNE ARCHIVES—What We Want, What We Believe: The Black Panther Party Library (4 DVD set)

HOWARD ZINN & ANTHONY ARNOVE (ed.)—Readings from Voices of a People's History of the United States

INSTITUTE FOR ANARCHIST STUDIES

The Institute for Anarchist Studies was established as a non-profit institution in 1996 in order to support the development of anarchist thought through a grant-giving program for radical writers. To date, the IAS has funded over fifty projects by authors and translators from around the world.

The IAS has grown significantly since its inception. In addition to supporting projects like the Latin American Archives Project, coordinating a Speakers Bureau, and co-sponsoring the annual Renewing the Anarchist Tradition conference, the IAS also publishes a biannual journal, *Perspectives on Anarchist Theory*, as a forum to frame, explore, and debate questions of significance to contemporary anarchist theory and practice.

The IAS relies entirely on contributions from generous individuals around the world to be able to carry out its programs.

Institute for Anarchist Studies
PO Box 15586
Washington, DC 20003

http://www.anarchist-studies.org
info@anarchist-studies.org

Renewing the Anarchist Tradition:
http://homemadejam.org/renew

PRESS
EDINBURGH · OAKLAND · WEST VIRGINIA

SUPPORT AK PRESS!

AK Press is a worker-run collective that publishes and distributes radical books, visual/audio media, and other material. We're small: a dozen people who work long hours for short money, because we believe in what we do. We're anarchists, which is reflected both in the books we publish and the way we organize our business: without bosses.

Currently, we publish about 20 new titles per year. We'd like to publish even more. Whenever our collective meets to discuss future publishing plans, we find ourselves wrestling with a list of hundreds of projects. Unfortunately, money is tight, while the need for books is greater than ever.

The **Friends of AK Press** is a direct way you can help. **Friends** pay a minimum of $20 per month (of course we have no objections to larger sums), for a minimum three-month period. The money goes directly into our publishing efforts. In return, **Friends** automatically receive (for the duration of their memberships) one free copy of every new AK Press title as they appear. **Friends** also get a 10% discount on everything featured in the AK Press Distribution catalog. We also have a program where groups or individuals can sponsor a whole book. Please contact us for details. To become a **Friend**, go to *www.akpress.org* and click on **Friends of AK** for more information.